Privatization in Central and Eastern Europe

Key Issues in the Realignment of Central and Eastern Europe

Series Editors:

Dr Stuart Stein, Centre for the Study of Central and Eastern Europe, University of West of England, Bristol and Professor Tony Saunders, Leonard N. Stern School of Business, New York University.

A series of specially commissioned essays covering key aspects of the economic, social and political transformation being undertaken in Central and Eastern Europe. Each volume brings together an international team of experts who assess the theory and practice of the reform process.

SAUL ESTRIN

Key Issues in the Realignment of
Central and Eastern Europe

PRIVATIZATION IN
CENTRAL
AND EASTERN EUROPE

LONGMAN
London and New York

Longman Group Limited,
Longman House, Burnt Mill,
Harlow, Essex CM20 2JE, England
and Associated Companies throughout the world.

Published in the United States of America
by Longman Publishing, New York

First published 1994

ISBN 0 582 22766 6 CSD
ISBN 0 582 22765 8 PPR

British Library Cataloguing-in-Publication Data

A catalogue record for this book is
available from the British Library

Library of Congress Cataloguing-in-Publication Data

Privatisation in central and eastern Europe / edited by Saul Estrin.
     p.   cm. – (Key issues in the realignment of Central and
Eastern Europe)
    Includes bibliographical references and index.
    ISBN 0-582-22766-6 (cloth). – ISBN 0-582-22765-8 (pbk.)
    1. Privatization–Europe, Eastern. 2. Europe, Eastern-Economic
policy–1989-   I. Estrin, Saul. II. Series.
HD4140.7.P725   1994
338.947–dc20
                                             94-9121
                                               CIP

Set by 16 in 10/12 Times
Printed and bound by Bookcraft (Bath) Ltd.

Contents

Notes on contributors   ix
Preface   xv

PART ONE   CONCEPTUAL ISSUES   1

CHAPTER ONE
Economic transition and privatization: the issues   Saul Estrin   3
1. Introduction   3
2. The developing privatization debate   4
3. Pre-conditions and outcomes   6
4. The aims of privatization policy   13
5. How to privatize and to whom?   20
6. Conclusions   27
   Notes   28
   References   28

CHAPTER TWO
**Privatization in comparative perspective: an overview of the
emerging issues**   Paul Hare   31
1. Introduction   31
2. Aims of privatization   32
3. Methods of privatization   34
4. Two-sector model of capital accumulation   38
5. Aspects of private sector development   43
6. Conclusions   47
   Technical appendix   48
   Notes   52
   References   52

CHAPTER THREE
Corporate governance in mass privatization programmes
Enrico Perotti   54
1. Introduction   54
2. The rationale for mass privatization   55

3. Structure of privatization sales   57
4. The role of creditors and outside shareholders   62
5. Conclusions   66
   Notes   66
   References   67

CHAPTER FOUR

Privatization and regulation of utilities in economies in transition   Martin Cave and Pal Valentiny   69
1. Utilities under central planning   69
2. Why regulate utilities?   71
3. Issues in regulating utilities in economies in transition   73
4. A Hungarian case study   77
5. Conclusions   80
   References   81

CHAPTER FIVE

Political dimensions of privatization in Eastern Europe
Judy Batt   83
1. Political aspects of systemic transformation   83
2. The problem of political legitimation   84
3. The raw material of politics   85
4. Constitutional blockages   87
5. The politics of privatization   89
   References   90

CHAPTER SIX

Privatization, distribution and economic justice: efficiency in transition   Amos Witztum   92
1. Introduction   92
2. The idea of transition   95
3. The immediate effects of transition   96
4. Reward and equity   102
5. Prices, liberalization and a note on sequencing   111
6. Rational behaviour and effort   113
7. Conclusion   118
   Notes   119
   References   122

PART TWO   COUNTRY STUDIES   125

CHAPTER SEVEN

Privatization and deindustrialization in East Germany
Wendy Carlin   127
1. Introduction   127
2. How has German reunification affected the context for transforming the enterprise sector?   129

3. The Treuhand's record on privatization   132
4. The primary method of privatization in East Germany: broad-brush
   restructuring and sale to 'competent outsiders'   137
5. Alternative methods of privatization used in East Germany   144
6. Reunification, privatization and deindustrialization   148
7. Conclusions and policy implications   150
   Notes   152
   References   152

CHAPTER EIGHT
The relationship between privatization and the reform of the
banking sector: the case of the Czech Republic and
Slovakia   Lina Takla   154
1. Introduction   154
2. Review of the main issues – the Czechoslovak experience   155
3. Czechoslovak privatization – a short description   156
4. Results of privatization: highlighting the problems   159
5. Conclusions   172
   Notes   173
   References   174

CHAPTER NINE
The privatization process – economic and political aspects of
the Hungarian approach   Anna Canning and Paul Hare   176
1. Introduction   176
2. From ownership reform to privatization   179
3. State-managed privatization   186
4. Decentralized privatization   192
5. Pre-privatization   194
6. Compensation and related matters   196
7. Institutional ownership and management of corporate assets   201
8. Recent developments – a turn-around in privatization policy?   207
9. Concluding comments   210
   Notes   212
   References   215

CHAPTER TEN
Privatization in Poland 1989–1993: policies, methods, and
results   Stanisław Gomułka and Piotr Jasiński   218
1. Growth of a private sector   219
2. The privatization debate and developments before September 1989   220
3. Policy controversies and the Privatization Act of 1990   221
4. Mass privatization of small-scale businesses   226
5. Methods and results of privatization in the narrow sense   227
6. Privatization in 1993 and prospects for 1994–1995   235
7. Constraints to privatization   238
8. A tentative assessment: concluding remarks   241

Notes   243
References   247

CHAPTER ELEVEN
Privatization in the former Soviet Union and the new Russia:
Alexander Bim, Derek Jones, and Thomas Weisskopf   252
1. An analytical framework   252
2. Privatization in the Soviet Union   256
3. Privatization in independent Russia   261
4. Conclusion   272
   Notes   276
   References   278

CHAPTER TWELVE
Economic system reforms and privatization in Romania
Avner Ben-Ner and John Michael Montias   279
1. Introduction   279
2. The Romanian economy under communism   280
3. The economy since 1990   282
4. Chances in the management of government-owned firms,
   privatization, and entry of new firms   287
5. Conclusions   299
   Notes   302
   Appendix 1   306
   Appendix 2   308
   Appendix 3   309
   References   309

CHAPTER THIRTEEN
Privatization in Bulgaria   Derek Jones and Charles Rock   311
1. Introduction   311
2. The economic context and privatization initiatives before spring 1992 311
3. Privatization since November 1991: the focus moves to large-scale
   privatization   315
4. Overall evaluation   317
   Notes   322
   References   323

Index   325

Notes on contributors

Judy Batt is Senior Lecturer in East European Politics at the Centre for Russian and East European Studies, University of Birmingham, was Research Fellow on the Soviet Programme, Royal Institute for International Affairs (Chatham House) 1990 and was on secondment to the Policy Planning Staff, Foreign and Commonwealth Office, 1992–93. Research interests focus on political aspects of economic reforms and transformation in Central and Eastern Europe. Her main publications are *Economic Reform and Political Change in Eastern Europe* (Macmillan, 1988), *East Central Europe from Reform to Transformation* (Printer/RIIA, 1991) and *Developments in East European Politics*, (1993), co-edited with S. White and P. Lewis.

Avner Ben-Ner is Professor of Industrial Relations at the University of Minnesota. His publications have concerned organization theory, the economics of employee-owned firms and non-profit organizations, and comparative economics. He has recently edited, with Benedetto Gui, *The Non-profit Sector in the Mixed Economy* (University of Michigan Press, 1993). He has taught and done research at Yale University, University of California-Davis, Haifa, SUNY at Stony Brook, and Northwestern University.

Alexander Bim was educated at the Moscow Institute of the National Economy and has worked at the Economics Institute of Gosplan and the Institute of Market Economy at the Russian Academy of Sciences. His main research interests are the role of the state in transitional economies and Russian privatization. He has published more than sixty books and papers, and is currently working as an adviser to the Russian Ministry of Privatization.

Anna Canning graduated in interpreting and translating at Heriot-Watt University, then worked in Hungary for three years for the Ecumenical Youth Council in Europe. Since joining CERT as a research associate in 1991, she has worked on privatization in Hungary and prepared a variety of other reports on Hungarian economic policy, including contributions to reports for the Economist Intelligence Unit.

Wendy Carlin has taught in the Department of Economics at University College London since 1986, before that she taught for three years at Christ Church, Oxford Univeristy. She has published and is currently engaged in research in three fields: (i) macroeconomics with imperfectly competitive product and labour markets, *Macroeconomics and the Wage Bargain*, with David Soskice, (Oxford University Press, 1990); (ii) the post-war economic development of the West German economy, 'West German Growth and Institutions, 1945–1990', *CEPR Discussion Paper No. 896*, (1994); and (iii) the economics of transition, 'Restructuring Enterprises in Eastern Europe' *Economic Policy* No. 15, (1992), with Colin Mayer, and 'The Treuhandanstalt: privatization by state and market', with Colin Mayer, in O. Blanchard, K. Froot and J. Sachs (eds) *Transition in Eastern Europe* (Chicago University Press and NBER, 1994). Dr Carlin is a participant in the CEPR's Network on Post-War Economic Growth, a Research Associate of the CEPR's Eastern Europe Project and a member of the CLARE Group of economists.

Martin Cave is Professor of Economics and Dean of the Faculty of Social Sciences at Brunel University. His principal interests lie in the fields of industrial regulation in Western economies and economies in transition, and the evaluation of public spending programmes. He has published a number of articles and contributions to books on regulation, especially in the broadcasting and telecommunications industries, and is co-editor with Saul Estrin of *Competition and Competition Policy: A comparative Analysis of Central and Eastern Europe* (Pinter Publishers, 1993).

Saul Estrin was educated in economics at Cambridge and the University of Sussex. He is currently Associate Professor of Economics at the London Business School, and Research Director of its Centre for Management Development in Middle Europe and the CIS. He was formerly lecturer at Southampton University and lecturer, then senior lecturer at the London School of Economics. He has written books on employee management in Yugoslavia, and French planning, as well as dozens of articles for scholarly journals. His current research is concerned with company adjustment from planning to markets in Central and Eastern Europe, and has led to consultancies with the OECD and the World Bank.

Stanisław Gomułka is Reader in Economics at the London School of Economics, where he has been since 1970. His main publications are: *Inventive Activity, Diffusion and the Stages of Economic Growth*, (1971); *Growth, Innovation and Reform in Eastern Europe*, (1986), and *The Theory of Technological Change and Economic Growth*, (1990). He has served as economic adviser to Poland's successive Finance Ministers since 1989. As a member of the Balcerowicz Group, he advised the Polish Government on the elaboration and implementation of the 1990–91 reforms, including privatization. He is Director of the research programme on post-communist reform at the LSE's Centre for Economic Performance.

Paul Hare was educated at Cambridge and Oxford Universities and has spent most of his subsequent academic career in Scotland, first at Stirling University and, since 1985, as Professor of economics at Heriot-Watt University, Edinburgh. He has also been Director of the Centre for Economic Reform and Transformation at Heriot-Watt University since 1990, and is a senior researcher at the LSE's Centre for Economic Performance. His research interests have always focused on the economies of Central and Eastern Europe, with occasional diversions into the economics of education and economic policy in the UK. Recently, his research has included studies of privatization, industrial competitiveness and industrial policy in various countries, supported by ESRC and other research grants, and with several projects being undertaken for international organisations such as the World Bank, the OECD and the EBRD.

Piotr Jasiński is Research Associate at the Regulatory Policy Research Centre, Hertford College, Oxford University, and Tutor in Economics, Campion Hall, Oxford University. His main research areas are privatization, post-communist economies and regulation of public utilities. He has published numerous papers in Polish and in English. The following books are to appear in 1994: *Privatisation and Foreign Direct Investment in Transforming Economies*, with Paul J. J. Welfens, (Dartmouth Press, Aldershot); *Back to Capitalism* (in Polish), (PWN/CASE, Warsaw) and *Competition in the Energy Industry* (in Polish), with A. Szablewski and G. Yarrow, (PAN, Warsaw).

Derek Jones is Professor of Economics at Hamilton College. He has published widely in the fields of the economics of transition, labour economics and industrial relations, and comparative economic systems. His current work focuses on transition and includes studies of the nature and the determinants of enterprise adjustment in Bulgaria and Russia, and labour market dynamics in several countries, but mainly Bulgaria and Russia.

John Michael Montias is Professor of Economics at the Institution of Social and Policy Studies at Yale University. His articles and books have dealt with the theory of economic systems, the economies of Eastern Europe, and the economics of the arts. His most recent books include *Comparative Economics*, with Avner Ben-Ner and Egon Neuberger, (Harwood Academic Publishers, 1994) and *Le marché de l'art aux Pays Bas – au seuil du l'ère moderne* (Flammarion, 1994). He is founding editor of the *Journal of Comparative Economics* and past president of the Association for Comparative Economic Studies. He has taught and done research at the Center for Advanced Study in Social Sciences, the Wissenschaftskolleg in Berlin, and other institutions.

Enrico Perotti is Professor of Finance at the University of Amsterdam. He has taught at Boston University and Central European University in Prague. His research is in corporate finance theory, underdeveloped financial markets, and privatization. He has worked as a research consultant to the World Bank and the IMF on financial market reform in Eastern Europe and China, and acted as an advisor to the Latvian government on privatization. Recent publications include: 'The Governance Structure of the Japanese Keiretsu' (with Erik Berglof) forthcoming in *Journal of Financial Economics* (1994); 'Credible Privatization' in

American Economic Review (1994); 'A Taxonomy of Post-Socialist Financial Systems' in *The Economics of Transition* (1994); 'Eastern European Financial Systems', *IMF working paper series* (1994) and 'Bank Lending in Transition Economies' in *Journal of Banking and Finance*, No. 17 (1993), pp. 1201–32.

Charles Rock is Professor of Economics at Rollins College, Florida. He teaches courses in the areas of labour, comparative, and alternative economics. His recent research includes work on financial aspects of economic democratization, description of organizations in the 'third sector', and the transformation of Central and Eastern European economies. During 1991–1992, with the help of an IREX research grant, he spent a year in Bulgaria beginning a project on comparative enterprise privatization in Bulgaria's economic transition.

Lina Takla graduated from the London School of Economics. Her current positions are Research Fellow at the CIS-Middle Europe Centre, London Business School, from 1993, and affiliated Research Fellow in International Economics at the Royal Institute of International Affairs. She previously held the post of Research Fellow in the International Economics Programme at the Royal Institute of International Affairs. She was first employed as a researcher at the Centre for Economic Performance in the Post Communist Reform Programme, and subsequently as a Visiting Research Officer at the Centre for Business Strategy at the London Business School. She has worked as a consultant to the World Bank on Czech enterprise adjustment. She is currently coordinating an EC funded ACE project on trade and competitiveness in the Czech Republic and Bulgaria. Her current research analyses enterprise behaviour in transition, privatization, corporate governance, trade and competitiveness and industrial restructuring in Central and Eastern Europe.

Pal Valentiny is Research Fellow at the Institute of Economics, Hungarian Academy of Sciences. His principal interests lie in economic history, business history, theory of regulated markets and state intervention and privatization policies. He has published articles and contributions to books on privatization from an international perspective.

Thomas Weisskopf is Professor of Economics at the University of Michigan, where he teaches in the fields of political economy, comparative economic systems and macroeconomics. After working for many years on problems of the US economy, he has shifted his attention more recently to problems of economic transition from administered to more market-oriented economic systems in the newly independent states of the former Soviet Union. Among his recent publications are several articles on economic reform and changes in property relationships in Russia. His most recent book is *After the Waste Land: Toward a Democratic Economics for the Year 2000* (co-authored with Samuel Bowles and David Gordon).

Amos Witztum studied at the Hebrew University of Jerusalem and the London School of Economics. He is now teaching at the London Guildhall University. He is a frequent visitor to Russia as a Visiting Professor to the New Economic School in Moscow, and the LSE-EC summer schools in Moscow and St. Petersburg. He works mainly on the ethics-economics relationship from the points of view of methodology and the moral dimensions of the rational individual.

Preface

This volume has been produced to fill a major gap in the literature on the economies in transition. There have been several studies which attempt to formulate the conceptual issues regarding privatization in the formerly planned economies of Central and Eastern Europe. There have also been numerous papers and books which describe the experience of privatization, to date, in one or a few countries. There has as yet been no book that seeks both to tackle the theoretical questions and to reflect upon the experiences in key privatization experiments. It is this gap which the present volume seeks to fill.

This ambitious objective explains the character of the book. It would be virtually impossible for one person simultaneously to combine the theoretical understanding and depth of institutional knowledge across a range of countries needed to produce a volume of this sort unaided. My approach has been to enlist the skills of colleagues, some of whom (namely Judy Batt, Martin Cave, Paul Hare, and Lina Takla) work with me in an ESRC East-West Initiative project, 'Transition to a Market Economy; Competitiveness, Ownership and Regulation'. I have been particularly fortunate in being able to recruit a group of authors who are both eminently capable of producing research to the standard and subject matter that I desired, and thoroughly professional in their academic work. I hope the fact that the book was conceived and edited as a unity will to some extent offset the intellectual fragmentation that so often characterizes edited volumes.

This book is not intended to be only a summary of the current privatization policy in most of the reforming economies of Central Europe plus Russia. Though the authors have sought to include the most recent information, and the publishers have worked very hard to produce the volume quickly, in practice things will have changed in certain dimensions more or less everywhere. We have sought in the country papers, however, to explain the economic, political, and social nature of the privatization process, so that the material will be more durable than any particular privatization policy or minister. This approach is supported by the theoretical section, which tries to consider the privatization process in the transitional economies thematically. Issues which recur in the country experiences, and which are treated in the first part of the book, include speed of privatization, finance and corporate governance, political questions, and income and wealth distribution.

The idea behind this book belongs to Stuart Stein, who persuaded me to take on the editorial role. My thinking on privatization has been greatly influenced over the years by Alan Gelb and I. J. Singh of the World Bank's Transitional Economies Research Unit, though they do not bear any responsibility for the final product. The Longman's side has been administered with great efficiency by the social science editorial department. Finally, the whole project has been organized at the London Business School by Eleanor Burke, to whom I and all the authors owe great thanks.

Saul Estrin

PART ONE

CONCEPTUAL ISSUES

CHAPTER ONE

Economic transition and privatization: the issues

Saul Estrin*

1. Introduction

This chapter is intended to serve as a brief summary of the issues discussed in greater analytical detail, or with reference to particular countries, in the remainder of this book. Privatization has of course been on the policy agenda of Western economies for well over a decade (see e.g. Vickers and Yarrow 1988), in which context it has both a narrow scope and a well-defined meaning. Privatization in the West refers to the transfer of ownership of public corporations from state to private hands, typically by public offering, auction, or tender. In contrast, state-ownership in the formerly socialist economies has been far more widespread and more varied in nature than in the West, so the shift back to private hands is likely to be both greater in scope and more diverse in character. Moreover, while basic objectives are the same — to increase corporate and thereby national efficiency and to raise revenue for the government — the problems arising for example from the shortage of domestic saving and the deficiencies of the capital markets cast the principal issues in a very different light.

It is important to stress from the outset that while privatization raises particular problems and dilemmas, it is merely one element, though an important one, in the process of transition from a socialist to a capitalist economy. A considerable literature has emerged to define the principal economic reform tasks during transition, as well as to propose an appropriate sequence of changes (see Lipton and Sachs 1990, Fischer and Gelb 1991, Portes 1993). The major other components in a reform programme are generally thought to be macroeconomic stabilization following price liberalization; opening the economy to foreign trade and competition; and institutional reform, including reform of the legal system and reform to the functioning of the state. Readers should therefore be aware that in all the transitional economies considered in this book, the fundamental changes to ownership arrangements which we are considering were being undertaken in conjunction with other microeconomic reforms, particularly regarding prices

* The author would like to thank Alan Gelb, Paul Hare and Lina Takla for fruitful conversations about privatization in Central and Eastern Europe. Any remaining errors or misinterpretations are his alone however. The work in this paper was sponsored by the ESRC East-West Initiative project 'Transition to a Market Economy: Competitiveness, Ownership and Regulation', no. Y3009/25/3007.

and international trade, and with attempts, whether successful or not, to stabilize the macroeconomy.

The remainder of the chapter is organized as follows. The main themes are briefly summarized in the following section. An important reason for differences in privatization policies, or for differential impacts of similar policies, lies in the initial situation of the reforming economies, or in differences in economic progress thus far. The formerly socialist economies were similar in their ownership arrangements, but differed enormously in initial conditions and recent economic performance, and this variation is the subject matter of the third section. The fundamental reasons for privatization in transition are examined in the fourth section, while the fifth discusses alternative methods of implementation in such economies. Conclusions are drawn in the sixth section.

2. The developing privatization debate

The question of privatization is a major one in economic transformation because the state sectors in the former socialist economies were so large and because the economic consequences of public ownership were perceived to be so baleful. According to Estrin (1991), around the time of reform the state sector produced the vast majority of national output, and virtually all industrial output, in every Central and East European economy. The only partial exceptions were Poland and Hungary, where the private sectors accounted for about 18 and 30 per cent of production respectively; in the former case because agriculture was still largely in private hands. Assuming that production will continue in the same organizations post-reform, these figures imply that the privatization packages in these countries will dwarf the programmes already undertaken in the West, entailing transfers of ownership covering perhaps 75 per cent of output, and 90 per cent or more of industrial output.

A major reason for the collapse of the socialist model throughout Central and Eastern Europe was the manifest economic failure of the system. Perhaps the crucial driving force was the gradual growth slowdown which commenced from at least the 1960s, and which brought economic progress to a virtual halt throughout the region by the 1980s (see Gomułka 1990). High on most lists of explanatory factors was the inefficiency of a state-owned enterprise sector which failed to invest or produce rationally; squandered material inputs, labour, and energy; and did not innovate (see Ellman 1989, Bergson 1991, Estrin 1993). Western analysts have been hard pressed to find convincing evidence of public sector inefficiency in their own countries, at least of a form unambiguously attributable to the absence of private owners rather than of market competition (see Borcherding et al. 1982 and Marchand et al. 1984). The situation in the socialist economies offers a far stronger *prima facie* case for the inefficiencies of public ownership.

Privatization of the former state sector is, however, not the only way, and may not be the best way, to ensure successful transition to a market economy, because reform also entails a significant degree of restructuring. Formerly planned economies have especially small service and non-productive sectors, with relatively over-expanded capacity in manufacturing, construction, mining, and agriculture. Within manufacturing industry, the stress has been on heavy industry or for products to trade within the socialist trading bloc — the Council for Mutual Economic Cooperation (CMEA) — rather than for international competitiveness (see Ellman 1989). One indicator of the structural problems is given by Hare and Hughes (1992). Using input–output tables to revalue sectoral activities at world prices, they find that only between 7 and 22 per cent of industry in Poland, Hungary, and Czechoslovakia (as it still was when the study was conducted) could actually make a profit in the new economic environment, where firms were subject to international competition. A further 60 per cent or more would require restructuring, sometimes of a drastic nature, to attain a level of profitability compatible with market levels. Finally, the remaining firms in each country were actually generating negative value added, and by implication could not survive once capital market forces were free to assert themselves. There have been numerous criticisms of this study, not least because it is based on the assumption of fixed coefficient technology. However, it makes the point that reform must involve restructuring as well as privatization. Thus it might reasonably be expected that many organizations will cease to exist during the transition period, and that new firms will spring up to fill the profitable niches opened up by the relative price changes.

Privatization is therefore not necessarily the sole component in the microeconomic adjustment of a transitional economy; one must also take into account restructuring by existing state-owned firms, and the growth of new private firms *de novo*, perhaps through the purchase at liquidation prices of the assets of bankrupt state firms. Indeed, it has been argued that the pre-existing state sector will be poor at restructuring to the new market circumstances, whether nominally in state or private hands. For this reason, some authors place particular significance on the pace of emergence of the new private sector (see Kornai 1991).

The literature on privatization in formerly socialist economies has already gone through several phases, reflecting deepening understanding of the problems at issue. Much of the earliest Western literature (see e.g. Lipton and Sachs 1990, Blanchard *et al.* 1991) was concerned with methods of privatization. The key problem at that time appeared to be the vast mismatch between the domestic supply of savings and the potential market value of the firms to be privatized. For example, as Estrin (1991) noted, in Czechoslovakia the value in 1989 of the industrial capital stock (valued in historic terms) was around 3,300 billion crowns. The stock of domestic savings summed to only 330 billion crowns, with even smaller flows; only 20 billion crowns. If nothing in the equation changed, and people could be induced to buy company paper with all their savings, either prices would have to be at around 10 per cent of historic valuation of assets (itself almost certainly an underestimate in many cases) or it would take many years, perhaps more than a century, to effect the privatization. The Western literature frequently concluded by backing an idea developed by two Polish professors, Lewandowski and Szomberg of Gdansk University, of privatization based on the free distribution of shares to the population as a whole.

The idea of voucher privatization simultaneously (and to some extent independently of the Western literature) took root in countries more advanced upon the reform path, such as Poland and Czechoslovakia, and has since been considered or introduced in most other transitional economies, most notably Russia. The key economic question thrown up by this policy was whether privatization of this form could engender the desired improvements in organization, management, and efficiency. This highlighted the issue of corporate governance: the mechanisms whereby owners exert influence over managers to act in the interest of profits rather than for example, the interest of managers themselves, or of managers and workers together (see e.g. Frydman *et al.* 1993).

A further theme which has been of growing significance in the Western literature recently has concerned the relationship between privatization, restructuring, and the role of capital markets. It had been a common assertion in the literature (see e.g. Lipton and Sachs 1990, Blanchard *et al.* 1991) that restructuring would be virtually impossible in the absence of privatization. However, some important empirical work for Poland (Pinto *et al.* 1993) has suggested that many state-owned firms in Poland have been restructuring despite continued lack of progress towards privatization. A similar finding emerged in a set of case studies for Poland, Czechoslovakia, and Hungary (see Estrin *et al.* 1993). The role of the Truehand in the five *Länder* in East Germany in restructuring firms prior to privatization represents an additional basis for the argument (see Carlin and Meyer 1992). If managers have begun to act in a profit-oriented way despite weak or deficient ownership rights, the reasons must lie either in their own motivation or in the effective imposition of hard budget constraints. The former explanation has stimulated work by Aghion *et al.* (in press) which considers the likely role of managers in the privatization process, and the benefits to be obtained from either foreign buyers or the state if the managerial group can establish its own competence through successful restructuring. The latter highlights the potential role of the financial institutions, most notably banks, in exercising control over managers despite the absence of formal ownership rights. The current state of the banking system in most of these countries gives only limited credibility to this explanation (see Estrin *et al.* 1992, Hncir *et al.* 1993). Such a line of enquiry leads to privatization and banking reform being viewed as necessarily simultaneous and inter-related, rather than as the sequence of earlier conceptions.

3. Pre-conditions and outcomes

The planning system in Central and Eastern Europe is normally described as a common feature of all socialist economies, with the exception of Hungary since 1968 and Poland during the 1980s (see Ellman 1989). However, there were great differences between the transitional economies prior to reform, and these have influenced the nature of the transformation programmes which have been introduced as well as their effectiveness. The main differences have referred to the level of development, the degree of macroeconomic stability, the extent of microeconomic decentralization and the exposure to international trade. The discussion here is with reference to Table 1.1, which is derived from a variety of sources.

TABLE 1.1 Initial (pre-programme) conditions

	Hungary	Poland(a)	Czechoslovakia	Bulgaria	Romania	Russia(b)
1. Population³ (In millions, mid 1989)	10.6	37.9	15.6	9.0	23.2	147.6
2. GNP per capita(c) (1989 US$)	2,590	1,790	3,450	2,320	2,290	5,394(d)
3. GNP Growth(e) (Average Rate in per cent at constant prices)						
1970s	4.5	3.5	4.6	7.0	9.3	4.95
1980s	0.5	-0.07	1.4	2.0	1.8	2.95
4. Administered Prices (per cent of total)	15%	100% (Excluding food prices)	100%	100%	80%	100%
5. State Ownership	90%	70%	Economy-wide	Economy-wide, except 15% of agriculture	Economy-wide	Economy-wide
6. Money(M1)/GDP, 1990	0.4	0.9	0.7	1.3	0.6	0.53
7. External Debt/GDP (1990, percent)	65	80	19	506	3	7.6
8. External Debt Service Ratio (1990)	57(f)	36	23	116		
9. Exports to CMEA (1990)(g)						
In per cent of total exports	43	41	60	69		48.9
In per cent of GDP	16	14	25	34		26

(a) M2/GDP and exports to CMEA in per cent of total exports are 1989 figures.
(b) Russian estimates are for 1989.
(c) World Bank: *World Development Report.* 1991; IMF staff estimate for Romanian GNP per capita; All of these data are highly sensitive to the choice of exchange rates.
(d) Purchasing Power Parity. Source: Economist Intelligence Unit.
(e) The Vienna Institute of Comparative Economic Studies: *COMECON Data,* 1990; Net Material Product.
(f) In per cent of merchandise exports.
(g) Estimates are highly tentative as they are sensitive to distortions in intra-CMEA prices and exchange rates. Data for exports are based on estimated world market prices (considerably above the official traded prices); however, the GDP data are based on actual official prices. For Romania export data are only available at official prices which would tend to underestimate the weight of CMEA trade; on this basis CMEA exports were 39% of total exports and equivalent to 6% of GDP.

The Czechs, East Germans, and to a lesser extent the Hungarians entered the communist era as relatively mature industrial economies. For Poland and Russia, and even more markedly Romania and Bulgaria, socialism was the engine of transformation from an agricultural to a predominantly industrial society. Though there was very rapid catch-up, differences in terms of income per head persisted until the 1980s. Countries like Bulgaria and Slovakia were also indus-trialized, in no small part, by building huge new factories to serve the whole Soviet-bloc market, and were therefore more exposed when the trading area disintegrated at the start of transition.

The 1970s and 1980s were a period of deteriorating economic stability through-out Central and Eastern Europe. An important reason was probably that the growth slowdown had implications for lower rates of growth of personal con-sumption which the unpopular communist regimes were unwilling to accept. So most of them exploited the easy availability of cheap credit in the 1970s, more to maintain consumption than to increase investment. When credit conditions became more stringent at the end of the decade, and real interest rates increased, the regimes followed one of two paths. Two countries sought to solve the international debt problems. In the Czechoslovak case this was for reasons of budgetary prudence and international reputation; in Romania it probably more reflected a dictator's fear of foreign dependence. Romania and Czechoslovakia thus followed a policy of sound money, slow growth, and repaying international debts for the 1980s, in the former case at considerable human cost. Both entered the transitional era, however, in a relatively strong macroeconomic position, with little foreign debt, approximately balanced bud-get, and low monetary overhang (indicated by M1/GDP ratio).

The remaining countries failed to address the fundamental imbalances ade-quately, leaving international debt to accumulate via unpaid interest and finan-cing continued money wage growth through monetary emission. In the context of planning and fixed prices, this led to longer queues rather than price increases[1], and to the forced holding of money by consumers — a growing 'monetary over-hang'. Polish international debt was therefore around 80 per cent of GDP in 1990, and the M1/GDP ratio perhaps twice that which would pertain in the West. An alternative indicator of macro-imbalance is given by the instantaneous increase in prices following price liberalization (which is determined by the size of the mone-tary overhang). This was more than 250 per cent in Russia (on this measure the most imbalanced economy), more than 100 per cent in Poland and around 50 per cent in Czechoslovakia.

One tends to imagine the countries of the Soviet bloc as uniform in their application of socialist principles and repression of the market. This is not cor-rect. Many countries briefly embarked on the path of reform in 1968, and the Hungarians have erratically stayed on it since then, with the consequence that economic transition has been for them an acceleration of a long-standing process rather than a dramatic shock. Thus the Hungarians had already by the late 1980s put in place many of the elements of a market economy, including significant price and trade liberalization, a fledgling private sector, and the shell of a Western banking system. With a relatively open economy, they had dramatically reduced their reliance on CMEA trade, and were beginning to export successfully to the

OECD. Though only beginning reform convincingly in the early 1980s, the Poles had also begun to rely on liberalized prices and an emerging private sector before their 1990 reform package. They had managed to reorient their trade pattern to some extent prior to the collapse of the CMEA but decision-making based on market-based criteria was virtually unknown. Private sector activity was at best semi-legal in all other countries in the region. Several of these were very open, most notably Bulgaria and Czechoslovakia, and heavily exposed to the CMEA.

This section has, of course enormously simplified a complex and varied recent economic history of the region. Interested readers can cover the issues more deeply by reading Portes (1993) or Frydman et al. (1993). The fundamental point is that reformers in the different countries, though wrestling with similar problems, faced them with differing orders of severity. In Hungary there was neither a macroeconomic crisis associated with price liberalization, calling for macroeconomic stabilization[2], nor a complete absence of experience and management to cope with the restructuring required to create an open market economy. The Poles also had some advantages on the latter front, but faced a macroeconomic environment so inhospitable that a draconian stabilization plan was implemented immediately. Approximately the converse situation pertained in Czechoslovakia, where planning-type arrangements to control firms persisted after the fall of the communists, yet sound macroeconomic fundamentals were further reinforced by an effective stabilization plan in 1991.

At the time of writing, the three 'more advanced' countries above had effectively used their lengthier period in transition (since at least 1988 for Hungary, 1990 for Poland, and 1991 for Czechoslovakia) and their slightly better initial situation on either the micro or the macro front to address problems in the other. Hence, inflation in Poland has been brought under control (see Schaffer 1993) and the Czechs have already established a relatively large private sector (see Chapter 8). The remaining transitional economies either started in a much more difficult position from the outset, like Russia or Bulgaria, or gradually moved in that direction because of weak government policies, like Romania. But as noted, they have not yet had so long, and they had more problems, and possibly deeper ones, to address. This distinction should be remembered when attempting to evaluate performance.

The first element in transition is therefore macroeconomic stabilization, and progress for the countries studied in this volume is summarized in Table 1.2. Initially, observers significantly underestimated both the magnitude of the output decline and the scale of the inflationary pressures (see e.g. *Journal of Economic Perspectives* 1991). Gross domestic product has been falling for three or four years consecutively in almost all the countries, with cumulative declines in excess of 20 per cent in the less affected countries, and more than 40 per cent in Russia. The output drop is graphed in Figure 1.1. The fall in industrial production has been even more marked, cumulating to more than 30 per cent in the Central European economies, and reaching more than 50 per cent in some parts of the former Soviet Union and the Balkans.

On the other hand, the differences between the two groups of countries are most noticeable in their recent growth performance. The recession bottomed out in Poland in 1992, and reasonably strong growth now seems firmly established.

TABLE 1.2 Economic progress 1990–1993

	Change in GDP (YOY)			
	1990	1991	1992	1993 (est)
Czech Republic	−0.4%	−15.9%	−7.0%	0.0%
Poland	−12.0%	−7.0%	1.0%	2.0%
Hungary	−4.0%	−12.0%	−5.0%	−2.0%
Romania	−7.0%	−14.0%	−15.0%	−9.0%
Bulgaria	−9.0%	−12.0%	−8.0%	−5.0%
Russia	−4.0%	−11.0%	−19.0%	−15.0%

	Industrial Employment			
	1990	1991	1992	1993 (est)
Czech Republic	40.0%			
Poland		21.6%	18.6%	22.6%
Hungary		28.2%	25.4%	31.1%
Romania				
Bulgaria	38.2%	37.1%	37.5%	39.1%
Russia				

	Inflation (CPI)			
	1990	1991	1992	1993 (est)
Czech Republic	18.4%	53.6%	11.0%	20.0%
Poland	586.0%	70.0%	43.0%	39.0%
Hungary	29.0%	35.0%	23.0%	23.0%
Romania	70.0%	161.0%	210.0%	200.0%
Bulgaria	26.0%	334.0%	83.0%	100.0%
Russia	6.0%	93.0%	1354.0%	1000.0%

	Unemployment			
	1990	1991	1992	1993 (est)
Czech Republic	1.0%	4.0%	3.0%	6.0%
Poland	6.0%	12.0%	14.0%	16.0%
Hungary	2.5%	8.0%	12.0%	13.0%
Romania	N/A	2.0%	8.0%	9.0%
Bulgaria	1.5%	10.0%	15.0%	16.0%
Russia	0.0%	0.0%	1.0%	4.0%

	Current Account ($Billions)			
	1990	1991	1992	1993 (est)
Czech Republic	−1.10	0.40	0.20	
Poland	0.80	−2.30	−0.03	0.50
Hungary	0.10	0.30	0.30	0.00
Romania	−1.70	−1.40	−1.20	−1.00
Bulgaria				
Russia	−7.30	1.90	−4.30	−5.20

Source: Economics of Transition, 1993, EBRD Annual Review, 1993
Plan Econ.

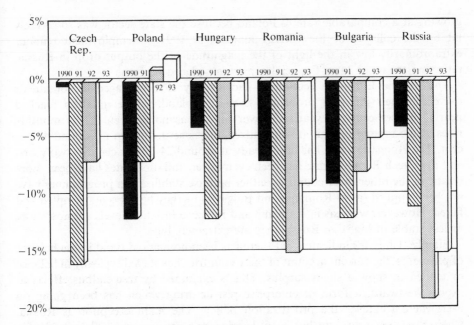

FIG. 1.1 Change in GDP 1990–1993* (Year on Year)
(1993 is estimated)

Forecasters assert that the same would have held for Czechoslovakia if the country had not decided to break up in 1993, which depressed consumer confidence and inter-republic trade and slowed growth markedly (see e.g. *PlanEcon* 1993). It is expected that the upturn will be established in 1994 there as well as in Hungary, which was dragged down in 1993 by restructuring and financial problems in the enterprise sector. Thus some 'green shoots' are visible after the long winter in Central Europe. The same cannot yet be said for Russia and the Balkans, where output continues its relentless decline.

As a result of the output drop, all countries have seen an increase in open unemployment, especially Poland and Bulgaria, though the rise in the private sector and a decline from the extremely high participation rates of the communist era have meant that unemployment has nowhere risen in proportion with the fall in output. The change in unemployment relative to output offers a useful indicator of the extent of company restructuring during transition, as well as the political pressures that might influence the privatization debate.

Of the three countries most advanced on the transition path, the Czech Republic is remarkable in maintaining a much lower level of unemployment, only 6 per cent in 1993, despite comparable falls in output and industrial production to Hungary and Poland, where unemployment has reached 16 per cent. Possible explanations include the particularly rapid growth of the private sector around the tourist industry in Prague, and continued tardiness in restructuring state-owned firms (see Svejnar 1993). Turning to three countries that can be viewed, whether by choice or circumstance, as being in the second wave of transition, unemployment has been rising more slowly in Romania than Hungary or Poland (though not the Czech Republic). However Bulgaria's unemployment has been growing at a comparable rate to Poland because the state sector was so severely hit by the collapse of the CMEA markets in 1991. Unemployment remains extraordinarily low in the light of the magnitude of the output drop in Russia, reflecting the much laxer financial constraints placed on firms.

The Central European economies had also by 1993 managed to contain or overcome their inflation problems. Even in Poland, where inflation reached nearly 600 per cent per year, and over one thousand per cent if the monthly rates at the time of reform are annualized, it has settled down to around 40 per cent. The Hungarian rate has been steady at around 24–26 per cent for two years, and the Czech Republic rate has been even lower. Inflation rates have been more erratic in the other three countries, either because stabilization programmes have not been applied (as in Romania and Bulgaria) or they have been attempted and failed. However, whereas in Romania and Bulgaria inflation levels are now more or less stable (if high), in Russia they are extremely high.

Finally, Table 1.2 indicates that there has been no marked trend in the balance of payments; the current account of these countries has stayed typically in balance or tended to show a slight surplus. This is explained by tremendous efforts to export westward, a form of enterprise restructuring which has been going on everywhere whatever the privatization policy. The main exception is Russia, where the current account has been deteriorating because of problems with raw material exports and disruption of trade following the collapse of the ruble area.

The second aspect of transition is microeconomic restructuring and privatization, and the progress in this area is summarized in Table 1.3. Though the data are patchy and not entirely reliable, it can be seen that the growth of the private sector has been truly remarkable throughout the region. Poland leads the way in the growth of the private sector, as in economic growth. Private sector employment

TABLE 1.3 Growth in the private sector 1989–1992

A.	Share of GDP (Output)			
	1989	1990	1991	1992
Czechoslovakia	4.1%	5.3%	8.1%	
Poland (includes cooperatives)	28.6%	30.9%	42.1%	
Hungary		19.0%	28.0%	33.0%
Romania	13.0%	16.4%	21.0%	25.6%
Bulgaria	7.2%	9.5%	11.9%	15.6%
Russia	5.3%	6.0%	10.0%	

B.	Share of Total Employment			
	1989	1990	1991	1992
Czechoslovakia	1.2%	6.4%	16.4%	35.0%
Poland (includes cooperatives)	44.3%	45.8%	51.1%	57.0%
Hungary			56.7%	
Romania	5.9%	8.2%	21.5%	
Bulgaria		5.9%	10.0%	14.1%
Russia	1.6%	2.6%	4.8%	

Source: Various statistical yearbooks

was already high in 1989 because of the large cooperative sector, but has grown to exceed 50 per cent of the total. Even in industry, private sector employment now exceeds 25 per cent and is continuing to grow rapidly (see Schaffer 1993). Hungary is another country in which, at least in one important sense, the transition process is virtually over, since a majority of workers are already employed in the private sector. Growth rates of the private sector have been even more dramatic in Czechoslovakia, where private sector employment has risen from around 1 per cent of the total in 1989 to 35 per cent in 1992, and is probably approaching 50 per cent by the end of 1993.

Despite their more tarnished macro-stabilization record, the second-wave transitional economies in this study are all also making very rapid progress towards private ownership. The share of output produced by the private sector had increased by 12 percentage points in Romania, 1989 –1992, and by eight percentage points in Bulgaria. In Russia, even before the major initiatives under Yeltsin in 1992 outlined in Chapter 11, the share of the private sector in output doubled, and in employment tripled in three years.

Not all of this, and often rather little of it, is due to privatization policies for the state-owned sector. The bulk of new firms everywhere, and of private sector jobs everywhere with the possible exceptions of Czechoslovakia and Hungary, have emerged *de novo*, and primarily in small-scale service, construction, transport, and retail firms. But privatization strategies for large state-owned firms greatly influence the shape, form and structure of the emerging private sector in transitional economies, and therefore the future prospects of the whole economy. Table 1.3 serves as a reminder that, while the political debate over privatization is furious for these reasons, such policies may not in fact have greatly influenced the surprisingly rapid rate at which the private sector has emerged in the early years of reform.

4. The aims of privatization policy

It is the opinion of almost all Western analysts of the transitional process that privatization must be an essential component of reform, but the reasoning is rarely spelt out. It is useful to distinguish between two categories of reason; the economic and the political. The former also apply to state-owned firms in capitalist economies, but can be made even more convincingly for situations when there is no private sector to exert competition. The latter ones are more specific to the transitional problem.

ECONOMIC REASONS

There are several important economic justifications for private ownership as a foundation stone of the market economy. The most important line of reasoning relates to managerial motivation. Other important factors include the role of entrepreneurs in innovation and growth, and the urgent need for government revenues in the early years of transition.

Traditional neo-classical economic theory can offer few convincing arguments for privatization, or indeed for preferring any one ownership form to another. In this framework, the crucial ingredient in a well-functioning economy is competition, and provided that this is maintained, the competitive equilibrium attained by the free market generates economic efficiency in the Paretian sense. This so-called first fundamental theorem of welfare is indifferent to ownership rights, and indeed the second welfare theorem essentially points out that any distribution of endowments, or ownership rights, can be supported by a competitive equilibrium (see Laidler and Estrin 1989). The point can also be seen in the modelling of alternative economic systems. Theoretical models of decentralized planning (see e.g. Heal 1973) or workers' self-management (see Dreze 1976) isolated equilibria identical to those attained under competitive capitalism. The underlying reasoning was clear; since competition erodes all profits, the distribution of ownership rights to those profits cannot affect outcomes; no flows above opportunity cost will be assigned to those rights.

Should one therefore conclude that the transitional economies need merely to create a competitive environment, for example by breaking up their highly concentrated industries into competing plants or units, and reducing trade barriers — that privatization is not a crucial component of economic reform? The answer is no, but the reasoning is subtle and the force of the argument in favour of free trade and competition remains overwhelming nonetheless.

The reason lies in the potential dissonance between the task of restructuring and the motivation of managers. It forms a strand of the substantial principal-agent literature (see Vickers and Yarrow 1988, for a discussion of the privatization problem in this context). In organizations where owners do not directly control decision-making, mechanisms of governance are required to ensure that managers are motivated to maximize profits. In the West, these problems are addressed, at least in Anglo-Saxon countries, primarily through the discipline of the capital market. The share price, which itself reflects a market-based evaluation of the future profitability of the firm, is publicly available information upon which to evaluate the performance of one management team against another. Share prices can also form the basis for managerial evaluation in the job market, and for managerial remuneration. Low share prices provide the trigger for takeovers; the replacement of one management team by another. The ultimate sanction for managerial deficiencies in the system is bankruptcy or associated financial restructuring. These mechanisms taken together are considered sufficient to ensure that managers focus their efforts on the maximization of profits; according to some, excessively relative to the development of their longer-term interests (see Blinder 1992).

In contrast, state firms in the West often operate in monopolistic markets, where the firm specific rents are anywhere potentially greater, and have no market-based evaluation of their performance. Perhaps most seriously, managers are aware that the governments themselves are not uniquely interested in profits, but in a variety of objectives, many political and social, the relative weights of which are constantly altering. They therefore exploit this lack of purpose to their own advantage, for example by concealing true tradeoffs so as to claim that failures to meet targets were the consequences of inconsistent plans rather than inefficiencies. Estrin and Perotin (1991) claim that it is the state's inherent disinterest in profit maximization as a goal, rather than the absence of appropriate instruments for monitoring and enforcement, that is the principal source of public sector inefficiencies in the West. In situations when the government as owner focuses solely on profits, public and private sector performance can be comparable.

Similar arguments apply in an extreme form in the transitional economies. The main initial task of management is restructuring. One example is financial restructuring, including the stripping away of social assets such as housing, health clinics, and crèches, as well as the more conventional disposal of peripheral activities. There may be many of these because planning made firms wasteful of all resources, including plant and land, and encouraged excessive vertical integration (see Ellman 1989). Another task will be reducing the labour force, estimated to be excessive by a factor of around 25 per cent (see Estrin 1993) even before the output drop. A third will be developing new products and finding new markets, especially in the West. However the interest of the state in these matters is mixed. It will, for example, be under increasing political pressure to slow or prevent restructuring, because of the consequential unemployment. Moreover, the communist era was characterized by excessive state involvement in the enterprise sector, and many of the governments in the region represent a political reaction to those excesses. Ministers may therefore be disinclined to use their authority to direct or influence managers at all, even in ways that reflect their own political interest. Finally, the collapse of planning has left the governments in the region with few instruments directly to control or monitor the behaviour of firms nominally under their ownership. In the short term at least, transition has increased rather than decreased the autonomy of managers from their nominal owners — the state — and legislation or other instruments may be required before the authorities could once again ensure that managers would be influenced by their wishes.

Thus the authorities in the transitional economies probably neither have the interest nor power to impose effective governance on company managers. The importance of privatization therefore hinges on the motivation of managers pre-privatization. If one can rely on mangers to act in a profit-oriented way while still under public ownership, then privatization can indeed take a back seat to other reform policies in the short run. Unfortunately, there is no reason to assume that the managers of state-owned firms have the right motives, and indeed some reason to worry that they may be motivated to act in perverse ways. The most likely interest of former socialist managers in the face of all the changes to the economic environment is to attempt to preserve the *status quo*, especially with respect to employment and the local community. Even if they had the appropriate skills and experience, such managers rarely have the incentive to restructure their organizations for competition on world markets. In the absence of effective governance from the nominal owners — the state — the managers will work in the interest of major stakeholders, that is, the labour force as a whole (including management itself); the local community to which the firm may be a major supplier of public goods, services and housing as well as jobs; and perhaps even to networks of suppliers of intermediate inputs. There is no one in this list concerned to defend the return to capital, which can be assumed to take a relatively low priority.

If managers in state-owned firms are concerned with short-term defensive rather than long-term strategic actions, the resulting enterprise responses to changes in the economic environment will be sluggish but not perverse. For example, changes in relative prices will only slowly bring forth a positive supply response because managers will be more concerned to resist the decline in output required in less profitable activities rather than to stimulate expansion in profitable ones. However, there are occasions when state-ownership and the absence of effective governance might have even more serious consequences for the transition process, namely when the players within the firm are motivated to play an end-game. For example, consider the situation in an enterprise which the reform process has left clearly non-viable; for example a supplier of defence components in the CMEA whose market has disappeared. Managers and workers may realize that when capital market forces are operating effectively, the company will be closed. In the interregnum, they have an incentive to decapitalize the company, and to use its (possibly not insignificant) credit lines in effect to absorb assets from more productive uses to the decapitalization process. It may be noted that negative net worth is no constraint because decapitalization applies to gross assets.

The need rapidly to introduce some weight in decision-making to the consequences for the level of profits, and to avoid the danger of perverse enterprise responses in the short term, are the principal reasons for the pivotal role of privatization in transition. The debilitated and dispirited state apparatuses in these countries cannot fulfil the function of owner, and weak managerial motivation means that the micro-economy may not respond as necessary to reform programmes.

There are two further practical reasons in support of privatization prior to restructuring state-owned firms, at least in the context of Central and Eastern Europe. First, restructuring involves investment, and because of the stabilization programmes the governments of transitional economies typically have few resources to make available to the enterprise sector. State-owned firms do of course have recourse to the commercial banking sector, but developments there have been even slower than in the enterprise sector, and government credit policy remains very tight everywhere (see e.g. Estrin *et al.* 1992). Privatization, at least in principle, holds out the promise of access to relatively cheap new funds from the new owners through the issue of shares. Perhaps even more enticing for a few select firms is the hope that the new owners will be foreign firms, in part or in full, bringing simultaneously capital and access to Western design, technology, markets, and managerial expertise.

Second, it is felt that private owners of firms will be more willing and able to withstand the pressures to increase money wages, and thereby prevent the persistence of inflation following price liberalization. This is, of course, an example of the general argument that privatization will bring owners concerned to defend the interest of profit. It carries particular weight in transitional economies because price liberalization everywhere leads to once-and-for-all price increases because of the monetary overhang, and an important determinant of the period and intensity with which inflationary pressures will persist is the degree of indexation of wages to prices. Old communist managers have few incentives to withstand wage pressures; indeed many factors might lead them to support them. For this reason, most successful reform programmes included incomes policies, supported by penal tax rates (up to 500 per cent of wage increases above the income policy norm in Poland for example). However, it is questionable that such policies can withstand wage pressures in the medium term, and even if they did so, they would introduce increasing distortions into the emerging labour market. An urgent task of policy is therefore to stiffen managerial resistance to wage claims, and this can probably best be achieved under private ownership. Interestingly, the British privatizations of the 1980s also viewed the weakening of worker power in public sector firms as an important objective (see Estrin and Perotin 1991).

Economists from the Austrian School, e.g. Hayek (1945), would be bemused by the neo-classical conundrum over the function of ownership. In this approach, private ownership is the crucial element of the market system. In the absence of effective property rights over productive assets, it would be impossible to set up and operate a private capital market. This is because in the absence of proper ownership rights, there is no agent responsible for the production process who is rewarded according to variation in the residual surplus. It is argued that the effective monitoring of the production process lies at the heart of company efficiency, and managers cannot be motivated to do this adequately unless they have rights in the residual of revenue over cost.

The Austrian approach views the operation of a market economy differently to neo-classical economics. The focus is on the dynamics of growth, which stems from the successful exploitation of new technological processes and products. The essence of the free market is that it allows entrepreneurs to experiment with their innovations, richly rewarding those who successfully discern the pattern of demand. Such an approach would clearly place particular emphasis on the emergence of new entrepreneurs as the foundation for the private sector in transitional economies, with less emphasis on privatization of state-owned firms (see Kornai 1991).

Privatization was originally conceived as a way for a financially strapped regime to generate revenues (see Vickers and Yarrow 1988). The first British companies to be sold (e.g. BP, Amersham and the National Freight Corporation) already had large private stakes or operated in competitive markets. The efficiency objective only came to prominence with the attempt to privatize the utilities, commencing with British Telecom in 1984, five years after the start of the programme. The same logic applies even more forcefully to the economies in transition, almost all of which face a short-term budgetary crisis.

The reasons for the straightened budgetary circumstances of governments in transitional economies are straightforward (see e.g. Gomulka 1991). The process of reform undermines the tax base, especially the generation of revenues from the profit tax (see Schaffer 1992), while simultaneously increasing the government's need for expenditure, most notably on a social safety net to counter the worst effects of emerging unemployment. In long-run equilibrium, it can be argued that privatization does not affect the long-term run financial position of the government. This is because the value of the public firms being sold can be assumed approximately to equal the discounted flow of net future profits. Hence in principle privatization merely leads the government to substitute current cash for a future income. This portfolio manipulation will only be attractive to governments at times when there are significant calls for short-term expenditures and limited recourse to alternative financial sources, as occurs in transitional economies.

POLITICAL REASONS

The fundamental political reason in support of privatization relates to securing the irreversibility of the reform process. To many Western observers, the collapse of communist rule was expected and just; the democratic overthrow of an unpopular tyranny. Such a perspective was reinforced by the apparent role of Soviet tanks in keeping local communist leaders in power throughout much of Central Europe. From this standpoint, the idea that the communists are a serious force post-reform, or that they could successfully regain power, is hard to understand.

However, there were only really (non-violent) revolutions to overthrow the communists in Poland, East Germany, and Czechoslovakia. The communists (under a different name) retained power after free elections in Bulgaria and after the bloody coup to remove Ceasescu in Romania. Power slipped formally from the communists' hands after the abortive August 1991 coup in Russia, but former communists' hold many of the levers of authority. The situation may change after the so-called 'second October revolution' of 1993, in which the deadlock between the largely former communist parliament and the pro-reform government was apparently resolved in favour of the latter. A similar situation applies in much of the rest of the former Soviet Union, where the current nationalist leaders are typically ex-communists, and the old elites continue to exercise power. Communist ideas, if not in any formal sense the Communist Party itself, thus continue to exercise considerable influence across the region.

Moreover, even in the countries where the communist path was firmly rejected at the start of the reforms, the enormous hardships suffered by the populations during reform have revived the political fortunes of parties of the left. Thus, in the 1993 Polish elections, the pro-reform coalition which has led the country since the fall of the communists was defeated by a left-leaning coalition containing successors to the parties that maintained communist party rule. Similarly, the disintegration of Czechoslovakia can be interpreted as being caused by differences about the pace and desirability of reform, with the Slovaks supporting a less rapid and free market approach. Thus the reform process itself can act to stimulate a resurgence in Communist Party support, and thereby renew the threat that reform will be aborted.

Probably the most important reason for the treacherous political waters in which reform politicians are swimming is that, at least at the outset, there is only a limited constituency of people who benefit from the transitional process. Reforms, it is true, bring in their train the eradication of shortage, the availability of goods, including Western goods, and the ability to travel. But they also bring lower real wages (sometimes markedly so), the destruction of savings through inflation, and the threat of unemployment. Crucial from the perspective of median voter theory is that the benefits from reform are diffused around the population as a whole, but the costs are concentrated among a vocal group — workers and managers of large industrial firms — who may have the interest as well as the power to slow reform.

At the outset, therefore, reformers are in a position ironically reminiscent of Lenin and the Russian Bolsheviks in 1917; ruling on behalf of an interest group which as yet hardly exists. But the group is no longer the industrial working class, which has been hugely expanded under the decades of communist rule. Now the missing interest group is the entrepreneurial class, upon whose appearance the economic as well as the political success of the reform will depend. The political problem is therefore rapidly to create a property-owning class committed from their own interests to the continuation of a market economy.

In consequence, the nurturing of widespread private ownership of assets is not a policy restricted to the large industrial firms. In many countries, it has started in the agricultural sector, where the creation of an independent land-owning peasantry can immediately represent a bulwark against the re-emergence of socialism. It has also been most visible in the rapid formation of small businesses in both town and country; shops, restaurants, hotels, taxis and other small-scale service firms. The new entrepreneurs are not merely filling critical gaps on the supply side of the formerly socialist economies. They are also creating an ever-growing group of gainers from the reform, whose political interests would not be served by a reversion to socialism. In several countries, the reforming governments are also following the classic British anti-socialist policy developed by Mrs Thatcher of encouraging private home ownership via the sale of government-owned property.

However, these policies leave out some of the politically most sensitive stake-holders in the previous regime; namely the workers and managers of state-owned industrial firms. An important element on the political side of the reform is therefore to motivate these groups in support of the process through privatiza-tion. An obvious way, though as will be seen below, not necessarily the one most in tune with the economic objective of improved company performance, would be to give ownership rights to existing managers and workers, for example through employee-manager buyouts. It would also not always be necessary or constructive to give a significant ownership stake to the labour force; transition may involve significant redundancies which worker-owners might be in a position to hinder or prevent. An alternative approach would be to privatize by distribution of shares to the population as a whole, so that managers and workers obtain ownership rights in the state-owned enterprise sector as a whole, rather than in their own particular firm.

These arguments do not merely support privatization , but provide a case for it being very rapid. A traditional economic analysis would regard privatization as a very slow and difficult process, likely to impact on behaviour only after liberal-ization has taken root and under pressure from international competition. The economic case for speed rests primarily with the dangers of managerial misbeha-viour in the early phase of transition. To this can now be added the danger that the reformers will fail to create for themselves an adequate body of political support to withstand the pressures later in the transformation process to slow down or abandon reform.

5. How to privatize and to whom?

In most of the Western literature on privatization, a discussion of the actual mechanisms of privatization firmly takes second place to the analysis of the objectives and possible consequences. In Central and Eastern Europe, the position is reversed. The reasons for privatization are clear to almost all observers; as a political symbol of reform and to address the manifest deficiencies of the enterprise sector. But the transitional economies are countries in which private domestic savings are scarce, capital market institutions are weak, and existing stakeholders in state-owned firms are very powerful. Traditional modes of privatization by the state divesting its assets through capital markets to individual and institutional private owners are therefore virtually impossible to implement. Much of the debate in the region has therefore revolved around alternative methods of privatization; how to privatize and to whom?

Our discussion revolves around Figure 1.2, which presents the main options available to reforming governments. The debate has focused around two closely related issues. The first is whether to attempt to sell state-owned firms for something approaching their market price, or instead to distribute the ownership rights in the enterprise for free, or for nominal sums. The second issue is whether to seek owners from the general population or from existing (or previous) stakeholders. Figure 1.2 summarizes the various options, and gives examples of the policies applied in different countries. Most countries have in fact followed several policies at once. For example, the Czechs have followed a strategy centred on voucher privatization but which includes restitution and a concern to ensure significant foreign involvement. Almost all transitional economies have sought to encourage foreign investment and observed differences in outcomes reflect problems more with the supply of willing partners rather than of demand. The two key distinctions are between countries that have based their policy on free distribution of shares or on sales on the one hand; and on either enhancing or reducing the authority of existing stakeholders in firms on the other.

There are no automatic parallels between policy decisions in the two areas. The Czechoslovaks chose free distribution, and seeking to bring outsider pressure to bear to counter the authority of existing managers and workers. The East Germans typically sold to outsiders, notably companies from West Germany. The Hungarians, at least until recently, also chose to sell firms but in the absence of foreign buyers tended to look favourably on bids from existing management. The Russians have opted for a free distribution scheme, but in its operation this has appeared to support the emergence of management-employee owned firms.

The arguments in favour of selling firms rather than giving them away seem in abstract totally convincing (see e.g. Bolton and Roland 1992). Most importantly, the new owners will be established via a process of financial exchange so that the people who obtain control will be those who are willing to bid the most, presumably because they believe they can achieve the most with the assets. The efficiency arguments in favour of distributing ownership rights to the highest bidder are therefore strong when capital markets function well. Unfortunately, of course, transitional economies have virtually no capital markets at all, so there is no reason to assume that the potentially highest bidders will in fact be able to

HOW TO PRIVATIZE	TO WHOM			
	Existing managers and workers	General population	Previous Owners	Foreign or domestic private firms
BY SALE	Employee management buyouts e.g. in Hungary, Romania	Stock market flotation. No examples as yet		Joint ventures, foreign direct investment, e.g. Hungary, East Germany
BY FREE DISTRIBUTION	'Spontaneous privatization', employee management takeovers of assets, e.g. Russia	'Voucher privatization', e.g. Czechoslovakia, Poland	Restitution e.g. East Germany, Czechoslovakia, Bulgaria	

FIG. 1.2 Alternative methods of privatization

enter the auction at all. Bolton and Roland have tried to address this deficiency. Their proposal entails the state loaning funds to people to buy shares, the sums to be repaid from the future returns in the company.

Selling has two further advantages. In the first place, it brings badly needed revenue to the government. As mentioned earlier, transition typically brings a budgetary crisis in its tail and the authorities would be foolish to forego a major source of revenue without good reason. Finally, if privatization is sequenced correctly, prior to price liberalization, it could be used to soak up much of the monetary overhang and thereby to reduce the inflationary pressures which are bound to be released when prices are freed.

The main problem with this traditional method of privatization is that it will be very slow, and indeed, given the paucity of funds in private hands, may not work at all for a substantial proportion of the enterprises currently awaiting privatization in the transitional economies. Even in the United Kingdom, with a technically competent and relatively honest civil service, sophisticated capital markets and where the privatization revenues were only a modest proportion of domestic capital formation in any year, each privatization project took several years to bring to fruition. Thus in the decade of frenetic privatization activity in the UK, the volume of output that was transferred from the state to the private sector was only in the order of 7 per cent of the industrial total. In contrast, the Czechoslovaks, Poles and Hungarians sought in their initial programmes to transfer ownership of around 50 per cent of industrial output in the first three years of reform. Their civil services were not trained to make business plans or assess profitable opportunities, capital markets were at best fledgling, and the required revenues exceeded domestic savings by a factor of 50 or more (see Estrin 1991). In short, these ambitions were not consistent with the careful restructuring, valuation and placement associated with traditional privatization programmes in the West.

A major practical problem was the process of valuation. There was no simple way to value firms, as a basis for reservation prices in tenders or auctions. There were at least three difficulties. In the first place, most socialist enterprises had not kept the kind of accounting information that would be required to establish a track record of past profitability upon which to base future expectations. Second, even if information about previous performance was available, its predictive power in the fundamentally different economic environment post-reform was highly questionable. Reform had meant major changes in input prices, especially for energy and material inputs, and for output. It had meant the collapse of old trading relations, most notably within CMEA and between the former republics of the Soviet Union, while opening up new prospects for trade with the West. The full implications of these changes, particularly the more positive ones, made estimates of likely future profitability even more speculative than usual. Finally, the future of firms depended more than anything on the reaction of managers and workers to the changes in the environment wrought by the reforms. This would typically not be fully established at the time when valuations were required, and brought into question the validity of any valuation exercise.

Finally, any privatization based on sales would bring issues of justice and equality to the fore. In many reforming countries most of the people with access to the funds to purchase enterprises were the *nomenklatura*, the former communist elite at the head of most enterprises, the army and local government institutions. If capital markets were perfect, or if a Bolton–Roland type scheme to mimic them were introduced, the bidders for state assets would be those who thought they could earn the highest return from them. With an inegalitarian distribution of income, with wealth based on previous position in the communist regime and/or black market links, and with the effective absence of instruments whereby other private individuals might borrow to purchase state assets, privatization by sale would probably involve transfer of ownership of industrial assets to the former elite. The danger was therefore that the revolution would not change the personnel of the ruling group at all; it would merely lead to the nomenklatura replacing communist-type inequalities, based on party membership, with capitalist-type ones based on ownership of productive assets. This might seriously undermine the reforming government's moral claim to legitimacy.

The idea of free distribution of the state's assets provides an apparently simple and appealing solution to these problems. There would be no need to find domestic buyers, nor to develop capital market institutions prior to privatization. In principle there would be no requirement to value the assets. Moreover free distribution schemes offer the potential of speed and could be highly egalitarian, or at least serve to reward key agents in the reform process. If, as argued above, the issue of speed is almost as important as the fact of privatization itself, then the appeal of free distribution schemes will be very strong to reforming governments bogged down in the detail of case-by-case privatization for sale in hundreds of enterprises simultaneously.

However, not all these advantages will occur automatically with all such schemes. In practice, most schemes have attempted to simulate capital market behaviour and therefore have required some valuation information. They have also not been as fast as was first hoped; the first wave of the Czechoslovak voucher privatization was delayed by months at every stage, and some three years after it was first proposed the Polish voucher scheme has not yet taken effect. Nonetheless, they are probably much faster than the alternatives, and do lead to a remarkably fast transformation in ownership arrangements, as was shown in Table 1.3. Most importantly, they provide the authorities with the option of preventing the accumulation of power and wealth in the hands of the nomenklatura, if they choose to exercise it. In this way, voucher schemes can give a popular legitimacy to privatization itself, for example by returning assets to people from whom they had originally been confiscated or by giving the general population a stake in the assets accumulated through forced saving in the communist era.

The disadvantages of voucher privatization are a mirror image of the case in favour of selling the state's assets. One problem is that the government will fail to realize the value of its portfolio at a time when revenues are sorely needed. This might be addressed by a capital gains tax to obtain revenues from the new owners after the noise in the system had worked its way through and market-based valuations had begun to gain credence. But the most serious problem remains that many free distribution systems will fail to ensure the emergence of adequate forms of corporate governance. It is unclear that free distribution to the population as a whole, for example, can ensure the emergence of real owners dedicated to the interest of profits. Political and economic pressures towards free distribution may therefore lead reforming governments towards privatization policies which affect the legal form of ownership rights while leaving the substance of managerial motivation and enterprise performance unchanged.

In part, the impact of a free distribution scheme depends on who are the beneficiaries. This leads us to the second important distinction in categorizing the privatization process in transitional economies. Turning for the moment from economic agents external to the system, who might be willing to play according to standard Western rules (e.g., foreign corporations who would in principle be willing to purchase enterprises at market prices, provided these could be fairly evaluated), this leaves the authorities with two sets of agents to whom they might sell, or freely distribute, shares. The first is agents inside the firm; either workers or managers or both. The second are members of the general population, either as a whole or those specifically injured by the previous nationalization and who seek redress from the new regime.

There are several aspects to this issue. The first is about who in principle will make better owners of firms — outside capital holders exercising their influence through the stock exchange and financial institutions along traditional Anglo-Saxon lines, or the existing stakeholder in the firm — managers, workers, and perhaps indirectly the debt-holders who will predominantly be the commercial banks. The latter approach, with powerful managers either as effective owners or divorced from weak owners, more closely resembles the situation which has emerged in Japan and much of continental Europe (see Carlin and Meyer 1992). While theory strongly supports the salutary influence of competitive capital markets on enterprise behaviour, much of the literature tends to favour the German–Japanese system, essentially on empirical grounds (see Frydman *et al.* 1993). The transition debate, however, is not only about long-run equilibria, but is also concerned with paths. In the case of privatization, the evolutionary question concerns which agents are best motivated and qualified to restructure state-owned enterprises. From this perspective, the apparently simple solution of making majority ownership rights available to existing stakeholders may be a fundamental error.

The advantages of distribution by whatever method to insiders are clear. The approach is potentially very fast, perhaps the fastest privatization scheme available; a view apparently confirmed by the current experience in Russia. Such a privatization method would also be very cheap to administer, since the target group of buyers is already identified, and it could even raise some revenue, since managers and workers might be willing to make some contribution towards the value of the assets that they were receiving. The insider approach also ensures that existing scarce managerial experience continues to be exploited. Finally, as noted above, such a privatization method guarantees the emergence of a relatively desirable final outcome in terms of ownership structure, namely a management-owned firm.

However, there are three major problems with this approach to privatization. In the first place, employee-management ownership raises numerous questions of enterprise motivation and performance. The first issue concerns the impact of significant employee shareholdings. Many regard employee ownership as inextricably linked to the consumption of assets by workers in the form of higher wages (see e.g. Hinds 1990), despite the absence of any convincing evidence of such effects in Western cooperatives or in the former Yugoslavia (see e.g. Bonin *et al.* in press). The dangers from managerial ownership are less dramatic, but in the absence of a capital market allowing successful managers to withdraw their equity in the future, the motivational effects are not clearly as positive as one might hope. Once again, one could imagine management being forced to consume capital at the end of their life cycle in order to recoup previous investments which, because of the ownership arrangements, were not marketable.

Even if managerial or employee-managerial ownership were a long-term ideal, it is not clear that it is the most suitable ownership form for enterprises about to embark on major restructuring. In the first place, it hands decision-making authority to groups of people who might quite possibly be removed, or at least find their position fundamentally altered, by more dispassionate analysts of restructuring needs. Thus workers in overstaffed plants will be reluctant to vote themselves out of a job, while traditional socialist managers, now owners of the firm, will be unlikely to countenance choices that further increase the importance of new colleagues in the hitherto insignificant finance, accounting, and marketing divisions. Moreover, privatization to insiders brings no direct new funds to the company, at a time when additional resources are the crucial ingredient for restructuring. The same criticism applies of course to other forms of voucher privatization, with the important proviso that the new external owners have both the instruments and the control to bring in additional funds if they consider them to be required. Management-owned firms may already be heavily indebted if the authorities decided to privatize by sale, and potential debt or equity holders will be aware that they have few sanctions against managerial abuses.

The final problem with distribution to existing stake holders concerns the political legitimacy of the programme. The argument applies with particular force if managers and workers are simply given ownership rights in their firms. As already noted, there are political and social dangers in appearing to reward the previous elites, a problem more marked in Central Europe than in the former Soviet Union. But the situation is hardly better if the state sells managers and workers their shares, because most observers realize that the insiders are likely to have a far better idea of the true value of the firm than the authorities, and are therefore likely to be able to obtain a very good price. Problems of this sort led to a public outcry against so-called spontaneous privatization, even in highly pragmatic Hungary which therefore introduced fairly strict state supervision of the privatization process (see Chapter 9). The political problems are hardly reduced if the privatization to insiders includes widespread employee ownership. The reason is that the prospects of particular firms are very different, and there is no fair reason to justify the allocation of rights to highly unequal streams of income to the working population as a whole on the basis of where they happen to be employed at a particular moment. Clearly privatization of this sort will in the long term lead to major disparities, with some winners and some losers from the privatization process as well as a group of workers, for example so-called 'non-productive' workers such as employees in the state, education and health sectors,

completely excluded from the resulting capital gains. Privatization in this form
may undermine the legitimacy of the privatization process, and therefore of the
whole reform movement.

The alternative approach is to distribute shares to outsiders. As already stated,
privatization to outside owners on the basis of an auction probably represents the
first best solution, but is probably impractical for the majority of firms in transitional economies. One is drawn down the route of free distribution, for which
there are two alternative methods. The first is to restore ownership rights to
previous owners — restitution. The second is to distribute shares to the population as a whole — a voucher or certificate scheme. Both methods have the
advantage of speed and in principle bring external capital market pressures to
bear on the restructuring process. Both also offer the possibility that additional
external funding might be made available by the new owners. This is because the
creation of external ownership rights will typically be associated with the formation of capital market institutions that permit shareholders to withdraw their
funds by selling their stake in the marketplace. However, in the short term the
prospects here are not necessarily much better than with insider privatization
because in neither case do the new owners have recourse to significant funds.
Finally, outsider privatizations have the advantage that they can be constructed
so as to be fair, and therefore to provide the political legitimacy so crucial in the
early stages of reform. However the two strands imply quite different concepts of
justice. With restitution, people get back what they had lost under the communists, while with vouchers the benefits of privatization are diffused, along with
ownership rights, across the population as a whole.

As mentioned above, the key problem with free distribution schemes to outsiders is that they may fail to create effective forms of corporate governance. In
the case of restitution, the problem may be that the individuals or families who
have suddenly been given ownership rights neither understand, nor are interested
to learn, the business which they have inherited. If there were perfect capital
markets, they would simply sell the business to the highest bidder. However,
this is not a likely outcome because the paucity of buyers and the asymmetries
of information in the capital market are the reasons for following the policy of
free distribution in the first place. The new owners may therefore have to take
control themselves, and may well be far worse at management and restructuring
than the existing managerial group. The alternative, which seems common from
case studies (see Estrin *et al.* 1993) is that the newly restituted owners will leave
decision-making authority in the hands of existing managers and workers. Restitution then leads *de facto* to the same outcome as free distribution of ownership
rights to enterprise insiders.

The problem of corporate governance in the context of voucher privatization
schemes has received much more attention in the literature (see e.g. Lipton and
Sachs 1990, Bolton and Roland 1992, Frydman *et al.* 1993). The difficulty here is
that successful privatization to the general public must imply that ownership
rights are widely diffused among the population as a whole. But highly diffused
ownership rights, and the absence of any dominant block of shares, means that
control over managers will necessarily be weak. The distributional objective of
voucher privatization — to spread the new ownership rights as widely as possible

among the new population — therefore conflicts with the aim of bringing effective external capital market pressures to bear on managerial decision-making. When ownership rights are widely diffused, so that managers do not need to fear the dissatisfaction of a controlling block of shares acting in unanimity to remove them from their jobs or to enforce, for example, more radical restructuring policies, they may feel empowered to resist threatening changes.

The architects of voucher privatization schemes have been very concerned to minimize such effects. They have therefore sought to encourage the development of intermediate capital market institutions standing between the general public as shareholders and firms, concentrating ownership rights and able to exert effective corporate governance. The Polish scheme, for example, envisages the simultaneous construction of investment funds which actually jointly own the former state-owned enterprise sector and the free distribution of shares in these funds to the population as a whole (see Chapter 10 on Poland). In contrast, the financial intermediaries were not an integral part of the Czechoslovak voucher scheme; instead investment funds sprang up on a competitive basis to exploit the profits available via economies of scale in information about firms and from concentrating ownership rights (see Chapter 8 on Czechoslovakia). In no country is it yet clear whether these groupings of ownership rights can actually offset the tremendous advantage in decision-making power offered to insiders from their superior access to information about the firm's production methods, markets, finance and prospects. We have also yet to see anywhere the emergence of a large-scale secondary market in these externally held ownership rights, which would permit both a concentration of final ownership rights, rather than the rights of the intermediaries. The secondary market is also crucial in that, by giving investors the right to take their funds out when they wanted, it might encourage them to begin to put some additional funds into the enterprise sector, thereby facilitating the restructuring process.

6. Conclusions

In summary, there is no simple answer to the question of how best to privatize firms in Central and Eastern Europe. An imitation of standard Western methods is very attractive, especially if the buyer is a Western firm bringing new technology, capital, markets and managerial know-how. However, while valuable in a few special cases, as a general method it is probably too slow for most reforming governments and in practice unfeasible for most firms. Free distribution solves the problem of speed and feasibility, but arguably at the cost of entrenching the authority of existing workers and managers, who will probably not be motivated to restructure or to defend the interest of profit. There is also a trade-off between speed and fairness; privatization by free distribution (or sale at nominal prices, for example based on the historic valuation of capital) to managers and/or workers can be extremely fast but may carry over inequalities from the previous to the new regime. Both privatization to the general population and restitution are potentially more complex and therefore will probably be slower, but have the advantage of building political support for privatization and, as a consequence, for the reform process as a whole. But it is not clear that any of the forms of free distribution can ensure the establishment of effective capital market disciplines on the behaviour of enterprise management.

Thus, the conflicts between the various objectives for privatization in transitional economies — especially between the political and the economic — are reflected in the debate over alternative privatization methods. The way that these conflicts have been resolved in practice depends in large part on the political and economic situation of the countries in question. For example, where the authorities have had access to foreign capital, either in the case of the former East Germany through unification with West Germany or in Hungary via trading and capital market links developed over the decades, the privatization agencies have pursued a policy of sale to the highest bidder, usually subject to certain guarantees about employment and conditions etc. Restitution has been important in countries like Czechoslovakia and Bulgaria, where the grievances of former owners are still relatively fresh in the public conscience, but much less prominent in the former Soviet Union, where former private property rights are a much dimmer memory. Free distribution has been pivotal in most of the countries that have wanted to privatize very quickly, most notably Poland and the former Czechoslovakia, and more recently Russia. The former countries have also been very concerned with the equity issues in privatization, as part of their quest to build political legitimacy for the reform process. Finally, the attempt to recruit outside rather than inside owners has clearly been associated with the authority and legitimacy of the reforming governments. In countries where the central government is pro-reform but weak, privatization has tended to be based on free distribution to insiders, for example in Romania and Russia. Regimes with a stronger popular base, or facing less effective opposition, have sought to sponsor external ownership, using schemes which also attempt to encourage effective corporate governance, for example, Poland and Czechoslovakia.

Notes

1. It also stimulated the emergence of a flourishing secondary market in most countries, with prices far higher than those on the official market.
2. However, Hungary suffered considerably from the need to maintain the payments on its foreign debt.

References

Aghion, P., Blanchard, O. and **Burgess, S.** (in press) The behaviour of state firms in Eastern Europe, pre-Privatization, forthcoming, *European Economic Review*.

Bergson, A. (1991) The USSR before the fall. How poor and why, *Journal of Economic Perspectives*, **5**, pp. 29–44.

Blanchard O. *et al.* (1991) *Reform in Eastern Europe*, MIT Press, Cambridge, Mass.

Blinder, A. (1992) 'Should the former socialist economies look East or West for a model?' Lecture at Tenth World Congress of International Economic Association in Moscow, August 1992.

Bolton, P. and **Roland, G.** (1992) The economics of mass privatization, *CEPR Discussion Paper*.

Bonin, J., Jones, D. C. and **Putterman, L.** (in press) Theoretical and empirical studies of producer cooperation: will ever the twain meet?, forthcoming *Journal of Economic Literature*.

Borcherding, T. E., Pommerehne, W.W. and **Schneider, F.** (1982) Comparing the efficiency of private and public production: the evidence from five countries. *Zeitschrift für Nationalökonomie*, Suppl. 2, pp. 127–56.

Carlin, W. and **Mayer, C.** (1992) Restructuring enterprises in Eastern Europe, *Economic Policy*, **15**, pp. 311–352.

Dreze, J. (1976) Some theory of labour-management and participation, *Econometrica*, **44**, pp. 1125–39.

Ellman, M. (1989) *Socialist Planning*, Cambridge University Press, Cambridge.

Estrin, S. (1991) Privatization in Central and Eastern Europe: the lessons from Western Experience, *Annals of Public and Cooperative Economy*, pp. 159–182.

Estrin, S. (1993) The inheritance, in Barr N. (ed), *Labour Markets and Social Policy in Central and Eastern Europe*, World Bank, Washington, DC.

Estrin, S. and **Perotin, V.** (1991) Does ownership always matter?, *International Journal of Industrial Organization*, **9**, pp. 55–72.

Estrin, S., Hare, P. and **Suranyi, M.** (1992) Banking in transition: development and current problems in Hungary, *Soviet Studies*, **44**, (5), pp. 785–808.

Estrin, S., Gelb, A. and **Singh, I.J.** (1993) Restructuring, viability and privatization, *CIS-Middle Europe Centre Discussion Paper*, No. 1, London Business School.

Estrin, S., Schaffer, M. and **Singh, I.J.** (in press) Enterprise adjustment in transition economies, forthcoming, *MOST*.

Fischer, S. and **Gelb, A.** (1991) Issues in socialist economy reform, *WPS* 565, World Bank, Washington, DC.

Frydman, R., Rapaczynski, A. and **Earle, J.** (1993) *The Privatization Process in Central Europe*, CEU Press, Prague.

Gomułka, S. (1990) *The Theory of Technological Change and Economic Growth*, Wheatsheaf, London.

Gomułka, S. (1991) The causes of recession following stabilization, *Comparative Economic Studies*, **33** (2), pp. 71–89.

Hare, P. and **Hughes, G.** (1992) Trade restructuring in Eastern Europe, in Flemming, J. and Rollo, J.M.C. (eds.) *Trade, Payments and Adjustments in Central and Eastern Europe*, RIAA and EBRD, London.

Hayek, F. von (1945) The use of knowledge in society, *American Economic Review*, **35**, (4), pp. 519–30.

Heal, G.M. (1973) *The Theory of Economic Planning*, North-Holland, Amsterdam.

Hinds, M. (1990) Issues in the introduction of market forces in Eastern European socialist economies, *EMENA Discussion Papers*, No. IDP-0057, The World Bank, Washington DC.

Hncir, M., Estrin, S. and **Hare, P.** (1993) The development of Czech banking during transition, *CIS-Middle Europe Centre Discussion Paper*, London Business School.

Journal of Economic Perspectives (1991) Special Issue on Economic Transition, Fall, 1991.

Kornai, J. (1991) *The Road to a Free Economy*, Norton Press, New York.

Laidler, D. and **Estrin, S.** (1989) *Introduction to Microeconomics*, (3rd Ed.), Philip Allan, London.

Lipton, D. and **Sachs, J.** (1990) Creating a market economy in Eastern Europe: the case of Poland, *Brookings Papers on Economic Activity*, **1**.

Marchand, M., Pestieu, P. and **Tulkens, H.** (1984) *The Performance of Public Enterprises*, North-Holland, Amsterdam.

Pinto, B. *et al.* (1993) Transforming state enterprises in Poland: microeconomic evidence in adjustment, *Brookings Papers*, pp. 213–270.

PlanEcon **Reports** (1993), various.

Portes, R. (ed), (1993) *Economic Transition in Central Europe*, CEPR, London.

Schaffer, M. (1992) The enterprise sector and the emergence of the Polish fiscal crisis, *Working Paper No. 280.* LSE Centre for Economic Performance.

Schaffer, M. (1993) Polish economic transformation: from recession to recovery to challenges ahead, *Business Strategy Review*, **4**, (3), pp. 53–72.

Svejnar, J. (1993) Czechoslovakia, in Portes, R. (ed), *Economic Transition in Central Europe*, CEPR, London

Vickers, J. and **Yarrow, G.** (1988) *Privatization: An Economic Analysis*, MIT Press, Boston Mass.

CHAPTER TWO

Privatization in comparative perspective: an overview of the emerging issues

Paul Hare*

1. Introduction

In each of the Central and Eastern European countries in transition towards a market-type economy, a privatization programme has been regarded as a crucial component of the policies required to bring about the transition, standing alongside macroeconomic stabilization, the liberalization of prices and foreign trade, and a variety of institutional reforms (see Portes 1991). While there is scope for argument about the most appropriate mix and timing of these policies, there is no doubt that the creation of a vigorous and expanding private sector is essential. This can result from the *ab initio* growth of the private sector under certain conditions, as appears to be happening in China, and as Kornai (1990) appeared to recommend for Hungary, but most countries (including Hungary) have concluded that the established state-owned sector cannot merely be left to 'wither away'. Hence the need for some form of privatization programme.

Such programmes are either under discussion or already in the process of being implemented in several of the Eastern European countries in which communist regimes collapsed in 1989. Privatization started in several countries in 1990 (or, unofficially, even in 1989 itself), and Hungary, Poland and Czechoslovakia had all prepared comprehensive programmes covering both small-scale and large-scale businesses by early 1991 (see Grosfeld and Hare 1991). These programmes involved the creation of new institutions to manage the process, extensive experimentation with alternative methods and approaches to privatization, and the setting of ambitious targets concerning the rate of privatization. In practice, while implementation of the 'small' privatization was usually quite rapid, 'large' privatization proceeded more slowly and several countries were obliged to re-think their initial strategies (e.g. for Hungary, see Chapter 9).

As early as 1988, even in the former Soviet Union, some initial steps had been taken, at least in the sense that parts of large state firms could be, and were being,

* A shorter and less developed version of this chapter was prepared for the workshop on **Economic Transformation in Central and Eastern Europe**, WZB, Berlin, May 13th and 14th, 1993. I am grateful to my discussant, David Stark, and other participants in the workshop for very helpful comments, and also to the editor of this volume, Saul Estrin. The research for this chapter was undertaken with the help of ESRC grant no. Y3009253007 (under the East-West Initiative), for which I would also like to express my appreciation.

converted into new forms of cooperative or leasehold enterprise which in many cases behaved as if they were private in all but name (see Hare 1990). Russia passed a general privatization law in 1991 and had, by 1992, established much of the institutional framework through which the programme was to be implemented (see Ash and Hare 1993).

In the former East Germany, reunited with the Western part of the country in an enlarged Federal Republic of Germany since Autumn 1990, control over most large enterprises was transferred to the agency set up to manage the privatization process there (the *Treuhandanstalt*). The agency is restructuring many firms, closing down others, and selling off as many firms as it can. It is privatizing firms by negotiation with individual buyers, by organizing auctions, and occasionally by public issue of shares.

This chapter reviews some of the important conceptual issues raised by the early experience of privatization in Central and Eastern Europe. Section 2 begins by discussing the aims of privatization, and section 3 then discusses the main methods of privatization being employed in Central and Eastern Europe; these provide a useful introduction to subsequent stages of the argument. Section 4 introduces a model of privatization which explains some of the financial constraints on the process, while section 5 reviews a number of aspects of private sector development which help to explain why rapid privatization may have both political and economic advantages, as well as potential costs along a number of important dimensions. Section 6 concludes.

2. Aims of privatization

As was implied above, one of the main purposes of privatization in Central and Eastern Europe is to contribute towards the creation of a well-functioning market economy, since it is hard to imagine such an economy without a large private sector. Clearly, though, for this objective to be achieved, it must be the case that privatization actually changes enterprise behaviour in important ways. Hence it is important to consider the form of privatization with some care, and to take account of the environment in which the newly privatized firms must function, in order to assess the likely impact upon firms' behaviour. The key role played by the context in which privatization occurs is emphasized in KPMG and CERT (1993), which shows that many newly privatized firms in Russia do not expect to change their economic behaviour much, if at all!

A second, not unrelated objective of privatization is to create conditions conducive to raising productive efficiency in all its dimensions: lowering costs of production (including unit labour costs), improving product quality and variety, improving innovative behaviour, fostering investment based on prospective profitability. This objective introduces considerations of the management structures and managerial incentives resulting from privatization, as well as issues of financial markets and the allocation of credit, and reforms affecting the labour market. It also, implicitly, raises questions about the relative importance of ownership change, and the nature of the ownership structures resulting from privatization, versus the creation of a more competitive economic environment as determinants of overall efficiency. Exactly this issue has arisen, for instance, in discussions of the economic impact of privatization in the UK, where the performance of both state-owned firms and those recently privatized improved during the 1980s, suggesting that the competitive environment was at least as significant as ownership changes; see Dunkerley and Hare (1991), and Molyneux and Thompson (1987).

Third, for governments facing difficulties in raising revenue and balancing the state budget privatization can, in principle, provide a means of raising some revenue. Naturally, this only works if firms and other state-owned assets can be sold in the market at more than give-away prices, and if the resulting revenue is not entirely absorbed by the administrative and other costs associated with carrying out the privatization. However, since these 'other costs' include some of the costs of cleaning up enterprise balance sheets (writing off or writing down some of their past accumulated debts), restructuring the business to create viable economic units, and dealing with formerly neglected environmental liabilities, it can be expected that the net revenue from privatization would be rather modest in practice. That has certainly been the experience to date for the *Treuhandanstalt* in Germany and the State Property Agency in Hungary, though the latter has produced some net revenue for the budget.

Fourth, and in contrast, if revenue considerations are not so central, then equity arguments may dictate that privatization should be conducted in such a way that the ownership of former state-owned assets should be distributed relatively uniformly across the population. This view of privatization is often motivated by a variety of important political or quasi-political arguments. Thus according to the former socialist ideology, all property was already 'owned' by the people, the state merely acting as the people's agent. If this view is sustained, then people should not, logically, be required to pay to acquire assets which, in this sense, they already own. Also, in several countries there is great concern to avoid a situation where former members of the *nomenklatura* become the private owners of most state-owned property, or where most state assets fall into the hands of foreign firms and individuals. In practice, given the transferability of shares and other financial instruments in the financial markets — formally or informally — it may be hard to avoid such an outcome. But some governments, such as that of the Czech Republic, have decided that this should not be the initial outcome of privatization. To achieve this, mass privatization through a form of voucher scheme is the chosen route for the initial distribution of many state-owned assets. This ensures that, even if concentration proves to be the ultimate outcome, as must be rather likely given the tendencies towards ownership concentration which arise in most market-type economies, the government itself should not attract much of the resulting opprobrium.

Finally, in constructing a market-type economy, recognition of the need for a large private sector has sometimes been used as an argument for extremely rapid privatization. The same conclusion has also been reached on political grounds, namely the point that the momentum of reforms can only be sustained if privatization is carried out rapidly, to create an irreversible and therefore credible commitment to a market-type economy. For discussion of this argument, see Blanchard *et al.* (1991). The argument has some appeal, but tends to underestimate the practical

problems — administrative and other — of organizing a large privatization programme. As a result, it may simply not be feasible to accomplish rapid privatization in a way that is widely perceived as being fair and equitable.

3. Methods of privatization

As will already be clear, different methods of privatization are most appropriate
for achieving different objectives. Whatever form of privatization is adopted in a
given case, the state-owned asset or firm will first have to be transformed into a
recognizable legal form. This stage is often referred to as commercialization (e.g.
see IMF *et al.* 1990), though sometimes that term is used only for the more formal
creation of a state-owned joint stock company. The essential point is that the
company, business or asset must be clearly identified, its ownership status established, a suitable management structure installed (including, where relevant, a
company board of directors) and a business form recognized in the relevant
commercial law created. For many state-owned firms in the traditional system,
even the list of assets belonging to and/or used by the firm was often not well-
defined. The latter is not, of course, a problem unique to Central and Eastern
Europe, since it commonly arose in connection with privatizations in the UK.
However, in Eastern Europe it can prove to be rather more complicated than in
the UK because:

1. The original nationalization process in Eastern Europe rarely created
   unambiguous legal title in the hands of the state to the property that
   was expropriated from the former private owners;
2. Many firms came to use assets 'owned' by a number of state bodies and
   thought of them as the firm's property, but when privatization is in prospect the state bodies concerned suddenly have an interest in identifying
   and reclaiming 'their' assets;
3. Certain important productive assets, notably land, were usually not valued
   at all, so that formal ownership was immaterial — on privatization, this,
   too, becomes a very important issue;
4. Many firms provided important and highly subsidized services to their
   workers — such as housing, child care, access to holiday homes and
   culture, etc. — and on privatization the proper status of this provision is
   suddenly called into question; and
5. Even when the above issues do not arise, there is scope for competition and
   conflict between different levels of the state concerning the ownership of
   different state-owned assets. In this context it is a serious mistake to think
   of the state as a single, all-encompassing entity.

The methods of privatization which have been proposed, and to varying degrees
implemented, comprise the following (see Blommenstein and Hare, 1993):

1. Sale by public offering of shares;
2. Sale by private treaty (closed or limited tender);

3. Sale by public auction;
4. Leasing assets or firms;
5. Management and/or worker buyout;
6. Free (or almost free) distribution of shares/vouchers to the population;
7. Free or subsidized distribution of shares to the workforce/ management;
8. Free distribution of shares to social institutions;
9. Restitution of property to former owners;
10. Privatization via liquidation or bankruptcy.

Naturally, for any given firm or asset, a mixture of methods can be used: some shares can be given away, others retained by the government, others transferred to, say, a state insurance company, the rest being sold, depending on circumstances such as the firm's own aims and the government's mix of objectives.

In addition, a variety of new owners can emerge, including foreigners (both individuals and firms), domestic residents, domestic firms and institutions, with the state itself possibly retaining a stake. The choice of privatization methods both influences, and is influenced by, the set of likely future owners.

Some countries have been concerned both about the risks of excessive foreign ownership, and about the possibility of so called *nomenklatura* privatization, as indicated above. The former risk does not appear, thus far, to be very serious, since only Hungary and the Czech Republic have attracted significant inflows of direct foreign investment (partly associated with firms being privatized, partly with entirely new business activities). On the other hand, the rate at which foreign investment can be attracted clearly affects the feasible speed of privatization, and so measures to encourage such investment can be regarded as part of a comprehensive privatization programme; this point is illustrated in the model presented later on.

The latter, *nomenklatura* privatization, is a more serious risk, but may be unavoidable in the longer term since those who had established leading positions under the old system may well possess at least some of the characteristics needed to succeed in business (including necessary or helpful contacts, and possibly financial resources, too). Eventually, such people are likely to acquire the more productive assets in one way or another, though an initial free distribution of shares might delay that outcome.

The other argument for free distribution (essentially, method 6, and to some extent 7) is that unless foreign investment reaches implausibly high levels, it is the only feasible approach if it is desired to privatize quickly. But aside from the administrative complications of this, which tend to slow it down, Hussain and Stern (1993) argue that for fiscal reasons, the rapid sale of public assets could be very damaging, that there are opportunities to improve performance even while firms remain in the public sector, and that in any case, partial privatization involving leasing and shared ownership is perfectly feasible.

Newbery (1991) and others also urge greater caution, arguing that a good deal of restructuring, including the elimination of the most entrenched monopoly positions, is an essential prerequisite for privatization, and that this would take time. However, this argument assumes that the state possesses both the resources and the competence to undertake effective restructuring, whereas this is frequently unlikely in practice. Indeed, one reason for voucher-type privatization, aside from the equity and speed arguments already advanced, is precisely the state's own recognition that it cannot do anything constructive with the firms it formally owns prior to their privatization. Moreover, the most appropriate form of restructuring almost certainly depends on who the new owner or owners turn out to be, suggesting that it may be better to leave all but the most natural and straightforward forms of restructuring (such as splitting a conglomerate into separate business units) until a specific privatization deal has been agreed.

This conclusion takes for granted that the country concerned is already committed to the creation of an increasingly competitive business environment, including a fairly high degree of openness to international trade and favourable conditions for new firms to start up. For these features ensure that any near-monopoly positions initially maintained or created as a result of privatization can only be sustained if the firm involved turns out to be efficient and competitive. If the environment is less conducive to competition, then more pre-privatization restructuring might be called for, though it must still take into account the problems of state competence referred to above.

Despite the early success of the voucher privatization in the CSFR (now the separate states of the Czech Republic and Slovakia), it is now increasingly accepted that the administrative complications associated with all forms of privatization ensure that it will normally take longer than initially envisaged. Among other things, this implies that some attention needs to be paid to managing those firms which will remain in the state-owned sector for some time (or indefinitely), as some governments already recognize (e.g. Hungary, by forming the State Asset Management Company in 1992). This is likely to become an increasingly potent issue as the 'best' firms are privatized, leaving behind in state hands a mixed bag of 'more difficult' firms, some of which (such as the public utilities, companies producing national specialities, etc.) can be partly privatized, while others (e.g. some of the older heavy industry, including some defence-related firms) may well, more or less rapidly, decline into ultimate liquidation. Designing and enforcing effective governance structures for these firms remains a very difficult problem, even in countries like Hungary which have at least started to construct a suitable institutional framework.

Of the methods of privatization listed above, methods 1 and 2 are those most widely employed in Western countries, with a limited role, too, for method 5. The other methods are rarely used. But the Western approach is predicated on the existence of well-developed and highly liquid capital markets, able to absorb substantial share offerings without great difficulty. It also presupposes that the public assets being sold only comprise a relatively small fraction of the nation's capital stock, since it is then plausible to assume that savings ratios and asset-holding preferences will be compatible with such public share sales. As we shall see in section 5, below, these conditions are not likely to hold in Central and Eastern Europe, at least for the time being. Nevertheless, by early 1991 there were three principal approaches to privatization emerging from the Eastern European economies in transition, though most countries actually used, or proposed to use, a mixture of all three.

1. That of the former East Germany, together with Hungary, involving conventional, British-style sales of the larger companies (the British approach); in the case of the former East Germany, this approach is often accompanied by significant restructuring of the firms involved.
2. That of Poland (at least in its initial intention) and Czechoslovakia (in practice) using vouchers as a device for giving away shares in the major companies to the population (the voucher approach). The Soviet Union had not then progressed beyond the earliest, semi-official stages of the process, but by late 1992 it, too, had opted for voucher privatization as one element in its programme (selling companies via auctions in which vouchers were used to buy shares), as had Romania and several other countries. The precise mechanisms and arrangements are rather different in each case.
3. A programme based largely on the use of management-worker buy-outs; in Russia, for instance, this is currently the main method of privatization, alongside voucher-based sales.

In addition, given the distortion to prices which prevailed before 1990, it is not surprising to find that many new business units in Central and Eastern Europe are rising upon the ashes of old, hopelessly unprofitable, state-owned enterprises. This means that method 10, privatization via liquidation or bankruptcy, is a widespread means of creating new private firms in the region.

In choosing between these approaches or some mixture of the three, an important question concerns the types of post-privatization management/governance structures which countries wish to establish at enterprise level. The central issue here is the balance between insider and outsider models of control (see Frydman and Rapaczynski 1993; Frydman *et al.* 1993). With insider control, firms are essentially run by a coalition of workers and managers, who are likely, also, to own the bulk of the firms' assets. As illustrated by the Russian experience, and by the decentralized implementation of privatization of many smaller and medium firms in Hungary and elsewhere, this can facilitate quite rapid privatization and ensures that productive assets remain in domestic hands; on the other hand, it provides no new funds for investment, no new management expertise, and in the absence of competition provides very weak incentives to change how the firm operates.

With outsider models, the firm comes to be controlled by new owners (domestic or foreign), probably bringing new technology, management skills and finance, as well as experience of operating in other markets. However, since the new owners are likely to have a more commercial approach than the former managers, they will often want the firm to change very rapidly. The question then is how rapidly it can adapt itself to the new conditions.

In Eastern Europe, though not so far in the former Soviet Union (except in the three Baltic States), the restitution issue has assumed great political importance, being seen as a way of righting past injustices and simultaneously signalling the new governments' intention not to perpetrate similar injustices in the future. However, in practice it is not easy to deal with the issue without creating new injustices and also creating a bonanza for the principal beneficiaries, namely the legal profession.

Some countries opted initially for the return of the physical assets which were formerly expropriated. This simple principle, though, is very hard to implement because: (1) existing users of the assets, who may bear no responsibility for the original expropriation, have to be dispossessed or at least subject to new contractual arrangements; (2) the assets themselves will almost certainly have been changed by subsequent investment, making it unclear what should be returned; (3) original owners may be dead or abroad and it is not clear what rights should be assigned to descendants or other relatives; and (4) there is a real risk that arguments over the ownership of specific productive assets could delay privatization.

All these problems arose in East Germany, though their potential damage was mitigated by legal provisions giving priority to privatization proposals in which a given firm's assets would be used productively: restitution would only be approved if the former owner could offer to make the most effective use of the assets, otherwise financial compensation would be available instead. In Hungary, the government initially sought to confine restitution to the return of agricultural land to private hands, but was obliged by the constitutional court to make a more general provision. It therefore adopted a compensation programme whereby restitution claims had to be submitted by a given date, and those claims which were accepted and verified by the office set up for this purpose would receive compensation in the form of privatization bonds; these could be used to purchase state-owned assets in subsequent privatizations, and already an active secondary market in these bonds has developed. In order to limit the potential future burden on the state budget, the maximum possible value of compensation to any one individual was set at a rather low level. This approach appears to represent an effective compromise between the demands of justice, the need not to impede privatization, and the requirements of public finance.

4. Two-sector model of capital accumulation

Several countries embarked upon their privatization programmes by announcing astonishingly rapid rates of disposal of state assets. Thus Czechoslovakia (as it then was) and Hungary both envisaged selling off and/or giving away about 50 per cent of state-owned assets within around three years. Experience since 1990 suggests that in practice time-scales are likely to prove more extended than this, for a variety of reasons: disagreements within some governments (e.g. Poland) over the details of the privatization model to be pursued, the administrative complexity of voucher schemes (though important lessons are being learned from the early experience), the collapse in demand in the region which makes many firms unprofitable and so hard to privatize without major restructuring, the difficulty of attracting foreign capital into such uncertain and unsettled environments.

In order to study some of the implications of different rates of privatization, and the trade-offs between speed and other variables, consider an economy comprising firms, households and a public sector (government expenditure and taxation). Some firms are publicly owned (sector denoted by the suffix, G), while others are owned by households (sector denoted by the suffix, P). The model of the government sector is a very simple one, with government spending fixed as a share of GDP, and with fixed tax rates on the profits of publicly owned firms (t_G), privately owned firms (t_P), and the wage income of households (t_W). The government accounts are balanced in each period by varying a lump sum tax allowance applied to households (H). The model is essentially closed (i.e. no exports or imports), though it is useful to make some allowance for the possibility of net capital flows from abroad, since these can play an important role in speeding up privatization. Accordingly, these are included in the model from the start, represented as an exogenous flow, F per period; it is assumed that they are used entirely for private sector asset accumulation.

At any given time, let K_G be the volume of capital in the public sector and K_P be the volume in the private sector (i.e., as indicated above, owned by households). Note that I assume suitable units of measurement can be found. This is despite the fact that valuation issues have figured prominently in recent discussions of privatization in Eastern Europe. But valuation is not my concern in this section, so I have simply set it aside.

Let L_G and L_P be the levels of employment in government (i.e. state-owned firms) and private sectors respectively, and Y_G and Y_P the corresponding output levels. It is then assumed that output, labour and capital are related through production functions, as follows:

$$Y_G = f(K_G, L_G), \text{ and } Y_P = a.f(K_P, L_P), \tag{1}$$

where $a > 1$ is an efficiency factor, denoting the greater efficiency with which factors of production are employed in the private sector. Obviously, if $a = 1$, then the two sectors are equally efficient. But when $a > 1$, [1] means that any assets employed in the private sector are used more productively than state-sector assets, reflecting improved x-efficiency[1].

A second source of inefficiency derives from imperfections in the factor markets. Thus the public sector is assumed to use *labour* relatively inefficiently, in that it employs more people than would be justified by the usual appeal to marginal productivity conditions, though not so many more that it fails to make any profits at all; this allocative inefficiency is possible in an environment of relatively soft budget constraints. In contrast, the private sector is assumed to employ labour efficiently, in that the standard marginal productivity condition is satisfied. The conditions just stated on the public sector's use of labour can be put more formally in terms of the underlying production function, [1]. Thus define L_G^1 from the condition,

$$\frac{\partial f}{\partial L_G} = w_G,$$

this being the level of employment which would arise in the public sector if it were profit-maximizing. Then define L_G^2 from the equation: $f(K_G, L_G^2) = w_G.L_G^2$, this being the maximum public sector employment compatible with avoiding losses.

Then our assumptions imply that public sector employment can be expressed in the form:

$$L_G = \lambda L_G^1; 1 \leq \lambda \leq \left(\frac{L_G^2}{L_G^1}\right). \tag{2}$$

The other factor market imperfection is that *capital* is not freely transferable between sectors, but only moves as a result of the purchases of public capital by the private sector which are modelled in equations [3] and [4] below. Moreover, even the new investment that goes on in the model is not based on considerations of the relative marginal products of capital in the two sectors, private and public.

Now let α be the proportion of private sector and household saving used to accumulate productive assets originally owned by the public sector; in other words, this is a measure of the rate at which privatization is going on in any given period. Let p be the price paid by the private sector for each unit of capital transferred from the state sector. Note that both α and p are treated as fixed parameters in what follows; thus there is no formal analysis of the demand for public sector assets by the private sector, though of course it is possible to calculate the implications of making different assumptions.

Asset accumulation equations can now be written for the public and private sectors of the economy[2]. They are as follows:

$$\dot{K}_P = \gamma S_P + F \tag{3}$$

for the private sector, where $\gamma = (1 - \alpha) + \alpha/p$; and, for the government-owned sector:

$$\dot{K}_G = (1 - t_G)\Pi_G - (\gamma - 1)S_P \tag{4}$$

To interpret equation [3], observe that the rate of increase of private capital equals the direct investment in the sector (i.e. $(1 - \alpha)S_P$) plus the capital transferred from the public sector; at price p for each unit of public capital, the volume of such transfers is obviously $\alpha S_P/p$. Combining these terms yields the stated equation. In equation [4] we have to consider three terms. The first is just the public sector's after tax profits, $(1 - t_G)\Pi_G$, which is assumed to be wholly invested in the public sector; the second is a deduction of $\alpha S_P/p$, representing the *number of units* of capital transferred to the private sector; and the third is αS_P, representing the *payment* made by the private sector for the capital transferred, a sum which is then used for investment in the public sector. Taking these three terms together, and rearranging a little, gives [4]. Note that depreciation was ignored throughout this discussion. For simplicity, it is ignored throughout this section.

These equations, together with the equation for public sector balance, determine the path of the economy. Thus if we regard the tax rates as given, there are three exogenous variables at each point of time, namely the lump sum payment to households, H, and the two capital stock variables, K_P and K_G. Given the complexity of the resulting equations, further analysis is not very fruitful unless specific functional forms are employed. Accordingly, the technical appendix linearizes the model and derives an equation for the path of x, the share of the economy's capital stock held by the private sector. With suitable assumptions (specified in the appendix), and adopting the convenient initial condition $x(0) = x_0 = 0$, implying that there is no private ownership of capital at the start, it follows that the private sector's share of the capital stock increases from zero (the initial position) up to 100 per cent in finite time. What is interesting, though, is to explore the sensitivity of this convergence to particular values of some of the more important parameters. This issue is investigated by computing a number of solutions for a special case based on parameter values not too far removed from those for Hungary.

Table 2.1 investigates the effect of changes in α and p on the time required to reach 50 per cent private ownership (t_{50}) and 100 per cent private ownership (t_{100}). As would have been expected, if public sector capital assets are transferred at a very low price, and the private sector is willing to use a substantial fraction of its gross savings to purchase public assets, then extremely rapid privatization is feasible, as is evident from the bottom left-hand corner of each sub-table. However, it must be remembered that Table 2.1 was calculated in the presence of $f = 0.02$, which is rather a rapid rate of foreign capital inflow (2 per cent of GDP each year). In practice, most countries are likely to find that f is much smaller, that p may not be permitted to fall as low as 0.1 (which would imply selling public sector assets at 10 per cent of their book value), and that the population (i.e. firms plus households) will not be willing to spend much more than 15–20 per cent of its gross savings on acquiring public sector assets. Under these conditions, it requires at least five years to achieve 50 per cent private ownership, and at least eight years to complete the privatization process.

TABLE 2.1 Varying α and p

(a) *The time to reach 50 per cent private ownership* (years)

$\alpha\backslash p$	0.1	0.3	0.5	0.7
0.1	3.46	5.80	6.82	7.41
0.15	2.76	5.15	6.39	7.17
0.2	2.31	4.65	6.02	6.96
0.25	1.98	4.24	5.70	6.75
0.30	1.74	3.92	5.41	6.57
0.35	1.56	3.64	5.15	6.39

(b) *The time to reach 100 per cent private ownership* (years)

$\alpha\backslash p$	0.1	0.3	0.5	0.7
0.1	4.83	9.68	13.24	16.86
0.15	3.72	8.08	11.51	15.13
0.2	3.04	7.00	10.31	13.90
0.25	2.58	6.22	9.40	12.94
0.30	2.25	5.61	8.68	12.16
0.35	1.99	5.13	8.08	11.51

TABLE 2.2 Variations in f and s_w

(a) *The time to reach 50 per cent private ownership* (years)

$f \backslash s_w$	0.05	0.1	0.125	0.15	0.175
0.0	13.24	9.73	8.66	7.82	7.14
0.005	10.35	8.26	7.52	6.90	6.38
0.01	8.80	7.29	6.72	6.24	5.82
0.015	7.75	6.58	6.12	5.71	5.36
0.02	6.98	6.02	5.63	5.29	4.99
0.025	6.37	5.56	5.23	4.94	4.67
0.03	5.88	5.18	4.89	4.63	4.40
0.035	5.47	4.86	4.60	4.37	4.16

(b) *The time to reach 100 per cent private ownership* (years)

$f \backslash s_w$	0.05	0.1	0.125	0.15	0.175
0.0	18.44	14.32	13.00	11.93	11.05
0.005	15.45	12.77	11.79	10.95	10.24
0.01	13.79	11.73	10.92	10.22	9.61
0.015	12.66	10.94	10.25	9.65	9.11
0.02	11.79	10.31	9.70	9.17	8.68
0.025	11.10	9.79	9.25	8.76	8.32
0.03	10.53	9.53	8.85	8.40	8.00
0.035	10.04	8.96	8.50	8.09	7.72

The effects of foreign investment and savings out of wage income are studied in Table 2.2, again with the results being presented for t_{50} and t_{100} respectively. In the least favourable case with zero foreign capital inflows, it can be seen that even with high rates of personal savings out of wage income, privatization is unavoidably slow. Indeed, for some countries with high debt burdens (especially Poland and Hungary), it might have been more appropriate to calculate further solutions with f negative, reflecting the costs of debt service.

In any case, privatization is evidently speeded up either by increased foreign investment, or by a higher domestic savings rate, or both. As an approximate equivalence, an additional foreign capital inflow amounting to 1.5 per cent of GDP has the same impact on the speed of privatization as a 10 percentage point increase in the rate of saving out of wages (with reference to Table 2.2 t_{50}), or a 7.5 percentage point increase in the rate (with reference to Table 2.2 t_{100}). These last two results imply that domestic savings are relatively more potent in the longer term, especially once the private sector is already large.

The final Table 2.3, examines the effects of levels of taxation and/or government spending on the speed of privatization. Interestingly, all the observed effects are rather small. However, as expected, increased government spending does increase the time required to achieve a given level of private ownership. Increasing the level of taxation has a modest tendency to *accelerate* the achievement of 50 per cent private ownership, while having practically *no effect* on the time taken to achieve complete private ownership. This intriguing result can be explained as follows. When the private sector is small, raising levels of taxation with a given

TABLE 2.3 Variations in tax rates (r) and government spending (g)

(a) *The time to reach 50 per cent private ownership* (years)

r\g	0.15	0.2	0.25	0.3	0.35
0.7	5.62	5.89	6.18	6.51	6.88
0.8	5.49	5.75	6.02	6.33	6.67
0.9	5.38	5.62	5.88	6.17	6.49
1.0	5.28	5.50	5.75	6.02	6.32
1.1	5.18	5.39	5.63	5.88	6.17
1.2	5.09	5.29	5.52	5.76	6.03
1.3	5.00	5.20	5.41	5.65	5.90

(b) *The time to reach 100 per cent private ownership* (years)

r\g	0.15	0.2	0.25	0.3	0.35
0.7	9.34	9.69	10.07	10.49	10.96
0.8	9.30	9.64	10.01	10.41	10.85
0.9	9.28	9.61	9.96	10.35	10.77
1.0	9.27	9.59	9.94	10.31	10.72
1.1	9.28	9.59	9.93	10.30	10.69
1.2	9.29	9.60	9.94	10.30	10.69
1.3	9.33	9.63	9.96	10.32	10.70

Note: r denotes a multiplicative factor applied to all the tax rates in the model (i.e. t_G, t_P and t_W); r = 1 means that all tax rates are just as in the numerical example set out for illustration in the technical appendix.

level of government spending actually transfers more resources to the private sector (via equation [A3] in the Appendix, which determines H), some of which is then directed to private sector investment, and the purchase of public sector assets. Moreover, at this stage, private sector profits are still quite low, so increased profits taxation does not itself exert a significant depressing effect on private investment.

As the private sector gets larger, however, these two effects operate differently. Public sector profits are already relatively much smaller, so their taxation only modestly slows down public sector accumulation. But while the transfer to the private sector through the tax system still tends to raise private sector investment, the taxation of private sector profits has the opposite effect. Hence the total resources available for private investment (including resources for purchases of public sector assets) increase more slowly than earlier. The net effect is to make the time required to achieve complete private ownership almost independent of the level of taxation, over a surprisingly wide range.

5. Aspects of private sector development

The assumptions of the last section ensured that under a wide range of plausible conditions, the private sector would eventually come to dominate the economies of Central and Eastern Europe engaging in large-scale privatization programmes, though it could take a very long time. There were, however, some important considerations missing from the model, which must be taken up in this section. These are as follows:

1. The growth of the *ab initio* private sector as an additional factor contributing to private sector growth;
2. Issues to do with the sequencing (by profitability or type of sector) and speed of privatization;
3. Factors *external* to the firm which tend to force changes in firms' behaviour;
4. Factors *internal* to the firm, notably governance issues;
5. Public finance consequences of private sector growth, including the implications of different privatization methods.

Having examined these elements briefly, we attempt to assess their net effect on privatization programmes.

On point (1), it is of course the case that in the countries which embarked on reforms first, especially Hungary and Poland, but increasingly in the Czech Republic and elsewhere, the growth of new, private sector firms has proceeded apace, to the extent that over 25 per cent of GDP is now generated in the private sector, only a minor part of that being accounted for by privatized firms. These new businesses provide services that were formerly under-supplied (or supplied through semi-legal and illegal channels), and to a limited extent also operate in small-scale manufacturing. This adds to employment at a time when the privatization discussed in earlier sections clearly results in a large drop in employment as a massive and long overdue shakeout of labour occurs. Thus politically, the growth of this part of the private sector can offset some of the initial pain of transition by absorbing some of the workers formerly employed in the state-owned sector of the economy. So far in Hungary and Poland, over half of the workers released by the state-owned sector (in preparation for, or in the course of, privatization) find alternative employment in this way. From a political and social point of view, therefore, it is important that these two tendencies — employment creation due to new firm formation, and job losses due to privatization of state-owned firms — should proceed at compatible rates, and policies should be designed to ensure this.

This brings us to point (2), since this last observation can have important implications for the desirable speed of privatization. In particular, in countries where, for whatever reason, the pace of new firm formation is very slow, it could be politically very unwise to privatize very rapidly because of the likely impact on unemployment. On the sequencing of privatization, the situation is more complicated. On the one hand, from a public finance perspective (on which there is more below, in the discussion of point (5)) there is some advantage in privatizing loss-making firms first, to end the need for further state subsidies; but from a political standpoint this could be exactly the worst thing to do. Instead, one might prefer to privatize profitable firms first, in order to widen popular support for the notion of privatization and hence make it easier for tougher decisions later on to be accepted. In practice, investors' interests have ensured that the most profitable firms, or those with the best long-run potential, are the ones to be privatized first, with the result that in the countries where most progress has been made, such as Hungary, most of the firms still in state hands are in very poor condition.

Another way of thinking about the issue of privatization sequencing is suggested in Husain and Sahay (1992), which considers whether it is best to start by privatizing input-producing or final-goods producing sectors, in a model with imperfect competition. Since successful transition implies a move towards a market-type economy in which agents are responsive to price signals, and competitive conditions cannot be assured immediately (even with trade liberalization), it turns out that 'the sector facing relatively less uncertainty and containing the relatively less concentrated industrial structure should be privatized first' (p. 823).

The model developed in the previous section simply took it for granted that the postulated efficiency gains associated with privatization would occur. But this is only assured if many other conditions are satisfied, both external (point (3)) and internal (point (4)) to the firm. The external factors include the policies of price and trade liberalization which have formed part of the early stage of transition packages in most countries in the region. More importantly, though, they include policies to harden enterprise budget constraints in various ways: (1) breaking down the traditional practice of providing subsidies (either via the government budget or through the credit system) to enterprises in financial difficulty on the basis of enterprise–ministry negotiations, and replacing this system with harder credits (among other things, this presupposes that there will be significant reform and modernization of the banking system) and very limited budget subsidies; (2) replacing negotiations over tax payments, associated with very high marginal tax rates for profitable firms, with lower general rates of taxes enforced more uniformly; (3) encouraging new firms to start up, and fostering competition by breaking up or otherwise regulating the worst monopolies; (4) enforcing bankruptcy/liquidation of the most persistent loss-makers, partly to give an opportunity for other managerial groups/owners to manage the relevant assets more profitably, but also to signal to other firms that they would no longer be permitted to continue running up large losses; and (5) cleaning up bank and enterprise balance sheets in a selective way in order to create conditions for viable operation in the future, to re-capitalize or restructure the banks, while doing this in such a way that it is credibly viewed as a once and for all operation (not something that may be repeated regularly), and also imposes only a modest burden on the budget. Some governments have already made very substantial progress in all these directions, but the measures required to do so are often complex, time-consuming to introduce and implement effectively, and politically risky. Consequently, others have so far made very little progress.

Internal to the enterprise, the key issues concern the ownership and management/governance structures which emerge as a result of privatization. Not surprisingly, that depends very sensitively on the precise model of privatization employed in a given country. As emphasized earlier, if privatization is to confer long-term benefits in terms of improved economic efficiency, it must change enterprise behaviour very substantially. However, workers and managers may not view the situation in such terms, preferring instead to operate in ways which protect their existing positions. Privatization by sale to new owners, bringing in new technology, management inputs, marketing skills, and so on, is unlikely to provide such protection, though the interests of a smooth transition may often be served by offering financial compensation to incumbents, making way for a new management team. On the other hand, rapid privatization by mass giveaway programmes (voucher privatization) makes it possible for existing worker–management coalitions to continue to dominate their firms, with very limited external control. This point was stressed by Bolton and Roland (1992). Not only in the Czech Republic, but also now in Russia, this seems to be a very real possibility; in the latter case, KPMG and CERT (1993) found that almost all of a small sample of recently privatized firms had done so by means of a worker-management buy-out with defensive motives very much to the forefront.

In such cases, what will be important for the success of privatization, therefore, is not just getting as many firms privatized as possible in a given time, but ensuring that these defensive attitudes are, sooner or later, proved to be wrong. This would require the external measures discussed above to come into effect, so that newly privatized firms were no longer so protected. Moreover, this should become politically easier since, whatever else it achieves, any form of privatization does at least separate firms from the state bureaucracy, thereby making decisions about closure and/or restructuring somewhat less politically charged.

The wider question of corporate governance in privatized firms was analysed by Frydman and Rapaczynski (1993), focusing upon the agency problems involved. It is necessary to create an environment in which the new owners can transmit their objectives to managers and monitor their implementation, with some prospect of redress (removing the manager, takeover of the business, etc.) in the event of non-fulfilment. The problem in Eastern Europe is the lack of effective owners in this sense, partly for lack of relevant experience and institutions on the part of domestic agents, and partly due to a reluctance to allow foreign owners to become too dominant (though in most countries the real risks of that appear to have been greatly exaggerated).

Finally, it is essential to address the public finance consequences of privatization in Central and Eastern Europe, another point referred to by Bolton and Roland (1992), as well as by Hussain and Stern (1993). Especially in the presence of deep recessionary conditions which both increase the demands on public spending (to finance the social safety net) while simultaneously reducing tax revenues, the countries of Central and Eastern Europe cannot afford to privatize in ways which make their public accounts even weaker than they already are[3]. From this point of view, it is clearly desirable to privatize by sale as much as possible, and for the public sector to dispose of loss-making businesses first (though a counter argument to this was already referred to above); this may well also imply that privatization should not be especially rapid, in view of the analysis of the previous section. A further point to reinforce this conclusion is the observation that extracting taxes from private sector firms is proving very difficult in Eastern Europe. Tax administration is not yet very well developed, tax codes are still only in the earliest stages of development, and there are many opportunities for inflating costs or hiding profits which enable firms to pay very low taxes. Naturally, this situation will slowly improve, but in the meantime privatization is almost certain to lower government revenues not only immediately (loss of any capital charge on state-owned assets), but also in the longer term (lower future tax revenues).

Overall, this discussion of aspects of private sector development suggests that privatization should not proceed at the breakneck pace advocated in the first months after the fall of communist governments, and that it must be supported both by external measures to enforce 'competitive' behaviour, as well as policies to foster effective corporate governance.

6. Conclusions

What do we learn from the sort of model set out in section 4, together with the analysis of private sector issues of section 5? Probably the main lesson is that except under very favourable conditions (high domestic savings rates, high willingness by the population to buy public sector assets, high rates of foreign investment), or near giveaway policies by the governments concerned (corresponding to very low p in the model), it will not be possible for the privatization programmes in Eastern Europe to proceed as swiftly as some governments have indicated.

Second, in the early stages of privatization, it appears that higher taxation (including of state-sector profits) both slows down accumulation in the state-owned sector (because there are lower after-tax profits there) and transfers resources to the private sector (because any reduction in the government deficit, or increase in the surplus, is reflected in a change in the 'lump sum' payment to households from the budget) in such a way that it speeds up accumulation there. In effect, this is like subsidizing private sector accumulation. Although not explicitly in the model, a similar effect might also be achieved by providing private sector investors with credit to help them purchase public sector assets; the credit could then be repaid from future profits which, from the assumptions of the model, are bound to be higher than those which could have been earned in the public sector. Such a model of purchasing public assets using credit, perhaps on favourable terms (therefore implying a subsidized price) is being considered in several countries.

Third, it is quite clear that foreign direct investment can play a decisive role in speeding up privatization in countries with a stable political and economic environment and where the government concerned is prepared to welcome such investment. Hence the more open policies of Hungary in this regard are to be welcomed. Other countries, which are more nervous about the possible loss of domestic control over their firms, and hence are less welcoming to foreign investors, will find it very difficult to achieve rapid privatization from domestic sources alone, unless they pursue more flexible approaches, such as leasing.

A basic assumption of the model discussed above is that private sector production using *any* of the present public sector assets will necessarily be more profitable than previously. But in view of the extensive distortions in prices, taxes, subsidies and trade flows which existed throughout Eastern Europe before 1989 (and even, to a lesser extent, thereafter), this is simply not correct. Some of the existing capital stock will prove to be completely ineffective, even if transferred to private ownership, because its output is uncompetitive internationally, and increasingly in the domestic market too.

On the one hand, this means that the assets which it is worthwhile to privatize amount to substantially less than the initial capital stock in the state sector. To this extent, privatization might proceed more rapidly than indicated in Section 4. On the other hand, in order to return to full employment after the recession which marks the beginning of the transition in the whole region, huge volumes of new investment will be required. Hence although private ownership may come relatively quickly, the return to a satisfactory, full employment equilibrium may take rather longer.

The analysis of these issues, which are increasingly important for policy-makers in Eastern Europe, requires a significant development of the model of section 4: to incorporate trade (and hence the balance of payments); to distinguish between competitive and uncompetitive production; and to deal with the labour market adequately. The private sector issues discussed in section 5 help to clarify some of the other aspects of privatization missing from the formal model.

In particular, they strengthen the argument for a moderate pace of privatization, with attention being paid to the external environment in which firms operate, to the public finance effects of privatization and restructuring, as well as to governance issues. Although not examined here explicitly, this analysis also implies that many firms will remain in the state-owned sector for far longer than would have been anticipated in 1990. Consequently, how to manage these firms and improve their performance is set to become one of the critical problems for the newly democratic states of Eastern Europe in the mid-1990s.

Technical appendix

In the simple economy of section 4, GNP is given by:

$$Y = Y_G + Y_P = W + \Pi \tag{A1}$$

where W is the economy's total wage bill, Π is total profits. Both of these can obviously be broken down further; thus:

$$W = w_G L_G + w_P L_P, \text{ and } \Pi = Y - W = \Pi_G + \Pi_P \tag{A2}$$

where $\Pi_i = Y_i - w_i L_i$ ($i = G, P$).

Let government expenditure on goods and services be denoted by $g.Y$, financed by taxes, which amount to a total, $T = t_G \Pi_G + t_P \Pi_P + t_W.W - H$. As indicated above, the allowance, H is chosen to bring about balance between expenditure and revenues, so that:

$$t_G \Pi_G + t_P \Pi_P + t_W.W - H = g.Y \tag{A3}$$

Let us assume that a fraction s_W of post-tax wage income is saved, and that private sector profits net of tax are all saved. Then savings by households and private sector firms, S_P, amount to $[s_W.((1 - t_W)W + H) + (1 - t_P)\Pi_P]$. For the sector of government-owned firms, again assuming that all post-tax profits are saved, S_G is just $(1 - t_G)\Pi_G$.

We now take the production function in equations [1] to have constant returns to scale, Cobb-Douglas form, namely: $F(K, L) = AK^{(1-\beta)}L^\beta$, where A is a productivity parameter reflecting the average productivity with which inputs of capital and labour are transformed into output, and the parameter β would be labour's share of total product if both factor markets were competitive. In view of [2], public sector employment can be written in the form:

$$L_G = b.K_G \qquad [A4]$$

where

$$b = \lambda\left(\frac{\beta A}{w_G}\right)^{\frac{1}{1-\beta}}, \text{ and } \left(\frac{1}{\beta}\right)^{\frac{1}{1-\beta}} > \lambda > 1.$$

Thus if $\lambda = 1$, employment in the public (state) sector is set at its most profitable level, determined by marginal productivity considerations, while λ at its upper limit yields the highest level of public sector employment consistent with the public sector not incurring losses. Now,

$$\Pi_G = (Ab^\beta - bw_G)K_G = \delta_G K_G \qquad [A5]$$

and $\delta_G > 0$. For the private sector, which chooses its employment level to maximize profits at each point, we find:

$$L_P = \left(\frac{aA\beta}{w_P}\right)^{\frac{1}{1-\beta}} K_P \qquad [A6]$$

and

$$\pi_P = \frac{(aA)^{\frac{1}{1-\beta}}}{w_P^{\frac{\beta}{1-\beta}}}.\left\{\beta^{\frac{\beta}{1-\beta}} - \beta^{\frac{1}{1-\beta}}\right\}K_P = \delta_P K_P \qquad [A7]$$

where $\delta_P > 0$.

With these preliminary calculations, a little further manipulation reveals that private sector savings can be written in the form:

$$S_P = s_W[(1 - g)W + (t_G - g)\Pi_G] + [1 - (1 - s_W)t_P - s_Wg]\Pi_P \qquad [A8]$$

where [A3] has been used to eliminate H. By using the last few results, this can be written in the more useful form:

$$S_P = \eta_P K_P + s_W(t_G - g)\delta_G K_G \qquad [A9]$$

where:

$$\eta_P = s_W(1 - g)w_P\left(\frac{aA\beta}{w_P}\right)^{\frac{1}{1-\beta}} + [1 - (1 - s_W)t_P - s_Wg]\delta_P \qquad [A10]$$

Assuming that foreign capital inflows can be regarded as a constant fraction of GDP, so that F can be expressed as:

$$F = f.Y = f.(\pi_P + \pi_G + W) \qquad [A11]$$

then equations [3] and [4] can be transformed into a very simple pair of linear differential equations, which take the form:

$$\dot{K}_P = c_{11} K_P + c_{12} K_G \tag{A12}$$

$$\dot{K}_G = c_{21} K_P + c_{22} K_G \tag{A13}$$

where:

$$c_{11} = \gamma.\eta_P + f.\left(\delta_P + w_P \left(\frac{aA\beta}{w_P}\right)^{\frac{1}{1-\beta}}\right)$$

$$c_{12} = \gamma s_W(t_G - g)\delta_G + f(\delta_G + bw_G),$$

$$c_{21} = -(\gamma - 1)\eta_P, \text{ and } c_{22} = [(1 - t_G) - (\gamma - 1)s_W(t_G - g)]\delta_G.$$

In an obvious matrix-vector notation, this system can be written in the equivalent form $\dot{K} = cK$. It is also convenient for the subsequent analysis to express [A12] and [A13] in the form of a single differential equation in x, the share of the private sector in the economy's capital stock (thus $x = K_P/(K_P + K_G)$). In terms of x, [A12] and [A13] become:

$$\dot{x} = u_0 + u_1 x + u_2 x^2 \tag{A14}$$

where

$$u_0 = c_{12}, u_1 = c_{11} - 2c_{12} - c_{22}, \text{ and } u_2 = (c_{22} - c_{21}) - (c_{11} - c_{12}).$$

Subsequent analysis can be conducted in terms of [A14] alone, or using [A12] and [A13] together. In either case, [A3] can be used to compute H along any particular solution path. Also, certain boundary conditions must be respected, namely that the accumulation equations only remain valid while $K_G > 0$ (or equivalently, $x < 1$). If the equations imply that complete private ownership of the capital stock is achieved at some finite time (as turns out to be the case), then from that point onwards a different model of accumulation would obviously be required, involving private sector accumulation alone (and similarly if some solution path implies that complete state-ownership is achieved, though with reasonable parameters in the model this should not occur). Such single sector models are not provided here.

We derive some properties of the coefficients $c_{ij}(i, j = 1, 2)$ and $u_i(i = 0, 1, 2)$ which appeared in equations [A12], [A13] and [A14]. The results obtained here are useful for the analysis of the model presented in section 4 above. Let us first of all review the definitions of the coefficients; thus:

$$c_{11} = \gamma.\eta_P + f.\left(\delta_P + w_P \left(\frac{aA\beta}{w_P}\right)^{\frac{1}{1-\beta}}\right), c_{12}$$

$$= \gamma s_W(t_G - g)\delta_G + f(\delta_g + bw_g), c_{21} = -(\gamma - 1)\eta_P,$$

and

$$c_{22} = [(1 - t_G) - (\gamma - 1)s_W(t_G - g)]\delta_G.$$

Also, $u_0 = c_{12}, u_1 = c_{11} - 2c_{12} - c_{22}, \text{ and } u_2 = (c_{22} - c_{21}) - (c_{11} - c_{12}.)$

Starting with c_{11}, it can be shown that:

$$c_{11} = w_P \left(\frac{aA\beta}{w_P}\right)^{\frac{1}{1-\beta}} \left[\gamma \left[s_W(1-g) + ((1-t_P) + s_W(t_P-g))\left(\frac{1}{\beta}-1\right)\right] + \frac{f}{\beta}\right]$$

[A15]

Similarly,

$$c_{12} = w_G \left(\frac{A\beta}{w_G}\right)^{\frac{1}{1-\beta}} \left[\gamma s_W(t_G-g)\left(\frac{\lambda^\beta}{\beta}-\lambda\right) + \frac{f}{\beta}\right]$$

[A16]

$$c_{21} = -(\gamma-1)w_P \left(\frac{aA\beta}{w_P}\right)^{\frac{1}{1-\beta}} \left[s_W(1-g) + ((1-t_P) + s_W(t_P-g))\left(\frac{1}{\beta}-1\right)\right]$$

[A17]

and:

$$c_{22} = w_G \left(\frac{A\beta}{w_G}\right)^{\frac{1}{1-\beta}} [(1-t_G) - (\gamma-1)s_W(t_G-g)]\left(\frac{\lambda^\beta}{\beta}-\lambda\right)$$

[A18]

Then u_0 is clearly also given by equation [A15], while u_1 and u_2 are more complicated combinations of [A15] to [A18]. From the above expressions, it can be seen that $c_{11} > 0, c_{12} > 0, c_{21} < 0$ and c_{22} is of ambiguous sign if $t_G > g$, though for sufficiently small s_W, or small or negative $(t_G - g)$, it will be positive. It follows, therefore, that $u_0 > 0$, and also that $(u_0 + u_1 + u_2) = -c_{21} > 0$. However, the signs of u_1 and u_2 are ambiguous, though the numerical example below suggests that the former is positive, the latter negative. Hence this is the case examined in detail in the main text.

In order to get a better feel for the behaviour of the system being analysed here, it is useful to insert some plausible parameter values into the above equations. On the basis of the resulting coefficient values, the subsequent comparative static analysis is likely to be rather better informed, and hence be more informative, than would be possible if we merely carried out the comparative statics without any guidance.

The following assumptions are made for illustrative purposes, the assumptions about tax rates, savings rates and government expenditure being in line with Eastern European experience. Thus:

$A = 1$ (by suitable choice of units), $a = 1.1$ (i.e. a 10 per cent efficiency difference between public and private sectors, probably an underestimate), $\beta = 0.6$, $t_G = 0.5, t_P = 0.4, t_W = 0.25, g = 0.3, s_w = 0.1, w_G = w_P = 0.5, \lambda = 1.2$ (implying that the public sector employs 20 per cent more workers than it should), $\alpha = 0.2$, $p = 0.5$ (implying $\gamma = 1.2$), and finally, $f = 0.02$ (implying foreign capital inflows amounting to 2 per cent of the GDP, a level which only Hungary shows any sign of achieving so far).

With these data it is straightforward to calculate that: $c_{11} = 0.606$; $c_{12} = 0.0388$; $c_{21} = -0.0954$; and $c_{22} = 0.258$. Hence, $u_0 = 0.0388$; $u_1 = 0.2704$; and $u_2 = -0.2138$.

To solve [A14] for a situation where the coefficients have the same signs and properties just established, we proceed by rearranging [A14], simplifying, and integrating for x. With the assumed parameter values, it follows that as t increases, the economy approaches a state with complete private ownership of the capital stock ($x = 1$), in finite time. Specifically, with the given parameters, the time taken to reach complete private ownership, $t_{100} = 10.5$ years (also, the time to reach 50 per cent private ownership, $t_{50} = 6.2$ years, which implies that the later stages of privatization proceed more rapidly than the earlier ones).

This convergence to complete private ownership always occurs in the present model. Hence what is of interest is to study how the time required to achieve a specified level of private ownership (say 50 per cent, or 100 per cent) depends on the model's underlying parameters. Such an exploration is provided in section 4.

Notes

1. To say that production is x-efficient means that there is no avoidable slack in the relationship between inputs and outputs, so that managers are constantly striving to economize on the use of all inputs. It may be contrasted with allocative efficiency, which implies that producers have responded properly to the prevailing relative prices, and chosen the cost-minimizing factor proportions.
2. Further details of this and subsequent derivations are contained in the technical appendix.
3. Not least because, in the absence of developed capital markets, most government deficits in the region are monetised, contributing to inflationary pressure. A further important factor is the easy access of many state-owned firms to credit to cover their continuing losses.

References

Ash, T.N. and Hare, P.G. (1993) An introduction and overview of the Russian government's privatization programme, in KPMG/CERT project, (1993).

Blanchard, O., Dornbusch, R., Krugman, P., Layard, R., and Summers, L. (1991), *Reform in Eastern Europe*, MIT Press, Cambridge, Mass.

Blommenstein, H. and Hare, P. (eds) (1993) *Methods of privatizing large enterprises*, OECD, Paris.

Bolton, P. and Roland, G. (1992) *Privatization policies in central and eastern Europe,* Economic Policy, 15, pp. 275–309.

Dunkerley, J. and Hare, P.G. (1991) Nationalized industries, in Crafts, N. and Woodward, N. (eds) (1991), *The British Economy since 1945*, Clarendon Press, Oxford, ch. 12.

Frydman, R., Phelps, E., Rapaczynski, A., and Shleifer, A. (1993) Needed mechanisms of corporate governance and finance in Eastern Europe, *Economics of Transition*, 1(2), pp. 171–208.

Frydman, R. and Rapaczynski, A. (1993) Insiders and the state: overview of responses to agency problems in East European privatizations, *Economics of Transition*, 1(1), pp. 39–59.

Frydman, R., Rapaczynski, A., Earle, J. *et al.* (1993), *The Privatization Process in Central Europe*, Central European University Press, London.

Grosfeld, I. and **Hare, P.G.** (1991) Privatization in Hungary, Poland and Czechoslovakia, paper prepared for the EC, *European Economy*, special edition no.2, Commission of the European Communities, Brussels.

Hare, P.G. (1990) Ownership, 'de-statization' and privatization, report prepared for G7 study of Soviet economy, mimeo.

Hare, P.G. (1991) Transition to a market economy, *Royal Bank of Scotland Review*, March, pp. 3–16.

Husain, A.M. and **Sahay, R.** (1992) Does sequencing of privatization matter in reforming planned economies?, *IMF Staff Papers*, **39**(4), pp. 801–824.

Hussain, A. and **Stern, N.** (1993) The role of the state, ownership and taxation in transitional economies, *Economics of Transition*, **1**(1), pp. 61–87.

IMF *et al.* (1990) *Study of the Soviet Economy*, report prepared at the request of the G7 Houston summit, IMF/World Bank/OECD/EBRD, Washington DC.

Kornai, J. (1990) *The Road to a Free Economy*, Norton, New York.

KPMG and **CERT** (1993) Study of privatization in Russia. Report prepared for HM Treasury, London, mimeo

Molyneux, R. and **Thompson, D.** (1987) Nationalized industry performance: still third rate?, *Fiscal Studies*, **8**(1), pp. 48–82.

Newbery, D. (1991) Sequencing the transition, Discussion Paper, Department of Applied Economics, Cambridge, mimeo

Portes, R.D. (1991) Introduction, *European Economy*, special edition no.2, Commission of the European Communities, Brussels.

Tirole, J. (1991) Privatization in Eastern Europe: incentives and the economics of transition, *NBER Macroeconomics Annual 1991*, MIT Press, Cambridge, Mass.

CHAPTER THREE

Corporate governance in mass privatization programmes

Enrico Perotti*

1. Introduction

Mass privatization is an urgent priority for Eastern Europe. The recent history of attempts at reforming state enterprises while still under political control suggests that they are not successful. As long as the state does not relinquish control, it does not separate itself from financial responsibility; it therefore remains vulnerable to political pressure to support unprofitable firms. Only private owners have an interest in establishing a hard budget constraint, and would impose cost reduction and restructuring on enterprises.

This chapter analyses the question of corporate governance in mass privatization. It examines the different approaches adopted in Eastern Europe in terms of their effectiveness in establishing legitimate and effective private control over enterprises, thus divorcing the state budget from corporate liabilities. Centralized and decentralized approaches to control transfer are compared. The experience suggests that without large subsidies, centralized plans are extremely slow in selling the bulk of industry. A free share distribution allows the state to divest rapidly; however, the resulting dispersion of ownership may fail to create private control over enterprises necessary to harden firms' budget constraints. On the other hand, the Polish solution of centralized assignment of control stakes to new intermediaries has failed to legitimize their control. Apparently, only broad decentralization of the process can overcome popular resentment and political resistance.

Since most firms to be privatized are highly leveraged, the governance role of creditors is crucial. Moreover, as banks are currently the only source of capital, their lending practices should be the proper source of financial discipline and supervision in thinly capitalized firms. Currently, state-owned banks are largely used as channels for covert subsidies; given the poor state of their portfolios, even after bank privatization there is a risk of greater and more concentrated loan losses. Therefore, an indirect role of banks in governance is probably advisable.

Section 2 examines the rationale for mass privatization. Section 3 examines the structure of sales adopted in Eastern Europe. Section 4 analyses the role of

* I thank seminar participants at the World Bank, the Central European University and the CEPR Conference on Privatization for comments on an earlier version. I remain responsible for all mistakes.

creditors, particularly banks, in the transition to private control, and discusses the emergence of capital markets in the region.

2. The rationale for mass privatization

THE CASE FOR RAPID MASS PRIVATIZATION

Opinions differ on the optimal speed and form of privatization sales. There is no question that gradualism has considerable advantages. It may enhance government credibility and therefore sale revenues, offer an opportunity to introduce proper regulation and demerge overly integrated companies, and grant the time to reform the banking sector.[1] Finally, it is logistically much simpler to privatize gradually.

In a few cases, gradualism in sales may also be preferred by investors, particularly in circumstances of high political uncertainty. For profitable firms enjoying limited competition, or light regulation, clarity over government policy is a delicate issue; in these cases, gradual sales may raise greater revenues, as prices improve over time alongside confidence over public policy.[2]

However, most Eastern European firms are not very profitable, are overstaffed and employ obsolete equipment; some incur significant losses. For such firms, the state has limited ability to resist political pressure for subsidies. Therefore, a more rapid privatization may lead to a greater confidence in the success of reform: by establishing a clear separation of the enterprise sector from the state, it would reassure investors about the risk of fiscal collapse. In addition, reduction in subsidies is indispensable for macroeconomic stabilization; failure to generate a sufficient supply response can undermine the stabilization process and result in hyperinflation. There may be significant spillover effects in privatization; a failure to attain a critical mass of privatized firms could lead to a much too slow improvement in productivity and to a collapse of the reform programme. Finally, speed may be required to overcome the effect of a control vacuum over the corporate sector. As plan discipline has disappeared, labour and management are *de facto* in charge of most decisions; in the limbo period after privatization is announced but prior to firm private control, they are led to decapitalize the firms by appropriating assets and seeking entrenchment through various schemes. Thus an approach to privatization which is too slow may be a recipe for financial disaster.

INTERNAL OPPOSITION AND THE DISTRIBUTION OF BENEFITS

There are formidable obstacles to rapid privatization in Eastern Europe. Contrary to the opinion of many early observers, the major problem is not the lack of developed stock markets. Equity markets historically emerge at the last stage of financial development (Goldsmith 1969).[3] Even if such markets existed, the delicate issue would be the current distribution of private wealth. Most citizens in Eastern Europe are unable to afford to invest in corporate stock; this is especially true during the early transition stage, when savings are required for subsistence or small-scale investment, and the risk involved in equity investment is likely to be undesirable. In addition, there is a very skewed distribution of income, and there is widespread cynicism on the source of wealth accumulated under the previous regime. Rapid sales would transfer control over most assets to foreigners or to a minority of questionable domestic investors, depriving most citizens of assets whose accumulation they had contributed to.

In order to achieve a rapid transfer of control, it is necessary to recognize the interests of many constituencies to oppose restructuring, since in the currently ambiguous state of property rights over enterprises, there is considerable scope for insiders to hinder the process. This ability depends on the degree of decentralization (or better, dispersion) of power over the economy. For instance, in recognition of the degree of effective control exercised by workers and other stakeholders, a stated goal of the Russian privatization policy is to win their approval for privatization by granting them most of the economic benefits of privatization (Shleifer 1992). Thus a realistic solution is to grant a fraction of stock to workers, which would produce longer-term incentives than social compensation. On the other hand, such compensation should not be confused with ownership:[4] the voting rights of these shares should be restricted, or at least suspended during the phase of restructuring, when opposition may be most damaging. An example is the current proposal for privatization in Bulgaria, which reserves a fraction of stock to workers (up to 10 per cent) but without voting rights for three years.

On the other hand, in most countries outside Poland, the ability of workers to resist privatization is limited, relative to the control rights exercised by the management, local authorities or founding ministries. It is often these groups that are the most entrenched opponents of privatization, as it would limit their scope of control or even question their position. Thus it is often the very institutions which are supposed to lead the privatization process that will (mostly tacitly) slow it down, often relying on the remarkable conflicts of competences over enterprises which result from decades of vague property rights. The result is a pervasive degree of uncoordinated rent-seeking by insiders.

Clearly, a division of benefits exclusively in favour of firm insiders and supervisors is politically unacceptable; thus any partial distribution to workers and managers may be combined with a programme of share distribution to the population, to create support for privatization. In order to offer maximum political legitimacy to the process, all citizens should share its benefits, to the extent they have contributed to capital accumulation.

However, it would be naive to believe that a free share distribution will produce an equitable division of benefits. One reason is that informed insiders will be able to direct their investment more wisely, and capture the more valuable assets. But an even more important reason is that in an economy with limited legal structure and imprecise property rights, not all shareholders in a company share equally in its value. The main part of value will inevitably be gained by those who obtain control, and therefore the discretionary right to decide on the use of assets. Nevertheless, inequality of gains is inevitable in a major reform; the advantage of share distribution is to ensure that at least some of the benefits are shared with the general population. To this purpose, it may be desirable to link large- and small-scale privatization, to ensure that individuals may choose to gain some small asset of immediate use. For instance, in Latvia the privatization certificates may also be used for land or housing purchases.

There is another rationale for mass distribution of shares, quite possibly even more important than its equitability: the creation of a popular interest in seeing privatization progress steadily, and with limited political interference. To this goal, a distribution of shares amounts to a fluidization of control rights, which can then be exchanged and accumulated freely, without explicit bureaucratic approval. The question of governance over the privatization process is a key consideration in the examination of the structure of the various privatization schemes in Eastern Europe.

3. Structure of privatization sales

THE MASS PRIVATIZATION PROGRAMMES IN EASTERN EUROPE

The essence of privatization is a transfer of control from the state to some individual or company with a strong interest in the residual value of the firm (i.e. the value of its equity). Even when the current management is the best team to operate the firm, its behaviour is not likely to be efficient unless it is closely supervised by some large shareholder, who must be able to exercise control over the firm. This requires the creation of sufficiently large stakes in firms, so that their owners own both sufficient income and voting rights to have the incentives and control to exercise their ownership title.[5] And because control is extremely valuable in a weak legal context with poor contractual enforcement, the power of deciding the allocation of control is very valuable.

There are different approaches to the assignment of control, which are classified by their degree of centralization. The extreme example of centralization is given by the German *Treuhandanstalt*. Its relative success in dismissing state property derives largely from the financial ability of Western Germany to compensate for the economic and social costs of rapid restructuring; these subsidies are clearly directed to speed up sales and ensure limited resistance. A similar structure is prevailing in Hungary, where a state agency (SPA) is in charge of determining the future owners. According to this classification, the Romanian approach, where only a small fraction of the voting capital stock (30 per cent) is distributed and the state retains control till the final sale, is almost equivalent.

The orderly privatization of East German industry has been made possible by very large subsidies: according to the more conservative estimates, over 50 billion DM in annual direct *Treuhandanstalt* transfers, which do not include hefty social and infrastructural spending. But no other country in Eastern Europe can afford to follow such a route. The choice by Hungary in 1990 to privatize gradually and under central control of the SPA, in part in response to a public outcry against opportunistic self-privatization, has failed to transfer control speedily, and the government is considering an alternative, more decentralized approach. This slow progress is probably due to the ability of special interests to resist restructuring, and to conflicts over the assignment of control. Even more alarmingly, the amounts raised have been little more than symbolic, around 1 per cent of book value (Estrin *et al.* 1992). The cost of maintaining unrestructured firms in operation is presumably much larger. It is hard to establish the extent of losses in the state sector; officially, the Hungarian state has reduced dramatically its direct subsidies to firms. However, it is becoming apparent that lending by state-owned banks has been used to channel financial support to unprofitable firms, a policy option which is becoming less and less sustainable.

These examples suggest that a privatization process which gives discretion to the government to decide on each control transfer is probably a serious risk for most young democracies of Eastern Europe. First of all, the state has few resources and little political strength to enforce cost control in the transition. Since the main benefits come from obtaining control, public discretion over its assignment unleashes formidable rent-seeking behaviour; the suspicion of corruption in sale transactions may lead to a popular delegitimization of the sale programme. In addition, political debate on each sale can lead to requests for pre-sale restructuring and cross-vetoes and result in the stalling of the process. Finally, reformers who used to oppose state-ownership will find that it has both financial and political advantages, and become reluctant to relinquish it.

The share distribution alternative offers a solution to the problem of speed, particularly as it rules out any political interference in the selling and restructuring of enterprises. However, the resulting extreme dispersion of ownership does not address the necessity of rapid creation of private control. Since owners need to be properly motivated and enabled to impose financial discipline, it is necessary that they possess sufficient entitlements to residual income and control. The major question then, is how to achieve rapid concentration of ownership for privatized firms.

A solution offered by various proponents is that the share transfer should be made immediately to newly created financial intermediaries, whose shares are privately owned; the Polish and Czechoslovakian approaches, among others, follow this principle. These schemes vary in the degree of centralization, depending on whether the funds are created by the state and are awarded shares in companies, or if the individual fund's size and identity are determined by citizens' choices.

Various proposals have been advanced, which vary in terms of structure of the investment funds and their life horizon. Lipton and Sachs (1990) and Frydman and Rapaczynski (1990) both propose the creation of a system of corporate governance based on financial intermediaries. Their proposals differ on the type of intermediaries, and more precisely on the role of capital markets. Lipton and Sachs propose the adoption of a German model, based on transferring control shareholdings to large banks. This would have the double advantage of recapitalizing the banks and attributing supervision over management to institutional investors with some financial expertise. Fischer (1991) observes that this approach may lead the banks to throw good money after bad, since banks which have already loaned funds to inefficient firms will attempt to keep them afloat with more loans, potentially undermining any stabilization programme. Frydman and Rapaczynski argue that capital markets do have a role to play in governance; and are in favour of establishing mutual funds, whose ownership will be diffused free of charge among the population. Investors could appraise   the performance of the different funds in monitoring managerial decisions by observing the price of the mutual funds, which would be traded on the stock market.

Blanchard *et al.* (1991) offer a further refinement. They suggest that financial holding companies may not be the final form of corporate governance, particularly as they are concerned with the risk of entrenchment by the managers of the financial intermediaries. Their solution is to grant shares in the firms to well-diversified holding companies, with a statutory limited lifespan. By some future date, these firms must have completely divested their holdings, after which they would dissolve. In other words, these institutions would really act as 'privatization agencies', run by the private sector, with the short-term task to supervise management and a long-term goal to search out and negotiate with future potential buyers. Thus the concentration of voting rights in the hands of pre-ordained institutional investors would be temporary; the market would determine the final allocation of control.

THE STRUCTURE OF THE POLISH AND CZECHOSLOVAK DISTRIBUTION SCHEMES

The two countries which have adopted the investment fund approach have been Poland and the former Czechoslovakia. However, their approaches differ precisely on the question of the governance of the control transfer. The Polish approach resolves the allocation of control *ex ante* and *ex imperio*; the Czechoslovakian approach delegates the task to private initiative and market coordination.

The Polish scheme is the result of fine-tuned elaboration by many Western advisors. To address the extreme separation of ownership and control, it ensures that control over each firm is attributed immediately to a holding company, in which citizens will own shares. In addition, to avoid an excessive concentration of risk, these mutual funds will be partially diversified with minority stakes in other companies, ensuring some contest over corporate control. Finally, the management of these funds is to be contracted to outside advisors, mostly Western experts on fund management and corporate restructuring, which will receive a fraction of capital gains. The most recent version of the plan calls for distributing 60 per cent of the stock of over 200 firms to the general population through the transfer of shares in a number of National Wealth Management Funds (essentially, closed-end funds) of which all Polish adults will be shareholders. A deeply discounted sale of an additional 10 per cent of the stock will be made to the firms' employees, while the state will retain the remaining 30 per cent for some time.

In contrast, the Czechoslovakian scheme entailed a complete transfer of shares and a decentralized process of control allocation. Each adult received coupons, with which to bid directly for shares in the companies up for sale. Alternatively, citizens could have chosen to attribute their coupons to one of the several mutual funds which had registered.

The initial response of most academic observers was quite favourable to the Polish scheme, and dubious at best about the complex Czech plan. However, this evaluation clearly needs to be reassessed after the early experience of the two plans. The Polish plan has been stalled by strong political opposition and popular resistance for over two years, until it finally obtained parliamentary approval. It has also been beset by difficulties in attracting the interest of foreign fund managers; to increase attractiveness, the number of funds to be created has been reduced progressively. What was hoped to become a competitive market for fund management is now likely to involve no more than a dozen funds. Finally, the number of companies involved has been reduced from 400 to 200, in part reflecting the deteriorating state of enterprise finance under the current form of self-management.

In contrast, the Czechoslovakian scheme has put more than 1700 Czech companies and 700 Slovak companies, amounting to about 50 per cent of industrial output, on the auction block. The barriers to entry to start a mutual fund have been kept extremely low, resulting in massive entry by over one hundred funds.

The main difficulty with the Polish privatization scheme seems to have resulted from its centralized allocation of control, and from the centralized creation of funds. The initial popular support for privatization in Poland has turned into suspicion, incomprehension, and mistrust of the scheme. Polish citizens apparently also resisted the notion of foreign managers being put in charge of the domestic industry. Besides a nationalist attitude, there is certainly a rationale for this feeling: in an uncertain legal framework, the exercise of control over an enterprise is easily most valuable, particularly relative to the vague rights of minority shareholders. In Eastern Europe, the value of control is considerable relative to the value of the dividend payout. Moreover, since the process of control transfer was kept at a highly centralized level, it encouraged internal opposition and political contrasts which have caused severe delay. Polish citizens had been disenfranchised of any say in the assignment of control over enterprises, and the result has been a lack of political legitimacy.

The historical legitimacy of property in Eastern Europe was destroyed under socialism; since ownership is ultimately a form of social contract, it needs to be regenerated through some process of collective legitimization. Clearly, if property is obtained by an individual or institution in a fair sale, the buyer can rightfully claim to have acquired legitimate title to the property. But when the capital is distributed free of charge, the population must be allowed to make the decision as to who should be in charge, in part so as to be able to receive some of the benefits.

There is a related consequence; the funds may not only fail to be accepted as owners, but not even as private entities *distinct from the state*; they may be seen as just another layer of state control. This implies that when they may attempt to restructure firms, the political resistance will still be directed at the central government in Warsaw which, after all, was the one to assign control to these (unrecognized) owners. But if these funds are not perceived as entitled to operate corporate restructuring, then there has been no effective privatization at all.

In contrast, in the Czechoslovak scheme the population was moved from a rather tepid attitude to a very active involvement with the programme: while only 2.5 million participants were expected, the final tally should be around 8.5 million, with over 470 mutual funds registered. By all standards, this has been a remarkable success in substituting private agents as the protagonists of the privatization process, and legitimizing the creation of private control through open competition for citizens' entitlements.

Admittedly, such enthusiasm has in part resulted from the shock created, in an economy which has scarce memory of speculation, by the speculative promises of some mutual funds, which aggressively collected coupons by promising high guaranteed rates of return (over 10 times the cost of participation) in one year's time. These may well turn out to be hollow promises, as it is impossible to see how the privatized sector will offer much short term profitability or, more importantly, liquidity. Thus it is plausible that the promise was made with the anticipation that the government would not allow a collapse in confidence as a result of a 'run' on mutual funds. Fortunately, most funds did not extend such promises, and recent regulation has clarified their nature as closed-end funds.[6] Clearly, there are risks of speculative excesses, as well as fraud; however, the advantages of an open market to collect vouchers are apparent. Nor should one under-estimate the financial caution of the voucher investors: in the end, the Czechoslovak investment funds which attracted the most subscribers were those organized by banks; eight out of the ten largest funds, including the three largest, were associated with banking or insurance institutions. This suggests that banks still enjoy the confidence of most individuals, either for their solidity or their expertise.

The main advantage of the Czechoslovak voucher scheme seems to have been the enlisting of popular support for rapid privatization. Its decentralized share-allocation mechanism and its free entry of mutual funds involved all citizens, and limited the scope of political rent-seeking and delay tactics by insiders. Finally, it has legitimized the final owner to an extent which cannot be achieved through direct attribution of control by the state.

One main flaw has been its ambition to derive market prices through a very complex computerized market game. The auction mechanism was complicated. The auction for shares of enterprises involved in the first wave (another wave is planned for 1993–94) took place over a number of bidding rounds, until all shares were distributed. Its purpose was to approximate a fair market, such that over-subscribed shares become more expensive and under-subscribed shares fall in price. A particular effort has been devoted to publicizing the rules of the auction, and to creating a computerized trading system, parallel to the stock exchange, to facilitate trading at a moderate cost.

An important difference with the Polish scheme is that the Czechoslovak version gave little attention to the rapid establishment of control blocks over the privatized firms. Large shareholdings are necessary to create both incentives and voting power to ensure that restructuring takes place; but starting from a decentralized allocation, the process of aggregating small stakes may have been very slow, as most shares are not actively traded.

The solution has come from the investment funds. The largest funds concentrated a large fraction of vouchers, and were very active in building up large stakes in the major firms. The law regulating the funds established a maximum of a 20 per cent stake in any one enterprise for any fund, and of 25 per cent for all funds managed by a single sponsor; however, these stakes are large enough, particularly in the presence of many small investors, to ensure corporate control by one or a very few funds. There are strong indications that the Czech system will resemble the German bank-centred system, with banks indirectly controlling large firms by affecting the voting of the stakes held by the investment funds they sponsor. There is also evidence of an active network of alliances and exchanges of shares among the smaller funds, in order to muster a more significant corporate governance role.

4. The role of creditors and outside shareholders

THE ROLE OF CREDITORS

The larger Eastern European firms have extensive bank and inter-firm borrowings. They will have, even after partial debt write-offs, minimal equity value, in part because they are being transferred free. Therefore, even a small fluctuation in value will cause default on existing debts.[7]

Transfer of equity is insufficient for the establishment of hard budget constraints when there is improper enforcement of debt claims. Creditors are an important source of financial discipline in market economies; in addition to the ability to refuse further credit or impose restrictive covenants, creditors obtain control rights over insolvent firms. This is aimed at avoiding value dissipation: because creditors of bankrupt firms are the residual claimants, they have better incentives to run the firm efficiently than its owners.

Currently, creditors in Eastern Europe are not exercising a strong disciplinary role. Bankruptcy proceedings are rare, largely because there is a long history of collusion among debtors and creditors; this became apparent once bankruptcy laws became available, for example in Hungary. In addition, there is a diffused perception among observers that state-owned banks in Eastern Europe are showing a marked preference to lend to their main borrowers, the large state-owned firms. For instance, Polish data suggests that credit to the private sector as a fraction of domestic bank assets is rising quite slowly: it was 16.6 per cent in December 1990, and rose to 17.3 per cent in mid-1991. This contrasts with the evidence of a vibrant private sector. As noted in Chapter 10, the Polish private sector accounts for more than half of total employment in 1993 (see also Johnson 1992). As a result, the state sector should reduce or at least stabilize borrowing, while the investing private sector should receive a rapidly increasing fraction of credit. Moreover, the private sector has to finance not only its working capital but its acquisition of assets as small-scale privatization gathers speed. The situation appears to be similar in Czechoslovakia and Hungary. Czechoslovak data indicate that credit to the private sector is rising fast, although nowhere near as fast as the importance of private activity. In the period January to September 1991, it rose from 5 to 40 billion korunas. However, at the same time the state sector increased its borrowing by 70 billion korunas, to a total of 600 billion (Dyba and Svejnar 1992). Recent data from Romania suggests that bank credit to the private sector is around 13–14 per cent of the total, while its share of output is at least one-fifth.

Currently, several reasons exist for excessive bank lending to state-owned firms. There may be reluctance by the bankers to cut off their former clients, since it also implies admitting the difficult state of their institutions. Certainly a major cause is the political fear of severe restructuring and layoffs which would follow a declaration of insolvency of the old state-owned sector.[8] The large banks in Eastern Europe are still largely controlled by the state. Thus, even when the former state-owned firms are privatized, the state *de facto* retains enormous indirect control and broad financial responsibility for these enterprises. In addition, perhaps as a legacy of the old order's bias in favour of producers, almost all banks are in part owned by state-owned enterprises.

It is a common assumption that this lending bias reflects political pressure on banks. This pressure does not need to be explicit, as legislation often grants them limited powers to enforce liquidation. This suggests that bank privatization and clear bankruptcy laws may resolve the problem of an efficient allocation of credit (Rybcinskzy 1990). However, banks are institutions with a special status; their privatization is not a sufficient condition to ensure efficient credit decisions, because their deposit liabilities are typically guaranteed by the state. Recognizing this feature, Perotti (1993) offers a formal model of lending behaviour by value-maximizing banks in a transition economy. The conclusion is that unless the banks' balance sheets are cleared of the stock of accumulated losses by state-owned enterprises, the incentive to maximize profits will lead them to continue to misdirect credit, as well as create a serious concentration of risks.

The analysis relies on some crucial features of the post-socialist economies with specific assumptions. First, banks are assumed to be currently the only source of capital for investment. On the other hand, banks are saddled with a large number of bad loans, which reflect their former role as suppliers of subsidies to the state-owned sector (Estrin *et al.* 1992); also, the portfolio of non-performing loans for each bank is rather concentrated. Banks can choose either to lend more to these firms or to lend to private entrepreneurs, who are more efficient and less risky. Only in the medium term, when the economy will have stabilized and property rights clarified, will other intermediaries or source of capital emerge.[9] Finally, bank deposits are guaranteed (implicitly or explicitly) by the state budget.

The alarming conclusion is that the effect of accumulated bad loans will cause a bias against lending to new, more profitable ventures. Banks have a perverse incentive to direct funding towards their former debtors because, although they are less likely to be profitable, if they are successful the bank receives the additional benefit of repayment of their previous debts. In other words, the distortion arises because the bank is the real residual claimant in the old firm and not in the new ones. As a result, the banks may actually increase their overall financial involvement with their debtors, causing an unnecessary concentration of risks, even though diversification would permit greater financial stabilization. This leads to an overall lower productivity of investment in the short term, as the expansion of efficient new firms is postponed, causing a slower recovery in the transition period. In addition, bank credit may allow a slower pace of privatization of firms and assets. The consequence may be a very inefficient outcome if a rapid transfer of resources is necessary to avoid the collapse of the public budget, or when significant spillover effects exist among private sector firms (Roland and Verdier 1991). The analysis is consistent with the evidence on the dominant share of bank credit received by state-owned enterprises, the large concentration of bad loans among the main banks and the persistent concentration of their lending to the same industries (see Varhegyi 1992).

The degree of insolvency of the old state-owned sector is likely to increase in the interval before a complete transfer of control from the state to private interests takes place. In this phase of transition the state-owned firms are damaged by the short-term orientation of their management and labour, who recognize the severe financial situation of their firms and can anticipate that they stand to lose under the future restructuring under private control (or in liquidation). It is rational for them to engage in self-interested monetization of firm assets, to appropriate firm value or simply to prolong its existence. This causes the collateral of banks' loans to shrink, transforming them into residual claimants.[10] Once banks are privatized and operate in a profit-maximizing fashion, they will retain a strong incentive to attempt to regain their capital by gambling more money on those firms which are heavy borrowers. Any strong role for banks in the control of large privatized firms must clearly address such potential risks. The Chilean and Argentinian experience, where through privatization banks became involved with industrial groups and collapsed after extending enormous sums, should stand as a serious warning.

In conclusion, it is necessary for the government to recognize the extent of the banks' bad loans prior to their privatization, and allow them to write them off against untaxed reserves. Since these bad loans reflect a history of subsidization of industry by the state, they should be recognized as a component of the budget deficit. In fact, recognition is little more than an accounting procedure if the state is indeed the ultimate guarantor of deposits. However, this should not be allowed to put in question the solvency of the banks: their role in the payment system should not be compromised.[11]

A specific solution has been advanced by Calvo and Frenkel (1991), namely to substitute these claims in the banks' balance sheets with long-term government bonds. My suggestion is that loans should be reduced to the point where they eliminate a strong residual role for the banks.[12]

The clearing of firms' balance sheets and the establishment of value-conservation incentives and skills in the lending process by credit intermediaries are barely less important than privatization, and may be essentially equivalent in many cases.[13]

THE ROLE OF OUTSIDE SHAREHOLDERS

What may be the role of public security markets in financing the restructuring of large enterprises? In principle, public financial markets may allow the raising of large funds from dispersed investors, diffusing risks and rewards. However, it is most unlikely that such markets will develop soon. To understand the reason, it is useful to review the modern view of control, as distinct from other types of contractual rights. Typically, an enterprise has a set of contracts in place which attributes the right to its financial return and to administer its assets. Corporate control is the entitlement to the right to determine the use of assets in the residual set of uncontracted contingencies. Because the agent in control has discretion over the use of the assets in the residual set of circumstances, it gains certain private benefits, which can be defined as the value of control.

In theory, the residual owner in Eastern Europe is the state; in practice, in most countries it has lost control over enterprises to insiders, who thus enjoy broad discretion over the use of assets. In fact, until privatization it was often impossible to impose any outside discipline on large state enterprises.

But even after privatization, once a large shareholder is in place, the weakness of the legal framework is likely to undermine the development of markets. The fraction of corporate income which can be appropriated by the controlling share-holders is largely a measure of the degree of enforcement of the rule of equal income rights per share. Then the ability of firms to raise outside equity financing is limited by two factors. In the first place, market prices for equity will reflect a discount relative to the underlying profits which accounts for the control benefit. In addition, since control is very valuable, the controlling shareholder will sell voting equity only up to a point where they retain a majority of voting rights (which may be below 50 per cent when the rest of the shares are held by dispersed investors). As the value of insiders' control increases, the value of outside equity claims decreases.

The poorer the degree of equal rights enforcement, the larger the proportion of profitable ventures which are not financed. The international evidence gathered by Modigliani and Perotti (1992) suggests that in countries with poor enforcement of minority shareholders' rights, the stock market remains very under-developed. As by common assessment the legal framework in Eastern Europe is still inade-quate and poorly enforced, firms are likely to be unable to finance themselves by selling stock to small investors. As a result, a considerable number of valuable investment projects will not be undertaken.

The lack of a developed equity market is a serious disadvantage also for the emergence and growth of new private firms, for which equity is essential. The disadvantage of bank credit lies in its incapacity to support rapid expansion based on future prospects as opposed to current net worth. It may also be particularly inappropriate in emerging industries, where risk capital is essential to redistribute the considerable risk of new ventures; and in ventures where the large fraction of intangibles (talent, investment opportunities) over tangible assets increases the cost of financial distress induced by debt financing and increases its moral hazard costs. As a result, new firms' expansion is too often constrained to be financed with internal funds, which in general will not correspond to the opportunities available.

As a consequence of the unreliability of equity financing, funding of investment will continue to be provided in the form of claims demanding unconditional payments of fixed amounts at a stipulated date; in other words, debt tends to dominate as a source of financing. In conclusion, in a context of unreliable contracts, banks have some comparative advantage over market financing. Bank financing of investment relies on repeated interaction and often long-term relations; as a result, they are in a better position to supervise borrowers through non-contractual enforcement, such as the threat of refusing further credit. Finally, while poor accountability and unreliable enforcement apply to debt claims as well, creditors usually require that their claims be secured with current assets rather

spective returns. Thus, intermediating organizations will prevail over
rkets not because of an inherent superior capacity to administer
...ng but because of the unreliability of security financing.

5. Conclusions

This chapter has considered the problem of corporate control in Eastern Europe
and presented an argument in favour of decentralized mass privatization programmes. It is to be expected that financial constraints will ultimately force
most countries to adopt a voucher privatization programme with a market-
based allocation of control. While this implies that the final allocation of the
benefits from privatization will not be very uniform among the population, this
is probably inevitable. A voucher scheme is still likely to be more popular and
offer more advantages to the average citizen than most centralized arrangements,
particularly if it is in some form connected with small-scale privatization.

These conclusions go against the flood of proposals aiming to promote diversified mutual funds as the protagonists of privatization: in the current economic
situation financial risk can be better reduced by exercising corporate control
rights than by diversifying. Banks are similarly not appropriate agents of direct
corporate governance. Their fundamental role in the payment system and as
providers of low risk investment should not be compromised by the attempt at
rescuing unprofitable corporations. The likely final outcome is a system of control
over enterprises dominated by individuals rather than institutional investors, a
process which should be encouraged. There is unlikely to be an important role for
the stock market in the transition. There is no doubt that Eastern Europe will
develop active equity markets; however, in the short term the emphasis should be
on identifying private owners to engage in value creation through corporate
restructuring. While an active secondary equity market is a sign of a well-developed financial system, it is not the essence of a market economy, whose main
character is decentralized decision-making by individuals. After all, most firms in
the West are managed by one or a few individuals, who own a large fraction of the
stock; they are financed primarily by own funds and bank lending.

Notes

1. Brainard (1991) has forcefully argued that ensuring a proper allocation of credit
   resources is of even more primary importance than privatization.
2. Perotti and Guney (1993) document how sale of profitable firms in Eastern Europe to
   foreign investors is usually gradual, as are most privatization sales elsewhere.
3. One reason is the gradual development of the regulation and practices necessary for
   legal protection of small investors, who individually have little ability and incentive to
   influence management. In the absence of adequate rules and enforcement, controlling
   shareholders can easily dilute the value of small investors, resulting in scarce participation and depressed prices.

4. Blanchard *et al.* (1991) list some objections to workers' control: 'the current workers do not get the proceeds from investment and have strong incentives to give themselves dividend and to opt for very liquid forms of investments... if workers are majority shareholders with full voting rights, they have the opportunity to exploit minority shareholders by relabelling part of profits as wages' (p. 52).
5. The question does not arise in sales made to a strong industrial partner or to a large investor, who can exercise control effectively.
6. However, this implies that investors will have limited protection from fund management, since they have no right to withdraw their entitlements.
7. The effect of high debt on incentives and its role in causing under-investment (Myers 1977) is not discussed here.
8. A related reason is the existence of economic costs of bankruptcy, in addition to social costs.
9. Possibly the only reason why technically bankrupt banks still attract funds is that private citizens perceive an implicit state guarantee behind their deposits.
10. This highlights the fact that privatization by share distribution of highly indebted firms is really a transfer of only a small fraction of their capital to the private sector. The major lenders (the banks) hold the residual control claims in most states of nature.
11. In addition, it would be very dangerous to discredit the basic store of value available to households, as it may devalue all investments implicitly or explicitly guaranteed by the state.
12. A reason for resistance to this solution may be the reluctance by the government to recognize the extent of its liabilities. It may be in the (short-term) interest of a government otherwise unable to raise debt finance to allow the banks to take a gamble on their loans.
13. Liquidation may be the ideal procedure to recognize the market value of the debt and remove the debt overhang which discourages investment; it may be shaped to serve efficiently the function of rapidly assigning control over the assets to their more efficient user.

References

Blanchard, O., Dornbusch, R., Krugman, P., Layard, R. and Summers, L. (1991) *Reform in Eastern Europe*, MIT Press, Cambridge, Mass.

Brainard, L. Reform in Eastern Europe: creating a capital market, *Economic Review*, January/February 1991, pp. 49–58.

Calvo, G. and Frenkel, J. (1991) Credit markets, credibility and economic transformation, *Journal of Economic Perspective*, 5(4), pp. 139–148.

Dyba, K. and Svejnar, J. (1992) Stability and transistion in Czechoslovakia, papers presented at NBER Conference on transition in Eastern Europe, Cambridge, Mass., February 1992.

Estrin, S., Hare, P. and Suranyi, M. (1992) Banking in transition: development and current problems in Hungary, *CEP discussion paper* No. 68, London School of Economics.

Fischer, S. Privatization in East European transformation, *NBER working paper*, No. 3703, May 1991.

Frydman, R. and Rapaczynski, A. (1990) Markets and institutions in large scale privatizations, *New York University Research Report*, No. 90–42.

Goldsmith, R. W. (1969) *Financial structure and development*, Yale University Press, New Haven, Connecticut.

Johnson, S. (1992) Private business in Eastern Europe, papers presented at NBER Conference on Transition in Eastern Europe, Cambridge, Mass., February 1992.

Lipton, D. and **Sachs, J.** (1990) Privatisation in Eastern Europe; the case of Poland, *Brookings Papers on Economic Activity*, **2**, pp. 293–333.

Modigliani, F. and **Perotti, E.** (1992) The rules of the game and the development of security markets, *Boston University Working Paper*, No. 91–16, March 1992.

Myers, S. (1977) Determinants of corporate borrowing, *Journal of Financial Economics*, **5**, pp. 147–175.

Perotti, E. (1993) Bank lending in transition economies, *Journal of Banking and Finance*, **17**, pp. 1021–32.

Perotti, E. and **Guney, S.** (1993) Successful privatization plans, *Financial Management*, April, **22**(1), pp. 84–98.

Roland, G. and **Verdier T.** (1991) Privatisation in Eastern Europe: irreversibility and critical effects, paper presented at CEPR Conference on Privatization of Public Enterprises, Milan, May 1991.

Rybczynski, T. M. (1990) The sequencing of reform, *Oxford Review of Economic Policy* **7**(4).

Shleifer, A. (1992) Privatization in Russia: first steps, presented at NBER Conference on Transition in Eastern Europe.

Varhegyi, E. (1992) Modernization of the Hungarian bank sector, presented at CEPR Conference on Hungary: An Economy in Transition, London, February 1992.

CHAPTER FOUR

Privatization and regulation of utilities in economies in transition

Martin Cave and Pal Valentiny

1. Utilities under central planning

In almost every country, whatever its economic system, the state has played an active role in creating the infrastructure necessary for economic development. Direct aid, government-guaranteed loans, investment projects financed by the central budget and direct public ownership were the basic elements of state intervention in the late nineteenth and in the twentieth centuries. Extensive state support in the development of railways, telecommunications and electricity supply was a major element in creating the prerequisites for a developed economy.

The promotional function of the state was even more prominent in infrastructure development in relatively backward countries. In the inter-war period, during the Second World War and during the post-war reconstruction, there were many examples of far-reaching state intervention, including nationalization in sectors considered critical for the development of the whole economy. The public utilities were always seen as performing functions vital for the attainment of government economic goals. The development of utilities became a regular 'chapter' of the national or sectoral plans in many post-war experiments with planning in Europe and elsewhere.

In Eastern Europe it was the specific role of planning and the particular role of infrastructure within the plans which determined the development and performance of utilities in the four decades from 1950 to 1990. In post-war Eastern Europe, as in the pre-war Soviet Union, planning became the basic instrument of control over the economy. Sooner or later, all Eastern European countries adopted Soviet directive planning methods. The fundamental objective of planning was an aggressive industrialization 'crusade' based on compulsory output targets and centrally allocated inputs. The medium-term plans were subdivided into yearly, quarterly, or shorter plans. Planning targets in physical terms became the basic tool of economic management, and prices lost their signalling and allocative functions. Enterprises were converted into units in an administrative hierarchy controlled by a monolithic party.

In most East European countries, national networks were created from regional utility companies in the late 1940s and early 1950s. Because of their size and importance, public utilities became departments of ministries or even constituted a whole ministry. The ruling ideology required that their services should be cheap and available to all. However, only the first part of this injunction was fulfilled. Tariff structures typically favoured households so that residential consumption was constantly under-priced compared to industrial use, and cross-subsidization of consumers became a permanent feature of the tariff structure. Moreover, tariffs in general failed to cover economic costs. This was sustainable due to the lack of a feedback mechanism between prices and investment. As occurred generally in these economies, investments were covered by the central budget through taxation without any reference to revenues raised by the utilities; the Planning Office's choices among new projects was not based on rate-of-return analysis but on administratively set output targets.

Prevailing economic doctrine and the needs of industrialization resulted in separation of 'productive' and 'non-productive' activities within the economy. The former were assumed to create wealth, while the latter were assumed to consume it. Giving preference to 'material' production or 'material' services was a characteristic feature of economic policy under central planning. Although most public utilities fell into the category of 'productive' activities, some of them were considered less productive than others.

Energy industries (gas and electric utilities) were in a more advantageous position as they provided an input central to material production. But given the system of central allocation of investments, their development did not go beyond what was regarded as strictly necessary, creating bottlenecks and 'black-outs' in periods of rapid growth. The transport and particularly the telecommunications industries suffered more from the rules of central allocation of investments, as planners first satisfied the requirements of 'material production' and services only received residual financial resources.

An equivalent hierarchy of customers could also be detected within each sector. While network expansion in electricity or gas supply already showed some sign of preferential treatment of industrial or bulk consumers, the development of transport and telecommunication services made the distinction between industrial and residential consumers more directly. The standard statistical classification of activities separated passenger transport, for example, as a non-material service, from the transport of goods, a material service (OECD 1991: 13). The chances of getting a telephone line were much better for an industrial than for a residential customer. These distinctions reflected the fact that the delivery of planned inputs and outputs constituted the fundamental priority of the command economy, not the satisfaction of consumer demand.

As a result, public utilities were relatively weak sectors in the centrally planned economies. Because of their low prestige, reflected in the investment allocation system, they were provided with fewer and fewer resources. The performance of the energy, transport and telecommunications industries lagged behind those of the market economies. In many areas their relative backwardness became a major factor contributing to the inefficient use of resources (Major 1992; Bicanic and Skreb 1991).

At the same time, inflexible and relatively low tariffs led to excess demand, and the intensity of service utilization was much higher in Eastern Europe than in the developed economies (Major 1992: 82). The intensity of goods transport (measured in ton-km per unit of GDP) ranged from 0.5 to 2.0 in Eastern

European countries while OECD countries' figures varied between 0.2 and 0.5 (OECD 1991: 26). The performance of the transport sector also influenced working capital requirements in the manufacturing sector. Reliance on railways for transportation hindered inventory minimization and increased costs in all the countries of the region (Grubler 1990: 238–9).

In telecommunications, too, Eastern Europe was and is at the bottom of the European league. The average number of exchange lines per 100 population is 43 in Western Europe. In the East it is between 10 and 20 per 100. Moreover, the networks also suffered from technological backwardness due to autarchic development. The lack of technology transfer eliminated competitive pressure, often raised costs and cut Eastern public utilities off from the rapid changes in technology in the West. The annual loss of GDP in Hungary due to the low level of telecommunications has been estimated as 4 to 5 per cent of GDP (Major 1992: 78).

Thus severe shortages, poor quality of service and lack of investment characterized the public utilities as they entered the era of transition to a market economy. The bureaucratic style of government of the previous system affected utilities in fundamental ways. The experience of four decades of total state intervention led many to argue against any form of intervention, as reducing the strength of the state came to be regarded as one of the most important tasks of government. However, an exaggerated belief in the omnipotence of market mechanisms could render the transition period more difficult. There are areas where markets do not necessarily function well and some kind of regulation is demanded. It is therefore necessary to review how utilities can and should be regulated in a market context.

2. Why regulate utilities?

Standard economic analysis suggests that perfectly, or workably, or even potentially competitive industries serve the interests of consumers through the operation of market forces: competitive markets are the best regulator. However, the legacy of central planning has left most East European economies with a relatively small number of giant enterprises, as the centre saw advantages in co-ordinating the production of a relatively small number of firms. In many sectors, concentration went beyond the point where further economies of scale could be realized.

In such over-concentrated industries, the natural solution is to restore competition by restructuring production in a number of competing units. Imports can serve as a further form of competitive regulation. When this approach is impracticable because current productive capacity cannot be broken up, the process of inducing competition through entry may take a longer period, but it is likely to be a desirable policy.

Some industries, however, are characterized by distribution networks which may have natural monopoly properties. In such cases, output is supplied most cheaply by a single firm serving a particular area. For example, duplicating a gas or water distribution network is likely to impose a considerable cost penalty compared with the operation of a single efficient network. This does not mean that the distribution network need necessarily be run as a unitary national monopoly, as the coexistence of local monopolies may have advantages. It does imply, however, that some parts of the industry in question — notably the distribution network — may never become competitive and may require regulation in the long term, even though prospects for competition may be better in other parts of the industry. For example, in the electricity supply industry, generation is potentially competitive, and the natural monopoly is likely to be confined to transmission. Technological change may also erode the natural monopoly property of a distribution network. Thus, the development of radio-based telecommunications has eroded what to many had seemed the permanent natural monopoly property of conventional wire-based networks. (For a discussion of utility regulation in general, see Vickers and Yarrow 1988 or Kahn 1988.)

Where a monopoly exists, regulatory intervention is required to ensure economic efficiency. However, many utilities serve social goals as well as the objective of economic efficiency. In capitalist or mixed economies, these social goals are often reflected in the imposition of universal service obligations. Thus an electricity, gas, water or telecommunications company may have an obligation to supply anyone who reasonably requires the service, normally at an average price which does not reflect differences in the cost of provision. Such social goals require specific regulatory interventions if they are to be achieved.

In Western economies a variety of methods has been employed in the management and control of network utilities. In Western Europe the typical practice until recently has been to take the network into public ownership at either the national or municipal level, and to impose certain rules of conduct upon its operation. In its most basic form, the utility is operated as a government department, and pricing and investment decisions are taken directly by government ministers or officials. In principle, this can lead to an efficient outcome if marginal cost pricing rules are followed, if appropriate investment criteria are employed, and if inefficiency in production is eliminated. In practice, the industries are likely to be characterized by inefficiencies, and pricing and investment decisions often are directed at short-term political objectives rather than at an efficient, or even an equitable, allocation of resources.

An alternative variant of a publicly owned utility is for it to operate as an independently managed public corporation, subject to general rules of conduct imposed by a sponsoring minister. This situation obtained with nationalized industries in the UK. Here, too, efficient pricing and investment are potentially attainable if the appropriate rules are followed. Given the existence of economies of scale, efficient pricing rules may involve the public enterprise in incurring losses, which can be made up by subsidy. Alternatively, the government may seek to impose a break-even constraint upon the public enterprise.

Separating the assets of the public enterprise from those of the government introduces the possibility of separating production and regulation. The sponsoring department can lay down ground rules, set targets and evaluate the corporation's performance. Alternatively, a regulatory agency can be established independently of the government department to discharge the regulatory function. Both variants of regulatory structure can be observed in Western economies.

Different forms of regulation are sometimes required when the utility is privatized. Unless the government provides it with a subsidy in order to ensure its long-term survival and the availability of investable funds, the utility has to generate enough revenues to meet all of its costs, including its costs of raising capital from private investors. Moreover, such investors will be aware that because the assets which they own in the distribution network are long-lasting and 'sunk', they are potentially subject to expropriation through the regulatory process. Accordingly, they may be unwilling to invest unless confident of a stable regulatory regime which allows the recovery of all costs.

In the USA, this security of expectations was often achieved by the operation of rate of return regulation, which explicitly allowed utilities to set tariffs at a level intended to provide a return equal to the cost of capital. However, because pricing was essentially cost-plus, there were few incentives to maintain productive efficiency. Accordingly, many privatized utilities in Western economies are now regulated on an incentive basis, with price-caps set over a period of five years or so, thus giving the firm an incentive to reduce costs. These incentive arrangements normally operate within the framework of an obligation on the part of the regulator both to protect consumers from monopolistic exploitation and to ensure that the incumbent firm can, if it operates efficiently, sustain its existence.

Thus the main objective of utility regulation, which is to protect consumers' interests in the long term, can be met in a number of ways, and Western countries exhibit different forms of ownership and different patterns of regulation. As a rather crude generalization, economies at a lower level of *per capita* income tend to favour public ownership and direct government control over utilities rather than privatization and indirect control through independent agencies. This may be for a number of reasons. In poorer countries, networks may only be at the development stage and require substantial investments which the private sector cannot undertake. Social objectives may also play a more prominent role in pricing policy.

For the reasons described in the previous section, the economic and financial background of utilities in economies in transition is particularly difficult. A legacy of under-investment has created excess demand in many sectors. Prices bear a very weak relation to costs, leading many utilities to make heavy losses. The governments of economies in transition thus face severe problems in getting from their current situation into something approximating the long-term equilibrium which characterizes advanced Western utilities. It should not therefore be a matter of surprise that they are likely to choose a variety of different strategies towards ownership and regulation, depending upon their starting point and upon the weights given by their governments to the various objectives of developing networks, maximizing privatization revenues, controlling inflation, and pursuing social pricing objectives. In the next section we analyse how these conflicting objectives are likely to work out in practice.

3. Issues in regulating utilities in economies in transition

In deciding how to manage the utilities, economies in transition face four major issues: (1) who should own the utilities, the state or private investors (domestic or overseas); (2) the nature of the regulatory structure, in particular whether regulation should be carried out by an independent agency, a branch of the ministry, or the enterprise itself; (3) the desirability of allowing entry and competition; and (4) how to choose procedures for the control of prices. These issues arise in any economy, but the relationships among them are rather different in economies in transition. We examine each of them in turn.

The most conspicuous but not necessarily the most important issue is that of ownership; should the utility be privatized in whole or in part, and if so, should the government look at home or abroad for investors?

The limited Western evidence available on the impact of privatization upon efficiency suggests that, once a utility has been placed on a commercial footing, with its own profit and loss account and an established regime for financial control, the simple act of transferring ownership from the public to the private sector has relatively little impact upon efficiency. The evidence suggests that a greater impact on efficiency is exercised by the stage of 'corporatization' (i.e. separating the utility's activities from those of a ministry or department) and — further down the road — by the introduction of competition.

However, two special factors operate in the case of economies in transition, predisposing the governments in question to favour some form of privatization. For reasons indicated above, in many cases the utilities have been starved of capital. In more favourable circumstances, this deficit could be made up by funding from borrowing, from revenue raised by the central government through taxation or by raising tariffs. However, the process of transition imposes heavy burdens on government finances, and it is unlikely that investable funds can be found through central government borrowing or taxation: there are many more urgent demands upon government funds, and the difficulties of raising tax revenue during a transition are obvious. The same reasons make privatization an attractive option. Compared with much of the capital stock of economies in transition, that tied up in utilities requires relatively little restructuring, and the revenues from it are reliable. The assets of utilities are thus relatively saleable.

But should they be sold at home or abroad? The weakness of capital markets and the absence of domestic savings in most economies in transition argue strongly in favour of selling utilities to foreign investors, provided that appropriate safeguards can be introduced. Moreover, there is a further argument in favour of an overseas sale. Large overseas utilities typically have managerial and technological expertise which is strongly in demand in economies in transition. Selling a controlling interest or a major stake to a single company or a consortium often provides access to that expertise. It is therefore not surprising that economies in transition typically look to this source for privatization proceeds and subsequent investment funds. At the same time, they are likely to look to international organizations such as the World Bank or the European Bank for Reconstruction and Development as a source of further capital. This may be more easily forthcoming when private direct investment is also available.

The process by which the sales of substantial stakes in utilities can be achieved is illustrated in the case study from Hungary considered in the following section. Governments in such cases typically use Western financial, legal and management advisers experienced in privatizations in their own countries. This facilitates the sale process, but the incentive system often used in such cases carries its own dangers. For example, paying financial advisers a percentage of the revenue realized may be appropriate when the government's aim is to maximize revenue, but may be less appropriate when a mixed objective is being pursued, such as a combination of revenue from sale and the introduction of competition into the sector as a means of promoting efficiency.

Whatever decision is made about ownership, it is likely that important changes will have to be made in the system of regulation, especially if the industry in question is still operating as part of a central government department rather than as a public corporation. Experience suggests that there are considerable benefits to be had from separating the regulatory and operational functions which, in many cases, were previously exercised by the same organization. Combining the two functions runs the risk of compromising policies aimed at promoting internal efficiency and reducing the likelihood of the development of competition. For this reason, there has been a strong tendency in the West in recent years to establish a framework which separates regulatory responsibilities from those of managing the business. The benefits of this policy accrue equally to economies in transition, and most discussions of appropriate forms of regulation there presuppose an equivalent separation.

But this leaves open the issue of whether the regulatory function should be discharged by an independent agency, as frequently occurs in the UK and the USA, or whether regulation should take place within the ministry (the French or German model). Within the framework of an economy in transition, there are advantages and disadvantages associated with each option. The principal benefit of an independent regulatory agency is that to some degree it removes regulatory decisions from the political, or party-political process. A regulator may be able to promote efficient entry or increase or rebalance prices with less opposition than a government would face. Moreover, private investors may have greater confidence in a regulatory process not subject to immediate political intervention, as they might see such an arrangement as furnishing them with a more satisfactory procedure for protecting their investments.

On the other hand, it may be quite unrealistic to suppose that key decisions relating to the pricing or structure of centrally important sectors in the economy can in practice be removed from political control. If this is the case, it may be preferable to separate the regulatory function from operation of the enterprises, but to locate it squarely within the responsible ministry. In such cases, an independent regulatory agency would be seen as a charade, which tended to hamper rather than support the attainment of the long-term objectives of efficient production and equitable prices. Moreover, an independent agency might be more subject to 'capture' by the firms it is supposed to regulate.

As in Western countries, the balance of advantage between the alternative approaches is likely to hinge upon the nature of a country's administrative, historical, political and social traditions, and its overall transition strategy. However, whichever structure is adopted, there are advantages in making regulatory procedures as transparent as possible. This is particularly important when competition is permitted. Capricious regulation increases perceived regulatory risk, raises the cost of capital and ultimately injures consumers.

The third issue facing economies in transition in the regulation of utilities concerns the approach they should take in encouraging or excluding competition. Competition can be achieved through a variety of means, the principal of which are the restructuring of existing assets and allowing or encouraging entry. In the UK, for example, the former approach was adopted in the case of the electricity supply industry, which on privatization was divided into a partly competitive generation sector (into which entry was permitted), a single grid company for high voltage distribution, and a number of regional electricity companies with local distribution monopolies to which competitors have mandatory access. In the telecommunications industry, on the other hand, the principal operator was privatized as a single unit and new entry was subsequently permitted. New entrants have built their own infrastructure, which has to interconnect with that of the dominant incumbent, on terms set by the regulator.

Decisions about whether to encourage or permit entry depend upon a variety of considerations. In some cases, the nature of the activity under consideration is such that facilities-based entry is uneconomic. Thus, it is unlikely to make economic sense to duplicate a water and sewerage system or an electricity grid. In other areas, the costs of duplication are less, and it is quite plausible that they may be out-weighed by improvements in efficiency and quality of service which may result from competition.

Decisions about the regulation of entry are sharpened in economies in transition by their effect on government revenues from privatizations. Assets privatized as a monopoly are likely to command larger sums from potential purchasers. Moreover, liberalization of entry may hamper social objectives, such as the cross-subsidization of some customers by others, as any entrant will have a strong incentive to supply profitable market segments (a practice known as cream-skimming).

The dilemma is thus acute, particularly in areas where experience in Western countries has demonstrated that competition is both practicable and probably beneficial. One particular advantage of the liberalization of entry is that it promotes the use of new rival technologies. This may be particularly important when the incumbent is wedded for traditional reasons to methods of production that may be uneconomic in the country's new circumstances.

Finally, economies in transition have to face the issue of how to control prices. The traditional concern about monopolies is that they will set prices too high, leading to a misallocation of resources. Accordingly, utilities in Western economies are subject to some price control regime, either in the form of a restriction on the allowable rate of return on capital, or — more recently — in the form of a price-cap, which allows the utility to raise prices in real terms at some predetermined rate over a given period. The latter approach is often regarded as having more satisfactory incentive properties, as it allows the company during the period of the price-cap to keep any additional profits which it makes as a result of increases in efficiency.

Economies in transition face a rather different problem. Both absolute and relative prices are typically inefficient. Overall, they are too low to allow the recovery of economic costs, and they embody substantial elements of cross-subsidy, typically in favour of residential customers.

As a result, the problem facing the government is often that of increasing and rebalancing prices, while at the same time maintaining incentives for efficiency. Price increases, particularly as they affect residential customers, are highly unpopular. Realistically, they may have to be introduced in a phased manner. At the same time, the restructuring of production and demand associated with the transition makes it particularly difficult to form an estimate of potential efficiency gains, suitable for incorporation in a price-cap.

As a result, prices are typically directly controlled by the government through an administrative process. In many cases, the government is tied to increased prices through agreements with international organizations such as the IMF: grants or loans are made conditional on the implementation of such policies. This linkage places the issues of privatization and regulation of utilities close to the centre of politics.

4. A Hungarian case study

As a general rule, public utilities were not in the first wave of candidates for privatization in Eastern Europe following the overthrow of the previous regimes. They were generally viewed as state-owned assets for the long term, as the state has and will continue to have a role in influencing the market and services offered by these firms. However, it soon became clear that the development of these services is vital for the economies' modernization strategies, and that the respective governments were not in a position to finance the huge investments required. Governments began to opt for selling stakes, mainly to foreign investors. Nevertheless, the progress in Eastern Europe towards new ownership structures and a balanced regulatory framework is painfully slow.

To provide deeper insight into the process of regulating and privatizing public utilities in Eastern Europe, we turn to the case of Hungary, where preparations are at the most advanced stage. The telecommunications, gas distribution and electricity sectors were scheduled for privatization before the end of 1993. Hungary has a good reason for being in a hurry. The country is slowly running out of saleable companies, and assets of public utilities are considered as a good investment. The sale is also pressing because of potential rival privatizations in Eastern and Western Europe due in the next few years. It is therefore useful to discuss the development of privatization and regulation in these sectors in Hungary.

INSTITUTIONAL FRAMEWORK OF PRIVATIZATION IN HUNGARY

A modest separation of ownership, management, and regulatory functions occurred during the 1990–1992 period and the decision-making process and responsibilities became more clearly defined. Parliament is responsible for the formation of general energy policy objectives and for the development of national telecommunications policy, and for codification of laws relating the implementation of these policies. In the energy sector Parliament has the authority to determine the type and site of new baseload power stations. The government as a whole is responsible for realizing opportunities to diversify imports in energy industries, for decisions on privatization, and for decisions on 'developments with national importance'. The government also controls the implementation of national telecommunications and energy policies. In all other matters responsibility is shared between the government and the relevant ministries — the Ministry of Industry and Trade (MOIT) for energy issues, the Ministry of Transport, Telecommunications and Water (MTTW) for telecommunications, local government bodies, and the public utilities themselves.

Several changes have also taken place in connection with the ownership structure of the industries. In 1990 the energy industry companies as state-owned entities were under the control of MOIT, while the Hungarian Telecommunications Company (MATAV) was controlled by MTTW. During 1991 and 1992, the major energy industry companies and MATAV were reorganized into joint stock companies. According to acts governing the functioning of the State Property Agency (SPA) — the governmental body, established in May 1990 for implementing and controlling privatization in Hungary (see Chapter 9) — the SPA became the owner of state-owned assets in these reorganized companies. At the same time the SPA entrusted MOIT with the management of energy utilities and MTTW with the management of telecommunications assets. Thus the control over the public utilities was divided between the SPA and the ministries.

As a result of privatization legislation enacted in 1992, the role of the SPA changed. It became responsible for the 'entrepreneurial properties' of the state (assets temporarily owned by the state). A new institution, the Hungarian State Holding Company (SHC), was established to hold assets intended permanently to remain in state ownership in the hands of a separate governmental body. The assets belonging to SHC are of strategic importance. They include the electricity supply industry, oil and gas production and transmission, regional gas distribution and telecommunications. The government intends to hold at least 25 per cent of shares plus one vote in the case of regional gas distribution companies, and 50 per cent plus one vote in the holding companies for electricity supply, oil and gas production and transmission and telecommunications. As a result of the creation of the SHC, the asset management functions of MOIT and MTTW have disappeared. The ministries remain responsible for formulation and implementation of energy and telecommunications policy and for price control.

PRICING ISSUES

Maximum prices of services provided by most public utilities are set by the MOIT and MTTW with the approval of the Ministry of Finance and implemented by ministerial decrees. The transition process has been accompanied by a shift in pricing policy. Previous rules generated underpricing mainly for households, and cross-subsidization of consumer groups, while investments were covered by the central budget through taxation. Low prices gave rise to excess demands and resulted in low maintenance levels and an obsolete capital stock. Tariffs in general did not reflect economic costs. Prices of coal, district heating, and electricity for household consumers covered less than 30 per cent of their economic costs in

1989. Even after several increases in electricity prices, household tariffs covered only two thirds of economic costs in 1992.

The situation is much better in telecommunications. Owing to large price increases in 1991 the public utility became highly profitable. It is not the level, but the structure of tariffs which now causes concern. The relative prices of local and international/long distance calls need amendment in the medium term. All charges need to be brought further into line with international practices. Over time, however, the current high profit margins will be reduced by the rising costs of installation as network expansion moves into rural areas.

The energy price system needs more radical changes. The Hungarian government agreed with World Bank officials to eliminate household energy subsidies from the state budget, to implement new tariff structures for gas and electricity and to raise energy prices to economic cost level by 1992. However, the Bank's suggestion that energy prices cover long term marginal costs has proved difficult to enforce, partly because of the lack of progress in the implementation of new tariff structures and partly because of the political sensitivity of the energy price issue. Despite high increases, prices for residential consumers in gas and electricity supply are still lower than those for large industrial consumers. After renegotiating the conditions of loans provided by the IMF and the World Bank, the Hungarian government approved a new deadline for completing the reform of energy prices. By mid-1995 energy prices will be set to cover the economic costs of production and distribution and to provide for new investments.

PRIVATIZATION AND REGULATORY OPTIONS

Although the Hungarian Parliament has passed a huge number of laws since 1990, basic legislation is still lacking particularly on the regulation of network utilities. Parliament approved an Act on Concessions in 1991. This law mainly provided a general framework for granting concessions, while the detailed rules of carrying on individual activities were left to sectoral regulation, which requires separate legislation on each sector.

In the energy sector, the Mining Act (passed in April 1993) is the only sectoral legislation so far. The main statutory provisions of the act in principle abolished the existing monopoly privileges of gas production and supply. The act empowered the Secretary of State and the Ministry of Industry and Trade to authorize producers and suppliers. Many details were, however, unresolved and were subject to government regulation. This has happened, for example, with the issue of 'open access'; in the future the government will regulate the access to 'excess capacities' of gas transmission and distribution networks.

The legislation on telecommunications is at a more advanced stage. A Telecommunications Act was passed in November 1992. Under the act, telecommunications services (for example, public switched telephony services, mobile radio, paging services) are to be provided by companies with concession licences. The Secretary of State for Transport, Telecommunications and Water is authorized to issue an invitation to apply for concessions for telecommunications services. No single independent regulatory body was established to monitor and enforce the terms and conditions of the concession agreements. Instead, the supervision of the telecommunications service providers is assigned to different bodies and divided between the government and ministries. Some functions are performed by the Telecommunications High Authority, while consumers' representatives and local governments may express their views at meetings of the Telecommunications Interest Reconciliation Forum, both under the auspices of MTTW. Price setting is the task of the Secretary of State (MTTW) but there is no provision in the law on pricing rules or disclosure of information.

Based on the existing legislation in telecommunications, the privatization of the Hungarian Telecommunications Company (MATAV) has speeded up. In accordance with the Telecommunications Act, the MTTW and the State Holding Company announced a tender for the national concession licence and for a minority stake in MATAV in August 1993. All bids were to be submitted before 20 October 1993. The duration of the concession licence is 25 years with an eight years' exclusivity right. The licence includes some obligations on network and service supply and quality of service targets. The minority stake sold should be more than 30 per cent. Keeping potential investors in uncertainty, the tender offer contained no information on expected pricing rules.

At present it seems that the privatization of the gas distribution and electricity companies cannot proceed before approval of new sectoral acts. The latest Electricity Act and Gas Acts, currently under revision, date back to 1962 and 1969 respectively. The new ones are due to be presented to the Parliament in 1993. Recent drafts are extremely short and feature a preference for regulation 'with a light hand'. Contrary to telecommunications, the drafts propose the establishment of a single regulatory body under the auspices of the Secretary of State of the Ministry of Industry and Trade. It is envisaged that the regulation of gas and electricity industries will belong to a single regulatory body with two different departments. However, the Secretary of State will continue to determine price formation. The proposed acts may empower the regulatory body to issue, modify or withdraw licences for gas and electricity supply and generation. Current drafts have opted for exclusivity in gas and electricity distribution within a given area.

The draft bills show little effort to encourage potential competition and improve incentives in energy industries. There are few or no recommendations on current and future industry structure and operations, on purchase arrangements and fiscal regimes from public utilities and on the extent of cross-subsidies between business segments. The planned regulatory framework will leave incumbent companies with a free hand in the contract market and provides no guarantee for third-party suppliers to get access to transmission networks. There are also few provisions for control and enforcement. It is questionable whether these bills, if accepted in their recent form, would serve either the short- or the long-term interests of consumers.

5. Conclusions

Economies in transition inherited from the previous system an inadequate infrastructure provided by under-capitalized and inefficient firms. They also inherited a disadvantageous tariff structure characterized by prices generally below economic costs and relative prices containing strong elements of cross-subsidy.

This situation has placed the new regimes in a difficult situation. Raising tariffs and correcting the tariff structure may increase prospects for raising new capital and returns from privatization, but it imposes heavy social costs, as it is residential tariffs which require the greatest increases to eliminate subsidies. Governments are therefore reluctant to incur the unpopularity and inflationary consequences of permitting such price increases.

Yet while the coalition ranged against price increases, typically containing both consumers and the workforce and managers of utilities, is strong, the pressures for the rationalization of prices and for privatization are equally powerful. Utilities are attractive to private investors, and the latter — especially overseas investors — are the only plausible source of funding for development of the infrastructure on the scale required. The governments of economies in transition are thus torn between their macroeconomic and social objectives and the need for access to Western capital and technology. This dilemma takes different forms in different countries. In Hungary, the government is now committed to selling substantial stakes in the country's utilities, whereas in other countries progress is much slower.

Whatever decision is made, a further key issue facing governments is how to structure the sector in question. The maintenance of a monopoly potentially increases privatization proceeds, but may deprive the economy in question of benefits from competitive entry, in the form of greater efficiency, more innovation, and lower prices. However, given the financing needs of the economies, prospects for the development of competition in the short to medium term are limited, unless it can take the form of provision of a new and technologically distinct service such as radio-based telecommunications.

It is also true that, irrespective of the form of ownership, the economies in transition are still groping for suitable institutions for regulation. Current evidence suggests that governments will continue to be directly and centrally involved in the regulation of entry and price, so that the scope for independent regulatory agencies is limited. However, we expect this situation to change as and when greater stability has been developed in policy-making institutions and in the structure of the utilities.

In summary, economies in transition face issues in the privatization and regulation of utility which go beyond those faced by Western market economies. The difficult state of the economies makes the conflicts between the various possible objectives — raising revenue, increasing efficiency, and holding down prices — especially acute. Yet unless the issues can be resolved satisfactorily, prospects for the development of the economies as a whole will be seriously damaged.

References

Bicanic, I. and **Skreb, M.** (1991) The service sector in Easten European economies: what role can it play in future development, *Communist Economies and Economic Transformation*, **3**(2), pp. 221–33.

Grubler, A. (1990), *The Rise and Fall of Infrastructures. Dynamics of Evolution and Technological Change in Transport*, Physics-Verlag Heidelberg.

Kahn, A. E. (1988) *The Economics of Regulation*, 2nd edn. MIT Press, Cambridge, Mass.

Major, I. (1992) Private and public infrastructure in Eastern Europe, *Oxford Review of Economic Policy*, 7(4), pp. 76–92.

OECD (1991) *Services in Central and Eastern European Countries*, OECD, Paris.

Vickers, J. and **Yarrow, G.** (1988) *Privatization: An Economic Analysis*, MIT Press, Cambridge, Mass.

CHAPTER FIVE

Political dimensions of privatization in Eastern Europe

Judy Batt

1. Political aspects of systemic transformation

The project of system transformation in the post-communist countries is essentially political. Its fundamental purposes are to redefine the state on the basis of liberal democratic principles, and thereby to secure the 'return to Europe', meaning an international realignment and reintegration into Western economic and security structures. The economic aspects of systemic transformation are inseparable from these broader political goals. The communist system was based on a fusion of economics and politics: the Communist Party's monopoly of political power rested on state-ownership of the vast bulk of productive assets, the replacement of the market by centralized planning, and Party control of the careers of enterprise managers and state bureaucrats via the *nomenklatura* system. The essence of the task of systemic transformation is to unravel this totalitarian fusion of economics and politics, and to refashion the relationship between the state and society, allowing a 'civil society' to emerge independent of the state, and to which the state must become accountable.

The reestablishment of private ownership of the means of production is central to this project. Privatization is not just a question of improving economic efficiency, but of diffusing the sources of power throughout society. It is not just a question of 'rolling back the state', but of creating the preconditions for transforming the communist 'totalitarian' state into a state which is liberal — that is to say limited, based on the rule of law and dedicated to upholding individual rights and freedoms, and democratic — representative of and accountable to the citizens in periodic free elections.

Post-communist governments confront the tasks of economic transformation and privatization in a peculiarly difficult, insecure political environment. The legitimacy of the new regimes which took over after the collapse of communism is weak; the breakdown of the communist system has left society in a state of flux, and political parties are correspondingly barely formed and highly unstable; the legislatures are poorly developed and in many cases serve to obstruct rather than to facilitate the passage of legislation. These problems are outlined in the following three sections of the chapter. In the final section, a schematic overview of the impact of these problems on the process of privatization is presented.

2. The problem of political legitimation

Post-communist regimes face formidable problems of political legitimation in the transitional period. It is not enough for governments to have submitted themselves to free elections and to present themselves as the antithesis of their communist predecessors. Communism was widely discredited by the time of its collapse on account of its economic failures, and outside Russia by its association with national subordination to alien Soviet power. But the fact that it lasted as long as it did allowed it to put down deep roots, shaping popular interests and expectations which have not disappeared overnight with the communist system itself. Communist regimes have one feature in common with Western-style liberal democracies, in that their claims to legitimacy rest mainly on modern, secular and rationalistic premises. Both thus claim to serve the interests of the people, and are therefore exposed at some point to the judgement of the people on their performance. Economic welfare has a high salience in the popular legitimation of such regimes.

Communist regimes were notoriously unsuccessful in living up to their promise of a society of abundance, but their coercive monopoly allowed them to suppress criticism. Moreover their control over economic resources allowed them to buy off mass dissent by guaranteeing job security and a basic minimum of welfare. Post-communist regimes, however, in embarking on radical economic reform, lack these advantages. Democratization exposes governments to the massive social pressures generated by high expectations of rapid satisfaction of pent-up consumer aspirations; liberalization entails the state divesting itself of control over the distribution of economic resources. The economic legacy of communist rule has left most post-communist states virtually bankrupt, lacking the resources to sustain even the modest basic social security offered under communism. Ralf Dahrendorf (1990: 85) has written of the 'incompatible time-scales of political and economic reform': whereas political change can be effected in a matter of months, economic recovery will take several years. In the intervening period, the passage through the 'valley of tears' of economic upheaval and social dislocation makes extraordinary demands on political leadership, and can threaten to derail the political transformation itself.

A further, related aspect of the problem of legitimation of post-communist regimes is the rise of nationalism which has become the dominant ideology in the region, filling the moral vacuum left by communism. This is a natural reaction against communist 'internationalism', which entailed the forcible suppression of national independence and subordination of states to the interests of the Soviet superpower. As such, nationalist ideology is an essential ingredient of the legitimation of new democratic regimes as representative of their people, and reference to the 'national interest' offers these regimes a potent and convincing formula for explaining to people why they should moderate their immediate economic demands in the interests of general welfare in the longer term.

But if it is to play this positive role, nationalism must be promoted in a form which is compatible with liberal and democratic principles, in which the 'nation' is understood as the collectivity of individual citizens with equal political rights residing on the territory of the state. But nationalism in Central and Eastern

Europe has historically been focused on the assertion of ethnic identity rather more than civic political rights. The goal of national independence has therefore been defined as achieving territorial statehood based on ethnic homogeneity, and the legitimacy of the state has come to be understood in terms of its role as the political embodiment and expression of the ethnic-national will. The collapse of the communist international imperium has reopened the vexed question of the legitimacy of existing borders between states, many of which are perceived as arbitrary and unjust, as well as the legitimacy of the multi-national states of the former Soviet Union, Yugoslavia and Czechoslovakia, all of which have broken up. Older national rivalries, predating the communist period, have resurfaced; the fear of German hegemony has reawakened; and the rights of ethnic minorities have once again become problematic.

3. The raw material of politics

The new governments face societies in a state of flux and upheaval. Social groups are in a process of decomposition and realignment, and there is a high degree of volatility and unpredictability about the reactions of society to the policies that governments are trying to introduce. This state of flux is a product both of the communist system and of its breakdown. The period of communist rule had a dramatic impact on society, sweeping away whole strata of the population in the process of expropriating private property. This led to the physical destruction by emigration or proletarianization of the old landowning and 'bourgeois' classes, the transformation of the independent professions into servants of the state, and a massive influx of the rural peasant population into the cities and into industrial employment to meet the needs of accelerating industrialization.

The post-communist governments find themselves in a situation curiously reminiscent of that in which the communist governments found themselves immediately after the revolutionary seizure of power, lacking a natural base in a solid, established social constituency. Communist revolution in the industrially underdeveloped countries of Eastern Europe put the communist governments in an anomalous position, claiming to represent the interests of an industrial proletariat which did not yet exist, and which had to be created in the subsequent 'revolution from above' of forced industrialization. The revolutionary overthrow of communism has brought to power new governments dedicated to restoring liberal market economies, which requires the re-creation of a class of property-owning entrepreneurs out of the existing mass of dispossessed former employees of the state, who lack both the capital to invest and the psychological propensity to take risks. The pattern of 'internal emigration' adopted as a means of self-protection against the demands of the communist state — the flight to the weekend cottage or the vodka bottle — could prove hard to break, especially in a period of economic dislocation and gathering pessimism about the prospects of rapid improvement in the conditions of life.

The stability of communist societies rested in a form of state corporatism, structured around the bureaucratic sectoral organization of industry in large, monopolistic enterprises. The interests of workers were bound up with their enterprises to a much greater extent than is found in the West: access to flats, recreational facilities, social welfare benefits, child care, and even scarce consumer goods was to a great extent conditioned by the resources of the enterprise. These in turn depended on the bargaining power of the firm's managers in the allocation of centrally controlled resources according to the political priorities of the regime. The interests of workers and managers to a significant degree coincided in their joint efforts to secure special treatment from the state.

These powerful coalitions still exist in the post-communist period, and pose a considerable political threat to the new governments. Because of the sheer size of many of the giants of communist industrialization, which often were the sole major employers in a given region, the prospect of closure or radical restructuring threatens to provoke massive social unrest. In Poland in particular, the working class of large enterprises developed as a uniquely cohesive and articulate social group, with a strong sense of proprietorship over their enterprises and a tradition of militant resistance to the government. The fact that the new government contains people who in the past were closely allied with Solidarity cuts little ice when its policies are, if anything, even more threatening to their vital economic interests than those of its more accommodating communist predecessors. In other countries, the regional concentration of unviable enterprises set up to meet communist political priorities — notably defence industries — intersects with ethnic tensions. For example, the communist industrialization of Slovakia left that part of the Czechoslovak federal state encumbered with a burdensome economic legacy, which made it much more vulnerable than the Czech Republic to the social consequences of the federal government's radical strategy for economic transformation. This heightened Czech–Slovak tensions and helped to provide the electoral support for Slovak separatists which eventually brought about the collapse of the federation. In the Baltic states, we find something similar — the working classes of the large-scale industry established under Soviet occupation are often mainly Russian immigrants. Reforming governments in that region thus face not only a class revolt but ethnic insurrection fired by the combined resentment at the prospect of both loss of citizenship and loss of jobs.

But there is also a propensity to change and adapt on the part of both workers and managers. As state enterprises slid into decline and became ever less able to guarantee the expected wages and benefits, workers diverted their efforts ever more into secondary earning and black market activities. The result of this was not the formation of a cohesive new class of small entrepreneurs: such development was blocked by political restrictions and the insecurity of the private sector as a sole source of income. Most people kept their job in the state sector and the secure minimum income that went with it. The 'second economy' was thus parasitic on the state sector: corruption of local officials and pilfering of state property to obtain materials, equipment and time was a vital condition of its existence. This led to the widespread popular association of private enterprise with dishonesty and cheating. The task of new governments is to convert this reservoir of entrepreneurial initiative into a respected and responsible social mainstay of the transformation process. Full legalization of the private sector is the obvious first step, but the evolution of a normal entrepreneurial culture, comprising firmly established business ethics, a preference for accumulation and reinvestment in the firm rather than immediate conspicuous consumption, and acceptance of the obligation to pay taxes to the state, will take time.

Paradoxically, the social group most amenable to rapid conversion into an entrepreneurial middle class is frequently the former communist *nomenklatura*, who, by virtue of their former positions in industrial management and administration, were able to accumulate the knowledge and expertise, and also the capital, necessary to take over and succeed as independent entrepreneurs in the new liberal environment. Many have seized the opportunity presented by sketchy legislation to convert their politically secured positions into secure legal ownership of state firms. In economic terms, this may be desirable as a rapid solution to the problem of finding new owners, but politically it is inevitably controversial, provoking widescale social reaction against the injustice of it, confirming popular prejudices about the inherent sleaziness of the market economy, and engendering a hostile reaction on the part of governments staffed by anti-communist crusaders. Moreover, in some cases, most notably Russia, a potent industrial lobby can represent a formidable challenge to government policies for thoroughgoing economic transformation. As noted by Arkady Volshky, leader of the Russian Union of Industrialists and Entrepreneurs, 'Power belongs to those who have property and money. At present it is not the government but industrial managers who have both' (quoted in Teague 1992: 1).

The formation of political parties in this unstable social context has been peculiarly difficult. It is very hard for political entrepreneurs to identify coherent social interests to whom to appeal in order to build support for a specific party programme. It is indeed very hard for individuals themselves to identify where their interests lie, when tantalizing new opportunities have opened up but very few are certain about the benefits to themselves of launching out and grasping them. Moreover, forming parties on the basis of coherent alternative programmes is difficult where there is in fact such a limited scope for alternatives, so all parties tend to proclaim their commitment to the same broad objectives of democracy, the market etc. In these circumstances, emotional appeals tend to prove far more attractive and meaningful than 'rational' interest-based appeals for party support. Parties tend to be formed by individuals who represent no-one but themselves, and the vast memberships claimed are highly suspect. The skills of organization-building are spread thinly in a society previously deprived of all rights and opportunities for such activities. Governments thus find it hard to mobilize the support of disciplined and coherent parliamentary groups, and instead face constant opportunist sniping and vetos on policy from a disparate variety of sources.

4. Constitutional blockages

The new post-communist governments, committed to the principles of constitutionalism and the rule of law, are usually bound by the rules of the game as defined in constitutions inherited from the communist period. These constitutions were not originally designed to work: real power was exercised by the Communist Party, and constitutions by and large had the function of a ceremonial facade (although in the exceptional case of Poland, the *Sejm* was on occasion able to exert a significant restraining influence). Many constitutions embodied spurious 'democratic' elements, notably, wide formal powers were attributed to parliamentary legislatures, especially in the ease with which governments and individual ministers could be recalled and motions of non-confidence passed. These provisions have posed extremely difficult obstacles to the practice of effective government in the new post-communist circumstances, especially where, as in Poland between 1989 and 1991, and Russia to the present, they contained a large proportion of deputies elected under the old communist regime who saw no reason to support new governments, and had strong incentives to use every opportunity to secure their futures by demagogic appeals to discredit the policies of economic transformation. Even after free democratic elections, the situation may not improve: in Poland, the electoral law was such that it resulted in 29 parties winning seats in the first free election, the largest of which held less than 12 per cent of the seats. This was a recipe for 'gratuitous obstructionism' on the part of parliament:

> Increasingly, the Sejm became a soapbox for opposition to everything the government proposed; parties would even oppose initiatives that matched their declared platforms. This forced the government to maintain a state of constant mobilization, lest vital legislation fail through the 'accidental' absence of one deputy or another.   (Vinton 1993: 8–9)

Constitutional reform is thus vital, but extremely difficult precisely because of the vested interests of parliaments in retaining their extensive powers, and the inability of governments to secure the necessary majority for change. A rather successful case has been that of Hungary, where the Round Table Agreement of 1989, which had prescribed that any major piece of legislation with constitutional implications would require two-thirds support, was modified by agreement between the main governing party and the main opposition party after the 1990 elections in the interests of effective government. This was indicative of the relatively high degree of consensus and maturity in Hungary's post-communist politics. Elsewhere, the experience has been less happy, notably in Russia, where the titanic struggle between President Yeltsin and the Russian parliament has dominated political life to the detriment of the economic transformation. Another unhappy example is that of Czechoslovakia, where the federal constitution prescribed that all major legislation, not only on constitutional matters but also on a wide range of fundamental economic questions, must win a two-thirds majority vote in the Chamber of the People and in each section (equal-sized Czech and Slovak sections) of the Chamber of the Nations. This gave an effective power of veto to the relatively small number of Slovak nationalists and former communist deputies, effectively paralyzing the economic transformation programme of the government and blocking negotiated constitutional reform of the federation, thus contributing in no small measure to the eventual break-up of the state itself.

Constitutional conflict between the executive and parliament has also spilled over into questions of the distribution of powers within the federation in Russia. The protracted paralysis at the centre has led to a *de facto* seepage of political authority away from Moscow to the regions. Many of these have asserted control over the local economy and claimed rights of ownership over state assets and natural resources located in their territory. President Yeltsin's attempts to cut the Russian parliament down to size by constitutional reform have led him to seek an alternative power base in an *ad hoc* alternative Constitutional Conference, drawing in representatives from Russia's autonomous republics and regions. In so doing, he may have bought support for a strengthened federal executive *vis-à-vis* the federal parliament at the expense of weakening the real capacity of the federal government in Moscow to implement a coherent economic strategy throughout the whole territory of the state.

5. The politics of privatization

Post-communist governments embarking upon privatization in the sort of political context broadly outlined above have only one consistent, effective and organized source of pressure in support of the policy: the international financial institutions backed by Western governments, which insist on the inclusion of privatization as a condition for financial support and technical and economic assistance. On the domestic front they are weak and embattled. The choice of approach to privatization, and consideration of the relative merits of restitution, direct sale, or free distribution of shares to the population, is conditioned as much, if not more, by domestic politics as by economic arguments, as governments search for allies and struggle to maintain their credibility and authority.

   Thus restitution of property confiscated by the communist regimes to its original owners has only the weakest economic justification (such owners, where they can be found, may still have the requisite skills and commitment to return to entrepreneurship), and many economic drawbacks (endless property disputes are thereby invited, which create uncertainty which delays privatization by other means and deters investors). But from the political point of view, the case for restitution is overwhelming: the legitimation of new post-communist regimes rests on their capacity to demonstrate their commitment to righting the wrongs of the past as far as they are able. Thus restitution features in all countries where the government is serious about privatization. But it can also in some circumstances raise further political problems, notably in the case of Czechoslovakia, where much property was confiscated in 1945–46 from ethnic Germans of the Sudetenland who were expelled from the country in reprisal for their role in the wartime occupation of Bohemia and Moravia by the Nazis. Restitution only applies to property confiscated after the communist seizure of power in 1948; but there is a certain inconsistency in this given President Havel's publicly expressed doubts about the morality of the expulsion of the Germans. This is exploited by German emigré groups abroad, and is a sensitive and as yet not fully resolved issue in Czech–German intergovernmental relations.

   The economic arguments for direct sale of state property to new owners are clear and convincing, but, given the shortage of domestic capital to invest, this approach runs up against practical problems which are highly political in nature. The controversial issue of *nomenklatura* purchases of state property has already been alluded to. The alternative is sale to foreign purchasers. This can be equally controversial in the context of reawakening nationalism: fear of a 'new hegemony' of Germany is a delicate issue in the politics of Poland, and can be exploited by nationalist politicians. On the other hand, German investment can be welcomed where it promises jobs, good pay and the long-term future of a firm, as was the case with Volkswagen's purchase of the Czech Skoda company. Every case of sale to foreigners is open to challenge where there is a wide discrepancy between the public's perception of the value, prestige, and strategic significance of a well-known national enterprise, and Western capitalists' hard-nosed calculations of its viability and prospects. In June 1993, the sale of the Romanian state shipping firm, Petromin, to the Greek company Forum Marine was greeted with a hail of press criticism: the Romanian daily *Adevarul* wrote that 'in any normal society, in any democratic country, a scandal such as the one triggered by the sale for a pittance of the largest segment of the merchant fleet would have shaken the parliament and forced the cabinet to resign' (Ionescu 1993: 28) The xenophobic tinge of the political campaign against the sale was guaranteed to draw a wide social response, and coming on top of a series of corruption scandals, such criticism has shaken confidence in the government and eroded its capacity for action.

The alternative of distributing shares in state enterprises to employees on the model of Western Employee Stock Ownership Plans (ESOPs) has found particularly strong advocates in Poland. Despite the misgivings of liberal economic experts engaged in drawing up the Polish privatization law, some element of employee share ownership was politically unavoidable in the Polish political context, where the working class had an unusually strong sense of its right to a share in the spoils, having played such a large part in securing the end of the communist system, and having wrung from the communist regime extensive *de facto* property rights in nominally state enterprises. But elsewhere, where the workers have been more passive, governments have been able to avoid this alternative.

The option of distributing shares equally to all citizens by means of privatization vouchers has been the most innovative approach put forward by economists to meet the peculiar challenge posed by the scale of privatization in the post-communist context. Its political advantages are potentially considerable, but these have to be set against the high risk of failure and widescale public disappointment. The fact that this high risk strategy has featured so largely in the Czech approach to privatization is an indication of the relatively secure political position of its government: Prime Minister Vaclav Klaus has proved an effective populist politician, selling his neo-liberal ideology as a clear break with the past and tapping the high expectations of the Czechs of rapid change for the better. The voucher scheme fits both his neo-liberal and his populist inclinations: everyone is promised a stake in the 'property-owning democracy'.

References

Dahrendorf, R. (1990) *Reflections on the Revolution in Europe,* Chatto and Windus, London.

Ionescu, D. (1993) Romanian corruption scandal implicates top officials, in *Radio Free Europe/Radio Liberty Research Report*, **2**(30), pp. 23–8.

Teague, E. (1992) Russia's industrial lobby takes the offensive, in *Radio Free Europe/ Radio Liberty Research Report*, **1**(32), pp. 1–6.

Vinton, L. (1993) Poland: governing without parliament, in *Radio Free Europe/Radio Liberty Research Report*, **2**(26), pp. 6–12.

CHAPTER SIX

Privatization, distribution and economic justice: efficiency in transition

Amos Witztum*

1. Introduction

The purpose of this chapter is to consider how privatization might affect the disposition of agents in the transition between forms of economic organization. I would like to argue that institutional changes associated with privatization, and in particular, the fundamental changes in the structure of income[1], might have an adverse effect on the willingness of individuals to participate. One form that such unwillingness can take is that of effort withdrawal. Consequently, the efficient outcome of the new system might be socially inferior to that which could have been achieved through a moderate structural change that would have taken into consideration individuals' disposition towards the change.

To be more specific, this chapter is about a somewhat unusual interdependence in economic reasoning: between income distribution, political conceptions of economic justice, and efficiency. It is particularly in transition that the interdependence between those apparent unrelated subject matters is highlighted, though there is, as yet, little reference to it in the literature[2].

The form of ownership in an economy naturally affects the principles of income distribution. Political systems generate moral approval of those principles. Against this background, individuals form opinions upon which they will act. Among other things, they will either increase or decrease their level of participation according to their pleasure or displeasure with the functioning of society[3].

Naturally, the question that will at once follow is whether effort really depends on such general considerations rather than being dependent on incentives in the narrow sense of the word. In terms of standard analysis it is evidently the latter case. The choice of effort, like that of labour, is dominated by the disutility that it generates. In such a case, the unusual triangular relationship mentioned above remains obscure[4].

However, the choice of effort is far more complex, with some 'positive' inputs — as opposed to the negative sense of disutility — to this decision. Many in the

*I am in debt to Victor Polterovicz, Alexander Friedman, Mark Levin and colleagues at the New Economic School in Moscow for sharing with me their experiences and opinions. Peter Orzag and Brigitte Granville also made helpful comments. Saul Estrin deserves special thanks, or blame, for his advice and encouragement.

West have always felt that labour effort under communism was depressed[5]. But Atkinson and Micklewright (1992) report that the economies of Eastern Europe 'have been guided by a principle of distribution according to contribution' (p.76)[6]. Moreover, at least as far as the Soviet Union is concerned, the distribution there 'suggests a degree of dispersion not dissimilar to that of Great Britain'(p.85)[7]. Yet, in as much as one can believe the data — and the technique — productivity was lower in the East than it was in the West.

An obvious source of this difference is capital. However, Bergson (1992), while reflecting on his earlier results (1987), suggests that when considering the variation in output per labour with the change in capital per worker[8], the difference in productivity between the East and the West is much more pronounced. He concludes that 'the variation in productivity relative to that in capital per worker must reflect efficiency differences as well' (Bergson 1992: 29).

However, as far as technical efficiency is concerned the evidence is by no means conclusive. Murrell (1991), who summarizes the various attempts to measure technical efficiency argues that 'clearly, these results do not allow one to conclude that technical efficiency is a particularly important problem for centrally-planned economies' (p.12). In fact, in some of the studies the East was doing better than the West[9]. Technical efficiency, therefore, is unlikely to explain the difference in productivity between East and West.

This leaves allocative efficiency. But there is no basis to argue that this is the sole cause of the differences in productivity. As Bergson himself admits, while it is almost impossible to analyse effort, it is also extremely difficult to establish allocative efficiency. Hence while the differences in productivity might be the result of allocative inefficiency, it is equally plausible to argue that those not explained by the difference in capitalization are due to differences in effort[10].

If there is a difference in effort between the East and the West with similar compensation principles[11], the difference in effort must be due to a different type of consideration[12]. One possible explanation is that while in both systems there were incentives to increase effort, there has been a significant difference in what I would like to call the levels of 'social participation'. Consequently, the effort, and productivity, in these two systems were different. One reason could be that people in the East felt a greater displeasure with their society than people in the West. However, this does not mean that people necessarily feel more comfortable with market economies than they do with central planning. To an extent, one's judgement of one's own society depends on what one expects from society. In Thatcher's Britain the expectation must have been low as the government itself reduced any expectation by a continuous withdrawal of government from society.

In the East, on the other hand, the level of expectation must have been very high as the government set itself such high ideological targets. Failures of central planning, coupled with inevitable corruption, must have brought about a far greater disillusion in the East than could have happened in the West. However, this does not mean that people in the West were much more satisfied with the underlying ideologies of individual liberalism than people in the East were with more metaphysical social ideologies[13].

The key element is therefore the notion of effort as a component of productivity. I intend to show that privatization will affect both income distribution and its relation to effort, and may therefore bring about a form of 'alienation' that will turn the efficient competitive outcome into a 'second best' type of a solution.

Even if one ignores contentious issues like technical or allocative efficiency, the move from a central planner who promoted certain ideas, to a system which, implicitly, promotes different ones, is bound to have an effect on individuals' behaviour. For instance, while under the central planner income was composed almost solely of earnings, under market systems, the fraction of earning in one's income is reduced significantly[14]. If people tend to associate earnings with reward for effort then the move from one system to another will signify that there are means, other than effort at work, of income generation, and that effort is relatively less rewarded. In itself, this should be sufficient for individuals to withdraw some of their effort.

I will show that such a response can be consistent with the behaviour of a self-interested rational utility maximizer. Even if income, in general, increases after privatization — which is obviously the aim of transition — whether or not effort will rise or fall depends on how much of this increase is due to better effort rewarding or to the opening up of other sources of income (notably, capital). Given the initial big increases in income from ownership, it is more likely that effort will be withdrawn.

Interestingly enough, the above mentioned type of individuals would have increased their effort in response to the proposed changes in the structure of income had the good of society played a significant role in their utility. However, rapid privatization violates the principles with regard to the role of effort. People may feel betrayed by society. Consequently they will reduce, rather than increase, the role of society in their utility.

What might be more difficult to capture with the individualistic nature of neo-classical economics is the possible effects of more general circumstances on individuals' choices. For instance, if the central planner promoted equality, the effect of privatization on equality itself might be sufficient in generating some disapproval that will cause people to withdraw[15].

The generation of inequality, however, is not unrelated to the process which will generate the new class of entrepreneurs. And this, in the end, may prove to be crucial to the success of privatization. In a more general framework Banerjee and Newman (1993), for instance, find that the emergence of 'contract employment' (i.e. business beyond the self-employed) depends on the distribution of wealth. In their static model they find that when there is inequality, contract employment (and therefore entrepreneurial activities) will flourish. With equal distribution the outcome will be either subsistence or self-employment.

However, unlike the general problem of class formation, in transition there are 'natural' candidates for the 'new' class. These are the administrators of the central planner. The main question, which will not be discussed here, is whether the inefficiency of the central planner is due to an over-sized administration. If so, the move to market economy will require the slimming down of this class. This, however, will prove to be very difficult to do. Incentive-wise it would require an inequality which is unlikely to emerge. Nevertheless, had such inequality been brought about, both the optimal size of the entrepreneurs' class and the stronger position of effort related reward will push towards an all round better situation.

However, the need to create a new class of entrepreneurs outside traditional institutions will require inequality to work in the opposite direction. Thus, the possible improvements in the division of labour will be countered by the displeasure of workers who might completely offset this improvement through reduced effort.

That effort and income distribution are important determinants of efficient outcomes is a lesson that can be drawn from other areas in economics and in particular, development economics. In less developed countries, nutrition (through income) becomes an important parameter in the determination of effort and consequently, efficient outcomes[16]. Dasgupta and Ray (1986, 1987), for instance, relate income distribution to effort and by means of efficiency wages suggest that involuntary unemployment will be a result of certain income distributions. In those countries there is a particularly nasty twist to problems of productivity and efficiency as they might lead to increased poverty and famine.

The 'fair wage hypothesis' is another example of the use of effort choice to suggest that some forms of perceived fairness may lead to market failures. Akerlof and Yellen (1990), for instance, show that fairness, understood as equal treatment, can lead to unemployment in a multiple skilled economy. In this chapter, however, the concern is less with market failures than with examining the outcome of a functioning market economy with what might be described as somewhat reluctant agents.

The chapter is divided as follows: the next section contains some general remarks on the problems of using traditional neoclassical models. The following section deals with the immediate effects of privatization when effort is taken as an aggregate (thus circumventing the problem of analysing individuals' behaviour). The fourth section deals with how relationship between reward and equity affects the process of transition. The fifth section introduced the question of sequencing (i.e. liberalization and privatization) in a framework where transition affects reward which, in turn affects effort. The last section will suggest that the general assumption regarding the effort function can be derived from a certain kind of rational utility maximizer, one who takes society into his or her heart.

2. The idea of transition

The transition in Eastern Europe is often taken to mean 'simply' a move from an inefficient organization of economic activities to an efficient one. The possible consequences of such transition to equity are of lesser concern. This reflects the neo-classical view that equity is not a parameter of efficiency but a social choice from a given set of efficient allocations. That deviations from what is socially desirable may have an effect on the behaviour of individuals — an issue highlighted in transition — is traditionally beyond the scope of neo-classical economics.

There is, however, a growing recognition that individuals do have moral dimensions which may influence their choices (see e.g. Hausman and McPherson 1993). Nevertheless it is not opinions which individuals have regarding economic outcomes that affect their behaviour. Rather, the economic consequences are determined by some *a priori* assumptions about the moral behaviour of individuals (e.g. altruism). In transition one moves from one institutional arrangement based on assumptions regarding human behaviour and their role in society, to a completely different one. The change relies on individuals not acting to disappoint the theory. Thus, the assumptions about human behaviour can no longer remain functional and there is a need to believe in their descriptive power to justify the policy recommendations that follow.

Consider for a moment precisely what collapsed in Eastern Europe: central planning. This does not mean a refutation of the theoretical background of such systems (i.e. Marxian theories), even if such theories necessitate central planning.

If the rational self-interested utility maximizer is the universal of human nature then the environment within which the individual operates has little bearing on the nature of his or her behaviour. Instead, the entire analysis of transition will be concentrated on specifying the difference in constraints which individuals confront. On the other hand, if there is no such thing as a one dimensional 'Homo Economicus', one must re-examine individuals in the light of the political environment within which they operate. This is especially true of Russia, where the system had been in place for more than 70 years[17].

Individuals whose behaviour is conditioned by their political system may react differently to the signals and incentives of a new system. For example, in market systems the pursuit of one's own interest has always been perfectly consistent with the advancement of society. In communist economies, the advancement of the good of society was external to individual's welfare. There seems to have been the political need as well as the ideological background to relate the good of society to the 'disutilities', rather than welfare, of the individual (i.e. hard labour and effort).

The crucial question is whether the Homo Economicus of Eastern Europe is the one we know or something fundamentally different. Is it possible that because of reforms the Eastern European individual finds himself in complete dissonance with the emerging new system? Can the 'moral capital' of these people be so depleted that reform might have an adverse effect on efficiency?

My proposed answer to the last question is yes. The reason for it, which is not only relevant to the question of transition, is that even if there is an aspect of Homo Economicus in the Eastern European soul, there is still another important dimension of social consciousness. Many readers will find nothing special in this and will even be willing to admit that Homo Economicus is only one aspect of a person's character. However, the difference between such views and my own is that I do not think that the two are separable. This, in turn, will mean that people's views of how well their society is operating (ethically) will affect their tendency to participate. Participation, in turn, is an important factor in the analysis of efficiency.

3. The immediate effects of transition

To focus on the income distribution–effort–efficiency relationship, an efficient central planner will be compared with an efficient market system. At various points I will indicate how an initial inefficiency of the central planner might affect the results but the qualitative nature of these results will remain largely unaffected.

Consider a two sector economy[18]. For simplicity's sake assume that there are only two means of production: labour and administrators (managers). The amount of labour hours is fixed (at L), but what is relevant to productivity is effort, denoted by ϵ, which is embedded in those hours. Figure 6.1 shows the marginal product functions of labour in the two sectors (measured in terms of the output of sector 1) and the efficient allocation of labour to the two sectors when the aim of a central planner is to maximize output.

Notice that the marginal product of labour is a function of the effort (ϵ) in each of the sectors[19]. Normally, ϵ, the accumulated effort, will depend on the mean and variance of the distribution of effort. I shall not deal with this point here. Instead, I will assume that all individuals are identical and thus ϵ will simply reflect each individual's choice of effort. However, assumptions willl be made about ϵ to reflect some of the attitudes that individuals in the East are likely to hold.

Assume that the collective, or aggregate, of ϵ is derived from the political conception of what is economically just. The simplest characterization of ϵ will be where it is dependent on the share of income which is earned, i.e. the income that appears to be related to effort (denoted by w/I). In the communist environment it would mean that if effort is properly remunerated, it is one's duty to increase one's effort to bring about the final stage of communism.

Another factor which is likely to affect the willingness to contribute is inequality in the distribution of income. To keep things simple, the question of inequality will be reduced to a question of the relationship between the earnings of managers (administrators) and workers. In the political environment of Eastern Europe, equality should be seen as one of the most important components of what is economically right. More so when there is a general belief that effort too, is equally exerted.

The marginal product of labour is also a function of the size of administration (A). Assume that the level of A, at the initial setting, is the optimal size of management for the given size of L. Let the product of sector 1 be the numeraire

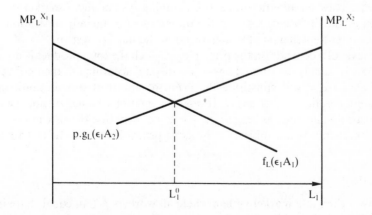

FIG. 6.1 Efficient allocation: output maximizing central planner

(say, foodstuff) and let p denote the price of the other sector in terms of those consumption goods.

Hence, the basic functions of the model are:

$$x_1 = f(L_1(\epsilon), A_1), \qquad x_2 = g((L - L_1)(\epsilon), A_2), \qquad [1]$$

where

$$\epsilon = \epsilon(w/I, w^m/w),$$

and

$$\frac{\partial \epsilon}{\partial \frac{w}{I}} > 0, \qquad \frac{\partial \epsilon}{\partial \frac{w^m}{w}} < 0 \qquad [2]$$

The greater the effort-related share of income, the more effort will be exerted. When for a level of equality everyone's income is more related to effort, a sense of community, if not self-interest, may drive individuals to increase their efforts. Naturally, the greater the inequality in the system, the more alienated people get and hence they are likely to reduce their effort contribution.

THE CENTRAL PLANNER

The bench-mark will be the efficient central planner. This will help focus the analysis on the fundamental change brought about by the move to the market system. It reflects the view that many in Eastern Europe (more so in Russia than anywhere else) are not necessarily convinced that the ideas behind central planning are flawed. Considering an ideal will make it possible to examine in a meaningful way the response to transition of individuals who are still loyal to the principle which the central planner was trying to implement.

Under an efficient central planner, L_1^0 labourers will work in sector 1 while the rest will work in the other sector. However, under central planning the planner need not associate allocation to distribution. The total output, in terms of 'consumption goods', is thus the area underneath the two curves. The entire cost of administration will be captured here in the payment to the administrator. The difference between an efficient central planning system and a market system can be seen as the difference between the optimal size of the administration and the number of entrepreneurs[20] (or managers) in the market system.

The level of ϵ depends on the principle by which the total product is distributed. If income is equally distributed or people are paid according to their contributions (in which case, ϵ will constitute the mean of an effort distribution), they will generate a certain level of effort. It does not matter whether or not the costs of administration are high as long as there is some sense that they are not wasted and that administrators are subject to the same principles of income distribution.

TRANSITION

We now switch to a market system where all workers get an equal share in newly created private firms.[21]

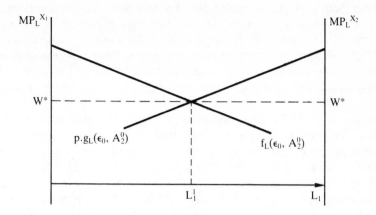

FIG. 6.2 A pure institutional transition: competitive allocation and its corresponding distribution

This will bring about a simultaneous determination of allocation and distribution. Labour will be allocated according to the same principle as under the efficient planner but with the additional outcome of a given distribution where workers now earn W^*. How precisely Figure 6.2 relates to Figure 6.1 depends on what will happen in the process of privatization. In any case, there will be an inevitable change in the sources of individuals' income.

Suppose that the central planner pursued a policy of equality in income distribution. The income per worker will be:

$$I^{cp} = \left[\int_0^{L_1} f_L(\epsilon, A_1)dL + \int_0^{L-L_1} p \, g_L(\epsilon, A_2)dL \right] \frac{1}{L+A} \qquad [3]$$

where, as in Figure 6.1, f is the production function of sector 1 (x_1) and g is the production function of sector 2 (x_2).

After privatization, assume that each individual gets an equal share in all newly formed private enterprises[22], so earnings depend on what will happen to the class of administrators. They might all become 'entrepreneurs', or managers of the newly formed firms; some of them may join the 'direct' labour market; some of the labourers may become entrepreneurs. On top of this there is the question of whether or not as managers they will take the same wages as workers. In any event, after privatization the income of a worker will become:

$$I_w^p = W^* \left[1 - \left(\frac{L+\Delta}{L+A} \right) \right]$$
$$+ \left[\int_0^{L_1^1} f_L(\epsilon, A_1)dL + \int_0^{L+\Delta} p \, g_L(\epsilon, A_2)dL - W^m M \right] \frac{1}{L+A} \qquad [4]$$

where M denotes the number of managers in both sectors, and Δ denotes the number of people who were administrators and who have now become labourers. L_1^1 reflects the new allocation of labourers between the two sectors.

Had there been a single labour market for managers and workers, the only condition under which a movement between managerial and labouring occupation will take place is when there is an income difference (stemming either from wages or from ownership differential). In such a case, there will be a single wage level in the economy and the analysis regarding effort will be entirely concentrated on the implications of equalizing moves across classes on the share of wages in income.

If, however, as shall be generally assumed, the work of administrator and managers is fundamentally different from that of labourers — that these are two different means of production — there is no need to assume a movement across 'classes' nor a unity of wages. The assumption of two separate markets, is consistent with the efficient working of the market system. The possible implications of various changes in 'class' structure will be briefly considered.

If $M = A$ then $\Delta = 0$ and $L_1^1 = L_1^0$ which means that there was no move across 'classes' after privatization and total output is unchanged[23]. Whether or not labourers, who have now to decide on their effort (ϵ), are better off depends on the wage level of the managers. If $W^* = W^m$, then the labourers' income is the same before and after privatization (i.e. $I_w^p = I^{cp}$). Nevertheless there are now two separate components to their income: that part which they earn as wages — the direct return to their effort — and income from ownership.

Before privatization, individuals considered their entire income as a reward to their effort. Now, only W^* is a reward to effort and it is clearly less than the income before transition. How such a change may affect individuals' choice of effort depends on how they feel about the relationship between their effort and the income that comes from ownership.

If, for example, they feel that profits, like wages, reflect their effort, there will be no change in effort. If, however, they do not believe that their efforts influence their income from profits, (e.g. because it comes from ownerships of firms in which they do not themselves work), there is a fall in the return to their effort. Consequently, it is quite plausible that they will choose to reduce their effort and thus bring about a competitive efficient outcome with a much reduced level of output and an even lower level of competitive wages (Figure 6.3)[24]. Note the ϵ_o corresponds to no change in effort and ϵ_1, to a reduced effort. *The corresponding wage* levels are shown as W_0^* and W_1^*, and the shaded area represents the loss in output.

Suppose now that there is a shift towards the class of entrepreneurs, $M > A$ and $\Delta < 0$. Total output will fall[25] and as a result, even if managers and workers earned equal wages (and ownership was equally distributed), total income per worker will be lower than under the central planner. Figure 6.4 depicts such a situation assuming, for the moment, no change in effort contributions and that the increase in the entrepreneurial class will have no adverse effect on productivity.

Even without a change in the effects of effort and management size, total output and thus earnings will be lower. There will be a certain collapse in productivity if we assume *a priori* that the optimal size of administration in a centrally planned system is greater than in a market system. If effort-related earnings are also lower, effort may be withdrawn, causing a further collapse in productivity.

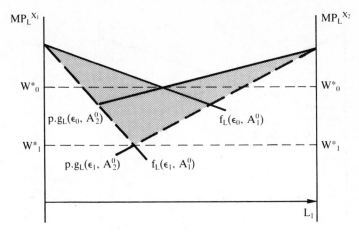

FIG. 6.3 Allocation and distribution consequences of effort withdrawal

In a dynamic setting this might look even worse. The fall in output, and subsequently income, will trigger a spiral of effort withdrawal (alienation?) and further collapses in output and earning. If labourers then escape into entrepreneurial activities, the number of entrepreneurs will exceed the optimal and will thus worsen the situation even further.

Nevertheless, one must be very cautious in dynamic considerations. It really depends on the expectations of individuals. If they do envisage a working market system at the end of the road — a system where effort is properly remunerated[26] — they might be willing to increase their effort in spite of some initial setbacks. But, it is hard to believe that a population that has been so long under a different impression can form such a precise view of the market system.

Many would argue that the role of the evolving entrepreneurial class is important not so much to substitute the 'old guard' but rather to explore new dimensions to the activity of the economy. The above framework naturally does not

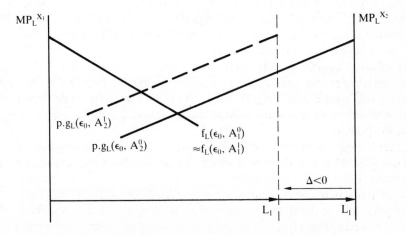

FIG. 6.4 Increase in entrepreneurial class without direct productivity implications

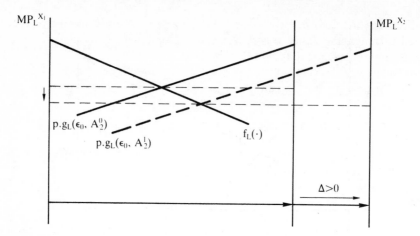

FIG. 6.5 Decrease in entrepreneurial class without direct productivity implications

capture this as the central planner was assumed to be efficient and thus we are merely considering the effect of privatization of existing industries.

If there is a fall in the number of managers $(M < A)$ then total output will initially rise (Figure 6.5) but the wage level will fall.

In such a case, although individuals' earnings have increased, that part which they associate with effort has evidently declined. If they choose to reduce effort, things can still deteriorate. Nevertheless, if one considers that the class of entrepreneurs is smaller than that of administrators, this could compensate for the loss of effort.

4. Reward and equity

This section considers the tension between reward and equality in the process of transition. In a world where all individuals are identical, there should not be, in principle, a tension between these two concepts. If all earn the same, and all put in the same effort, then whether or not equality is consistent with reward is an institutional question. The level of equal returns may or may not satisfy some principle of proportional remuneration.

The efficient central planner can easily satisfy both equality and reward. Indeed, as already mentioned, the two principles are fundamental to Socialism as a stage to Communism. Equality stems from the non-individualistic nature of Marxian theories, while reward reflects the transitional stage as explored in the Gotha Programme.

Market systems, however, are far less conducive to the co-habitation of these two principles. This is, obviously, a subject on its own but I will discuss it here in the context of the basic framework.

One assumes two rather simplistic parameters of reward and inequality. The former parameter is the share of wages in a person's income. For a given level of effort — assuming that effort is only present at someone's contracted employment — it can easily be argued that the greater the share of wages (w/I) the greater is the direct reward. In other words, one can say that the greater the share of effort related earnings, the easier it is to associate income with effort and to perceive income as a reward for that effort.

For inequality, I make use of the fact that in this model there are only two classes of people. Inequality can be represented by the ratio between their respective wages (w^m/w).

In the case of the efficient central planner, income was equally distributed and the share of wages in it was 1. After transition, the structure of income changed and from Equation [4] can be derived the following feasible relationship between shares of earned income and the distribution parameter (w^m/w) when shares in firms are equally distributed. At this stage one assumes that the level of effort is given:

$$I = w\left(1 - \frac{L+\Delta}{L+A}\right) + \left[\int_0^{L_1^1} f_L(\epsilon, A_1)dL + \int_0^{L+\Delta-L_1^1} p\, g_L(\epsilon, A_2)dL\right]\frac{1}{L+A} - w^m\frac{A-\Delta}{L+A}$$

[5]

Hence:

$$\frac{w}{I} = \frac{1}{1 - \dfrac{L+\Delta}{L+A}} - \frac{\left[\displaystyle\int_0^{L_1^1} f_L(\epsilon, A_1)dL + \int_0^{L+\Delta-L_1^1} p\, g_L(\epsilon, A_2)dL\right]}{A-\Delta}\frac{1}{I} + \frac{w^m}{w}\left(\frac{w}{I}\right)$$

[6]

let

$$\int_0^{L_1^1} f_L(\epsilon, A_1)dL + \int_0^{L+\Delta-L_1^1} p\, g_L(\epsilon, A_2)dL = Y \qquad \text{(total income)}$$

then:

$$\frac{w}{I} = \frac{L+A}{A-\Delta} + \frac{w^m}{w}\frac{w}{I} - \frac{Yw}{wI}\frac{1}{(A-\Delta)} \Rightarrow$$

$$\frac{w}{I} = \frac{L+A}{(A-\Delta)\left(1 - \dfrac{w^m}{w}\right) + \dfrac{Y}{w}}$$

[7][27]

One can now investigate the equilibrium relationship between rewards (w/I) and equality (w^m/w)[28], with effort and managerial wages exogenous. From [7] it follows that for a given level of output, the greater is the inequality (namely, the more the managers take as salaries) the greater will be the share of wages in income[29].

Figure 6.6 depicts the immediate effect of privatization assuming that there was no move across classes $(\Delta = 0)$, that the distribution of ownership shares remained equal and that managers' wages are higher than those of labourers.

Under the efficient central planner the economy is at point A. With privatization that is not accompanied by a change in the number of labourers, the economy moves at once to point B which is given by Equation [7] when $\Delta = 0$. For a given

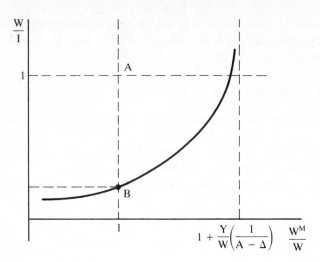

FIG. 6.6 Reward–inequality relationship and the immediate effect of privatization

class division the inequality that can be generated is limited. One finds that $(Y/w)(A - \Delta)^{-1} + 1 = w^m/w$ is the vertical asymptote of (w/I) as:

$$\lim_{\frac{w^m}{w} \to \left[\frac{Y}{w}\frac{1}{(A-\Delta)} + 1\right]} \left(\frac{w}{I}\right) = \frac{(L+A)}{(A-\Delta)\left(1 - \frac{w^m}{w}\right) + \frac{Y}{w}} = \infty \qquad [8]$$

Therefore the vertical asymptote shifts to the right whenever Δ increases. As more people leave the entrepreneurs group and join direct labour, the greater is the inequality that can be sustained by the system.

Preserving equality here has therefore 'cost' in terms of proper reward; the move to a decentralized system has inevitably reduced the degree of freedom in handling the two welfare parameters.

One may choose to reduce equality and increase managers' salaries. As a result of such a move, wages will remain unchanged but income will be reduced because less is left to be distributed, and thus effort-related earnings will have a greater share in people's income. But in such a case, a move across classes similar to the one described above might begin.

Suppose now that there is a move across classes ($\Delta \neq 0$) as a result of privatization. The possible implications will be considered with reference to Figure 6.7.

The vertical asymptote will move to the right when $\Delta > 0$. There is a greater potential for inequality now: for a given labourer's wage level and an equal share in profit, fewer managers will now be sharing the same 'residual'. Hence managers' salaries will be greater and inequality will increase. The effect on the equilibrium levels of wages' shares and inequality depends on how such a change will affect total output:

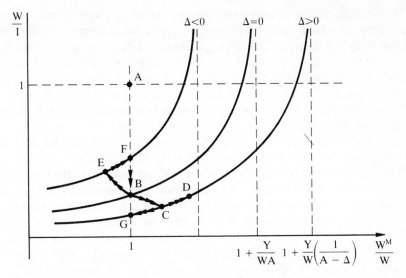

FIG. 6.7 Privatization and class mobility: effects on reward–inequality relationships

$$\frac{\partial\left(\frac{w}{I}\right)}{\partial\Delta}=-\frac{\left[\frac{\partial Y}{\partial\Delta}\frac{1}{w}-\frac{\partial w}{\partial\Delta}\frac{Y}{w^2}-(A-\Delta)\frac{\partial w}{\partial\Delta}\frac{w^m}{w^2}\right](L+A)}{\left[(A-\Delta)\left(1-\frac{w^m}{w}\right)+\frac{Y}{w}\right]^2} \qquad [9]$$

Hence,

$$\operatorname{sign}\left(\frac{\partial\left(\frac{w}{I}\right)}{\partial\Delta}\right)=-\operatorname{sign}\left[\frac{\partial Y}{\partial\Delta}\frac{1}{w}-\frac{\partial w}{\partial\Delta}\left((A-\Delta)\frac{w^m}{w^2}+\frac{Y}{w^2}\right)\right] \qquad [10]$$

which means:

if $\quad\dfrac{\partial Y}{\partial\Delta}\dfrac{1}{w}>\dfrac{\partial w}{\partial\Delta}\dfrac{1}{w^2}[(A-\Delta)w^m+Y]\quad$ then $\quad\dfrac{\partial\left(\frac{w}{I}\right)}{\partial\Delta}<0$

which means $\quad\dfrac{\partial Y}{\partial\Delta}>\dfrac{\partial w}{\partial\Delta}\dfrac{1}{w}[(A-\Delta)w^m+Y]$

as $\quad\dfrac{\partial w}{\partial\Delta}<0\quad$ while $\quad\dfrac{\partial Y}{\partial\Delta}>0$

then $\quad\dfrac{\partial\left(\frac{w}{I}\right)}{\partial\Delta}<0$

and this explains the positions of the curves in Figure 6.7 above.

It is quite reasonable to suppose that total output will rise as a result of slimming in the managerial layer and an increase in direct labour. This means

that if privatization was accompanied by an immediate move across classes —
while managers' salaries remain unchanged — then the economy will fall to point
C (through B) in Figure 6.7[30]. Allowing managers' salaries to increase will move
the economy to points like D. An income distribution policy which aims at
sustaining equality will push the economy to point G. At the same time, if there
was an increase in the entrepreneurial activity ($\Delta < 0$) then the economy would
have moved to point E when managerial reward is unchanged, and F if there is a
simultaneous increase in w^m.

Notice that while the process whereby there is an increase in the size of the
entrepreneurial class brings one closer to the initial position, it is, perhaps, the
least likely direction of privatization. It would imply that the optimal size of the
managerial layer is greater under a market economy than under a central planner.

To consider the implication of all this to efficiency, it is now necessary to add
effort functions to the framework. Assume that the aggregate of effort would be
affected by two variables: effort compensation and inequality. Effort will increase
with the share of effort-related earnings and decrease with a higher degree of
inequality. One can therefore describe iso-effort curves in the $(w^m/w), (w/I)$
plane in Figure 6.8.

Assuming that the slopes of the iso-effort curves are fairly steep, reflecting a
social aversion to inequality, the immediate impact of privatization can lead, in
Figure 6.8, to B (if there is no move across classes) or to C (if $\Delta > 0$ and w^m is
unchanged).

Therefore, if privatization means a reduction in the managerial layer, the
supply of effort will be considerably reduced (from ϵ_0 to ϵ_4). Allowing managers
to increase the gap between their earnings and those of workers (point D) will
make things even worse. On the other hand, government policy to keep the gap to
a minimum (point G) will reduce the negative impact of privatization on effort but
the level will still be much lower than under the central planner. In the unlikely

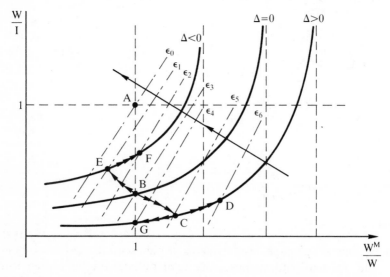

FIG. 6.8 Privatization, class mobility, and income policy: effects on effort

event where privatization is accompanied by an increase in the managerial layer, distributional consideration can only make things worse (point F)[31].

Thus, if the economy moves initially to B, there will be two reasons to keep inequality under control. One is that as long as there is no class mobility, the emergence of inequality will reduce effort contribution beyond what might be necessary (the move from A to B). The other reason is that the emergence of an income gap in favour of managers will only bring about a move across classes which will lead to a much worse outcome (point D). If that process has already begun, it will still be perfectly reasonable to carry on implementing an income distribution policy so that the damage is confined (a move to G). From the point of view of class formation, there might nevertheless be a reason to have some inequality. That is, if the process which one wishes to begin is that of a 'changing of the guard', it might be desirable for managers' income to be higher so as to attract new people, while forcing the 'old guard' to join the labour force. However, even if this is the aim, not controlling the gap means a move to D while control may confine one to G.

As things are, it seems that some economies are either at B or, at worse, at G. The little available evidence does not suggest the emergence of a tremendous gap between managers and workers. In a World Bank survey, Commander et al. (1993), find that 'relative wages had shifted surprisingly little by 1992. Over the period 1991.3–1992.3 we find rather close convergence in the rates of increase across the main grade categories.....while 40 per cent of sampled firms reported an increase in wage differentials, the remaining 60 per cent reported either no change or a decline in differentials' (pp. 27–9). Nevertheless, the move from A to B is the most significant cause for collapse of effort. Without further considerations to income distribution, things might soon deteriorate.

I shall now examine the simultaneous determination of effort, wage share, and output. With only managerial salaries exogenous, the effect of effort on the equilibrium levels of wages' share in income for a given level of w^m is:

$$\frac{\partial\left(\frac{w}{I}\right)}{\partial\epsilon} = -\frac{\left[\frac{\partial w}{\partial\epsilon}\left((A-\Delta)\frac{w^m}{w^2} - \frac{Y}{w^2}\right)(L+A) + \frac{\partial Y}{\partial\epsilon}\frac{1}{w}(L+A)\right]}{\left[(A-\Delta)\left(1-\frac{w^m}{w}\right) + \frac{Y}{w}\right]^2} \qquad [11]$$

Hence

$$\text{sign}\frac{\partial\left(\frac{w}{I}\right)}{\partial\epsilon} = -\text{sign}\left(\frac{\partial w}{\partial\epsilon}\frac{1}{w^2}[(A-\Delta)w^m - Y] + \frac{\partial Y}{\partial\epsilon}\frac{1}{w}\right) \qquad [12]$$

As both total output (Y) and equilibrium wages (w) increase with an increase in effort, the sign of equation [12] is ambiguous. It shall soon be established that this does not really matter, but first look at the conditions for the equilibrium level of w/I to fall with effort.

Rearranging the numerator, one gets the following condition for w/I to be decreasing with effort:

$$\frac{\partial\left(\frac{w}{I}\right)}{\partial\epsilon} < 0 \quad \text{if}: \quad \frac{\partial w}{\partial\epsilon}\frac{1}{w^2}[(A-\Delta)w^m - Y] + \frac{\partial Y}{\partial\epsilon}\frac{1}{\epsilon} > 0 \qquad [13]$$

This means that:

$$\frac{\partial Y}{\partial\epsilon}\frac{1}{w} > \frac{\partial w}{\partial\epsilon}\frac{1}{w^2}[Y-(A-\Delta)w^m] \qquad [14]$$

But,

$$I = w + \left[\frac{Y-(A-\Delta)w^m}{L+A}\right], \quad \text{which} \Rightarrow Y-(A-\Delta)w^m = (I-w)(L+A) \qquad [15]$$

so

$$\frac{\partial Y}{\partial\epsilon}w > \frac{\partial w}{\partial\epsilon}(I-w)(L+A); \quad \frac{\partial Y}{\partial\epsilon}\frac{w}{I} > \frac{\partial w}{\partial\epsilon}\left(1-\frac{w}{I}\right)(L+A);$$
$$\frac{w}{I} > \frac{\partial w}{\partial Y}\left(1-\frac{w}{I}\right)(L+A): \qquad [16]$$

This suggests that the smaller the influence of output on equilibrium level of wages, the more likely it is for the share of wages in income — for a given level of salaries that is kept by the managers — to fall when there is an increase in effort.

In Figure 6.9 below, the WI curve represents the feasible equilibrium levels of w/I and ϵ, for a given level of w^m. Added to the graph is a supply-of-effort function, which is not necessarily derived through an analysis of individual behaviour; it can represent group behaviour. I thereby avoid the limitations of neoclassical analysis when dealing with individuals who might still be convinced of the existence, and relevance, of social classes. The supply function is constructed along the lines explained at the beginning of Section 2 and in conjunction with Figure 6.8. However, instead of an inequality measure it is related directly to the level of managerial salaries. The shape of the curve suggests that when there is an increase in the share of earned income, people will be willing to put in more effort provided that their sense of satisfaction is not marred by an increase in managerial salaries. One has thus, in a way, combined inequality with envy.

The important thing about Figure 6.9 is that it allows an interaction between decisions of a group and economic equilibrium outcomes. Naturally, within neoclassical traditions there is a need to generate the group's response function from individual behaviour. The separation that is created here between individuals and group on the one hand, and group and equilibrium on the other, reflects the fact that there are outside considerations that need to be applied as indeed I believe the case of some Eastern European countries requires. The question that will immediately arise is whether there is a stable equilibrium to such an interaction, but I will only hint at it in this chapter.

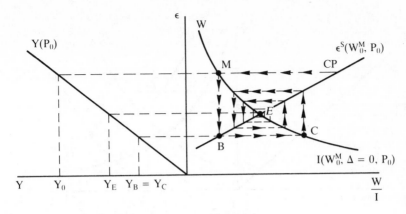

FIG. 6.9 Effort/reward equilibrium: fixed managerial earnings

For a given behaviour of managers who keep a certain level of salary, there is one level of effort which people want to invest in and which is consistent with the equilibrium conditions of the system. The central planner point (CP) is to the right of the intersection point because, as in Figure 6.8, for the same effort, the w/I of the central planner was higher than the one that is generated by an efficient move to a market system.

Privatization will bring the economy to point M. Here, the share of wages in income is such that labourers feel that instead of putting effort into work, they might be better off enjoying the trickle down of the fruits of other people's effort through the distribution of profit. In other words, as that part of one's income which is associated with effort shrinks, so must the will to produce that effort. Once effort falls, output will fall, wages will change, and as long as managers keep their salaries unchanged, the economy will move to point C (via B). Here again there will be adjustments in effort and so on. The stability of the system depends on the elasticity of effort supply and its relation to the elasticity of the WI curve. More importantly, when the only free agents are the managers and when there is no move across classes, privatization leads to point E with less effort and less output than under the efficient central planner[32].

If the process of privatization is accompanied by an increase in the level of inequality (still assuming no move across classes) the consequences can be considered through Figure 6.10.

An increase in w^m means that for a given level of w/I labourers will feel that the equality principle is violated. This may be coupled with a feeling that the work of managers reflects less effort; such a view could stem from the belief — hammered in by the political authorities — that there is only one type of productive endeavour. It is quite possible that the response of labourers to an increase in managerial earnings will be a withdrawal of effort. The supply curve of effort will therefore shift downward.

As can be seen from Figure 6.8, the WI curve will shift to the right. For a given level of output, an increase in managerial wages will reduce the level of income of

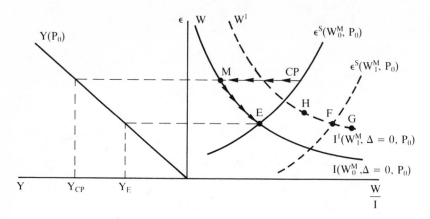

FIG. 6.10 Effort/reward equilibrium: the effect of increased managerial earnings

labourers. As the level of wages is unchanged, the share of wages in the lowered income must increase.

The consequences for the final equilibrium depend on the strength of influence that inequality considerations will have on effort decision. It is not inconceivable to think that people who have spent their entire lives in a political culture of equality will find these changes offensive. Hence, the shift of the supply curve will be far greater than that of the WI curve. As a result the economy ends up at G in Figure 6.10. The less significant inequality is to the labourers (and this, perhaps, might be the case in traditionally market cultures), the less will be the impact on the supply of effort. In such a case one will end up at a point like H in Figure 6.10. There, the collapse of output as a result of privatization will be minimal.

Had the population been exposed to Western thinking for longer, the shape of effort supply curve might have been different. There would be less impact of the internal structure of income on the way in which individuals feel that they were remunerated. In the neo-classical tradition people are both labourers and capitalists. The income we generated from capital is a well deserved return and we should not isolate one source of income as the only reward to our effort. Such a view may be strengthened by marginal productivity theories of distribution. Thus it is the relationship between wages and marginal product which matters rather than the proportion of wages out of total income[33].

But while the structure of income may not be relevant for individuals who were brought up with the rhetoric of neo-classical economics, inequality may still carry some weight in the determination of how pleased they are with the performance of their social system. In such a case, as inequality grows, they might feel somewhat alienated and reduce the effort supplied. Thus, even under this view of the difference between agents in the different systems, transition in which inequality emerges will be a cause of a 'second best' competitive solution (see point C in Figure 6.11).

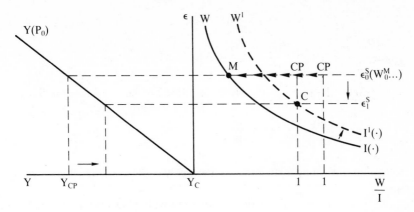

FIG. 6.11 Effort/reward equilibrium: a marginal productivity theory of reward

5. Prices, liberalization and a note on sequencing

Prices have not yet been discussed, and the chapter will not deal at all with the question of how the new prices are formed. But it will consider the possible consequences of price changes.

In the previous framework, the numeraire was the 'consumer good' produced by sector 1. This consumer good can be considered as necessary, in the sense that without it, individuals cannot even begin enjoying the satisfaction of their wants (i.e. good 1 satisfies *needs* as distinct from *wants*). Sector 2 produces 'luxury consumption' and p measures the exchange rate between luxury consumption and necessity consumption.

The relationship between prices, under the central planner and in the competitive economy, is complex. Prices under the efficient planner could either direct allocation or distribution, but not both simultaneously. Prices set to direct allocation would be generated by a simple programming method, with distribution determined by different principles. Here, I assume that allocation is conducted by means of directives while prices are set to support the equal distribution. It would not be surprising if the price of necessity goods was lower and that of luxury goods higher than in the market.

Price liberalization also meant the withdrawal of subsidies which had a greater impact on the price of sector 1 than of sector 2. Hence a drop in p will be assumed.

One must now analyse how price changes affect equilibrium relationship between the reward and distribution parameters and the supply of effort. Begin with the w/I function:

$$\frac{\partial\left(\frac{w}{I}\right)}{\partial p} = -\frac{\left[\frac{\partial w}{\partial p}\left((A-\Delta)\frac{w^m}{w^2}-\frac{Y}{w^2}\right)(L+A)+\frac{\partial Y}{\partial p}\frac{1}{w}(L+A)\right]}{\left[(A-\Delta)\left(1-\frac{w^m}{w}\right)+\frac{Y}{w}\right]^2} \qquad [17]$$

Hence

$$\text{sign} \frac{\partial \left(\frac{w}{I}\right)}{\partial p} = -\text{sign} \left(\frac{\partial w}{\partial p} \frac{1}{w^2}[(A - \Delta)w^m - Y] + \frac{\partial Y}{\partial p} \frac{1}{w} \right) \qquad [18]$$

This is exactly the same as the effect of effort on the w/I function. Therefore:

$$\text{sign} \frac{\partial \left(\frac{w}{I}\right)}{\partial p} = \text{sign} \frac{\partial \left(\frac{w}{I}\right)}{\partial \epsilon} \qquad [19]$$

and following the same reasoning as before, we shall assume that sign to be negative.

Figure 6.12 depicts the effects of privatization which has been preceded by price liberalization. Privatization alone would take us to point M first and then to A with dY^A as the loss in output (given no movement across classes and fixed managerial salaries). Liberalization, which brought about a fall in p, will shift WI to the right. This would increase the quantity of effort supplied (due to the larger share of the effort related remuneration) up to point B. However, as total output — in terms of the necessity good — falls, the loss of output may be greater, smaller, or the same depending on the responsiveness of output to the change. Allowing managers to increase their salaries (w^m)will shift WI back to the left, with a greater loss of output as a result of privatization and liberalization (as, for instance, at point A').

If the supply of effort is affected by prices directly then things become worse. The price ratio, p, reflects the command individuals have on the necessity goods. If this drops, people might feel that to get necessities, more effort is required. However, the impact of this extra effort depends on how much of people's income responds to effort. The higher is w/I, the more effect, one might think, effort will have and thus people might tend to increase their effort. If, however, w/I is low one might be inclined to believe that effort, if anything, is wasted. On the whole, I feel it is reasonable to suppose that as necessities become more difficult to obtain, there will be more anger and withdrawal rather than a will to continue effort. Hence, I shall assume that for any given level of w/I people will withdraw effort as

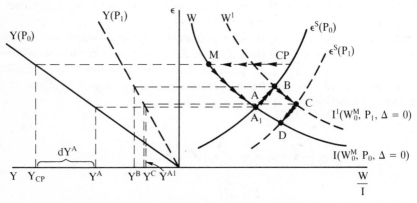

FIG. 6.12 A question of sequencing: privatization preceded by liberalization

p falls. This implies that the economy will move from point B in Figure 6.12 to point C. If managers also respond to the price increases by increasing their salaries, w/I will shift to the left and the economy will move to point D.

What it all boils down to is that a disregard for the reaction of individuals to the structural change in their income might have serious efficiency implications. Given the disposition of individuals who lived in a society which stressed contribution, and which justified income distribution on these grounds, a structural change that does not allow for sufficient time for 'human absorbtion' is bound to backfire. The lesson from this section therefore, is that privatization must precede liberalization and must be gradual.

6. Rational behaviour and effort

Finally, I return to a more or less standard neo-classical analysis and examine whether the above analysis could be consistent with the behaviour of the rational utility maximizer. I will examine the response of a rational utility maximizer to the situation where income is split into two components, one directly perceived as related to effort and the other not. Will the increase in the non-directly related part in income cause a *rational* reduction in effort?

I commence with a more general exposition of the role of the share of effort-related remuneration in the considerations of utility maximization. Consider an individual who consumes a composite good x, works given hours (t) and exerts effort of ϵ. The choice variables are ϵ and x and the constraint is comprised of wages per day (wt), and an effort related earnings function $f(\epsilon)$.

The individual's problem is therefore:

$$\begin{array}{c} \max\limits_{x\epsilon} \quad U(x,\epsilon) \\ s.t \quad p_x x = wt + f(\epsilon) \end{array} \tag{20}$$

First order conditions suggest that:

$$\frac{u_x}{p_x} = -\frac{u_\epsilon}{f'}$$

$$\text{but} \quad p_x = \frac{wt + f(\epsilon)}{x} \tag{21}$$

$$\text{hence} \quad -\frac{u_x x}{u_\epsilon} = \frac{wt + f(\epsilon)}{f'}$$

Also $I = wt + f(\epsilon)$ $\omega = f(\epsilon)$

and some rearrangement results in:

$$-\frac{u_x x}{u_\epsilon} = \frac{f(\epsilon)}{f'}\left(\frac{1}{\frac{\omega}{I}}\right) \tag{22}$$

which means that for a given reward function, as the share of unearned income increases (i.e. ω/I decreases) the first order conditions will hold only if effort is reduced.

A simultaneous change in the reward function will better reflect the neoclassical view that institutional changes are nothing more than changes in constraints. Then the impact on effort will depend on the relationship between the change in the function $(f(\epsilon))$ and the change in the marginal reward of effort (f'). The framework is consistent with the result that effort will be reduced by a change in the income structure which reduces the share of earned income.

The constraint and its effect can be examined closer through an example. Consider an individual with a specific utility function who confronts an exponential constraint function. This type of constraint may be more representative of a non-market system, because marginal compensation for effort is rising and is individually assigned. In a market system, the marginal reward for effort should be independent of the individual's choice[34].

The individual's problem is therefore:

$$\begin{array}{ll} \underset{x,\,\epsilon}{max} & U(x,\epsilon) = x^a (t^\epsilon)^\gamma \\[2mm] s.t & p_x x = wt + be^\epsilon \end{array}$$

$$\text{where} \quad \alpha > 0 \qquad \gamma < 0 \tag{23}$$

In the neo-classical tradition, labour reduced utility. Hence an increase in compensation to effort (i.e. an increase in b) might invoke a reduction of effort (through some kind of an income effect). However, effort will be increased by an increase in income which is unrelated to effort.

The first order conditions will be:

$$U_x - \lambda p_x = 0$$
$$U_\epsilon + \lambda be^\epsilon = 0$$
$$\therefore \quad \frac{U_x}{p_x} = -\frac{U_\epsilon}{be^\epsilon}$$

also : $\quad wt + be^\epsilon - p_x x = 0$

Hence:

$$\frac{\alpha x^{\alpha-1} t^{\epsilon\gamma}}{p_x} = -\frac{\gamma x^\alpha t^{\epsilon\gamma}\ln t}{be^\epsilon}$$

$$\text{but} \quad p_x = \frac{wt + be^\epsilon}{x}$$

$$\therefore \quad \frac{\alpha x^{\alpha-1} t^{\epsilon\gamma} x}{wt + be^\epsilon} = -\frac{\gamma x^\alpha t^{\epsilon\gamma}\ln t}{be^\epsilon} : \tag{24}$$

simple manipulation and re-arrangement results in:

$$\alpha b e^{\epsilon} = -\gamma(wt + be^{\epsilon})\ln t$$

$$\therefore \quad e^{\epsilon} = -\frac{wt(\gamma \ln t)}{b(\alpha + \gamma \ln t)}$$

$$\epsilon = \ln \left[-\frac{wt(\gamma \ln t)}{b(\alpha + \gamma \ln t)} \right]$$

hence $\quad \dfrac{\partial \epsilon}{\partial b} < 0 \qquad \dfrac{\partial \epsilon}{\partial w} > 0$ $\qquad\qquad$ [25]

This implies that an increase in that part of income which is related to effort (b) leads the rational individual to reduce the amount of effort contributed. On the other hand, an increase in that part of income which is unrelated to effort will bring about an increase in effort contribution, by allowing for much more utility enhancing activities.

In transition, the increase in non-effort related income together with the collapse of effort rewarding must bring about a renewed vigour in production. But this will be true only if the reward function remains unchanged. In this framework, the only way to investigate the response of rational individuals is to examine their reaction to the change in constraints.

The constraint appropriate to a market system will have a fixed return. The constraint becomes $wt + be$ and the individual's choice does not affect the marginal reward:

$$U_x - \lambda p_x = 0$$

$$U_{\epsilon} + \lambda be = 0$$

$$\Rightarrow \frac{U_x}{p_x} = -\frac{U_{\epsilon}}{b}$$ $\qquad\qquad$ [26]

also : $wt + be - p_x x = 0$

However:

$$\frac{\alpha x^{\alpha-1} t^{\epsilon\gamma}}{p_x} = -\frac{\gamma x^{\alpha} t^{\epsilon\gamma} \ln t}{b}$$

but $\quad p_x = \dfrac{wt + be}{x}$ $\qquad\qquad$ [27]

$$\therefore \frac{\alpha x^{\alpha-1} t^{\epsilon\gamma} x}{wt + be} = -\frac{\gamma x^{\alpha} t^{\epsilon\gamma} \ln t}{b}$$

again, some manipulation and re-arrangement results in:

$$\alpha b = -[(\gamma \ln t)(wt + be)]$$

$$\epsilon = -\frac{\alpha}{\gamma \ln t} - \frac{w}{b} t$$ $\qquad\qquad$ [28]

hence $\quad \dfrac{\partial \epsilon}{\partial b} > 0 \qquad \dfrac{\partial \epsilon}{\partial w} < 0$

which is exactly the opposite to the previous case. When a rational utility max-imizer moves from a system where effort was compensated according to non-market values, to a system where it is more in tune with them, he or she will change their response to the change in the structure of their income. A fall in the effort related pay, which might have brought about an increase in effort under a non-market system, will now bring about a fall in effort.

The impact on effort can be seen from equation [22] above. Effort will change as a result of a fall in ω/I ratio according to the relationship between the change in the reward function and its derivative. One has moved from:

$$\frac{f(\epsilon)}{f'} = \frac{be^\epsilon}{be^\epsilon} = 1$$

to

$$\frac{f(\epsilon)}{f'} = \frac{be}{b} = \epsilon.$$

to accommodate an increase at the extreme right hand side of [22], whatever the level of effort before the change effort must come down.

To emphasize the significance of the different responses of rational utility maximizers, one can fix the constraint and then consider whether there is any-thing in the objective function which may overturn the result in a similar way. In such a case, one might have a better insight into the nature of this apparent inconsistency in the behaviour of the rational individual.

Suppose a competitive environment where the reward function is linear. It has been assumed that individuals will reduce effort when there is an increase in the unearned income. Let us suppose that although the individual is exposed to the disutility of effort, he or she gains satisfaction from social approval. Hence though the exertion of effort is a cause of disutility, when social consciousness is high there may be some benefit from knowing that one has advanced society through some personal sacrifice. Assume separability to keep the social domain distinct. Then

$$U(x, \epsilon) = x^\alpha (t^\epsilon)^\gamma + S^{\delta\epsilon}$$

we shall call $\hat{u} = x^\alpha t^{\gamma\epsilon}$ private utility   [29]

$\bar{u} = S^{\delta\epsilon}$ socially derived utility

where the first order conditions are:

$$U_x - \lambda p_x = 0$$
$$U_\epsilon + \lambda b = 0$$
$$\Rightarrow \frac{U_x}{p_x} = -\frac{U_\epsilon}{b}$$

also : $wt + b\epsilon - p_x x = 0$

and as before:

$$\frac{\alpha x^{\alpha-1}t^{\epsilon\gamma}}{p_x} = -\frac{\gamma x^\alpha t^{\epsilon\gamma}\ln t + \delta S^{\delta\epsilon}\ln S}{b}$$

but $\quad p_x = \dfrac{wt + b\epsilon}{x}$

$$\Rightarrow \frac{\alpha x^{\alpha-1}t^{\epsilon\gamma}x}{wt + b\epsilon} = -\frac{\gamma x^\alpha t^{\epsilon\gamma}\ln t}{b} - \frac{\delta S^{\epsilon\delta}\ln S}{b}$$

which we can write as: $\dfrac{\alpha\hat{u}}{wt + b\epsilon} = -\dfrac{\gamma\hat{u}t + \delta\bar{u}\ln S}{b}$ [30]

rearranging:

$$\alpha\hat{u}b = -(wt + b\epsilon)(\gamma\hat{u}\ln t + \delta\bar{u}\ln S) \qquad [31]$$

Define $\quad F(b, \epsilon, w) = \hat{u}[b(\alpha + \epsilon\gamma\ln t) + wt\gamma\ln t] + (wt + b\epsilon)\delta\bar{u}\ln S = 0$ [32]

hence $\quad \dfrac{d\epsilon}{db} = -\dfrac{\dfrac{\partial F}{\partial b}}{\dfrac{\partial F}{\partial\epsilon}} = -\dfrac{\epsilon(\hat{u}\gamma\ln t + \delta\bar{u}\ln S) + \hat{u}\alpha}{\delta\bar{u}\ln S[b + \delta\bar{u}\ln S(wt + b\epsilon)] + \hat{u}b\gamma\ln t}$ [33]

similarly $\quad \dfrac{d\epsilon}{dw} = -\dfrac{\dfrac{\partial F}{\partial w}}{\dfrac{\partial F}{\partial\epsilon}} = -\dfrac{t(\hat{u}\gamma\ln t + \delta\bar{u}\ln S)}{\delta\bar{u}\ln S[b + \delta\bar{u}\ln S(wt + b\epsilon)] + \hat{u}b\gamma\ln t}$ [34]

That the numerator in [33] is positive is easy to establish.
From [31] it is clear that:

$$\alpha\hat{u}b = -(wt + b\epsilon)(\gamma\hat{u}\ln t + \delta\bar{u}\ln S)$$

hence $\quad (\gamma\hat{u}\ln t + \delta\bar{u}\ln S) < 0$ [35]

rewriting $\quad \hat{u}\alpha b + b\epsilon(\gamma\hat{u}\ln t + \delta\bar{u}\ln S) = -wt(\gamma\hat{u}\ln t + \delta\bar{u}\ln S)$

hence $\quad b[\hat{u}\alpha + \epsilon(\gamma\hat{u}\ln t + \delta\bar{u}\ln S)] > 0$ [36]

Similarly, in [34] the numerator is always negative (it is [35] multiplied by t).
Hence:

$$\text{sign}\frac{d\epsilon}{db} = -\text{sign}(\delta\bar{u}\ln S[b + \delta\bar{u}\ln S(wt + b\epsilon)] + \hat{u}b\gamma\ln t) = -\text{sign}\frac{\partial F}{\partial\epsilon}$$

$$\text{sign}\frac{d\epsilon}{dw} = \text{sign}(\delta\bar{u}\ln S[b + \delta\bar{u}\ln S(wt + b\epsilon)] + \hat{u}b\gamma\ln t) = \text{sign}\frac{\partial F}{\partial\epsilon}$$

However, the sign of this derivative depends on the relationship between private utility ($\hat{u}$) and socially derived private utility ($\bar{u}$):

$$\delta\bar{u}\ln S[b + \delta\bar{u}\ln S(wt + b\epsilon)] + \hat{u}b\gamma\ln t > 0$$

if $\quad \dfrac{\bar{u}}{\hat{u}} > -\dfrac{b\gamma\ln t}{\delta\ln S[b + \delta\bar{u}\ln S(wt + b\epsilon)]}$

which means that the greater is the socially derived utility, that is, the more important to the individual is his or her contribution to society, the more likely it is that the denominator in both [33] and [34] will be positive. Hence, an increase in the direct payment to reward (perhaps interpreted as the more selfish side of effort consideration) will bring about a reduction in effort, while an increase in non-related income will yield an increase in effort. This would mean that in spite of a fall in the share of one's effort related income, one would still be willing to increase effort as one assigns greater value to the social consequences of effort contribution.

Notice that these results are exactly the opposite to the one established when there was no social component in the individual's utility and the reward function was exactly the same. They are, however, similar to the ones obtained when the reward function reflected a different *social attitude* towards individuals' effort contribution. By keeping the constraint unchanged, the change in the results can be explained by the properties of the objective function. Clearly, individuals who care much for society will respond to a collapse in the share of effort related earnings by increasing their total effort. The reason why such people may change their response even without an institutional change in the reward function, appears to be a decline in their social consciousness.

In the case of transition there seem to have been two effects on the rational utility maximizer. First, the change in the reward function and second, the collapse of the social order which has alienated individuals and wiped out the socially derived utility from their considerations. The two changes will bring about the outcome that has been assumed without direct reference to the individual utility maximizer. The collapse in share of effort related income will bring about a general fall in effort contribution when the social consciousness of individuals is being stifled.

7. Conclusion

The main point of this chapter is that transition may bring about a solution of a 'second best' nature. When there is a move from a system where social consciousness meant one thing, to another where it means something entirely different, individuals are likely to judge and react in terms of their previous beliefs and convictions. As it is far from clear that people in the East felt displeasure with the social messages of socialism, it is only reasonable to expect a response from them which is in line with those beliefs.

The discussion has concentrated on individuals' perception of social justice through their perception of reward to effort. Privatization means that economies move from a situation in which all income is perceived as effort related to a situation where income is only in part a reward for effort. A significant part of income may now come from what was considered as an illegitimate form of reward (profit). People who associated effort with a collective move to a better society and who saw in it a sacrifice which was rewarded through social standing will tend to withdraw from the newly emerging society. Transition which pays little attention to the disposition of these individuals would lead to a decline in performance. Naturally, there is an underlying hope that, in the end, the people of Eastern Europe will learn to accommodate the messages of market systems. Whether or not this will be the case, or, which is almost the same thing, whether the premises of neoclassical economics are really universal, remains to be seen.

Notes

1. In terms of its sources.
2. That income distribution, for instance, plays an important role in the effects of privatization is recognized by McKinnon with regard to China. He argues that in China it was easy to break up big farms into natural family units. 'Hayek's spontaneous order', he writes, 'could emerge because [the small units] were unaffected by distribution'. (Mckinnon 1992: 35).
3. This pleasure, or displeasure, may reflect either one's view of the underlying ideology or one's view of how successful the authorities have been in implementing it. Unsuccessful implementation may be a reason to review the entire ideological base but it is by no means a necessary outcome of such an event.
4. In fact, the case is really that the attitude which connects (or not) effort to income distribution is in itself part of the political culture or ideology. Hence, an argument that assumes that effort is independent of other things than compensation, is an argument which is confined to a given political system and is not valid either in comparative analysis or in the analysis of transition.
5. See a discussion in Bergson (1992: 28), where he uses this view to explain the apparent difference in productivity between West and East. Nevertheless, Bergson also says that 'unfortunately this is a matter that has yet to be demonstrated empirically'.
6. This, as was noticed by Atkinson and Micklewright, is not in contradiction with the communist ideology after Marx's *Critique of the Gotha Programme*.
7. Note that the distribution under consideration is that of earnings. The change in dispersion that might result from adding other sources of income (like capital etc.) is not taken into account.
8. Thus somewhat circumventing the problem of capital quality.
9. Danilin *et al.* (1985) studied cotton refining enterprises and found that they were 92.9 per cent efficient. Schmidt and Lovell (1980) found that generating plants in the US are 90.4 per cent efficient while Meeusen and van der Broeck (1977) rank French efficiency between 71 per cent and 94 per cent. The techniques of these studies differed and therefore, the comparison is questionable. Nevertheless, one can see from this that there is nothing about the East which is strikingly different as far as technical efficiency is concerned.
10. It will be shown later that difference in effort implies difference in efficiency. Hence, it is not that I disagree with Bergson but rather, I suggest an explicit relation between effort and efficiency.
11. Although there might be some differences in the actual incentive schemes, it is unlikely that the principles of reward were fundamentally different. Of course one might wonder whether the difference in the level of reward qualifies the comparison between the effects of these similar distributions on effort. However, in my view, effort is a relative concept. It can be shown that for a rational utility maximizer, it is the relative share of effort related earnings in one's income which determines the level of one's effort contribution (I will refer to this point in the last section of the chapter). However, even without referring to the rational utility maximizer (which simply might be

inappropriate in this context), I do not feel that people decide on how much effort to exert on the grounds of international comparisons. Decisions on effort are naturally relative to the society within which one operates. Those on the lower end of reward might exert themselves less simply because other people, in their own society, are getting more. Another person may put similar effort into his or her work for exactly the same reason although the level of reward of the two individuals might be different. The relativity of effort and the similarity of the actual distributions of earning suggest, I believe, that the incentive structures in the two economies were proportionally similar.

12. There is further support to the view that standard incentives cannot be used to explain difference in effort contributions in the Brada and King (1991) article. Their study is confined to one economy (Poland) and they compare state and private farms (presenting difference in incentive schemes and levels). They found little difference between them in terms of productivity and efficiency.

13. In a study of social attitudes conducted by Rose and Haerpfer (1993) they reveal a difference in the perception of the economic system and the political one. In Eastern European countries (not including Russia) 57 per cent have rated positively the working of the socialist economy; only 36 per cent rated positively the present system (p.43). At the same time, only 44 per cent considered positively the past political system (p.47). This, I believe, supports the view that what people did not like in Eastern Europe was the political manifestation of central planning. They do not seem to associate this disappointment with a rejection of socialist economics as a social programme.

14. This will be the case if equality of income is maintained. Namely, ownership is equally distributed. Otherwise, although some people will earn only wages (the share of effort related income is almost 1), the mere knowledge that others can live from ownership will have a similar effect.

15. In more neo-classical terms such a disapproval may be the reason for the above-mentioned reduction in the role of society in one's utility function.

16. See, for instance, Bliss and Stern (1978), Dasgupta and Ray (1986 and 1987), and Moene (1992).

17. Nevertheless, as was mentioned earlier, Rose and Haerpfer (1993) found that even in Eastern Europe, excluding Russia, people still rank the socialist programme positively at the same time as they rank its political manifestation negatively.

18. Sections 3 and 4 do not require a two sector model. This will become relevant in section 5 where sequencing is considered. Nevertheless, I will conduct the entire analysis in a two sector model to reduce 'entry cost'.

19. One can complicate the story considerably by allowing effort to vary across sectors but at this stage this will not necessarily help the inquiry.

20. What exactly one means by entrepreneurs and what is the difference, if any, between this word and 'managers' may be a cause for an interesting separate investigation. Here I will use the words interchangeably. Walras, who had raised the importance of what he considered as the fourth class, described an entrepreneur as 'a person (natural or corporate) who buys raw materials...leases land...hires the personal faculties...borrows capital...*having applied certain productive services*...sells the resulting product..' (p.227 my italics). I therefore assume that the role of administration in an efficient central planner is equivalent to the role of the entrepreneur in the market system; it is the organization of production. As such, the distinction, if it exists, between entrepreneurs and managers is uninteresting for our purpose.

21. Assume at this stage that the relative price p remains unchanged. Given that the product of sector 1 is the numerative and that the central planner is likely to have kept the price of necessities low, the possible competitive outcome will be a lower p. In

any case, at this stage I do not consider what will happen to relative prices and I will return to this point in section 5 below.

22. I deliberately ignore here the question of how such a distribution of ownership can come about or what will be the outcome of the creation of a capital market in terms of the distribution of shares.

23. In such a case it is quite possible that the number of managers $(M = A)$ can no longer be the optimal level of management. Hence, the productivity curves will move inward and will bring about a collapse in output. Nevertheless, at this stage I will assume that this is not the case, in order to concentrate on what I believe is the more important point, namely, the structure of income.

24. If on top of this we assume that number of managers is no longer optimal, this will only accentuate the argument.

25. If we assume that A was the optimal size of the managerial input and, in addition, suppose that in a competitive system the optimal size of this factor is smaller, then evidently an increase in that class will reduce relative productivity of the other means of production. In such a case, there is little doubt that output will fall after such a change.

26. I do not believe that market systems do offer a proper remuneration to effort (see Witztum 1992). I assume it is a form of expectation because it is, unfortunately, the popular view. As such, it might have a much greater impact on the behaviour of individuals than many theoretical considerations.

27. The sign of [7] is always positive. For this to be the case, it must be shown that $(A - \Delta)(1 - w^m/w) + Y/w > 0$. This is straightforward as it implies that $Y > (A - \Delta)(w^m - w)$ which is always true. Total output is always greater than the total earnings of managers; and certainly greater than a smaller sum.

28. Bear in mind that at this stage the exogenous parameters in our model are effort and, in the absence of capital markets, the wages of the managers.

29.

$$\frac{\partial \left(\frac{w}{I}\right)}{\partial \left(\frac{w^m}{w}\right)} = \frac{(A - \Delta)(L + A)}{\left[(A - \Delta)\left(1 - \frac{w^m}{w}\right) + \frac{Y}{w}\right]^2} > 0$$

$$\frac{\partial^2 \left(\frac{w}{I}\right)}{\partial \left(\frac{w^m}{w}\right)^2} = \frac{2\left[(A - \Delta)\left(1 - \frac{w^m}{w}\right) + \frac{Y}{w}\right](A - \Delta)}{\left[(A - \Delta)\left(1 - \frac{w^m}{w}\right) + \frac{Y}{w}\right]^4} > 0$$

30. This is because w will fall when $\Delta > 0$.

31. Had we assumed that the initial inefficiency of the central planner is in the size of the administration, the move towards a market economy should be characterized by the move from A to C, D or G. While the improved efficiency should present itself through a greater income (I), it is not clear how it will affect wages. Evidently, if the benefits of transition are mostly channelled through capital, w/I will fall and C, D and G will be located lower in the graph. This means that effort withdrawal will be even greater.

32. Evidently, if the process is accompanied by a slimming of the managerial layer, the WI curve will shift to the left. This will make the outcome much worse. Even if the change in the size of 'administration' does not reflect a move from one optimal setting to another, the efficiency gains may still move WI to the left (as I might rise by more than w). In such a case, those gains might be offset by the collapse of effort.

33. If wages reflect marginal products, the supply of effort curve will be horizontal as described in Figure 6.11 below and the move from an efficient central planner to an efficient market structure will have no effect on output.
34. If there is a special scheme in the market system, it is more likely that some attention will be given to productivity of effort which, most likely, will be diminishing.

References

Akerlof, G. A. and **Yellen, J. L.** (1990) The fair wage-effort hypothesis and unemployment, *Quarterly Journal of Economics*, **CV**, pp. 255–83.

Atkinson, A. B. and **Micklewright, J.** (1992) *Economic Transformation in Eastern Europe and the Distribution of Income*, Cambridge University Press, Cambridge.

Banerjee, A. V. and **Newman, A. F.** (1993) Occupational choice and the process of development, *Journal of Political Economy*, **101**(2), pp. 274–98.

Bergson, A. M. (1987) Comparative productivity: the USSR, Eastern Europe and the West, *American Economic Review*, **77**, pp. 342–57.

Bergson, A. M. (1992) Communist economic efficiency revisited, *American Economic Review*, **82**(2), pp. 27–30.

Bliss, C. J. and **Stern, N. H.** (1978) Productivity, wages and nutrition,1: the Theory, *Journal of Development Economics*, **5**, pp. 331–62.

Brada, J. C. and **King, A. E.** (1991) Is private farming more efficient than socialized agriculture?, Arizona State University.

Broeck, J. van den, *et al.* On the estimation of deterministic and stochastic frontier production functions: a comparison, *Journal of Econometrics*, **13**, pp. 117–38.

Commander, S., Liberman, L., Ugaz, C. and **Yemtsov, R.** (1993) The behaviour of Russian firms in 1992: evidence from survey, *working paper, WPS1166,* The World Bank, Washington DC.

Danilin, V. I., *et al.* (1985) Measuring enterprise efficiency in the Soviet Union: a stochastic frontier approach, *Economica*, **52**, pp. 225–33.

Dasgupta, P. and **Ray, D.** (1986) Inequality as a determinant of malnutrition and unemployment: theory, *Economic Journal*, **96**, pp. 1011–34.

Dasgupta, P. and **Ray, D.** (1987) Inequality as a determinant of malnutrition and unemployment: policy, *Economic Journal*, **97**, pp. 177–188.

Hausman, D. H. and **McPherson, M. S.** (1993) Taking ethics seriously: economics and contemporary moral philosophy, *Journal of Economic Literature*, **31**(2), pp. 671–731.

Lovell, C. A. Knox and **Wood, L. L.** (1989) Monitoring the performance of Soviet cotton refining enterprises: sensitivity of findings to estimation techniques, University of North Carolina, Spring 1989.

McKinnon, R. I. (1992) Spontaneous order on the road back from socialism: an Asian perspective, *American Economic Review*, **82**(2), pp. 31–6.

Meeusen, W. and **van den Broeck, J.** (1977) Efficiency estimation from Cobb-Douglas production functions with composed error, *International Economic Review*, **18**, pp. 435–43.

Moene, K. O. (1992) Poverty and landownership, *American Economic Review*, **82**(1), pp. 52–64.

Murrell, P. (1991) Can neoclassical economics underpin the economic reform of the centrally-planned economies?, Mimeo, University of Maryland.

Roemer, J. E. (1982) *A General Theory of Exploitation and Class*, Harvard University Press, Cambridge, Mass.

Rose, R. and **Haerpfer, C.** (1993) Adapting to transformation in Eastern Europe, *Studies in Public Policy*, University of Stathclyde, **212**.

Sachs, J. D., Privatization in Russia: some lessons from Eastern Europe, *American Economic Review*, **82**(2), pp. 43–8.

Schmidt, P. and **Lovell, C. A. Knox** (1980) Estimating stochastic production and cost frontiers when technical and allocative inefficiency are correlated, *Journal of Econometrics*, **13**, pp. 83–100.

Walras, L. (1984) *Element of pure economics*, Orion Editions, London.

Witztum, A. (1992) The lost status of desert, Mimeo, London School of Economics.

PART TWO

COUNTRY STUDIES

CHAPTER SEVEN

Privatization and deindustrialization in East Germany

Wendy Carlin*

1. Introduction

This chapter starts from two facts about changes in the enterprise sector in East Germany. The first is that privatization of state-owned enterprises — including large ones — has taken place extremely rapidly, and the second is that an equally dramatic process of deindustrialization has occurred. Both of these changes mark East Germany out from its neighbours in Eastern Europe. In brief, between mid-1990 when German economic and monetary union occurred and mid-1993, nearly 6,000 enterprises and another 6,000 parts of enterprises had been sold. The initial portfolio of the privatization agency, the *Treuhandanstalt*, was 8,500 state-owned enterprises. Moreover, the great majority of privatized East German enterprises are genuine capitalist firms in the sense that there is an owner with the incentive and the power to exert the control necessary to change the behaviour of management and raise the efficiency of the enterprise. Of course, this is no guarantee of survival as the well-publicized failures of East German privatized firms testify.

The Treuhand (THA) began with 4.1 million employees (nearly half of total employment in the GDR); by the end of 1993 there may be as few as 1.2 million people employed in THA and former THA firms (Kühl 1993: 12). The term *deindustrialization* is particularly appropriate since employment in manufacturing and mining has fallen from 3 million to 0.75 million and the share of employment in manufacturing has fallen to one half the share in West Germany.

The chapter begins in section 2 by setting out the context within which the transformation of the state-owned enterprise sector in East Germany has taken place. An understanding of this context is helpful in identifying aspects of privatization which are unique to East Germany. In particular, the consequences of reunification for East German competitiveness lie behind much of the job losses. It is not the new private owners of former Treuhand enterprises which have engaged in large-scale labour-shedding but rather the Treuhand itself. Somewhat

*I would like to thank UCL for providing a travel grant and the following people for their advice and assistance: David Audretsch, Robert Bischof, Andrea Boltho, Saul Estrin, Volker Färber, Thomas Frisch, Richard Gardner, Andrew Glyn, Ulrike Grünrock, Jens Kammerath, Harald Kroll, Christian Magirus, Colin Mayer, Peter von Richthofen, Friedrich Seifarth, Christian Schmidt, David Soskice, Markus Rauschnabel, Winfried Rosenkranz, Frank Stille, Frank Thiesen, and Ian Zilberkweit.

paradoxically, the Treuhand has also provided employment subsidies to the purchasers of its enterprises. In negotiating the terms of the sale of an enterprise, it was required to take account of the opportunity cost of labour. A discount on the sales price of firms was provided according to the number of jobs guaranteed by the purchaser and the amount of investment guaranteed. The employment subsidy varied according to the availability of alternative employment opportunities in the area and the regional importance of the enterprise (e.g. for local suppliers). The scale of investment guaranteed can be interpreted as an indicator of the permanence of the jobs provided. In section 3, the Treuhand's record in privatizing, restructuring and closing enterprises is set out. The characteristics of the new owners of East German business are identified. The problem of the manufacturing sector stands out very clearly in an examination of the stock of enterprises remaining unsold.

In section 4, the focus turns to the Treuhand's primary method of privatization: the sale of its enterprises to 'competent outsiders'. This is a 'top-down' method of privatization through which the Treuhand has sought to find buyers who have a knowledge of the industry in which the core activity of the enterprise is based and the access to finance required to make the firm competitive. The reasons why this strategy was chosen are explored, and what it has entailed in terms of pre-sale reorganization and restructuring of the enterprise — including employment shedding — is discussed. Issues of private efficiency and the need to establish effective corporate governance in former state-owned enterprises are highlighted along with the notion that Treuhand ownership should be used to deal with market imperfections prior to sale to the private sector.

In section 5, a series of secondary privatization methods is presented, including the East German version of 'insider privatization': the MBO (Management Buy-Out). MBOs are mainly small enterprises of less than 20 employees. For larger enterprises failing to attract a buyer through the primary privatization method, a number of alternatives to closure have been developed by the Treuhand and by private, public, and hybrid institutions. Institutions have been designed to take advantage of economies of scale in providing close control over enterprises. The aim is to enable forward-looking or strategic restructuring to take place which has not generally been possible in the Treuhand.

Section 6 returns to the problem of deindustrialization. Given its budget constraint and policy instruments, it is difficult to argue that the Treuhand could have prevented such a scale of job loss in manufacturing. However, it appears inconsistent from the perspective of the economy as a whole for the Treuhand to be offering employment subsidies associated with enterprise sales (using a shadow price of labour) whilst cutting jobs to control its own deficit (using the market wage). Section 7 concludes with a brief consideration of the policy implications of the analysis.

2. How has German reunification affected the context for transforming the enterprise sector?

All transitional economies have experienced dramatic falls in industrial output. The fall in East Germany was the largest of the Central European countries. Industrial output halved between the first half of 1990 (before monetary union) and the first half of 1991. Since then it has fallen further and stabilized at one third of its original level.

For the other countries in Central and Eastern Europe, a substantial proportion of the fall in output was caused by the reduction of aggregate demand associated with stringent macroeconomic stabilization packages. East Germany is quite different since aggregate demand has been sustained by transfers from West Germany: for example, between 1990 and 1991, GNP fell in real terms by 28 per cent in East Germany, whilst domestic demand rose by almost 10 per cent. A dramatic indication of the divergence between domestic demand and output is reflected in East Germany's current account deficit — 88 per cent of GNP in 1992.

Output fell not because loss-making enterprises were closed down but because demand for the products of East German firms collapsed. West German and 'world market' goods were immediately available and East Germans could afford to switch their consumption basket to Western products. East German real wages jumped from being similar to those in the former Czechoslovakia to being of the order of 10 times as high. Investment demand too was buoyant in East Germany in contrast to the situation elsewhere in the transitional economies. It increased by nearly 30 per cent in 1991 in East Germany. On the whole, East German producers were unable to compete successfully for this business so that high investment as well as consumption demand was associated with low sales by East German enterprises.

Elsewhere in Eastern Europe, large depreciations offered protection to domestic producers in markets both at home and abroad. In East Germany, there was a large real appreciation. At the post-unification real wage, Akerlof et al. (1991, Table 8: p.27) estimated that less than 10 per cent of employment was profitable. Table 7.1 presents the operating results for Treuhand firms in 1991 and 1992 showing losses to the extent of nearly one-fifth of turnover.

Akerlof et al. (1991) argue convincingly that wages rose because of the efforts of the West German unions — sanctioned at the time by the government and the West German employers — to move East German wages rapidly to parity with those in the West. The government's decision to convert Ost-Mark wages into

TABLE 7.1 Operating results of Treuhand enterprises

	1991	1992 (prelim. data)
Turnover per employee (DM)	54,300	54,500
Profit or loss per employee (DM)	−10,200	−10,350
Profit or loss (% of turnover)	−18.8	−19.0

Source: Lichtblau (1993) Table 7, p.27

Deutsch-Marks at 1:1 may have sped up the convergence of wages but was not decisive. This view is supported by the fact that East German wages *increased* after currency conversion.

Prior to reunification, it was estimated that industrial productivity in East Germany was 40–50 per cent that of the West (see Beintema and van Ark 1993, Table 11 for a summary). However, recent research suggests a much lower value of 30 per cent per person and 28 per cent per hour (Beintema and van Ark 1993, Tables 11, 12). It appears that the physical capital stock was in poorer condition than previous estimates had assumed and the labour force far less well-trained relative to their West German counterparts than their paper qualifications would suggest (Birnie *et al.* 1993). Hourly labour costs in the East German engineering industry were 40 per cent of those in the West in mid-1991 and 57 per cent in the spring of 1993 (Bispinck 1991: 474, 1993: Table 6). With labour costs on a trajectory to reach 80 per cent of West German levels by 1996, it is clear that without massive investment in physical capital and retraining, profitable employment in the tradeable goods sector in East Germany is bound to remain far below the labour available.

Prospects for the East German firms sank further with the break-down of the COMECON trading system and the collapse of output in the economies of Eastern Europe and the former Soviet Union. Enterprises faced simultaneously a four-fold real exchange rate appreciation and the loss of major markets.

The government's privatization strategy was based on an over-optimistic view of the competitiveness of existing East German plant and equipment and of the likely magnitude of investment in East Germany by West German companies. The idea was that the privatization agency, the Treuhandanstalt, would rapidly find Westerners with management expertise and access to finance who would buy the East German enterprises, take control of them and turn them around into high productivity firms competitive in the European market. This optimism is reflected in the initial estimate made by the first West German head of the Treuhandanstalt of the value of the enterprises in its portfolio: DM600 billion (see Table 7.2). Instead, the portfolio has been officially valued in the Treuhand's opening balance sheet (published in October 1992) at DM81 billion. However, in order to sell these enterprises, a cost of DM215 billion is expected, confirming that enterprises typically had a negative value at the market wage.

The government's optimism about Western engagement in East Germany lay at the heart of its macroeconomic strategy for transition. Productivity convergence

TABLE 7.2 Estimates of the value of the Treuhand's original portfolio of enterprises

Date of estimate	Estimate in billion DM	Estimated by
Early 1990	1,365	Modrow administration of the GDR
Spring 1990	600	Treuhand-president Detlev Rohwedder
October 1992	81*	Opening balance sheet of the Treuhandanstalt

Source: Kühl (1993) p.1, Treuhandanstalt (1992)
*The net equity capital of enterprises is estimated at DM81 billion; the cost of privatizing, restructuring and closing them is DM215 billion.

with West Germany was to occur through huge flows of investment so as to equip East German workers with capital per head equivalent to that in West Germany. Estimates of the amount of investment required to achieve productivity convergence between East and West Germany within 10 to 15 years, range from DM100bn to 200bn per year. However, total investment spending in 1991 was DM83bn (in 1992, DM 109bn), of which investment in the enterprise sector[1] was DM 40.5 million in 1991 and DM60 million in 1992 (Sachverständigenrat 1992: 93).

Convergence of productivity levels between Eastern and Western Germany would also be assisted by migration and commuting[2]. There is evidence, for example, of a very high incidence of training being undertaken by commuting employees. This suggests that commuters can accumulate additional human capital in the West which could be very productively used in the East as conditions improve there (Pischke *et al.* 1993: 15).

Why would Westerners and in particular, West Germans, wish to buy East German enterprises? The optimistic scenario for rapid transition assumed that the bulk of Germany's large companies would commit themselves to major investment in the new Federal States, either in the form of greenfield investments or through the purchase of Treuhand enterprises. The motive for the large companies was the availability of a skilled workforce (cheaper, at least for some years, than in West Germany) and either existing production facilities or easier planning permission for greenfield sites than would be the case in West Germany. But their decision to move into East Germany via a Treuhand company often hinged on the assumed value of the Treuhand firm's sales contacts in Eastern Europe. Retail and distribution networks familiar in Western economies are very underdeveloped in Eastern Europe and made very attractive the idea of acquiring enterprises with distribution networks in place and/or with strong 'brandnames' in those markets.

Indirect support for the hypothesis that this was the key motivation for West German firms comes from a survey of the investment motives of large Western investors and potential investors in Eastern Europe. They found that the principle motive for *all* investors was to establish a market share in the region (Business International/Creditanstalt 1992).

Initially, West German companies expected to achieve rapid access to the new Eastern European markets by the purchase of East German firms. With the collapse of the COMECON trading system, the deep recessions throughout the region and the disintegration of the Soviet Union, the value of East German contacts with the former communist economies shrank rapidly. Far from offering markets to companies prepared to invest in East Germany, it became clear that many Treuhand enterprises lacked not only management skills, adequately trained workers, and capital equipment but also markets. Higher than expected unit labour costs and lower than expected value of East German contacts with the former planned economies has led German companies to scale down their investment in East Germany relative to initial plans.

Two policy instruments have been used by the government to promote investment and privatization. Investment grants and subsidies are available which can reduce the cost of an investment project by up to 50 per cent. Second, subsidies are provided in conjunction with the privatization of state-owned enterprises by the Treuhandanstalt. The price at which the enterprise is sold by the Treuhand depends on three factors: the number of jobs the investor is prepared to guarantee, the amount of investment guaranteed per employee, and the amount of enterprise debts and environmental burdens the investor takes on. *Ceteris paribus*, the higher the number of employees taken on, the greater the discount on the sales price for the enterprise.

Had the Treuhand not provided employment subsidies in the course of its privatization deals, the loss of jobs in East Germany would have been even more rapid. One method of preventing the haemorrhage of jobs would have been to provide general protection to employment in East Germany, for example through an employment subsidy (Akerlof *et al.* 1991, Begg and Portes 1992, Paqué 1993). Only the government and not the Treuhand could have implemented such a policy.

3. The Treuhand's record on privatization

SALES

There is general agreement that the Treuhand has been successful in one respect: it was set the objective of rapid privatization and this has been achieved. Table 7.3 highlights the run-down of its portfolio. The Treuhand began with 8,500 enterprises comprising some 44,000 plants. Privatization has taken the form either of the sale of an enterprise as a legal entity or of part of an enterprise as a so-called asset deal. In Table 7.3, it is shown that around six thousand sales of each type had occurred by mid-1993. In addition to sales to the private sector, the Treuhand's stock of enterprises has been reduced through several other routes. In particular, as part of the restitution programme, more than a thousand enterprises have been returned to those who owned them prior to their nationalization by the communist authorities. Another set of enterprises — mainly public transport and utilities — has been transferred to local authorities. There are almost 3,000 enterprises scheduled for closure. In summary, nearly 17,000 enterprises or parts of enterprises has been sold, returned to a previous owner, closed or transferred to a local authority. The Treuhand still has over 1,500 enterprises on its books.

Measuring the Treuhand's progress in numbers of enterprises is very crude. The data available is still very poor but a clearer impression of the meaning of these numbers comes from an examination of the results of privatization in terms of the receipts from sales and the amount of investment and number of jobs guaranteed by the purchaser of the enterprise. Later in this section an inspection of the enterprises remaining in the Treuhand shows where success has been very limited.

As noted in the introduction, the Treuhand has valued its assets at DM81 billion. This valuation was based on the revenue achieved on sales to the middle of 1992. Table 7.4 shows that investment guarantees far exceed privatization receipts. The time profile for the investment guarantees is bell-shaped with its peak in 1994-95 with respectively 19.9 per cent and 17.4 per cent of investment

TABLE 7.3 The transformation of the Treuhand's portfolio of enterprises

1. Treuhand's original portfolio: 1/7/1990	
Enterprises	8,500
Plants	44,000
2. Transformations of Treuhand's portfolio: 30/6/1993	
Privatized,	12,195
of which:	
enterprises	5,831
parts of enterprises	6,364
Enterprises returned to former owner (restitution)	1,360
Enterprises transferred to local authority	259
Enterprises closed or in the process of closure	2,857
Total of transformed units	**16,671**
Enterprises remaining in Treuhand's portfolio	**1,668**
3. Other activities	
Transfer to local authorities of enterprise facilities,	
of which:	8,809
educational facilities	585
kindergartens, crèches	728
sports facilities	914
Sales of real estate	16,405 objects

Source: Treuhandanstalt 1993.

TABLE 7.4 The revenue from sales and the amount of investment and number of jobs guaranteed by purchasers, data to the end of June 1993

Cumulative from July 1990 to mid 1993	Number of firms and parts of firms sold	Sales receipts DM billion	Employment guarantees '000	Investment guarantees DM billion
1. Main privatization activity (sales of enterprises and parts of enterprises)				
	12,195	32.0	1,030	122.7
2. Other major activities				
Sales of land released from enterprises (e.g. as business parks)	10.2		282	34.6
Agricultural and forestry land	1.0		138	19.1
3. Total for Treuhand (including minor activities)	43.5		1,468	180.1

4. Memorandum items				
Data for East Germany, 1992	GDP DM billion 247		Employment '000 6,297	Total investment DM billion 109 Investment in the private enterprise sector 60

Source: Treuhandanstalt (1993), DIW (1993) Table 2, p.133, Sachverständigenrat (1992) Table 23, p.93.

guarantees falling due (Lichtblau 1993, Figure 1: p.13). By the end of 1992, only 2 per cent of guaranteed investment was to have taken place but by the end of 1995, almost 50 per cent should have occurred. (For almost 20 per cent of the investment guarantees, no date was fixed for their implementation.)

The time profile of the Treuhand's sales is presented in Figure 7.1. In Figure 7.1a, the record of monthly sales of firms and parts of firms since the inception of the Treuhand is shown. The peak of sales was in the first half of 1992 and there was a halving of sales activity in the first half of 1993. Over time there has been a clear decline in the number of jobs guaranteed per firm (or part of firm) sold — from more than 200 per firm up to mid-1991 down to about 60 since mid-1992. Investment per job guaranteed has remained fairly constant (Figure 7.1c). As Figure 7.1(d) shows, the sales receipts per job guaranteed have increased. To some extent, this simply reflects the fall in jobs per sale (Fig. 7.1b). However, a further factor behind this pattern is that as financial restructuring has proceeded (see section 4 below), enterprise debts have been written down or written off. Early on, it was much more common for enterprises to be sold at a negative price, leaving the new owner to discharge the old debts.

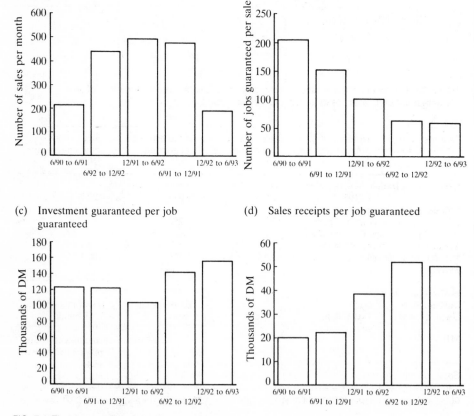

(a) Monthly sales of firms and parts of firms

(b) Jobs guaranteed per firm or part of firm sold

(c) Investment guaranteed per job guaranteed

(d) Sales receipts per job guaranteed

FIG. 7.1 The time profile of the Treuhand's sales
Source: Lichtblau (1993), Table 1, p. 11. Treuhandanstalt (1993)

NEW OWNERS

Privatization in East Germany has produced an ownership structure quite different from elsewhere in the transitional economies. The basic type of privatization in East Germany shares key characteristics with some kinds of foreign direct investment elsewhere — namely, the new owner with a majority ownership stake is a Western enterprise. The most common form of ownership of larger privatized East German companies (with at least 100 employees) sold by the Treuhand is one in which there is a dominant owner (with a stake of at least 50 per cent) which is a West German company. In other words, privatization has created subsidiaries of West German companies (Carlin *et al.* 1993).

Of sales to foreign companies, a majority stake by a West German subsidiary of a foreign company is as common as the purchase by a foreign company without such previous involvement in Germany. New foreign participation as a means of entering the German (and for some companies, the EC) market is relatively infrequent (Frisch 1992). Table 7.5 indicates that 700 firms or parts of firms have been sold to foreigners — the larger than average size of these firms is clear from the comparison between the foreigners' 5.7 per cent share of sales compared with a share of 15 per cent of sales receipts and investment guarantees. The receipts from sales of Treuhand firms to foreigners is of the same order of magnitude as the foreign direct investment attracted by its most successful Eastern European neighbours (Hungary and Czechoslovakia).

East Germans have played a very limited role in the purchase of larger enterprises. Their ownership of firms stemming from the activities of the Treuhand is limited to so-called MBOs — management buy-outs of usually small parts spun off from Treuhand firms (see Table 7.5 and section 5 below).

Ownership by the state (outside the THA) is confined to utilities (apart from the well-known case of Jenoptik from the former Zeiss Kombinat) but would be

TABLE 7.5 The role of foreigners and East Germans in privatization, data to the end of June 1993

	Number of firms and parts of firms sold	Sales receipts DM billion	Employment guarantees '000	Investment guarantees DM billion
Total	12,195	32.0	1,030	122.7
of which to foreigners (% of total)	700 (5.7%)	4.8 (15.0%)	138 (13.4%)	18.5 (15.1%)
MBOs*/MBIs	2,364 (19.5%)			

Source: Treuhandanstalt (1993) *Niederlagsungs-Berichte* 12.92
* In general these are sales to the East German managers/employees. There are 200-300 cases of MBIs where a West German manager has become the owner in a spin-off (see section 5).
    Two-thirds of the 1,733 MBOs which had taken place by the end of 1992 were firms with less than 50 employees (Treuhandanstalt (1992) *NL-Report* 12.92, p.15).

expected to increase in the light of the creation of the state holding companies described below (section 5).

There has been only one case of stock market flotation and even in this case, a West German company in the same sector held 51 per cent of the equity. The East German company Sachsenmilch AG went into liquidation in July 1993. This case exemplifies the magnitude of the task faced by management in achieving a successful turnaround of an East German firm. Even with a controlling interest held by a Western firm and with the backing of the Deutsche Bank, control of costs during the phase of new investment was inadequate to prevent bankruptcy.

The equity of privatized East German companies is thus mainly held very tightly, indicating that considerable control over management by the owners is viewed as necessary.

DEINDUSTRIALIZATION

Employment in East Germany has fallen by over 3 million from over 9 million before reunification to 6.3 million in the last quarter of 1992 (DIW 1993, Table 2). The great majority of lost jobs have been in manufacturing with a decline of 2.25 million. In manufacturing, the sectors in which output growth has begun are those which supply the construction industry, and those which supply local consumers (printing industry and food and drink). Investment goods and especially machinery have been hardest hit with the share of mechanical engineering in manufacturing output falling from 24 per cent to 11 per cent (DIW 1993, Table 3).

The continued presence of the Treuhand in manufacturing remains very important as enterprises in this sector have been hardest to privatize. By the end of 1992, the proportion of total employment which was in Treuhand firms was less than 10 per cent but over one fifth of manufacturing jobs were still in the Treuhand (see Table 7.6). For firms with more than 20 employees, one third of all manufacturing jobs were in THA firms — down from one half in the middle of 1992. Table 7.6 highlights the problem industries within manufacturing. Machinery accounts for nearly one third of all jobs left in the Treuhand and 45 per cent of jobs in this sector in East Germany were still in Treuhand firms at the end of 1992. As Table 7.6 indicates the losses of Treuhand machinery firms increased between 1991 and 1992.

The other notable characteristic of the firms still owned by the Treuhand in mid 1993 is that the bulk of employment remaining (300,000) is in very large firms: just under 50 per cent of jobs are in 29 mining and manufacturing firms with more than 1,500 employees (Treuhand 1993).

Although labour shedding has produced rapid productivity growth in manufacturing (a doubling from the first quarter of 1991 to the last quarter of 1992), this has been almost matched by the equally rapid growth of wage costs. Thus unit labour costs in East Germany remain on average nearly double those in West Germany (DIW 1993). Since there is no protection for tradeables, output prices are at best the same as in West Germany and the price-cost squeeze identified by Akerlof et al. (1991) persists.

TABLE 7.6 Manufacturing: the importance of the Treuhand as an employer, the role of large enterprises and the magnitude of losses

	% East German employment in THA-owned enterprises	% THA employment in enterprises with > 1,000 employees	Profit or loss as % of turnover	
	end 1992	Feb. 1993	1991	1992
Manufacturing	31	41	NA	−21
Machinery	45	29	−17	−32
Chemicals	47	87	−58	−38
Iron and steel	44	54	−26	−11
Vehicles and shipbuilding	38	53	−43	−14
Electrical engine and electronics	25	55	−43	−37
Metal fabrication	21	41	6	0
Textiles and clothing	47	0	−64	−37
Food and drink	10	0	−13	−6
Mining	74	NA	−16	−30
Economy (incl. enterprises with < 20 employees)	8			
Manufacturing (incl. enterprises with < 20 employees)	21			

Sources: Column 1: Lichtblau (1993) Table 3, p.16; Column 2: DIW (1993) Table 6, p.139; Column 3: Lichtblau (1993) Table 8, p.29
Note: From a sample of 2,647 enterprises in 1991 and 812 enterprises in 1992 (samples may not have been fully representative)

4. The primary method of privatization in East Germany: broad-brush restructuring and sale to 'competent outsiders'

Privatization in East Germany has taken place almost exclusively from above. Compared with elsewhere in Eastern Europe, it has been very fast and has involved much more restructuring ahead of privatization. Two objectives have dominated the process: speed and the matching of management to assets. The work has been done by the privatization agency — the Treuhandanstalt. This institution was created by the East German reform government of Hans Modrow. All state-owned enterprises were to be transformed into companies, either AGs (German public stock corporations) or GmbHs (limited liability companies) fully owned by the Treuhandanstalt. The very early and comprehensive programme of corporatization (which preceded reunification) was possible because the central authorities in East Germany had maintained their power over enterprise decision-making. It seems that the East German path to privatization would have been quite distinct from that of its neighbours even in the absence of reunification.

The West German authorities took control of the THA in July 1990 when German economic and monetary union took place. Once under West German control, the THA became a statutory body directly accountable to the Federal Government and in the responsibility of the Finance Ministry. The Federal

Government appointed an administrative or supervisory board for the THA comprising representatives of the main interest groups in the German economy. The Ministries of Finance and Economics were represented, a number of large German companies, foreign business, the trade unions, the East German federal states and the Bundesbank. Experienced managers were recruited for the THA's management board.

When the Federal German authorities took over the THA, there were 600 employees. Even at that stage, this represented a privatization institution on a scale not seen anywhere else in the transitional economies. At its peak, the THA employed close to 4,000 workers, three-quarters of whom were East German. But it must be recalled that with reunification, the bureaucratic apparatus of the East German state had been completely dismantled; elsewhere in Eastern Europe (even in Czechoslovakia) the ministries continue to exist and to play a major role in the privatization process. East German privatization is taking place within an entirely new institution.

DECENTRALIZATION AND DEVOLUTION OF CONTROL TO THE PRIVATE SECTOR

The THA decentralized its work load in two main ways. First, by assigning smaller enterprises (with less than 1500 employees) to its 12 regional subsidiaries. The regional subsidiaries have operated with considerable autonomy. The larger enterprises were assigned to one of the industry divisions of the THA's main office in Berlin.

The second method of decentralization centred on the creation of supervisory boards for all enterprises with more than 500 employees. German corporate law requires the establishment of such second-tier boards. Supervisory boards play a vital role in the governance of German companies and are especially important when major investment and strategic decisions face a company (e.g. Schneider-Lenné 1992). In the context of privatization, the supervisory board was an institutional route through which East German enterprises could be brought into direct contact with the West German corporate world. In general, supervisory boards were chaired by West Germans and had one or two other West German members. The aim was to use supervisory boards:

1. To gather and diffuse information to managers and employees within the enterprise on how the East German enterprise would have to be reorganized in order to have a chance of survival. (As in West Germany, employees comprise one-third of members of supervisory boards and one-half (minus one) of members of boards in companies with more than 2,000 employees.)
2. To provide contact with potential investors from the same industry in West Germany.
3. To provide advice on internal reorganization of the enterprise and its management.

The incentives for supervisory board members to fulfil these functions were far from perfect. Board members received a fixed fee — far below the fee for service on a board in West Germany in circumstances in which the demands on members' time were much higher. Many cases have been reported by the German weekly *Der Spiegel* in which supervisory board members used their position to reduce rather than enhance the enterprise's survival chances. It was in the interest of some enterprises in West Germany to eliminate competition from East German firms.

In other cases, supervisory boards — often those appointed before reunification — colluded with the management to prevent the Treuhand from restructuring firms. The THA was unable to prevent entirely the exercise of such insider power although it has been very limited in scale as compared with elsewhere in the region. The efficient functioning of supervisory boards relied on the importance of reputation to board members. The large German companies and banks nominated employees to sit on supervisory boards to demonstrate their contribution to the reunification effort. Such nominees voiced their reluctance to take on the position of chair of the supervisory board precisely because of their concern that subsequent failure of the enterprise would damage the firm or bank's reputation.

For all its shortcomings, the implementation of two-tier boards provided a decentralized method for introducing market-economy expertise and contacts into state-owned enterprises at an early stage.

EVALUATING ENTERPRISES, FINANCIAL RESTRUCTURING AND IDENTIFYING ENVIRONMENTAL LIABILITIES

One of the THA's initial tasks was to establish the value of its portfolio. Enterprises were instructed to provide opening balance sheets in DM for 30 October 1990. Although initially viewed as a straightforward accounting exercise that would be completed within months, this task was transformed into a major project of enterprise evaluation and financial restructuring which lasted two years. For the reasons discussed in section 2 above, enterprise balance sheets based on GDR data were seen to bear no relation at all to the market value of firms. The THA responded to this by setting up a team of Western experts (managers, accountants, management consultants), formally employed by the Ministry of Finance, not the THA, to evaluate each enterprise.

Each enterprise was classified on a six-point scale according to its potential viability in the market economy. The implicit assumption throughout this exercise was the negotiated trajectory to convergence with West German wage levels. The evaluation of potential viability depended on three key elements: the existence of a market for the enterprise's output, the capabilities of management, and the existence of partners in the West. The evaluation resulted in some 70 per cent of enterprises being deemed potentially viable - but this must be interpreted with caution. It means that in 70 per cent of enterprises there was deemed to be at least one potentially viable core business. This may have comprised only a fraction of the firm's original employment.

Enterprises which were classed as *sanierungsfähig* (potentially viable) had their balance sheets restructured so as to give them a capital structure (debt:equity; and debt:turnover) similar to a West German firm with the same projected turnover in the same industry. (For a theoretical rationale for this practice see the discussion of debt write-off in Aghion *et al.* 1993). Financial restructuring entailed the writing down or writing off of old debts inherited by the enterprise from the GDR era. In addition, it was often necessary to recapitalize the asset side of the balance sheet. As well as financial restructuring, the THA has engaged in environmental audits of its enterprises to evaluate the burden of environmental liabilities.

EFFICIENCY RESTRUCTURING: BREAKING UP ENTERPRISES

In tandem with the evaluation of enterprises and financial restructuring, enterprises have been split up. In principle, the huge Kombinats[3] of the former GDR were to be broken up as part of the corporatization process which had begun before reunification. However, over one third of the Kombinats remained intact. Since July 1990 the process of splitting up large concerns has continued with the result that the number of enterprises which are or were owned by the THA continues to grow. It began with 8,500 enterprises and this number has risen to 16,671. In addition to simply splitting up the Kombinats and hanging the former subsidiary enterprises directly on to the THA, a great deal of breaking up of individual enterprises has also taken place. An indicator of this is that in addition to the sale of enterprises as legal entities, over 6,000 parts of firms have been sold in asset deals.

The motivation for breaking up the Kombinats and for splitting up enterprises was to increase efficiency. Allocative efficiency requirements to reduce horizontal integration have played a relatively limited role in East Germany in the light of the strength of competition in the product market coming from West German suppliers.

The need to improve private productive efficiency has dominated the splitting up process. The Kombinat structure was intimately linked in many industries with the mode of sale of enterprise output. Sales to the COMECON area often comprised orders for a set of related output from a series of members of the Kombinat. The frequently discussed synergy between member enterprises of a Kombinat appears to have value only in the context of the now-defunct COMECON trade arrangements and to a limited extent in sales of turn-key projects (i.e contracts for the planning, construction, and running-in of a production plant) to less developed countries. The criteria for efficiency restructuring have been dominated by the need to create rough units which make sense in market-economy terms. As ever in the East German case, West German structures have formed the explicit standard of comparison (see Bischof *et al.* 1993 for details of how this was effected in one case of restructuring).

Opposition from insiders to the break up of Kombinats has been particularly prevalent in cases where the Kombinat was managed by a holding company with no core business of its own and where the supervisory board was weak. As enterprises were broken up, land not required for business purposes was separated from the enterprise and made available for new activities.

SELLING CORE BUSINESS ACTIVITIES

The THA has focused its sales strategy on finding investors able to complete the turnaround of a THA enterprise by undertaking sufficient investment to give the firm a secure future. The strategy was therefore directed exclusively toward Western investors, from the former West Germany or from elsewhere in the capitalist world. Although in the early days of the THA's activities, there was some truth in the accusation that German investors were favoured over those from abroad, this soon ceased to be the case. In particular, the THA discovered the usefulness of having a foreign bidder interested in an enterprise as a method of introducing competition into the sale (Frisch 1993 provides several examples). It remains true that German firms or the German subsidiaries of foreign firms were better acquainted with the Treuhand's activities and benefited from proximity.

As noted in the Introduction, industrial employment in East Germany has not been preserved. Nevertheless, the sales strategy of the Treuhand was based on the preservation of the core activities of enterprises. Its aim was first to match the assets of East German enterprises — rebundling these assets when necessary — to the management skills of potential purchasers. A potential purchaser had to demonstrate knowledge of the industry and, in particular, that there was a market for the enterprise's output. Second, the purchaser had to demonstrate that it had the financial and managerial resources necessary to carry out the remaining restructuring tasks, in particular strategic restructuring in the form of new investment and the development of new products.

One reason for the close interest of the Treuhand in the experience and qualifications of a potential investor was that the sale of an enterprise typically involved payment of a subsidy to the purchaser. For example, a negative price or a positive price offset by some element of subsidy. If a negative present value enterprise is 'sold' and the purchaser given a subsidy, the rational thing for the purchaser to do is to abandon the enterprise and walk away with the money. To prevent this, the THA has included employment and investment guarantees together with penalties for failure to fulfil the conditions in the contracts of sale of its enterprises.

Employment subsidies have been a key component of the sales strategy. Investors have been given a discount on the sales price of the enterprise according to the number of jobs guaranteed by the investor. In some cases, the price becomes negative (i.e. the investor receives the enterprise plus a grant). The basic rule of thumb is: ensure that the investment per head will be sufficient to make the enterprise competitive (assuming West German wages within three to five years), then give a discount on the current asset value based on the number of jobs guaranteed. There was no centrally determined scale of subsidies used in negotiations, but subsidies varied according to the availability of alternative job opportunities in the area and the external effects of employment in the firm in supporting employment elsewhere. For example, in the sales associated with enterprises from one Kombinat, discounts per job guaranteed varied from DM 10,000 for an enterprise on the outskirts of Berlin to DM80,000 for one near the Polish border (Bischof et al. 1993). In addition, in industries identified as of strategic importance, such as microelectronics, or subject to particular political pressure (such as ship-building) larger subsidies were provided (over DM250,000 per job guaranteed in microelectronics, Bischof *et al.* 1993).

The advantage of this approach is that regional and industrial external effects can be taken into account. The disadvantage is that investors face market wages and prices *ex post facto* at which they would, in the absence of the contracts, choose lower employment. Thus, the THA is required to monitor its employment and investment contracts and therefore to maintain contact with its former enterprises for the length of the contracts.

THE DIFFERENCE BETWEEN TREUHAND AND PRIVATIZED ENTERPRISES

One key difference between firms privatized according to the 'basic method' and enterprises still owned by the Treuhand relates to the type of restructuring undertaken. Enterprises which have been privatized have typically already undergone considerable restructuring under THA ownership as described above. But usually, *strategic* restructuring has begun only once the enterprise is in the private sector. Until very recently, the view of the Treuhand has been that it should not carry out forward looking or strategic restructuring. By strategic restructuring is meant the reorientation of an enterprise toward new markets requiring major investment in fixed capital and the development of new products. Such decisions should, in the view of the THA, only be taken by agents who would bear some risk. This was reflected in the very limited willingness of the THA to give permission for investment expenditure. It exercised tight control of enterprise access to finance for investment by rarely giving guarantees for investment credits. Banks were very unwilling to lend to Treuhand firms without such guarantees because of the extent of uncertainty hanging over the future of the enterprise.

Aggregate data reflect the fact that investment in THA firms is much lower than in privatized firms. For firms owned by the THA in October 1992, investment in 1992 was just DM 7bn, with one quarter of enterprises carrying out no investment at all. In privatized firms, investment was DM 30.3 bn representing three times as much investment per employee (Kühl 1993 p.18). Another survey has found for manufacturing that although 55 per cent of employment was in THA firms, these firms carried out only one-quarter of investment in the sector in 1992. Manufacturing firms with West German owners accounted for 17 per cent of employment but 43 per cent of investment (DIW 1992b). Table 7.7 shows the difference in investment per employee in manufacturing firms owned by the Treuhand, privatized, and newly founded firms.

As noted above, employment shedding in East Germany has largely taken place under THA ownership. This marks a striking contrast with developments elsewhere in Eastern Europe where mass lay-offs have been rare and largely limited to the few purely defence related enterprises which have been completely closed (e.g. in Slovakia and Poland).

Regular questionnaires have been conducted of THA firms and of the same firms once privatized and are the best available source of information on enterprise behaviour. The data is still far from perfect because of the complications introduced by the splitting up of enterprises. With this caveat in mind, one can examine the behaviour of enterprises which have remained in the Treuhand — i.e.

TABLE 7.7 Manufacturing. Investment by Treuhand, privatized, and newly founded firms. Investment per employee (DM)

	Treuhand firms	Privatized or reprivatized (former THA firms)	Enterprises founded since 1989
1991	11,070	23,340	47,360
1992	12,900	29,900	132,400

Source: DIW (1992b) Table 8, p.718

the 'long-stay' firms — from the time of the original questionnaire in April 1991 until the most recent questionnaire in October 1992. Employment in these firms has fallen by just over one half during this period. A rather disturbing aspect of the pattern of job losses in these long-stay cases is that large-scale employment shedding has left the structure of employment as between production, administrative, research and development, and sales/purchase workers unchanged (Kühl 1993, Table 5). This is one indicator of a passive management of firms.

There is also information on the expectations of enterprises as to future employment changes. Firms privatized by October 1991 expected a decline of only 6 per cent in employment over the course of 1992-93 whereas THA firms expected a decline of more than 25 per cent (Kühl 1993, Table 3). This provides some confirmation of the view that investors will only buy enterprises once employment shedding has largely occurred.

In a large survey of Treuhand and privatized firms in manufacturing industry conducted in the summer of 1992, managers were asked to identify the major problems facing them (DIW 1992a, Table 7). To sharpen the focus, the comparison here is confined to Treuhand firms and those privatized according to the 'basic method', i.e. with West German and foreign owners. For both sets, the most frequently mentioned problem was the rapid rise of wages and salaries, though this was a problem for a smaller proportion of the privatized ones. This reflects the expectation of a more rapid transition of privatized firms to West German productivity levels. For THA firms, of equal concern as wage costs was the lack of access to finance for investment. This was a relatively low-ranking concern for privatized firms just as one would expect of subsidiaries of West German companies which are in a position to exert control over management, and which have established reputations with their bank.

A different survey of East German enterprises focused on their perceived competitive advantages and disadvantages as compared with their Western competitors (Boden and Zimmerman 1992). The most commonly ranked disadvantage was that the East German enterprise was not known in the market (65 per cent of firms), whereas being known in the market was viewed as an advantage by only 4 per cent of firms. This highlights the problem of market entry and the limited value assigned to market access to home or Eastern European markets. It is striking that whilst 48 per cent of firms perceived cost disadvantages *vis-à-vis* their Western competitors, another 38 per cent saw cost advantages.

The ranking of urgent tasks is also quite different between the two groups (DIW 1992a, Table 8). It shows that the greatest difference between the two groups lies in the extent to which breaking up and spinning off has been completed — the reduction of vertical integration and spin-offs is virtually complete in privatized firms. Thus although often very substantial changes in the structure of enterprises have been undertaken in firms still in the THA (groups of enterprises brought together from one or more former Kombinats, parts of enterprises split off etc.), further restructuring is foreseen (see, for example the sets of case studies reported in DIW 1992a, 1992b). For privatized firms, however, there was far less concern with finding Western markets. This supports the idea that privatization has often been associated not only with finding management and access to external finance but also with finding markets.

5. Alternative methods of privatization used in East Germany

MBOS — SALES TO INSIDERS

As a consequence of the THA's basic strategy — to sell enterprises to buyers who have Western management expertise, knowledge of Western markets and technology — East Germans have been largely excluded from participation. They lack access to finance as well as to Western networks. East German involvement developed as the threat of unemployment prompted existing managers of THA enterprises or parts of enterprises to propose the spinning off of a part of the enterprise as an independent business. This is the clearest example in East Germany of 'privatization from below' where the initiative for a privatization project has come from the Eastern management itself. This has provided a route to the creation of indigenous small and medium sized businesses, although the likelihood of survival of these so-called management buy-outs is not judged to be very high (DIW 1992b). The Treuhand did not initiate the MBO route as a deliberate strategy. They began to emerge in the regional subsidiaries of the THA and it was only in the Berlin regional branch that a properly worked out policy to support the preparation and screening of projects occurred. Only in autumn 1992 did the THA establish a fund to provide MBO candidates with access to consultancy advice.

To date, there have been almost 2,400 MBOs accounting for just under one fifth of the total number of sales of enterprises or parts of enterprises. Two thirds of MBOs have been small firms with less than 50 employees; six MBOs have between 500 and 1,000 employees; 45 per cent are in manufacturing (Treuhandanstalt, *NL-Berichte* 12.92). Some of the sales registered as MBOs are in fact MBO/MBIs where a Western partner is involved. Banks and funds have been much less willing to provide external finance (debt or equity) to MBOs which lack a Western partner.

MBIS (MANAGEMENT BUY-INS) INVESTMENT FUNDS AND BANK HOLDING COMPANIES — SALES TO OUTSIDERS

The Treuhand ran a programme in 1992 to try to attract mainly Western managers to establish an independent business in East Germany by taking over a

Treuhand enterprise. This can be thought of as a variant on the basic THA strategy — the key difference here being that rather than attracting a West German or foreign company to take over the THA firm, the MBI route is designed to open the way for individual entrepreneurs. The advertizing campaign elicited 2,800 responses and applicants were screened according to four criteria: availability of at least two annual salaries as start-up finance, managerial experience, a track record in the industry, and a willingness to resettle in East Germany. As a result of the screening, 400 highly qualified candidates emerged and were then matched with firms. Some 3,000 THA enterprises had been identified as potentially suitable. The candidates were then put in contact with a series of West German and foreign 'venture capital funds' in order to secure participation by a financial institution in the risk capital of the enterprise. By the spring of 1993 there were 210 MBIs. Fifteen funds took part in the programme and have contributed DM 0.5bn as equity finance.

The Deutsche Bank established an industrial holding company in 1991, the Deutsche Industrie Holding, with the objective of purchasing 100 per cent of a set of THA firms. The idea was that the DIH would provide 'hands-on' management to enable the turnaround of the enterprises. After a very slow start, it sharply increased its commitment with the purchase of 13 Treuhand firms in July 1993 taking its total employment guarantees to nearly 3,500 and doubling its investment guarantees to DM150 million (*Financial Times* 2.8.93: p.15). There are a number of other private sector investment funds operating in a similar way — e.g. the Ermgassen fund, EGIT, and Robert Flemings of London.

The THA has sought to increase the involvement of private sector institutions in providing combined management and finance for East German enterprises through offering an incentive to the seven major management consultancies involved in East Germany to enter the finance side. The Treuhand proposed that a management consultancy branching out into the provision of equity finance would have to pay only 50 per cent of the purchase price of the enterprise initially with the remainder to be repaid at a fixed interest rate of 5 per cent over several years. To date, only one consultancy has taken up the offer: Arthur D. Little has established a new fund.

Treuhand experience here and elsewhere underlines that the scarcity of management capabilities appears to be a binding constraint on the pace of transition of the enterprise sector. Even in East Germany, methods for economizing on managerial resources have proved necessary.

THE MANAGEMENT KGS

In the spring of 1992, the THA embarked on an experiment by setting up two new companies to introduce high-powered (i.e. market driven) incentives into the restructuring and privatization process whilst retaining the ownership of enterprises in state (THA) hands. The THA believed that a new strategy was necessary because large numbers of 'potentially viable' enterprises had failed to attract a buyer. Prolonged parking of enterprises in the THA was undesirable and new institutional forms for state-ownership were required which would provide more time for the enterprise to prove its viability and clear incentives for effective restructuring, including the forward-looking strategic restructuring typically denied to THA firms. There was a clear political objective for the THA as well: it is working to a time constraint and is due to have wound up its mainstream privatization activities by the end of 1993. Without creating new institutions for many of its 'potentially viable' enterprises, the THA would be forced to close them down.

The outcome was the creation of a new institutional form for state-ownership known as the Management KG. The German corporate form of the 'limited partnership' *Kommanditgesellschaft* (KG) was chosen as the vehicle for setting up a restructuring company since it permits the separation of management from ownership which remains with the THA. An individual experienced Western manager takes on the responsibility for turning the group of enterprises around and can earn a large bonus from a successful privatization. The Treuhand provides the finance for restructuring needed in the KGs and sets the budget constraint. The managers of the KGs negotiate directly with the Treuhand's vice president.

The Management KG was designed to deal with medium-sized (*Mittelstand*) enterprises and to effect privatization within three years. This is not a structure set up to provide for prolonged periods of maintenance in the state sector.

Enterprises were chosen for Management KGs by the THA according to four criteria: judgement of potential viability, requirement for a large amount of restructuring, no immediate privatization prospect, and a minimum of 250 employees. The entire portfolio of a KG has a turnover of between 0.5 and 1bnDM. The first two Management KGs were set up as pilots with one having a set of enterprises from related industries and the other a broad mixture of industries. Industry concentration has proved the superior method because it allows for the concentration of expertise in the management of the KG. Three further KGs have been set up reflecting this experience. Total employment in all five Management KGs is 31,000.

The theoretical advantages of the Management KG structure as compared with the THA hinge on the fact that the KG provides the enterprise with continuity of concentrated managerial attention. In the best cases under THA administration, a combination of talented THA case officers and active and constructive supervisory board involvement achieved successful restructuring. But it is difficult to imagine that the devolution of responsibility to supervisory boards for the oversight of enterprises in need of substantial restructuring can provide a solution when the time scale is five to seven rather than one to three years. Second, as time has passed, enterprises remaining in the Treuhand have become stigmatized. Because the Treuhand's objective was rapid privatization, 'failure to find a buyer' has come to signal poor quality and great uncertainty about an enterprise's future. This feeds back to worsen the enterprise's ability to find markets for its output since purchasers have no confidence that continuing supply will be forthcoming. For investment goods suppliers where service and spare-parts guarantees for years are necessary to achieve a sale, this has become crippling.

Finally, a critical difference as compared with THA firms is the attitude of the Management KG toward investment. THA firms have typically invested considerably less than privatized firms as discussed above. The Management KG is designed to provide a channel through which public sector funds can be directed to new investment in enterprises within the context of a strategic restructuring of the firm.

5.3 JOINT INITIATIVES OF THE THA AND THE FEDERAL AND STATE GOVERNMENTS

It was with the 'Revival of the East' (*Aufschwung Ost*) programme of spring 1991 — a joint statement by the Federal and state governments, the unions and business associations — that the Treuhand was obliged to take account of the employment and regional development consequences of its privatization activities. This programme also launched a massive flow of government resources to rebuild the infrastructure. However, it did not constitute a general structural policy for the region of the kind the unions had been demanding from the early days of reunification.

Policies for industries and, given the structure of GDR economic development, often also for regions were developed piecemeal in response to political pressure. The chemical industry was the first to be openly identified as needing a 'plan' in order to ensure its survival. The technological and economic indivisibility between the large enterprises meant that the standard THA incremental approach was inappropriate.

Microelectronics was also identified by the Federal Government as a sector which would be retained. But in this case, the likelihood of generating a coherent plan for the industry was much lower because (unlike the chemical industry) the key microelectronics plants were located in several of the New *Länder*: there was no supra-regional body capable of coordinating the reorganization of the industry. The THA had the capability for doing this but would not intervene in such 'structural' policy. The result was fragmentation and perhaps a greater downscaling of the industry than necessary (see Bischof *et al.* 1993 for a more detailed discussion).

By mid 1992, there was considerable public concern that the rapid pace of employment shedding apparently necessary to achieve rapid privatization was denuding East Germany of its industrial core. Even with large cuts in employment within the THA, manufacturing enterprises were particularly hard to sell and prone to closure. This prompted the Federal Government to announce its commitment to retaining the 'industrial cores' of East Germany. As yet this term has not been defined. But it has been reflected in initiatives from the *Länder* to tighten the link between THA decisions and the Federal States in which enterprises are located.

One approach has been to set up a procedure for identifying enterprises still owned by the THA which are considered essential to the maintenance of a minimum industrial core in the region. For example in Saxony, the ATLAS project has been launched as a joint initiative of the *Land*, the unions and the THA. ATLAS is an acronym for 'Treuhand enterprises chosen by the *Land* for restructuring'. The *Land* government will support the modernization of these enterprises with the policy instruments available to them — funds for the improvement of the regional economy, guarantees for loans, and labour market policy instruments. Enterprises chosen must be judged by the THA to be salvageable and the restructuring concept for the enterprise must maintain existing employment or create new jobs. Particular emphasis is given to enterprises with important links to other enterprises in Saxony. The ATLAS team (led by two managers, one nominated by the *Land*, the other by the unions) is advised by a council with equal representation of the *Land*, the industry associations and the unions.

ATLAS was established in November 1992 and by January 1993, 16 enterprises had been designated ATLAS firms, mainly from textiles and machine building; 50 more are being processed (Nolte 1993a).

The pledge to 'save the industrial core' has lent renewed momentum to the creation of holding companies at *Länder* level to which the ownership of THA enterprises would be transferred. The holding companies will take on enterprises with industrial and regional significance which are too large to be dealt with through a Management KG and too important to close. It appears that this is the institutional structure which will provide longer term state-ownership and within which strategic restructuring will take place. Several *Länder* have moved to set up such holding companies (e.g. Berlin-Brandenburg, Saxony). Joint private sector (bank) and public sector (*Land*) funds are also being formed (e.g. the Sachsenfond) (Nolte 1993b).

INITIATIVES OF PRIVATE BUSINESS

As argued above, the implicit strategy in the government's approach to transition was based on the spontaneous involvement of large businesses from West Germany. Such large companies would bring with them the infrastructure of the business associations. But engagement of large companies both as buyers of THA enterprises and on greenfield sites has been less than anticipated.

The West German corporate sector will become more closely involved in East Germany as a consequence of the 'Solidarity Pact' hammered out between Federal Government, *Länder*, unions and business associations in the spring of 1993. Two concrete initiatives have come forward. First, 30 of the largest West German companies have formed a group which has committed itself to doubling each company's purchases from East Germany over the next year. Second, the business association of the banks has committed its members to providing an additional DM 1bn to support enterprises in the East. Of this, the private banks (including the big three — Deutsche, Dresdner and Commerz) will establish a new investment fund with capital of DM400mn with which to purchase enterprises from the Treuhand and organize their restructuring and privatization.

6. Reunification, privatization and deindustrialization

Full economic and monetary union between two regions at quite different stages of development and with different economic and social systems has proved extremely costly. It is impossible to look at the East German privatization process in isolation from this context. Rapid privatization through the Treuhand was based on the assumption that East German enterprises represented valuable platforms from which West German companies could develop markets in Eastern Europe. As the value of these market networks shrank, the Treuhand was faced with a portfolio of enterprises which had lost both their domestic and export markets. East German firms were squeezed in Eastern and EC markets by Eastern European enterprises desperate for orders and with costs a fraction of those in East Germany, and in their home market by Western and especially West German suppliers.

There are two separate reasons for the massive run-down of employment by the Treuhand in its enterprises (prior to sale): (1) in order to create saleable units and (2) in order to control the Treuhand's deficit. The Treuhand took the view that in order to sell enterprises to outsiders, a drastic slimming down of the workforce was necessary. In other words they believed, probably correctly, that western and in particular, West German, companies would not take on the task of implementing mass lay-offs. The reason for this is clear for West German firms or those foreign firms with subsidiaries in West Germany. Employment security constitutes an important feature of the set of implicit contracts which defines the operation of the German economic system (e.g. Houseman 1991). It is unlikely that companies would have been prepared to engage in forms of behaviour in East Germany unacceptable to their West German works councils since cooperation between employers and their workforce is highly valued. Lay-offs would also be more expensive for private employers because the Treuhand had fixed a maximum severance payment at a low level for employees of its enterprises. The labour-shedding associated with enterprise sales in East Germany cannot be attributed solely to the high level of wages. The Treuhand has provided substantial employment subsidies as a discount on the purchase price of an enterprise (section 3 above). Experience in Eastern Europe demonstrates that a low wage is not a sufficient condition for achieving sales to outsiders. Foreign investors in Eastern Europe have required steep cuts in employment (a typical figure used in relation to foreign acquisitions in the former Czechoslovakia is a cut in employment of 30–40 per cent) and the kind of financial restructuring, environmental audits and breaking up of enterprises discussed above, before they have been willing to buy (see, for example, the survey results in Business International/Creditanstalt 1992).

The second reason for job-shedding was to control Treuhand expenditure. Employees on short-time work or laid off or working in job-creation and retraining schemes became the financial responsibility of other authorities, in particular, the Federal Labour Office. The Federal Labour office spent DM 45bn in East Germany in 1992. For the THA it was worthwhile to lay off workers when their value added was below the gross wage. For the government, *given* the level of unemployment benefit, employment of a worker with value added greater than the difference between the net (of tax and social security contributions) wage and unemployment benefit is worthwhile. The required value added threshold for the government would be a fraction of that for the Treuhand.

Thus on the one hand, in line with its obligation to take account of the regional and employment consequences of its *privatization* decisions, the THA has been using a shadow price for labour in its sales negotiations (implicitly recognizing the social cost of unemployment). On the other hand, the actual price of labour has been used as the decision variable for its own enterprise management with no systematic procedures for taking account of regional, agglomeration and other external effects.[4]

A wage subsidy would have afforded East German industry a measure of the kind of transitional protection available to other East European countries where sharp devaluations and real wage cuts have taken place. The sectors of East German business which are showing signs of life are the ones with some natural protection in the home market: construction, building materials, services, parts of the food and drink industry. Some form of protection is necessary to give East German industrial enterprises a chance to reestablish themselves in the home market as the basis for seeking markets abroad.

Combined with the Treuhand's basic strategy of bringing in effective management and corporate control and undertaking financial restructuring and the break-up of enterprises, a wage subsidy would have enabled a broader-based process of enterprise transformation to take place. The population of 'fast-track' enterprises with Western owners, rapid movement to West German levels of productivity and high survival chances would probably be little different from under current policies (given the subsidies already on offer when enterprises are sold). But employment in the remainder of enterprises would be much higher than at present.

This broader based process of transformation would have required not only the introduction by the *government* of a wage subsidy, but also the recognition by the *Treuhand* that the primary method of privatization — i.e. selling firms to Western companies — could not be relied on to produce sufficient sales of enterprises and thus guarantees of investment and jobs, especially in industry.

The Treuhand has recognized that greater use must be made of economies of scale in management and control in newly created institutions to achieve the strategic restructuring of its remaining portfolio. But this has come too late to prevent the excessive contraction of the industrial sector. Theoretical justification for the common ownership of groups of enterprises both by the state and in private institutions during transition comes from the literature on vertical integration (discussed in Carlin and Mayer 1992). It arises primarily from the fact that many enterprises in the transitional economies consist of rather arbitrary collections of assets and are in need of extensive restructuring. Institutional structures involving private, public and mixed forms of ownership are emerging which can fulfil this task. The role of private investment/venture capital funds in MBI/MBOs, the private management/public ownership combination of the Management KG and the bank and state (*Land*) industrial holding companies are examples.

7. Conclusions and policy implications

The transformation of state-owned enterprises into capitalist firms has proceeded very slowly in Eastern Europe. A much more rapid pace has been achieved in East

Germany as several thousand subsidiaries of German and foreign companies have been established through the Treuhand's sale of former state-owned enterprises. Success with finding new owners has been paralleled by a catastrophic collapse of industrial employment. Labour shedding has occurred in response to the hardening of budget constraints facing enterprises. Enterprises have usually found it impossible to borrow from the banking system without guarantees provided by the Treuhand and the Treuhand has kept tight control over its guarantees. As a consequence, insufficient cash flow has led to lay-offs. The opposition of the workforce to redundancies has been muted by the extent of the social safety net and early retirement and labour market programmes financed by the West German tax payers.

As emphasized throughout this chapter, the whole thrust of privatization in East Germany has been toward finding a solution to the problem of corporate governance. The first step taken by the Treuhand was to bring in outsiders on to the supervisory boards of Treuhand enterprises. Although not always successful, the intention was to subject the management of large East German enterprises to scrutiny by outsiders and to provide a flow of information about required changes in organization. The great majority of enterprises with more than 100 employees which have been privatized have been sold to a West German or foreign company. In most cases the owner has a large majority stake, often 100 per cent. This provides an indication of the extent of restructuring which is envisaged by investors as being necessary in order to turn the enterprises into profitable firms competitive in the European market.

Participation in the Treuhand's 'sale of the century' by Western and especially West German companies has been less than initially expected and less than necessary to secure the industrial base of the East German economy. Political volatility and uncertainty about the economic environment appear to be the major reasons behind the low levels of foreign direct investment in Eastern Europe (Business International/Creditanstalt 1992). By extension, the economic weakness and uncertain prospects of the economies of the former Soviet Union and Eastern Europe help to explain the lower than expected involvement of West German and foreign companies in acquisitions of East German companies. The principal attraction of East German enterprises in the tradeables sector was the value of their access to markets in the former planned economies.

The Treuhand's success in finding new owners who will exert effective control over management in the core businesses of many of its enterprises is due both to its extensive restructuring and rebundling of assets and to the provision of subsidies. In spite of the availability of employment subsidies in the form of a discount on the price of the enterprise for each job guaranteed, sharp cuts in employment have accompanied virtually all privatizations. The conclusion from this is that even if a general wage subsidy had mitigated East Germany's labour cost disadvantage, complete reliance on early sales to Western companies would not have preserved the bulk of employment in East German enterprises. The Treuhand moved too slowly to create or foster the creation of institutions which will deploy to best effect the managerial resources available. The Management KG appears to have the right incentive structure to engage in the strategic restructuring essential for the survival of enterprises for which there appear to be no immediate prospect of sale and which are not scheduled for closure. However, there appears to be no alternative to lengthier periods of state-ownership for some enterprises than the three years permitted in the current Management KG structure. Greater use of combined *Länder*-THA-private sector institutions will be necessary and serious evaluation of these alternatives is a priority.

Notes

1. Excluding the post office, telecommunications and railway enterprises.
2. 3 per cent of the East German population moved to West Germany before monetary union. Migration then rapidly stabilized to a level of about 20,000 per month (about twice the level of migration between West German states). By 1991, a reverse flow had begun amounting to 7,000 per month. Commuting from East Germany to work in West Berlin or West Germany has built up to a significant level of half a million (Pischke *et al.* 1993: p.1).
3. The organization of the enterprises of the GDR in three hundred giant multi-enterprise groups or *Kombinate* had taken place in the 1970s. This process was far more comprehensive and systematic than was the case elsewhere in Eastern Europe.
4. New initiatives such as the ATLAS project in Saxony implicitly introduce the shadow cost of labour into the Treuhand's enterprise management decisions.

References

Aghion, P., Blanchard, O., and **Burgess, R.** (1993) The behaviour of state firms in Eastern Europe, pre-privatization, *EBRD Working Paper*, London.

Akerlof, G. *et al.* (1991) East Germany in from the cold: the economic aftermath of currency union. *Brookings Papers on Economic Activity*, 1, pp. 1–105.

Begg, D. and **Portes, R.** (1992) Eastern Germany since unification: wage subsidies remain a better way. *CEPR Discussion Paper*, No. 730, September 1992.

Beintema, N. and **van Ark, B.** (1993) Comparative productivity in East and West German manufacturing before reunification, Paper presented to CEPR Workshop 4/5 June, Berlin.

Birnie, E., Hitchens, D. and **Wagner, K.** (1993) Productivity and competitiveness in East German manufacturing: a matched plant comparison, Paper presented to CEPR Workshop, 4/5 June 1993, Berlin.

Bischof, R., von Bismarck, G. and **Carlin, W.** (1993) From Kombinat to private enterprise: two case studies in East German privatization, *UCL Discussion Paper 1993–02*, in Heath, J. (ed) *Revitalizing Socialist Enterprise: A Race Against Time*, Routledge, London.

Bispinck, R. (1991) Alle Dämme gebrochen? Die Tarifpolitik in den neuen Bundesländern im 1. Halbjahr 1991, *WSI-Mitteilungen 8*, pp. 466-478.

Bispinck, R. (1993) Collective bargaining in East Germany between economic constraints and political regulations, mimeo, Düsseldorf.

Boden, S. and **Zimmerman, H.** (1992) Schwieriger Weg der ostdeutschen Industrie zur Wettbewerbsfähigkeit, *IWH Konjunkturbericht 8-9*.

Business International/ Creditanstalt (1992) *1992 East European Investment Survey*, Vienna.

Carlin, W. and **Mayer, C.** (1992) Restructuring enterprises in Eastern Europe, *Economic Policy 15*, pp. 312–52.

Carlin, W., Mayer, C. and **von Richthofen, P.** (1993) Ownership of large East German privatized enterprises, unpublished data set, University College London.

Deutsches Institut für Wirtschaftsforschung (1992a) Gesamtwirtschaftliche und unternehmerische Anpassungsprozesse in Ostdeutschland, Sechster Bericht, *DIW-Wochenbericht* **39/92**, pp. 467-92.

Deutsches Institut für Wirtschaftsforschung (1992b) Gesamtwirtschaftliche und unternehmerische Anpassungsprozesse in Ostdeutschland, Siebter Bericht, *DIW-Wochenbericht* **52/92**, pp. 709-38.

Deutsches Institut für Wirtschaftsforschung (1993) Gesamtwirtschaftliche und unternehmerische Anpassungsprozesse in Ostdeutschland, Achter Bericht, *DIW-Wochenbericht* **13/93**, pp. 131-58.

Frisch, T. (1992) Privatisierung und Unternehmenskäufe in Ostdeutschland, *HWWA-REPORT* Nr. 104, Hamburg.

Frisch, T. (1993) Unternehmenszusammenschlüsse in den neuen Bundesländern, *HWWA-REPORT* Nr. 119, Hamburg.

Houseman, S. N. (1991) *Industrial Restructuring with Job Security: The Case of European Steel*, Harvard University Press, Cambridge, Mass.

Kühl, J. (1993) Unternehmensentwicklung von Treuhandunternehmen und privatizierten ehemaligen Treuhandfirmen vom Ende der DDR bis Ende 1992, paper presented at ZEW workshop, 'Arbeitsdynamik und Unternehmensentwicklung in Ostdeutschland - Erfahrungen und Perspektiven des Transformationsprozesses', Mannheim, April 1993.

Lichtblau, K. (1993) Privatisierungs- und Sanierungsarbeit der Treuhandanstalt, *Beiträge zur Wirtschafts- und Sozialpolitik*, Institut der deutschen Wirtschaft Köln, Nr. 209.

Nolte, D. (1993a) Das 'ATLAS'-Projekt - ein Modell zur Sicherung industrieller Kerne in Sachsen, unpublished ms. WSI-Institut, Düsseldorf.

Nolte, D. (1993b) Zwischen Privatisierung und Sanierung: Die Arbeit der Treuhandanstalt. *WSI-Materialien*, Nr. 32. WSI-Institut, Düsseldorf.

Paqué, K-H. (1993) East/West wage rigidity in United Germany: causes and consequences, *Kiel Working Paper* No. 572, Kiel Institute of World Economics.

Pischke, J-S., Staat, M., and **Vögele, S.** (1993) Let's go West! Do East Germans commute for wages, jobs or skills? unpublished ms., Mannheim.

Sachverständigenrat zur Begutachtung der gesamtwirtschaftlichen Entwicklung (1992) *Jahresgutachten*, Bonn.

Schneider-Lenné, E. (1992) Corporate control in Germany, *Oxford Review of Economic Policy* **8**(3), pp. 11-23.

Treuhandanstalt (1992) *DM Opening Balance by July 1, 1990*, Berlin.

Treuhandanstalt (1993) *Monatsinformationen der THA 06.93*, Berlin.

The relationship between privatization and the reform of the banking sector: the case of the Czech Republic and Slovakia

Lina Takla*

1. Introduction

Privatization is the mechanism which redefines property rights and should thus bring about '*de novo* the basic institutions of a market financial system including corporate governance of managers, equity ownership, stock exchanges and a number of financial intermediaries' (Lipton and Sachs 1990). The former Czech and Slovak Federal Republic[1] led the way with voucher privatizations for large firms, based on (virtually) free distribution of shares to the population at large. This achieved a rapid change in the share of output nominally in state hands and provides the opportunity to evaluate the link from ownership change to the establishment of corporate governance and financial market institutions. The problem of creating effective corporate governance has been raised by many observers. To some extent, these fears might have been allayed by the apparent emergence of ownership concentrated in financial institutions often owned by commercial banks. A major theme of the chapter is therefore the relationship between privatization and the reform of the banking system. This chapter will investigate how the restructuring of the banking sector will affect the adjustment of enterprises. In the context of mass privatization one must also anticipate the impact of the direct reduction in bank lending, which subtracts liquidity. It is not clear whether enterprises can generate enough internal liquidity to counterbalance the credit squeeze.

Section 2 reviews the main issues of privatization in what was, at the start of transition, Czechoslovakia, discussing its objectives and the main reasons for the choice of voucher privatization. Section 3 provides a brief description of privatization legislation. The benefits and dangers of such a privatization strategy are analysed in Section 4, where the interactions between privatization, bankruptcy

*Financial support for this work was provided by an ESRC grant under the East-West initiative, grant number Y3009/25/3007. The author wishes to thank Lenka Flašarova, Eva Klvaćova, Libor Kudlaćek and Peter Galbraith for helpful comments and information and the members of COEX and of CERGE for their assistance and hospitality when I was in Prague. Discussions with Istvan Abel and John Bonin helped me highlight the link between debt, bank restructuring and enterprise restructuring. Lastly, I wish to thank Saul Estrin and Wendy Carlin for invaluable editorial assistance and thorough comments. The views expressed in this paper do not necessarily reflect the views of the persons/institutions mentioned above. Any remaining errors are my own.

legislation, banking sector reform, foreign direct investment, and the role of the state are surveyed. Possible policy responses concerning credit legislation and industrial policy are surveyed in the final section.

2. Review of the main issues – the Czechoslovak experience

When analysing the overall Czechoslovak reform package of 1991, one is struck by the pivotal importance attached to privatization, and to the originality of the voucher privatization programme. To understand the weight placed on privatization, it is important to bear in mind the initial economic and political setting. Czechoslovakia was a country that had suffered the overpowering influence of party bureaucracy and was deficient in individuals with experience in entrepreneurial activities (see Estrin 1991). Fast privatization was advocated for political and economic reasons. It stemmed both from the failed experience of attempted mild reforms within the old system and from the desire to remove all traces of socialism, such as state-ownership. However, the former system was also characterized by an egalitarian ethos which may have influenced the choice of voucher privatization.

The Czechoslovak government believed that the absence of effective ownership rights was at the heart of the old system's inefficiencies (see also Fischer and Gelb 1990; Lipton and Sachs 1990; Hinds 1990). Right from the start, the consensus in Czechoslovakia was that privatization was necessary. The initial problem was formulating objectives and deciding on how to proceed. Early theoretical discussion in the West tended to stress provision of incentives for better resource allocation (Ben-Ner and Neuberger 1990; Estrin 1991), the fiscal benefits from revenues from sales, and monetary considerations about the absorption of the monetary overhang.

Lessons from privatization in Western Europe, however, appeared limited. Privatization there was on a smaller scale and primarily involved the utilities. It usually took the form of the direct sale to the private sector of public assets through the capital market by offer of stock to the general public, domestic and foreign. Such methods were not the obvious way to proceed in the Czechoslovak case.

An important practical obstacle concerned valuation of enterprises which depends on judgements about future profitability. The enterprises to be privatized did not have a market track record on which to base valuation and there were no expert financial institutions to underwrite the process through bearing and trading risky assets. Imperfect information about policy regarding prices, taxation, credit and the treatment of outstanding debts aggravated the difficulty in formulating predictions of future profitability.

Valuation of companies was deemed *a priori* impossible and direct sale of equity too lengthy. Valuation problems apart, there did not seem to be any apparent buyers for the state's industrial assets. Perhaps the most obvious way to privatize medium and large size enterprises is to sell them to foreign investors without any prior restructuring. But foreigners appear to have been unwilling to bid for most of the state-owned enterprises (SOEs) offered for sale, and foreign control was often politically sensitive. Domestic savings, however, were simply not available to buy the state-owned firms at prices reflecting more than a fraction of their value[2] (Begg 1991; Dyba and Svejnar 1992). The Czechoslovak government concluded that the state must primarily distribute its holdings in the enterprise sector to the population at large for free.

Nevertheless, the Czechoslovak government still wanted to ensure that privatization would improve management, the pricing system, the structure of industry and the allocation of capital. Liquidation of companies and questions of long-term viability were therefore intertwined with changes in ownership and the clarification of ownership rights.

First, corporate governance had to be created to ensure that managers adjust their behaviour from the reliance on orders from 'planners' to those from shareholders. Principal-agent theory suggests that in the private sector contractual discipline is enforced by potential bidders and by the bankruptcy discipline enforced by creditors. Second, pressures on management were to be made effective by enterprise restructuring and the introduction of market competition through free trade and anti-monopoly legislation. Ownership reform was not intended to deal with the adjustment process by itself. It was to do so hand in hand with new bankruptcy and competition laws and with the restructuring of the banking and foreign trade systems.

A series of reforms was introduced in Czechoslovakia from the beginning of 1991. Measures directed at the enterprise sector have included price liberalization (January 1991), the drafting of bankruptcy legislation (July 1991), the start of 'small-scale privatization' (October 1990 Law No. 427/90) and 'large-scale privatization' (February 1991 Law No. 92/91 and the 1 April 1991 Law). The programme also stressed a comprehensive liberalization of foreign trade and the convertibility of the currency.

The weakness of SOE adjustment rapidly manifested itself in the wake of transition. The drop of output was greater than expected; GDP declined by 16 per cent in 1991 as opposed to the 5-10 per cent forecast. Industrial output fell even further but employment rather less. This drop in output has been mainly attributed to a fall in demand (domestic and foreign), with the inflexible response of the state-owned sector to changing demand conditions as a contributory factor.

3. Czechoslovak privatization – a short description

The Czech and Slovak republics have been implementing a two track policy, comprising both 'small-scale privatization' and 'large-scale privatization'. 'Small-scale privatization' consists of the auction of shops and service establishments to individuals, mainly implemented at a 'local' level. It envisages transfer to Czechoslovak citizens in the first instance and, only failing that, acquisition by foreigners. 'Large-scale privatization' involves no such discrimination against foreigners. It is aimed at manufacturing, banking, and insurance organizations which often have a domestic monopolistic character and invariably operate on a large-scale. It involves a voucher scheme[3] to put large state enterprises into the hands of private owners. Former Czechoslovakia is thus moving towards allowing individual share ownership in most large and medium-sized firms both directly and through mutual funds. Privatization has also been the main way to ensure enterprise restructuring.

The voucher scheme is intended to ensure the rapid transfer of state-owned property to the private sector and to offer Czechoslovak citizens a stake in the reforms. Excluded from the impact of the Large-Scale Privatization Act 27 February 1991[4], are properties to be restored to former owners by special legislation and all Church property confiscated after 25 February 1948 (Restitution Act 22 February 1991). The corporatization of SOEs is a precondition for their inclusion in the voucher privatization programme. Corporatization entailed the transfer of 100 per cent of the share capital of enterprises to National Property Funds (NPFs). There were three such funds: one for the Czech Republic, one for the Slovak Republic, one for the federation. The organization and activity of the Federal National Property Fund is determined by the Act, which also leaves the republican legislatures to determine the legal relations and activity of the Republican National Property Funds. The federal and republican governments had a time period to issue guidelines for ministries and local government which were called upon to submit lists of enterprises which should be privatized for governmental approval.

For enterprises included in the large-scale privatization programme, a privatization project has to be developed by the enterprise itself, and the company's management has the main input in its formulation. Foreign buyers are also allowed to collaborate with Czech firms in the formulation of the basic project. If the enterprise is too slow, it can be given a time limit by the Supervisory State Agency, described in the Act as the 'founder' (usually a ministry responsible for a particular sector of industry). Anyone can put forward a privatization project. Most competing projects propose the break-up of the existing SOE. This could be a positive development if it creates medium and small enterprises. On the other hand, some projects have sought to divide indivisible property. The Ministries of Privatization reviewed projects involving voucher privatization first, in order to approve enough property by the start of the first wave on 18 May 1992. With the exception of voucher privatization, there is a two month waiting period after a particular privatization project has been submitted so that competing privatization schemes can be prepared.

Not surprisingly, management has been reluctant to deliver the necessary information for outside parties to develop their own competing projects and withholding information was made illegal by the amendment to the law on 'large-scale privatization', passed in February 1992. This legislation also corrected a loophole which had allowed existing management to sign long-term rental agreements. Such agreements would *de facto* predetermine the fate of the property before privatization. The inherited coalitions and hierarchies between the government and state enterprises are largely still in place. Branch ministries are sometimes at odds with the privatization ministries in their evaluation of projects, and have often supported existing management.

Although drafted by the enterprise, the project is the responsibility of the 'founder'. The founder selects the project it deems to be most suitable and recommends it for approval. The legal status of the National Property Funds, as well as their competence and that of the Privatization, Finance and 'Founder' ministries are summarized in Table 8.1. The winning privatization project is generally chosen by a team consisting of officials from the Ministry for Privatization and officials of the relevant founder ministry in whose jurisdiction the particular enterprise initially finds itself. Exceptions to this rule are instances where the selected project recommends sale of some or part of the property to a private owner or any sale to a foreign investor. In these cases, it is the national

TABLE 8.1 Structure of State regulation of privatization 1991–end 1992

Federal Finance Ministry	**Role 1** Approves projects of enterprises founded by 'federal' ministries. No more than 10 per cent of total book value among voucher privatization projects in the first wave fell into this category. **Role 2** Is *solely* responsible for organizing the demand side of the voucher programme, overseeing the distribution and registration of voucher booklets. **Role 3** Coordinates the work of other government bodies in the process of privatization and sets the timetable.
Privatization ministries	**Role 1** Most influential in both the selection of enterprises to be privatized and the methods of privatization. **Role 2** They thus approve privatization projects for enterprises which fall in their jurisdiction. **Note** The approval of projects is concentrated in the hands of a small number of people. The Czech Ministry of Privatization was initially staffed by 20 people. That number rose to 160 by mid-1992.
Founder ministries	**Role 1** Responsible for the preparation of the privatization projects of their enterprises. They may either prepare a project or require that management prepare it. **Role 2** They must pass on all projects proposed to them, including those they do not recommend, and their recommendations to the Finance or Privatization ministries. Their role in the approval of projects may have increased since mid-1992.
National Property Funds	Under Act no. 92 of 1991, NPFs were set up at the federal level and at republican levels. They are legal entities appearing in the Company Register, 'mutually independent, with jurisdiction over a precisely defined sphere of enterprises'. **Role 1** They hold the shares not yet sold of corporatised enterprises. **Role 2** After voucher privatization, have remained large shareholder in key companies which have been only partly privatized, including the Czech electricity company and the major banks and insurance companies. As a shareholder the NPFs appoint the Supervisory Board and Board of Directors. After partial privatization they participate as owners. **Role 3** Are supposed to privatize the shares remaining after voucher privatization within the next five years. **Role 4** Prepare the offering for the second wave of privatization. **Note** While there is a legal and organizational distinction between NPFs and the Privatization Ministries, in practice the funds are under the direct supervision of the ministries and formal parliamentary oversight is performed by five-member Supervisory Boards.
The Consolidation Bank	Founded by the Ministry of Finance and the Central Bank in March 1991. **Role 1** A type of recovery agency. Its aim was to take over 'working capital loans', acquired prior to 1990, from the balance sheet of commercial banks. **Role 2** Linking the financial restructuring of companies with their privatization, e.g. the role of NPFs is linked to that of the Consolidation Bank. This role arose under pressure, when the commercial bank started charging the current rate of interest at the beginning of 1991.

Source: Frydman *et al.* 1993

government which makes the final decision. This principle also applies for the sale of enterprises with a large number of employees (over 3,000 workers).

The founder also has to submit to the ministry those projects it does not recommend. The National Property Fund administrates a special account in which revenue from privatization sales is concentrated, which is strictly separated from the state budget and may only be used for privatization in the form of a joint-stock company or other commercial company, sold or switched over to local government or social security funds. It can also be utilized to meet the obligations of enterprises which will be privatized. Enterprises, whether sold by contract or auction, always involve the transfer of all connected rights and obligations including those in respect of employment relations. The transfer of ownership does not require the agreement or approval of the enterprises' creditors. However, the National Property Fund guarantees with all its property the new owners will meet their obligations towards their 'inherited' creditors. The new privatized company inherits all rights of ownership as well as all risks. The National Property Funds will act in regard to the privatized enterprises essentially as shareholders. The revenue from sales of enterprises is used among other things for the settling of restitution claims, government-approved financial assistance to selected enterprises, financing expenditures for remedying environmental damage, and contributions to the social safety net.

'Large-scale privatization' employs a broad range of privatization methods, apart from voucher privatization. The nature of the enterprise involved, and the time factor, are the decisive influences when deciding the method. Prior to initiating the process of large-scale privatization, enterprises were divided up into three broad categories. The first category contained enterprises included in the first wave of privatization, characterized by the perceived relative ease and speed of their privatization. The second category was second-wave enterprises, dominated by large engineering, chemical and metallurgical companies. Also included in the second wave are key branches of the power sectors as well as public utilities and infrastructure. Finally, the third category contains businesses to be kept in state hands for at least another five years, for example railways and airports. These shares will be formally held by the National Property Fund, although rights are entrusted to other state bodies (for example, ministries).

Privatization of large enterprises has rarely involved leveraged buy-outs. Management buy-outs were only common in small-scale privatization because managers took long-term leases in 1990, so 'a buy-out was a logical solution to avoid a gridlock' (ECE 1993: 3–12).

4. Results of privatization: highlighting the problems

The discussion will focus on 'large-scale privatization'. 'Small-scale privatization' has been proceeding relatively well[5]. By the end of October 1992, 69 per cent of all assets designated for 'small-scale privatization' in the Czech Republic were sold and 81 per cent in Slovakia. Sales revenues for the Czech Republic were of the order of Kcs 28.5 b ($1.4 b) and Kcs 13.7 b ($0.5 b) for Slovakia.

LARGE-SCALE PRIVATIZATION

The Large-Scale Privatization Act came into force on 1 April 1991. In the context of the voucher scheme, shares were to be acquired by voucher holders (individuals or investment funds) through a complex bidding process. A basic privatization project (submitted by the enterprise management) included a statement of the proposed disposition of shares: the proportion available through voucher privatization, the proportion for direct sale, etc. A considerable number of SOEs were set aside to be privatized through the sale of shares within the framework of the voucher scheme. Most enterprises used corporatization as a first step in their privatization project. Through their projects enterprises were also able to divide up their shares between different privatization methods, including standard options such as direct sale, public auction or more unique measures such as vouchers. Table 8.2 charts this distribution for the Czech Republic; 62 per cent of all shares privatized up until the end of 1992 were in the form of coupons. In Slovakia it was even more common to allocate equity to voucher privatization (74 per cent). Heavy reliance on the voucher method was chosen by the enterprise management in four types of firm; companies that are financially troubled and are too large for alternative methods; companies where workers saw privatization as a form of worker buyout as they could choose to place their points in their own firm; firms where managers sought the voucher method as a way of maintaining control; and those where management could not find an alternative to the voucher scheme (e.g. could not find a foreign partner).

Large-Scale Privatization is a two stage programme (preparation and implementation), with the second stage having started in 1992. Privatization is compulsory and in the first wave 1,700 enterprises in the Czech Lands, 700 firms in Slovakia, and one 'federally owned' firm had until the end of 1991 to submit business plans to their 'founder' sponsoring ministries. Basic details of voucher privatization are summarized in Table 8.3.

Adult citizens, over 18 years of age, were allowed to buy a 14 page book of vouchers entitling them to 1,000 shares in a maximum of 10 listed privatized enterprises for about $30[6]. They had the alternative of turning the vouchers

Table 8.2 Distribution of shares by 31/12/1992 – Czech Republic

	%	Value in mn Kcs
Coupons	62.19	238,345
Direct sale to domestic buyers	1.74	6,683
Temporarily held by NPF	15.49	59,354
Permanently held by NPF	0.09	327
Free transfer	11.33	43,406
Direct sale to foreign investors	1.73	6,647
Employee-owned shares	1.53	5,846
Indirect sale	1.59	6,099
Restitution	4.32	16,540
Total	100	383,247
		($13,405 mn)

Source: Ministry of Privatization, Czech Republic

TABLE 8.3 Voucher privatization

Objective	Systemic (fast)
	Political (motivated owners)
	Social (equitable distribution)
Status	In progress
Sale stages	Two waves
Designation	Coupon
Law passed	02/1991
Distribution started	10/1991
Per cent of state assets	25 per cent
Number of medium and large sized enterprises included	+4,200
Eligibility	All citizens of 18 years old and above
Numbers of points per person	1,000
Approximate nominal par value	1 point = 35 Kcs at the start of round 1 of 1st wave
Nominal issue price	1,035 Kcs
Validity	10 months
Acceptable as cash for buying	Shares in firms or equity in investment fund
Funds function	Originally close ended, maybe open in future
Shares obtainable through vouchers in any SOEs (%)	15–97
Allocation mechanism	Centrally regulated
Method of allocation	Computer iterations to achieve supply = demand
Restrictions	Depends on project, 20-40 per cent of equity maximum for investment funds*
Secondary trading allowed	No
Auctions started	05/1992

Source: ECE 1993; Jermakovicz and Jermakovicz 1992
*An individual fund can manage up to 20 per cent of the shares of a single enterprise. A legal entity which may own several funds cannot manage or own more than 40 per cent of the shares of one firm.

over to mutual funds which would then bid for shares. The voucher book came with a 30 page instruction book. Most of the eligible population, about 8.5 million adults, purchased these books. Vouchers are not transferable, though they can be transferred to heirs. They cannot be used as security for a loan.

The obvious problem with this scheme lay in the fact that voucher holders would need information to appraise the enterprises on offer. Property to be privatized was separated into joint-stock companies; a list of enterprises involved in voucher privatization was published along with basic data on the share of stock offered for voucher sale. Balance sheet information was also printed in daily newspapers. All the major banks as well as numerous other institutions and individuals have set up investment privatization funds (IPFs). Voucher book holders could allocate part or all of their points to one or several of the 437 privately formed IPFs, or bid directly for the shares. Funds could not hold more than 20 per cent of shares in any individual company, however.

The exact number of bidding rounds within each wave was not predetermined. Rather it was anticipated that the process would end when a 'decisive share of the property would be sold and further continuation would not lead to the sale of the remainder' (Skalicky 1992). Bidding for shares was to proceed as follows. First, shares of all enterprises were offered at the same 'nominal' value, expressed in investment points per share. In the first wave, this price was set at 100 investment points per three shares. As the bidding process proceeds, the demand of shares by investors was supposed to reveal the 'true' value of the firm. Bidders know the calling price of a share of an enterprise (in terms of points) and bid accordingly. If the supply of shares exceeds the demand for shares, shares are exchanged for points. When demand exceeds supply by 25 per cent, shares are first allocated to the bidding individuals and the remainder is rationed amongst bidding IPFs. If excess demand is over 25 per cent, points are not converted into shares and the price of shares is raised by the government before a new round of bidding; the process continues until excess demand is below 25 per cent.

Drawbacks to the voucher scheme are comprehensively listed in Dyba and Svejnar (1992) and Svejnar and Singer (1993). To summarize, bidding generally occurs in disequilibrium. Individuals who are unable to convert their points into shares in the cases of excess demand forgo the opportunity to regulate the excess supply as they have to wait until the next round of bids. The best firms also risk being withdrawn as firms whose share prices are bid above 1,000 points are removed from the lot. The government took note of these problems, but did not deem them important enough to change the bidding rules. Another problem with the scheme is that the IPFs are not fully regulated. Conditions for starting up IPFs were easily met by a number of reputable and less reputable organizations. IPFs sought to attract investors by promising a fixed return in one year (10–15,000 Kcs). The danger of a run on funds was perceived and a law was enacted. However, the law does not explicitly require the IPFs to deposit their promised fixed pay-outs with the government. The system remains unstable with the likelihood of a rapid fall in share prices and insolvency of funds looming by the end of 1994.

In the first wave, property worth over $23 b was put up for sale, $7 b of which was through vouchers. Only 7.2 per cent of shares remained unsold and 277.8 million shares were sold to private investors. Of 1,471 companies, 291 were fully

TABLE 8.4 Timetable of voucher privatization

26 February 1991	Legislation enacted
1/10/1991 - 15/02/1991	Registration of coupons
Federation	
First Wave	
17/02 - 27/04 1992	Pre-round of auctions
18/05 - 22/12 1992	Rounds 1 to 5
29/05/93	Start of physical distribution of shares
Czech Republic	
June 1993	Secondary market opened .
	Registration of coupon books
Second Wave	
October 1 1993	Intended completion of voucher privatization
January 1994	First round expected to start
Mid 1994	Second wave expected to be almost completed

sold. The unsold shares are temporarily being held by the National Property Fund, which will dispose of them mainly by arranging direct sale through an intermediary. Table 8.4 charts the timetable of voucher privatization to the end of 1993.

The final results of the first wave appear to be successful. Around 93 per cent of total share supply was sold and 99 per cent of all disposable voucher points were used. Table 8.5 shows the distribution of shares purchased in individual rounds by type of investor, noting the success rate of orders and the instances of excess demand. In the first round, bids were mainly oriented to high value companies. 92 per cent of disposable points were bid, indicating a high participation rate. Only about 30 per cent of the shares bid for were sold. The success rate plummeted in the third round, as the price of shares was set too low at the start of the round. Only 24.5 per cent of shares ordered in this round were sold. Interestingly, individual voucher holders (IVHs) generally invested better than IPFs buying the same shares as IPFs at lower prices, as they waited for later rounds to invest (second and fifth rounds as opposed to first, see Table 8.5).

TABLE 8.5 Distribution of shares purchased by round and type of investor in the first wave of privatization in per cent

Round	1	2	3	4	5
Individual voucher holders	19.1	26.7	12.7	19.7	21.8
Investment Privatization Funds	39.7	28.8	11.1	9.7	10.7
Success rate of orders defined as supply = demand	38.0	37.0	11.8	34.7	86.5
Rate of excess demand defined as over 25 per cent	0.0	9.5	3.0	61.0	2.0

Source: L. Flašarova

Progress has been slower than expected, though investors will have received their shares by summer 1993. Their decision to purchase would have been taken 12–15 months earlier, and on the basis of 1991 balance sheets. In the interim, the country has split up, relative prices have changed and Czech and Slovak investors could now own property in a foreign country[7]. The second wave involves 2,100 companies worth potentially $17 b. Up to $5 b will be sold through the voucher method.

PRIVATIZATION PROJECTS

The original intention of the government was that most projects would be presented by the firm itself and that the privatization process would concentrate on the voucher method.

Some 16,000 privatization basic and competing projects of about 3,500 enterprises or their parts had been submitted for the two waves by the beginning of 1993. By the end of 1992, the Czech Privatization Ministry had already considered almost 10,000 privatization projects for more than 2,000 enterprises. There were no common criteria for the approval of privatization projects. Uncomplicated rules were followed in the first wave where the aim was to privatize quickly through voucher privatization, so a high percentage of shares were allocated to voucher privatization. Privatization legislation was drawn up on the assumption that privatization projects would be suggested by the enterprise itself. In actuality, only 26.3 per cent of submitted projects were proposed by the firm. The remainder were competitive bids; the number of competing bidders for one individual firm reached 20–30. The second wave will be more intricate. Among the enterprises to be privatized in this wave are infrastructure, energy, transport, and steel companies as well as gas lines, refineries, pipelines, and power stations.

INVESTMENT FUNDS

The first round of voucher privatization was supposed to start in January 1992. In autumn 1991, the Czech Ministries of Industry and Privatization demanded postponement of this deadline for large-scale privatization, including both the voucher scheme and other methods. A two month postponement was granted because early purchases of privatization vouchers were sluggish. Sales picked up suddenly because some investment funds had aroused the keen interest of the population[8]. One such fund, Harvard Capital, by promising 10 times the purchase price of the booklet by the end of 1992, was able to secure one fifth of all the voucher books sold. Thus investment funds which were only intended to play a minor role emerged spontaneously as a major player in the Czechoslovak privatization programme. This went counter to all fears of a dispersed ownership result, however well founded they were[9].

Any legal entity can set up an investment fund, if it follows certain rules directed by the privatization ministries. Investment funds and associations of small investors (investment clubs) now hold around 70 per cent of shares sold through voucher privatization. Some of the investment clubs are very large, holding 8–10 per cent of some companies (the intention to consolidate this number of shares was voiced prior to privatization) and the relationship between funds and managers will determine the strategy and future of privatized enterprises. The remaining 30 per cent of shares are in the hands of individual shareholders, and many companies have ended up with more than 25,000 investors. Common rules have been set up for the first meeting of shareholders.

CORPORATE GOVERNANCE

The outcome of privatization and the emerging role of investment funds and their parent banks can be assessed in the context of corporate governance. Difficulties of valuing 'acquired' companies, the definition of proper rules, and the resolution of bad loan portfolio problems lie at the heart of these discussions.

Table 8.6 lists the key players in the first wave of voucher privatization. The nine largest funds control almost 50 per cent of all investment points. Of these, six are subsidiaries of well-known state banks, one is owned by an American expatriate and only one is a domestic private joint venture. Of all voucher points placed, 37 per cent are in the hands of the IPFs created by state-owned commercial banks[10].

Even before shares were issued to them, funds were encouraged by the government to become involved in the management of the companies in which they hold

TABLE 8.6 Key players in the first wave of voucher privatization

Fund	Managed/Controlled by	Points Held (mn)	Share (%)
IPF Czech Savings Bank	The Czech Savings Bank*	790-950	9.3-11.1
IPF Investicni Banka	Investicni Banka	700	8.2
IPF Harvard Investment Funds	Harvard Capital and Consulting	638	7.5
IPF General Credit Bank	owned by V. Kožen‎ý**	550	6.4
IPF Komercni Banka	Credit Bank in Bratislava	450-510	5.3-6.0
IPF Czech Insurance Company	Komercni Banka[†]	334	3.9
IPF CreditAnstalt	Czech Insurance Company	260	3.0
IPF Prvni Privatizacni	CreditAnstalt[††]	150-170	1.8-2.0
IPF Zivnobanka	First Investment Company[†††]	140-160	1.6-1.9
Other Smaller Funds	ZivnoBanka	1,868-2,128	21.9-24.9
Individual Investors		2,400	28.1
TOTAL		8,540	100

Source: PlanEcon 1992, 1993

* The Czech Savings bank offered to lend immediately 10,000 Kcs (around $364) to all investors who have invested all their 1,000 points in its fund against their share in the investment fund. As many as 75 per cent of these investors did take up this offer.

** Only major fund not controlled by a financial institution. This fund is the single largest private investor in the Czech Savings Bank and in Komercni Banka as banks were prohibited from directly investing in any financial institution

[†] Komercni Banka and Investicni Banka are heavily exposed to Czech industry. By early 1993, 97 per cent of Komercni Banka's loans were to the state sector. Komercni Banka is the biggest lender to the corporate sector. According to the management of the bank its fund will require a good deal of capital. In view of this, the bank has set up another mutual fund 'Universum', which aims to supply additional capital to the companies in the IPF's portfolio.

[††] Foreigners were also allowed to establish investment funds and this Austrian Bank set up one of the largest.

[†††] First Investment Company offered a loan of $517 against a portfolio purchased for 1,000 voucher points.

significant stakes. The funds have already nominated one of their number to the board of their companies. Newly privatized shareholding companies are governed by a two-tier board system with proportional representation of shareholders. The main players are six large funds who must work together on many company boards since 'an individual fund can manage or own up to 20 per cent of the shares in a single firm' (McDermott 1993). There is a fragile alliance, which may be threatened in the future because there is no protection for minority shareholders from a hostile takeover. An informal market has sprung up among the funds in forward agreements to trade or swap shares to rationalize their holdings (subject to the 20 per cent ceiling). As they begin to trade on the stock exchanges, funds still do not exactly know how the market will price their shares.

Funds have the capacity to demand management change. Harvard Capital is a vociferous and controversial fund which has boldly stated that it aims to replace management in one third of the 51 companies in which it has a stake. It also wants to cut employment by a third. But there is a danger inherent in the possible behaviour of funds. Most of the enterprises were loss-making in 1992. How will small firms be able to pay their shareholders? This problem may yet be passed over to the government. A freeze on dividends has already been decided for the first year of privatization, though Harvard Capital, which is also the only fund without a bank's backing, is opposed to this. It was offering new investors a guaranteed 28 per cent dividend in the first year, while most other funds propose to reinvest dividends rather than to distribute them.

Re-capitalizing enterprises is another challenge faced by the new funds. Enterprises are moving from an owner (the state) which at least possessed a budget, to owners with no capital to invest. There is a danger that these new owners will not be able to supply their enterprises with working capital and that they will want immediately to offload their assets. Funds are worried about market liquidity when they start trading their shares on the stock exchange. Many of the smaller funds could go bankrupt once trading begins.

Another danger could come from a run on the funds' guarantees, by nearly four million small investors who now own, through the funds, shares in 1,471 companies. The only source of liquidity open to the funds is the sale of some of their portfolio. This could lead to loss of investor confidence and plummeting share prices. The law on investment funds came too late on 28 April 1992. The law includes disclosure rules, rules regulating conflict of interest and stipulations of diversification requirements. It alleviates the danger of a run by splitting funds into open and closed funds with the latter not obliged to fulfil their promises. Funds were originally set up as close-end funds, 'meaning that they would not be obliged to redeem their own shares' (Frydman *et al.* 1993: 87). These funds may be open in the future. Good reasons for keeping them closed include the fact that the stock market on which shares will be traded will not be functional for some time and more importantly, 'the funds themselves will have very low liquidity initially' (Frydman *et al.* 1993: 87). There is also concern over conflicts of interest and insider dealing. Government officials are on the board of investment funds, while senior managers in 'privatized companies' are also sometimes on the boards of funds. The lack of information and transparency combined with the uncertainty about behaviour of many funds, could jeopardise the future of the privatization process.

Funds have no trading expertise in shares and there will probably be little trading. They are likely to act as dormant funds. Despite all this, there will be a need to open forward markets for funds to meet their operating costs. Forward markets are still not permissible in Czech law as you cannot establish a price prior to the settlement of a contract; the Commercial Code states that transactions have to be settled on the same day. Whatever the procedure, transactions will be difficult due to a lack of knowledge of equity markets and settlement trading. A new Securities Act came into force in 1992 and was followed in the Czech Republic by a Czech Act which supersedes the old Act where contradictions exist. The Act is briefly outlined in Table 8.7.

BANKRUPTCY LAW

Most of the companies privatized in the first wave have been largely given away. The government did not want to implement bankruptcy legislation before the new owners took possession, because newly 'privatized' firms could have been liquidated before the new owners had been given the opportunity to take control, since

TABLE 8.7 Trading in privatized companies shares: the Czech Securities Act

• Legislation	Federal Securities Act 591/1992
	Czech Republic Act of 24/2/1993
	If two acts are contradictory, the Czech Act prevails
• Stock exchanges	Prague Stock Exchange
	RSM Electronic Share Market
• Maximum share held by fund in a company	20 per cent
• Takeover rules	No legislation to protect minority shareholders
• Admission to trade	Securities dealers licensed by Finance Ministry
• Shares allocated under voucher method	Issued as registrations with the Securities Centre, expected to be mainly paperless
• Guidelines for exchange trading licences	Licence under the Banking Act, Minimum capital requirement of Kcs 200,000
• Specific information to be included in application for licences to trade	Extent of any foreign ownership and applicant's internal measures which aim to prevent conflict of interest
• Provision of golden shares	None, no special powers for the shares held by government bodies in privatized companies

many firms entering voucher privatization have had bad debts. The government has loosely linked the forgiveness of bad debts to enterprise privatization and to bank privatization, in order partly to solve the valuation problem and to avoid bad loans leading to on-going expected bail-out.

The domestic recession and the collapse of CMEA markets left many Czech and Slovak companies saddled with debts. Strict monetary policy has sharpened this plight. The decision of a company to restructure its productive capacity relies on its ability to raise finance. The state has to balance its tight monetary policy with credit incentives to restructure; otherwise as credit from the banking system is tightened, the problem of bad debts is transferred to inter-enterprise credit accumulation. With credit expensive, many companies that were financially strained did in fact begin to issue credit to each other. Inter-enterprise secondary debt more than tripled from Kcs 45 b at the end of 1990 to Kcs 145 b at the end of 1991. As can be seen in Table 8.8, by mid-1992, inter-enterprise credit was valued at one fourth of total bank credit. This development shielded many other state enterprises from bankruptcy. Looming insolvency actions will be complicated as the distinction between creditor and debtor is ambiguous. A case against a specific firm could set off a chain reaction, ultimately driving many other companies into bankruptcy as well.

The Czech Parliament amended the Bankruptcy Law which took effect on 22 April 1993 (see Table 8.9). The main reason for the change was the need to allow promising companies to break out of the chain of inter-enterprise debt. Another reason was to avoid the liquidation of newly privatized companies. Proceedings against privatized companies can only begin two months after shares have been distributed. Firms facing a bankruptcy petition are protected from their creditors for three months and can then negotiate an additional three months. A privatized company thus has eight months reprieve in total. The government has declared its reluctance to provide assistance to ailing industries, but with markets still nascent, it cannot afford the fiscal or political costs associated with mass bankruptcies.

TABLE 8.8 Credit to enterprises, end of year (quarter) data, (Kcs bn)

	1990	1991	1992 q2
Bank credits to state enterprises			
CSFR	529.8	575.3	564.9
CR	383.0	403.7	390.5
SR	146.8	171.6	174.4
Bank credits to private enterprises			
CSFR	3.4	71.4	125.7
CR	2.8	55.5	94.4
SR	0.6	15.9	31.3
Inter-enterprise debt			
CSFR	44.9	145.5	123.7
CR	31.8	101.7	79.3
SR	13.1	43.7	44.4

Source: Dyba and Svejnar 1992

TABLE 8.9 The Bankruptcy Act

• Law Passed	Act 328 / 1991
• Law Amended	Act of 25/3/1993
• Law Effective from	22 April 1993
• Trigger	Application made by creditor
• Moratorium	Generally applicable
	3 months, an extra three months can be negotiated
	Application within 15 days of receipt of the application for bankruptcy from the court
	Debtor may apply for voluntary arrangement with creditor
• Some cases where bankruptcy may not be declared	• legal entities established by law where the state has taken over their debts or has given a guarantee for them
	• privatized state enterprises where at least 50 per cent of shares were offered through vouchers, an additional two month respite is granted.
• Managing the insolvency	• creditors committee elected
	• managers forbidden to acquire assets for three years after completion of bankruptcy proceedings

The amendments in the bankruptcy law amount to government intervention in an *ad-hoc* manner, in response to financial crises or political pressure, as a result of *ex-ante* negligence. The government has licensed three companies to match debtors with creditors via computer. The Ministry of Industry is threatening to sack directors of state firms that refuse to register and cooperate.

The impact of bankruptcy law is further diluted by the fear of social unrest. The Ministry of Industry has already declared that 'under no circumstances will there be a massive wave of bankruptcies that would harm the economy' (*Economist* 1993: 72). Had the act come into force without any protection for insolvent companies, large volumes of assets would have been put up for sale, which would have depressed already weak demand. The purpose of the moratorium[11] is to give the insolvent company an opportunity to rescue itself by obtaining further credits from banks, entering a voluntary arrangement with its creditors, or receiving financial support from the state. The grace period is also intended to give companies time to reach out of court settlements, since trained bankruptcy judges, lawyers, and administrators are in short supply. The state is expected to provide financial help subject to certain criteria: viability of the company, its strategic importance to the industry, the temporary nature of its financial difficulties and social policy. The Consolidation Bank will be one of the main institutions in the provision of support for buying bad debt from creditors at a discount. It is likely to be funded by contributions from the National Property Fund out of the proceeds of direct sale of state-owned enterprises.

HIGHLIGHTING THE BAD DEBT/PRIVATIZATION/RESTRUCTURING LINK

The National Property Fund claims that it will selectively offer loan guarantees to several industrial companies (see discussion on privatization above). Creditor banks will typically be given shares in these companies. The Consolidation Bank could use the money put up by the National Property Fund to buy uncollected receivables at a discounted rate. In February 1993, the National Property Fund said it would commit Kcs 10 b to be used by the Consolidation Bank to acquire equity in or to write off debts of certain companies. It is likely that such debt will be again resold by the bank on secondary markets. This policy is limited to loans guaranteed before 1990.

The government has also approved loans to a handful of the most troubled heavy industrial firms. For example, Skoda Plzen received Kcs 915 m from a bond issue to cover its debts. The bonds were bought by Komercni Banka and Investicni Banka. The money was only released after the Finance Ministry was convinced that progress had been made in restructuring including the break up of the company into 25 units[12]. Other 'giants' (for example the steelworks) caught in the debt chain may ask for similar help. These companies are likely to be difficult to privatize because of the size of their debt. The National Property Fund would remain their sole shareholder. Some of these companies' shares could be used as collateral to clear up their 'bad debt' portfolios, i.e. debt would be swapped for equity. According to the Czech National Bank, total enterprise debt is valued at Kcs 130 b, of which 100 b is not being serviced.

Several programmes have been initiated to write off debt and relieve enterprises and banks of their bad debt, without subsidizing poorly performing enterprises. The first step taken involved easing the burden of 'working capital loans', debt forced on enterprises under the previous regime. These credits were extended in the early 1970s and have accumulated over the past two decades within the monobank system. They were inherited by the new commercial banks, especially Komercni Banka (Prague) and General Credit Bank (Bratislava) (Hrncir et al. 1993). Four billion US dollars worth of loans were thus transferred to the Consolidation Bank, i.e. almost a fifth of total bank credits to enterprises at that time. These loans were transformed into eight-year loans with a relatively modest interest rate of 13 per cent. The $12.5 b bond issue by the National Property Fund was intended to help banks entering voucher privatization clear their portfolios of bad debt. The second step aimed at tackling the banking sector. The third step tried to address inter-enterprise debt with $12.5 m worth of debt being cancelled out. This is a small amount, but it was hoped that around $12.5 b of secondary debt will be wiped out as the programme widens[13].

Bankruptcy procedures are not solely about the problem of enterprise debt. They also hinge on questions of asset restructuring. The conundrum to be solved is whether to reorganize or liquidate. Questions linked with liquidation are concerned with determining the point at which one can judge enterprise performance sufficiently to justify closure and thus opt for definite closure against restructuring. They also involve trying to find substitutes in the medium term for guaranteed employment. Another decision to be taken is how to dispose of the remaining capital assets. In some cases, financially troubled enterprises may have a continuation value in excess of their liquidation value. Such firms may be able to effectively reorganize operations and restructure debt so as to ensure future profitability and viability. Czech bankruptcy law seems to allow secured creditors rights to demand that assets be sold to satisfy their claims. In insisting on liquidation, creditors may obstruct the enterprise from retaining and using essential assets. Reorganization is more attractive than liquidation, especially in the case of a small group of very large Czech holding companies. Potentially viable subsidiaries are saddled with the inefficient management and burdensome debt loads of the parent company. These units could be viable if separated from the parent company and restructured so as to retain certain property and assets.

The government is thus striving for a piecemeal application of the bankruptcy law, rescuing a number of companies which have inherited debts from the malfunctioning planned economy. Government action does not, however, seem to follow a clear policy, but appears as concessions which are a function of economic or political pressures. In conclusion, the new Bankruptcy Act gives insolvent companies strong protection and the government significant powers of intervention.

Faced with the threat of bankruptcy, many debtor companies will be seeking to restructure so as to generate revenue to meet their financial obligations. This could also mean the sale of numerous assets at low prices. However, companies may be willing to sell at low prices because they need the money. In such cases, banks themselves might have to buy assets in debtor companies. Banks since 1990, partly in anticipation of such a situation, have been increasing the amount of collateral they hold in debtor companies. Komercni Banka, the largest and partly privatized commercial bank, claims that it now has security attached to about 50 per cent of its pre-1990 loans.

As the governor of the Czech National Bank remarked: 'Banks could be very cautious, over-prudent in lending when the economy needs credit. It is necessary for us [Czech Republic] to find, to support and encourage banks and avoid a credit crunch... We have to [find a] balance between economic needs and liquidation and the health of the banking sector'. These words capture the essence of the defect of voucher privatization. It is neither the emergence of funds, nor the inadequacies of an unsophisticated credit market, but unavailable credit and management know-how that are hindering restructuring and are highlighting the limitations of the privatization programme. Firms cannot afford to restructure and there has been no input of new management know-how. The role of foreign capital is crucial.

THE ROLE OF FOREIGN CAPITAL — A SOLUTION FOR THE FUTURE

Foreign participation in privatization can make an indispensable contribution to the development of industry. In addition to needed capital, foreign investors would endow enterprises with new technology, capital goods, managerial know-how and market economy experience. The inflow of foreign capital is swiftly increasing. Table 8.10 maps foreign transactions in the CSFR from 1989 to 1992. Transactions totalled 86, most were carried out by US and German companies (Ministry of Privatization). Now that the first wave of voucher privatization is terminated, foreign investors face new conditions. Foreign investment in the Czech Republic amounted to $1 b in 1992. Although most came from the US and France in that year, Germany remains the top investor since 1989, with its total investments peaking at $1 b. Foreign investors can directly negotiate with the new private owners on establishing joint ventures as well as on the purchase of a stake in the enterprises. They can also purchase from the National Property Fund their allocated shares from particular privatization projects.

A large number of shares have remained in the hands of the National Privatization Funds. The relevant ministry is supposed to regulate the sale of these shares. For some enterprises, the original privatization project stipulated that a certain amount of shares will have to be set aside for foreign investors. In others, a number of shares were set aside for future flotation on the stock market. Time consuming negotiations, bureaucratic hurdles and problems of unresolved debt, cross ownership etc. still have to be faced by foreign investors. Deals require negotiations with enterprise management, branch ministries and their advisers, and perhaps with the government. In an effort to diminish administrative delays in the endorsement of joint ventures and foreign acquisitions, a special inter-ministerial committee was set up. In March 1993, Czechinvest, a foreign promotion agency was also launched.

The Skoda–VW deal, and to a lesser extent the Philip Morris and Nestlé deals, are a unique case where taxes and tariffs were used to protect the company's dominant market position in exchange for a large amount of government revenue. Such a transaction cannot easily be replicated. In addition, special tax

TABLE 8.10 Foreign Investment in the Czech Republic, 1989-92

	Total Amount ($m)	Germany (%)	USA (%)	France (%)	Belgium (%)	Switz (%)	Austria (%)	Italy (%)	Others (%)
1989-92	1,600	37.4	21.8	15.1	7.6	5.0	4.9	4.3	4.1
1992	1,000	15.8	28.8	20.8	8.8	7.4	6.6	4.1	7.8

Source: EIU 1993

incentives to foreigners are to be removed under the new tax system introduced in January 1993.

If shares allocated for voucher privatization are not sold and are kept in the hands of NPF, then the NPF is to sell them freely on the stock exchange. If a high percentage of a company's equity is floated, then a single buyer has to acquire the whole amount. In addition, as soon as large volumes of shares have been distributed, foreign investors will be allowed to acquire them freely. The Czech legislation contains no regulation of takeovers. Already many foreign investors have entered agreements on future purchases of shares from investment funds means. There seems to be considerable scope for gainful transactions. A number of investment funds are keen to pre-sell their shares to secure their future cash-flow.

5. Conclusions

Privatization in Czechoslovakia has correctly been treated as part of a broader process of structural change. It is clear from the setting up of both the National Property Fund and of the Consolidation Bank that policy-makers have realized that while some assets and enterprises are not viable, others have a future if restructured or liquidated. Creditors, through their involvement in IPFs and through some debt-equity swaps, have already emerged as co-owners of enterprises[14].

It is evident that if debt-equity swaps are to be arranged, they should involve all banks concerned and be supervised. One can also conclude that without an inflow of funds from abroad, it will be hard for privatization to yield the expected results. The existing financial system is unable to finance the transformation to a market economy. Banks are trying to recapitalize and operate in profit-maximizing ways and the implied high cost of borrowing has shattered bad companies and pushed the obviously good ones towards foreign investors. Privatization, until now, has not fully resolved the problems of most companies which lie somewhere in between. As Abel and Bonin (1993c: 4) claim, it is important to separate the objectives of financial sector reform from those of enterprise sector reform, namely 'recapitalizing banks, consolidating loans to facilitate workout, and restructuring large loss-making enterprises. Separate procedures should be designed, to deal with each problem'. The problem of bad loans is largely 'a confusion of financial policy and industrial restructuring' (Abel and Bonin 1993c: 4). Remedies to both the enterprise sector and the banking sector must however, go hand in hand. Inter-enterprise debt might have replaced access to bank credit and might have left enterprises that are servicing their debt subsidizing enterprises with bad loan portfolios. The bankruptcy law when applied will affect both banks and enterprises.

In conclusion, voucher privatization, through the emergence of investment funds, has created a complex net of cross-ownership. For example, though under the privatization rules, banks are not allowed to bid for shares in other banks, all of them have done so through subsidiaries. There is a need to control the connection between banks and enterprises. A legal gap also exists in the monitoring of the link between banks and funds. The question revolves around how the behaviour of funds affects or constrains the behaviour of banks. One of the main drawbacks of Czechoslovak-style privatization is that it does not guarantee access to financing for restructuring to the individual enterprises. The success of privatization in Czechoslovakia lies in its flexibility. Privatization in Czechoslovakia has mostly been distinguished by its wide variety of methods and its speed.

Notes

1. On January 1st 1993, the Federal Republic of Czechoslovakia was separated into two constituent parts: the Czech Republic and Slovakia. There were economic difficulties associated with this division, some being connected with the privatization process, i.e. the continuation of voucher privatization and solving the repercussions of the fact that the first wave of privatization took place at a federal level, with cross-republican investments.
2. Bolton and Roland (1992) refer to this problem as the stock-flow constraint: 'Briefly, in a closed economy without pre-existing private wealth or capital markets, the most the government can get from selling the stock of state assets is selling a flow of savings'.
3. No fixed equity must be set aside for the voucher programme. However, all equity not sold to a buyer must be privatized through the voucher programme. Besides, 3 per cent of equity automatically goes to the restitution fund.
4. The Federal Ministry of Finance classified firms at the inception of the programme as follows. Category A consisted of public utilities and other regulated SOEs which were not to be privatized in the near future. This included at the federal level 30 per cent of state-owned companies in sectors such as defence and some public utilities. Category B covered state-owned medium to large heavy and light industry firms. These firms were to take part in the large-scale privatization process. Category C covered property which took part in the small-privatization or 'municipalization' process (restaurants, local services, flat rentals etc.).
5. Much better in numerical terms than in Hungary, whether or not adjusted for population size.
6. In the first quarter of 1992 the average monthly wage was $135.9, the average weekly salary was thus about $34 (Ham *et al.* 1993).
7. Czech investors only placed 3.5 per cent of their investments in the Slovak Republic, while Slovak investors invested 23.1 per cent of their points in the Czech Republic. Slovaks hold 11.1 per cent of equity in Czech companies, while Czechs only hold 7.9 per cent of equity in Slovak companies.
8. Bad loan portfolios of companies probably intensified the initial reluctance of the population to take up shares if only for a nominal price.
9. Jan Winiecki 1992 holds that such arguments were weak. A large — if not dominant — portion of individual voucher holders would have sold their shares quickly and acquired assets with a more stable flow of income. Underlying this is evidence from patterns of asset holding in market economies, which derive from the risk preference structure of households, only a small proportion of which is usually willing to hold risky assets, i.e. shares. This also arises from the existence of a well-developed capital market in market economies.
10. A positive feature about investment funds in Czechoslovakia is that they are not led by government appointed figures. 'The funds were not organized directly by the state, and

they were supposed to be a purely private activity. But state-owned joint stock companies were allowed to establish intermediaries and the state banks took advantage of this possibility.'(Frydman *et al.* 1993). However, these banks were also included in the voucher privatization process. There is therefore less danger of funds becoming vehicles of state intervention as may be the case in Hungary or the Ukraine.

11. This is a protective period between the filing of a bankruptcy petition and the commencement of bankruptcy proceedings.

12. There have been other instances of government led restructuring. CKD, the holding company, had some of its units completely separated from it. The Ministry of Industry split up the company along product lines instead of marketing lines. Units have thus not been transformed into independent units outside the holding as they depend on the head office for sales contacts (especially in exports) and the main product programmes create a high degree of synergies across product groups (McDermott 1993).

13. Secondary debt is defined as debt which the enterprise is unable to pay only because of illiquidity of its accounts receivable.

14. One such deal was initiated recently and involved Investicni Banka acquiring a 34 per cent stake in Aero Praha, a soon to be privatized company, in exchange for its Kcs 500 mn debt. The plan was contested by Komercni Banka which is owed a larger amount by the company.

References

Abel, I. and **Bonin, J.** (1993a) Capital markets in Eastern Europe: the financial black hole, *Connecticut Journal of International Law*, **13**.

Abel, I. and **Bonin, J.** (1993b) State desertion and financial market failure: is transition stalled?, mimeo.

Abel, I. and **Bonin, J.** (1993c) The failure of credit markets in Hungary: are there any solutions? Paper presented at a conference organized by the Blue Ribbon Commission meeting, Budapest, 18 June.

Begg, D. (1991) Economic reform in Czechoslovakia: should we believe in Santa Klaus?, *Economic Polic*, **13**, pp. 243–87.

Ben-Ner, A. and **Neuberger, E.** (1990) Privatization and entry of new firms in Eastern Europe and the Soviet Union, *Jahrbuch der Wirtschaft Osteuropas*, **14**, pp. 178–81.

Bolton P. and **Roland G.** (1992) Privatization policies in Central and Eastern Europe, *Economic Policy*, **13**, pp. 275–309.

Dyba K. and **Svejnar J.** (1992) Stabilization and transition in Czechoslovakia, *Cerge Working Paper No. 7*, Prague, June.

Economic Commission for Europe, (1993) Progress in privatization 1990–92, ECE Geneva, April.

Economist (1993) 19 June 1993.

Economist Intelligence Unit (1993) Country forecast, Czech Republic, Third Quarter.

Estrin, S. (1991) Privatization in Central and Eastern Europe: what lessons can be learnt from Western experience, *Annals of Public and Cooperative Economics*, **62**, pp. 159–82.

Fischer, S. and **Gelb, A.** (1990) Issues in socialist economy reform, *WP 565*, The World Bank, December.

Flašarova, L. (1993) Voucher privatization: targets, intentions and preliminary results, Institute of Economics, Prague.

Frydman, R., Rapaczynski, A., Earle, J., *et al.*, (1993) *The Privatization Process in Central Europe*, Vol 1, Central European University Press, London.

Ham J., Svejnar J. and **Terrell K.** (1993) The Czech and Slovak labour markets during the Transition, paper prepared for the World Bank Conference on 'Unemployment, Restructuring and the Labour Market in East Europe and Russia', October 7 and 8.

Hinds, M. (1990) Issues in the introduction of market forces in Eastern European socialist economies, The World Bank, *EMENA Discussion Papers*, No. IDP-0057.

Hrncir, M., Estrin S. and **Hare, P.** (1993) Banking in transition, *Working Paper*, CERT, Heriot-Watt University, October.

Jermakovicz, E. and **Jermakovicz, W.** (1992) Business evaluation in the privatization process in Central European economies: the case of Poland, University of Southern Indiana, Evansville, October.

Lipton D. and **Sachs J.** (1990) Creating a market economy in Eastern Europe: the case of Poland, *Brookings Papers on Economic Activity* **2**, pp. 293–341.

McDermott, G. (1993) Rethinking the ties that bind. The limits of privatization in the Czech Republic, paper presented at a conference on 'The Social Embeddedness of the Economic Transformation in Central and Eastern Europe', Social Science Research Centre Berlin (WZB), September 24–25.

PlanEcon Report (1992) Results of Czechoslovak voucher privatization: Part I Overall review and statistical data, Number 50—51–52, December 31.

PlanEcon Report (1993) Results of Czechoslovak voucher privatization: Part II Sectoral and industry branch reviews, Number 3–4, February 16.

Skalicky, J. (1992) Policy of privatization in the Czech Republic, Ministry of National Property Administration and Privatization of the Czech Republic, Prague.

Svejnar, J. and **Singer M.** (1993) Using vouchers to privatise an economy: the Czech and Slovak case, paper presented at the 1993 Meetings of the American Economic Association, January.

Winiecki, J. (1992) *Privatization in Poland: A Comparative Perspective*, Mohr, Tübingen.

The privatization process — economic and political aspects of the Hungarian approach

Anna Canning and Paul Hare*

1. Introduction

Hungary's transition to a market-type economy is widely regarded as one of the most successful and best coordinated of all the former centrally planned economies (CPEs) in the region. It is also one of the longest standing, having begun with the introduction of the New Economic Mechanism (NEM) in 1968, in the same year when similar liberal reform efforts were crushed in Czechoslovakia[1], taking that country into another 20 years of socialist atrophy. However, the reform package, which released enterprises from the strict dictates of central planning and gave enterprise management more autonomy in terms of investment and trade decisions, was only moderately successful. The role retained by the central administration in allocating resources, including credits and subsidies, and a highly differentiated system of taxation, along with the continued orientation of production towards the Eastern European and Soviet markets, and a high degree of central control over foreign trade, prevented the programme from achieving a significant change in enterprise behaviour (Hare 1990). The NEM did, nevertheless, set Hungary on a slow-rolling path of economic reform; this in turn produced an organizational, legislative, and intellectual legacy as a result of which, by the late 1980s, Hungary was in a unique position, well ahead of its other former socialist neighbours when the wave of reform broke over the region. This legacy proved durable, if not always entirely advantageous (as we hope will become apparent in our more detailed discussion below), and has profoundly influenced political and economic decisions in Hungary's transition. Indeed, it has often determined the policy options themselves.

Despite initial scepticism from some quarters in East and West regarding the 'unambitious' nature of Hungary's reforms post-1989, the gradualist approach inherited and continued by the country's first post-communist government seems on the whole to have proved its worth, particularly in the light of the mixed results of the 'big bang' and other radical approaches to reform adopted elsewhere (e.g. in Poland and the former Soviet Union) and the consequent political upheaval

*This paper has been written with support from the ESRC under the East-West Initiative, grant no. Y3009/25/3007, for which the authors are most grateful. The paper was originally prepared for the Initiative's conference in Budapest, March 26-27, 1993, and then revised in the light of comments received there. The authors are also grateful to Saul Estrin for his helpful suggestions.

and erosion of public support for the reform programmes. While Hungary is not free from political problems or from social tensions, the situation has remained fairly stable: the coalition government elected in March 1990 is still in power (to the surprise of many observers who initially predicted that it would not survive for long), there have been no major social or industrial (or, for that matter, ethnic) upheavals, and the cogs of the legislature have continued to grind relatively smoothly.

The fact that Hungary, of all the countries which embarked on the process of transformation to a market economy in the late 1980s, has attracted around half of the total direct foreign capital investment in the region so far[2], reflects the confidence of Western investors in the political stability and economic potential of Hungary. Although there are some inevitable, transition-induced cracks in the economic edifice — a continuing decline in GDP (around 5 per cent in 1992) and in industrial output (a further 13 per cent in 1992), unemployment hovering around a painful 12.5–13.5 per cent (December 1992 – June 1993) without yet having reached its expected peak of around 16–17 per cent, and a budget deficit in excess of 7 per cent of GDP — the international business community appears to have undiminished confidence in Hungary's overall performance. Various surveys and a plethora of business guides to the region consistently rank Hungary highly in most categories related to political, legislative and economic security.

The evolutionary approach and the legacy of earlier reforms which have marked Hungary's economic transition in general are clearly evident also in the process of privatization. Hungary's chosen path of privatization is unique in its aim of selling off state-owned assets rather than opting — as in the neighbouring Czech and Slovak lands and Poland — for the distribution of shares among the populace at a nominal price or free of charge. This option was not so readily available to Hungary, given the government's international commitment to service its external hard currency debt[3], which was the highest in the region in per capita terms, but also due to the complex distribution of ownership rights (or rights of disposition) established by previous reforms. Although there were calls for a 'clean slate' approach[4], it was clear that two decades of reform would prove exceedingly difficult to wipe away with one sweep of a legislative brush, and it was generally felt that such a move might be a step backwards in the reform process, and perhaps even be damaging to Hungary's already considerable standing as a country open to reform and as an attractive and welcoming destination for Western investment.[5]

Privatization in Hungary is also unique in its pragmatism, in the astonishing variety of models and approaches which have been developed to cover almost every eventuality, and in the high degree of apparent responsiveness and flexibility on the part of the government and its agencies when one set of measures or particular privatization programmes have failed to produce the expected results. Another interesting feature of Hungarian privatization is that it has relied predominantly on 'home-grown' models. While it was clear from the outset that models of privatization adopted in Western countries and in some developing countries would not be appropriate, due to the scale of the task and to the fundamental differences between socialist state enterprises and public sector corporations in developed market economies, most of the models being tried in

Hungary have been drawn or adapted from a rich seam of intellectual debate which developed during the 1970s and particularly during the 1980s in Hungary's comparatively liberal environment.

However, what appears as a pragmatic and flexible response to one observer may look like mere political expediency and lack of cohesion to another; certainly, there has been a discernible process of trial and error in Hungary's privatization, and there can be no doubt that political bargaining and compromise have played their part. To what extent the rather piecemeal, and perhaps excessively eclectic approach to privatization which has resulted has been successful is as yet unclear. The measure of 'success' has also shifted with the realization that original expectations with regard to the speed and implementation of privatization were rather naive and required some adjustment. At the same time, as practical experience and deepening economic recession have made it increasingly clear that privatization will not take place as quickly or as smoothly as originally anticipated, a growing cause for concern has been the decline in value of state-owned assets as a result of the delay. In an attempt to combat the worst economic effects of the decline — and boost flagging public confidence in the privatization process — a new round of measures was introduced in the wake of long-awaited privatization legislation passed at the end of August 1992. However, at the time of writing, some of these are still in the process of being formulated, so it will be some time before their effectiveness can be assessed.

In terms of the progress achieved to date, privatization in Hungary can be summed up in the following terms. Out of a total estimated socially owned capital stock of the order of 2000 bn HUF, the (approximate) disposition at the end of 1992 is indicated below (see Voszka 1992):

- 100 bn HUF of former state assets have been sold;
- 1000 bn have been transferred to the State Assets Management Company (SAMCo.);
- 300 bn are to be given to the Social Security administration (TB);
- 100 bn are to be given to the local municipalities;
- 100 bn are to be given to employees under the various schemes in operation (ESOP, MBOs);
- 200-300 bn estimated as the value of assets which will become the property of creditors as a result of bankruptcy proceedings;
- 60 bn promised to cover compensation claims;
- 40 bn under offer currently to various potential buyers.

This may only be a rough breakdown of the assets, but it is clear even from this that most of the original HUF 2000 bn worth are spoken for. In the light of the above, Voszka (1992) raises an interesting question, namely where are the assets which are supposedly in excess supply, and for which buyers must be found urgently according to the government's privatization programme?

This chapter examines how the process of privatization in Hungary has developed, reviews the progress of privatization at different levels, and explores some of the underlying, less evident aspects of the process in the light of Hungary's reform heritage. The chapter also assesses the more recent developments in privatization and the recent policy directions initiated by the Hungarian government, which is now in the final year of its normal term of office before the general elections of 1994.

2. From ownership reform to privatization

Although privatization as such did not figure on Hungary's official reform agenda until early in 1989, considerable thought had been given much earlier to the possibilities of introducing some kind of ownership reform as a means of improving the economic efficiency of existing socialist ownership structures. The question may be raised as to whether these early proposals for reform of ownership rights within the socialist framework are relevant to a discussion of privatization. There are several reasons why they are.

First, some elements of the models proposed were built into the earlier reforms, notably those of enterprise organization in the early 1980s, and thus had a direct effect on the process of privatization. Second, the variety of models developed and the debate surrounding their feasibility left academic circles very much divided, which encouraged the new government to opt for a 'pluralistic' approach rather than a single, cohesive privatization programme. Third, and arguably most importantly, the issue of what to do with state-owned assets to ensure their efficient operation has remained topical, since privatization has not produced the rapid and radical reduction of state-ownership which had been hoped for. This was due to the lack of capital or lack of interest among a cautious population which prefers to invest in new ventures rather than in former state-owned assets, and due to the realization that for strategic and practical reasons most developed market economies also include elements of state-ownership and institutional forms of ownership similar to those which had been proposed by earlier reform thinkers.

While a study of the present scope cannot hope to do justice to the great body of scholarly work produced by Hungarian economists on the subject of ownership reform, which has in any case been exhaustively recorded elsewhere (Köhegyi 1991; Lengyel 1988[6]), by outlining the basic precepts and arguments (and counter-arguments) of some of the proposed models in the context of the privatization policies followed in Hungary since 1989, some useful insights can be gained into the progress and problems of privatization. The rest of this section is therefore devoted to illustrating the main strands of the early academic debate on ownership reform in Hungary, studying how elements of these were implemented prior to 1989 and the implications of this on the state of affairs inherited by the first democratically elected government.

CONCEPTS

Academic debate on ownership reform prior to the 1989 turning point can be divided — very broadly, since there are overlapping elements — into four main lines of thought:

1. Institutional ownership of state assets with a view to separating asset management from day-to-day economic management (asset management bodies, holding companies, financial institutions, pension funds, local municipalities);
2. Cross ownership: corporatization of SOEs allowing equity participation by state administrative bodies, state funds, financial institutions, other enterprises and private shareholding;
3. Individual entrepreneurship/share ownership (socialist entrepreneurial society, 'people's shares' programmes, leasing, 'small privatization');
4. Self-management (enterprise/workers' councils, cooperatives, employee share ownership).

When the 1968 reform package was being drawn up, some reform economists were already advocating the transformation of state enterprises into joint-stock companies and the management of the shares thus created by a separate ownership body in order to rationalize the allocation of investment funding and improve capital flow among the enterprises. Such proposals were not in the end incorporated into the NEM, but the idea was resuscitated in 1972 by Márton Tardos, although this time without including corporatization and shares. His idea centred around the formation of a number (unspecified) of financial institutions which would act as holding companies, taking over certain 'ownership' functions on behalf of the state, including the appointment and supervision of enterprise management and strategic decisions regarding the allocation of resources among the enterprises under their control (Köhegyi 1991).

Several other economists took up the idea in the years that followed, proposing various forms of institutional management of state assets, the main purpose of which was to separate the public administration functions of the state from its role as owner of economic assets (well documented in Lengyel 1988). Kevevári suggested a type of 'asset bank' (*vagyonpénztár*), which would contract out the actual management of shares in state enterprises to specialist asset management bodies (Kevevári, 1988). Tardos himself later came to the conclusion, along with many of his critics, notably Károly Attila Soós, that the holding-type institutions he had originally envisaged would be open to political manipulation unless their managers had a genuine interest in increasing the value of the assets in their hands. Soós pointed out that the state in its present form would not be able to create profit-oriented 'quasi-capitalists', and that it would therefore be a 'grave mistake' to set up asset management bodies (Köhegyi 1991: 84). Matolcsy held that 'any ownership solution involving the authorities — especially if the number of ownership bodies was very limited — would be easy prey for government intervention' (Matolcsy 1988b: 115).

Matolcsy's own model was that of 'cross-ownership', based on the principle of corporatizing state enterprises as smaller units (limited liability and joint-stock companies) with the possibility of involving external capital investment, each of which would be given equity stakes in the others; the enterprise headquarters would then in effect become a holding company which, ideally, should likewise transform into a corporate entity (joint-stock company), and which could sell shares to external institutions, to other (former) enterprises or even to domestic or foreign private investors. The advantages of the cross ownership model, as Matolcsy saw it, were the decentralization of state enterprises through the clear separation of owners, equity managers, and operational managers while at the same time obviating the need to establish separate 'artificial' ownership or asset management institutions; the possibility of creating a capital market through the involvement of external investment; the creation of profit motivation.

Critics of cross ownership, on the other hand, pointed out that such a scheme would not necessarily create strong owners, since equity management would be concentrated in the hands of the former enterprise managers; these would not be making decisions based on risk calculation, since it is not their own investment which is at stake (Köhegyi 1991: 94). In addition, it is unlikely that the management of the new concerns (former enterprise headquarters) would be willing to allow an outside investor, be it another company, a bank or a foreign investor, to acquire a majority stake and therefore an effective say in the management of the companies. Tardos also mentions the problem of monopolies, which would be reinforced rather than lessened by cross ownership, due to the high degree of concentration of the existing large enterprises and to the lack of incentive to encourage competition (Tardos 1989). Even Matolcsy recognized that the model contained elements which were fundamentally unfair, in that managers of larger enterprises with more valuable assets would acquire the dispositional rights over more shares than in the case of smaller enterprises (Köhegyi 1991: 92.).

Another economist whose ideas have been influential in the evolution of ownership reform in Hungary was Tibor Liska. He was openly critical of the economic logic behind traditional socialist forms of public ownership from early in the 1960s, but the alternatives he proposed did not gain recognition outside intellectual circles until much later.[7] Central to his thinking was the notion of a socialist entrepreneurial society, though avowedly populist rather than 'capitalist' in orientation, based on what he termed the 'social birthright' of socialist citizens. He proposed that this could be brought about by leasing out state assets to individuals. Close to, though not derived from, his model were the measures introduced in the early 1980s which permitted the development of (semi-) private businesses, especially in the retail, catering and services sectors; a substantial number of shops, restaurants, and bars were leased or 'contracted out' by the parent enterprise to private individuals. By 1988, around 11 per cent of shops covering a wide range of goods and services, and 44 per cent of catering establishments functioned in this way. In industry a parallel development was the institution of the VGMK (enterprise work association), through which work was subcontracted to groups of enterprise employees. In agriculture, similar sub-contracting developed through the 'ancillary branch plants' attached to agricultural cooperatives.

This de facto support for private business was motivated not so much by long-term economic policy considerations as by the desire to ease the immediate economic crisis and social discontent; but it also had the consequence of partially 'reprivatizing' the economy, reintroducing elements of balance after years of exaggerated centralization (Csillag 1988: 129) and creating a group of people within Hungary who gained useful experience of entrepreneurship largely independent from state directives and less reliant on the state for protection.

While studies of the Yugoslavian experience of enterprise self-management and of cooperatives in Hungary left Hungarian economists divided as to the benefits of self-management, it was widely felt at the time to be more feasible than some of the other models on offer.[8] In the immediate post-Brezhnev years, in the early 1980s, together with the dangerous economic decline which had put Hungary on the brink of bankruptcy, the mood was ripe for further reform. Tamás Bauer (among others) argued convincingly that the main obstacle in the path of enterprise efficiency was the umbilical link to the state administration; the most immediate, practical solution was to break this link by giving enterprises the possibility and the responsibility of managing the assets in their hands. Other options, he argued, such as 'holding' organizations or asset banks, would be too easily manipulated by the state.

LAWS AND LOOPHOLES

With the Enterprise Act (1984), a form of self-management (enterprise or workers' councils) was introduced into the majority of state-owned enterprises. This, in effect, transferred a considerable degree of control over enterprise assets, and the exercise of certain ownership rights, to the enterprises themselves. The Act affected nearly 70 per cent of SOEs, giving them decision-making powers over restructuring, mergers and de-mergers, the right to set up joint ventures, etc; the remaining 30 per cent, mainly enterprises in strategic sectors[9], were placed under the supervision of the branch ministries.

From around 1987 onwards, enterprise managers had realized that a loophole in the legislation, the existence of unrepealed, pre-communist laws on commercial companies dating from before the First World War, permitted enterprises to found subsidiary companies (either wholly owned by the enterprise or as a joint venture with a domestic or foreign partner) with up to 10 per cent of enterprise capital or assets in kind. This presented opportunities for management to gain control, and indeed, virtual ownership over a portion of state assets. Moreover, the parent company's liabilities were not simultaneously transferred to the new company, and additional tax relief offered to new company foundations (50 per cent, for a period of three years) from 1988[10], as well as exemption from wage regulation and export-import controls, provided further incentives to transform in this way. The Company Act of 1988 created the legal framework according to which state enterprises managed by enterprise councils could form such commercial entities, and effectively legalized the process which was already taking place. It should be pointed out, however, that it was not merely self-interest on the part of enterprise management that motivated these partial transformations. Tight monetary controls, the introduction of a two-tier banking system (1987) and a new fiscal regime introduced over the period 1987–88, placed the SOEs under considerable pressure, leaving them increasingly in a position of having to fend for themselves in the midst of cuts in subsidies, limits on investment finance from central funds and from the government budget, increased interest rates on loans (which now had to be negotiated with the commercial banks and backed by collateral), reduced subsidies on rouble exports, and later the administrative restriction of these. Setting up one or more virtually liability-free subsidiaries, using real estate or other enterprise assets frequently under a type of leasing arrangement, brought opportunities to raise fresh capital, particularly when a joint venture partner could be found. For some SOEs at least, it was a matter of survival (Voszka 1991b, 1991c).[11]

Nevertheless, the formal introduction of corporate forms was greeted as a major step forward in the process of economic reform initiated with the NEM, since it brought with it the prospect of decentralization of the mammoth state enterprises and their transformation from loss-making concerns into more manageable units, able — and indeed compelled — to respond more flexibly and efficiently to market forces rather than relying on the impoverished state for funding and 'bailing out' of their financial predicaments. It was hoped that the company form would create an effective profit motivation, de-politicize the enterprises and make them more publicly accountable in their operations (Matolcsy 1988a). At the same time, it was felt (particularly by those advocating even more radical reform) that the emergence of the elements of asset valuation and the issue of shares, that is, the possibility of dividing up the assets into smaller units, would facilitate the participation of private capital at a later stage and thus prepare the way for privatization proper.

The new legislation was therefore generally regarded as a logical and necessary continuation of the earlier reforms, the process of moving away from centralized planning towards a devolution of power from the state apparatus to the enterprises, and as a means of ensuring that the limited results of the earlier devolution of control would be improved upon by forcing the enterprises into new patterns of behaviour.

At the same time, however, the intention was not to 'strip the state of assets', but to provide 'a more developed, more modern framework' for their use (Varga 1988). During the debate on the draft of the Company Act, Miklós Németh reassured the Central Committee, saying, 'It is an indisputable fact that the basis of our socialist society is social ownership of the vast majority of the means of production and the decisive role played by state and cooperative ownership. Our most important task now is to find ways and means of using the assets in these forms of ownership in a much more effective manner than at present'[12]. The nature and extent of state-ownership was not in question at this stage, and the role of private capital, although it seemed to be recognized as a necessary evil, was expected to be relatively minimal and would therefore present no threat to the 'social ownership' form. In an interview in the economics weekly Figyelő, (Varga 1988), Tamás Sárközy, head of the committee established by the Council of Ministers to prepare the draft legislation, took pains to stress that the majority of 'shareholders' in the transformed enterprises would be other state institutions rather than private interests: other state-owned companies (through exchanging debt for equity — cf. Matolcsy's 1988b, concept of cross-holding), holding-type bodies, banks, pension funds, local authorities, and various foundations set up for the purpose.

However, the ownership rights of the state and the enterprises were left unclarified at this stage, and this was to cause problems later as increasingly widespread use of the mechanism provided under the Company Act became immersed in controversy and was dubbed 'spontaneous privatization' as fears grew that the old, party-appointed enterprise managers were exploiting the possibilities provided under the Enterprise Act and subsequent legislation to perpetuate their power and secure an income for themselves.

The basic assumption at the time was that ownership of the assets themselves (means of production) remained unquestionably in the hands of the state, but that the much-needed improvement in economic efficiency could be achieved by decentralizing and redistributing 'bundles' of ownership rights and duties within the state. Privatization, that is the sale or transfer of assets out of state hands, and the radical reform of ownership structures that this would imply, had not yet been fully accepted by the Németh government as a logical and necessary continuation of the reform path upon which it had embarked.

By summer 1989 the focus had substantially shifted, but for the time being, transformation remained the primary issue, and this was assumed (based on the existing legislation as well as on the spirit of reform) to be the rightful task of the enterprises themselves. Attitudes on the part of state representatives to intervening more directly in the process appear to have been ambivalent and, in cases where the state did intervene, this had little impact on the decisions or actions of the enterprise management.[13]

The January 1989 amendment to the Company Act provided an added incentive for the enterprises — and for foreign investors — by allowing handsome tax concessions for joint ventures (20 per cent for foreign participation of a mere 5 million HUF, irrespective of the size of the company, and more if the level of foreign investment was higher). An absolute tax exemption was permitted in the case of certain activities — specified in the Foreign Investments Act of 1988 — for up to five years, with further tax allowances for a subsequent five years (State Property Agency 1991: 6).

Intended to complement the Company Act, the Transformation Act of 1989 was already regarded by some as anachronistic when it was finally passed at the end of May 1989, since, if anything, it further enhanced the autonomy of enterprise management in the transformation process (Bokros 1989). The new legislation provided for the corporatization of whole SOEs (not just bundles of their assets), including those SOEs not run by enterprise councils. It was supposed to go some way towards clarifying the confused issue of who owned SOE assets, since after conversion to a corporate form the state became the clear owner of the new company's shares. It was also hoped that the new legislation would help to eliminate some of the abuses connected with the Company Act (empty shell companies — see below), since the old enterprise would cease to exist and the new entity would inherit not only the assets, but also the liabilities of its predecessor. However, the Transformation Act also allowed the new entity (insiders) the right to purchase 20 per cent of the company's shares on preferential terms (at a discount of up to 90 per cent). Although this provided an incentive to transform, the temptation to undervalue enterprise assets was obvious, and the way was hence opened for further abuses by enterprise insiders.

The role and the behaviour of enterprise management in the process of transformation, and the emerging position of managers as 'quasi-owners' as a result of this process thus became a major source of public concern. In brief, the problem concerning the transformation of the large state enterprises into a series of smaller, independent corporate units, was the following: although after transformation a proportion of the shares in the newly formed joint-stock company were registered with parties external to the company — commercial banks, insurance companies, other enterprises, and a few foreign and domestic investors — the vast majority remained in the hands of the old administrative headquarters of the enterprise, which then functioned as a kind of holding company (sometimes referred to as a 'shell' company). In other words, the former enterprise managers and a few dozen employees had become virtual owners of huge assets without having had to take the personal (or corporate) risk that real investment normally involves. The main fear was that these ownership rights — including the right to sell, and therefore the possibility to under-value, shares in the company — were now in the hands of managers 'whose personal profit-gaining motives might not necessarily coincide with the interests of developing the company's — or the nation's — wealth' (Réti 1989: 66. For details of the main arguments against 'spontaneous privatization', see Auth and Krokos 1989).

In summer 1989 some (now well-known) cases of transactions where enterprise managers were 'caught in the act' of selling assets at a conspicuously under-valued rate, and without open bidding, came to the attention of the press. These included the hotel chain, Hungar-Hotels, and the chain of stationery shops, Apisz. Cases such as these caused public outcry and furious political debate. The government came under fire from all quarters; months earlier, highly-placed officials within the state bureaucracy itself, notably from within the Ministry of Industry (see Auth and Krokos 1989) and the National Bank (see Bokros 1989), had called attention to the danger 'enshrined in the legislation' of the ownership powers of the enterprise managers. Henrik Auth, Deputy Minister for Industry, had consistently called for 're-nationalization' of the self-managed enterprises as a precondition of privatization, in order to establish a clear distinction between the ownership role of the state and the management function of the enterprise directors (Auth and Krokos, 1989; Hajnóczy 1989a).

Now sections of the political opposition, originally averse to any measures which would increase state intervention in the microeconomic sphere, had also begun to exert pressure on the government, making enterprise transformation into a national issue. The government and its offices had not only lost control of the situation, they seemed to have little information about what was happening. In September, the Ministry of Industry was unable to supply the press with data on the number of enterprises or the proportion of their assets which had been taken into joint stock or limited liability companies (Réti 1989: 67)[14]. The government was finally forced to take more rapid steps to regain control as 'owner' of the enterprises' assets, and to establish some form of body to supervise transformation and privatization.

In late 1988, the government reform proposals, as worked out by its Consultative Committee on Economic Management, still referred to 'the creation of a socialist market economy' (A Consultative Committee 1988). By spring 1989 the insistence on 'socialist' market reforms was conspicuously missing from the draft 'three-year programme for economic transformation and stabilization' of the now renamed Economic Reform Committee. In a report by one of the working groups of this Committee, published on 4th May 1989, which gave a summary of the work of the Committee (Gazdasági Reformbizottság 1989), the establish-ment of a state 'Property Fund' (PF) was recommended. 'The activities of the PF should be managed by a small board of experts selected by parliament', and its purpose should be to solve 'the question of what should happen to the shares [in state-owned enterprises] not registered by external shareholders', to 'keep account of all the state's business assets and to handle strategic questions related to the use of those assets'. The report also proposed that 'the PF should transfer a portion of the state shares which make up its property to holding bodies and asset manage-ment bodies on a contract basis', and stressed that it was a matter of the utmost urgency to establish such a body by the end of the year. The programme put privatization firmly on the agenda, recommending the formulation of a separate government programme on privatization of state-owned assets, to be undertaken as rapidly as possible, and even proposing that the first steps towards privatiza-tion would be 'most warranted' in the retail, catering, and services sectors. This programme was to pave the way not only for the formation of the State Property Agency, but also for the privatization strategy later followed by the government of József Antall.

3. State-managed privatization

Draft legislation on the State Property Fund, on the management of state assets, and also for the privatization of retail, catering and consumer services outlets, was ready in November 1989, bearing the title 'Ownership Reform and Privatization Programme'. The new body came into being on 1 March 1990, with the somewhat altered title of State Property Agency (SPA), under the chairmanship of István Tömpe, who had been the government's Privatization Commissioner. Its primary task was to supervise the transformation and privatization of state enterprises and to safeguard state assets from plundering through 'spontaneous' privatization by increasing the publicity and transparency of such transactions and ensuring proper evaluation of the assets.

The number of state-owned enterprises intended for transformation and priva-tization under the management of the SPA was in the region of 2200; the total book value of their assets was estimated at over 2000 billion HUF. Of these enterprises 63 per cent were founded by ministries and 37 per cent by municipa-lities; 32 per cent were under state administration and 56 per cent self-managed, while the remaining 12 per cent had been transformed into companies in 100 per cent state-ownership (State Property Agency 1991: 7).

Initially the SPA was set up with a small staff to meet the immediate need for a body to 'represent the state as owner', primarily as a means of monitoring transformations initiated by the enterprises, to carry out the transformation of state-administered enterprises to company forms and to ensure appropriate man-agement of state-owned shares in transformed companies by independent holding companies. It was to take over from the enterprise councils the function of decision-making regarding the use to which profits could be put, investments and the enterprise managers' salary (Henrik Auth, see Hajnóczy 1989b). How-ever, the SPA was responsible to parliament and had no power of its own to 'alter ownership relations ... and initiate ownership reform' (Sebök 1989); it had the right to veto enterprise transformation, but its decisions could be contested in court.

At the time there were several arguments against setting up a larger, more independent body with wider-ranging powers. Despite the controversy over the abuses of 'spontaneous' privatization, many economists still felt that privatization should be left largely to market forces, arguing that it was inconceivable that the state, which had mismanaged the assets in its ownership for four decades, should now be able to manage them in a rational manner (Réti 1989: 67). It should not be forgotten that by November/December 1989, when the debate on the proposals for the SPA was under way, major political changes had taken place; the opposition parties had gained places in parliament (July 22) and agreement had already been reached (September 18) on holding multi-party elections in the spring of the following year. The government was already in effect an interim one and its legitimacy had been considerably eroded. On the one hand, as discussed above, the government was under pressure to bring the enterprises under closer control as a matter of urgency, while on the other hand it now lacked the legitimacy — and stability — to do much more to settle the issue of property ownership rights than to set up a watchdog body which would operate according to 'Temporary Property Policy Guidelines'. The task of preparing legislation on ownership reform and privatization would fall to a new government.

In addition, although it might have seemed logical from an economic point of view to set up a body with the authority to manage all the assets belonging to the state, the scale of such an institution would pose certain risks: apart from the difficulty of finding sufficient experienced personnel to handle such a task, unprecedented anywhere, there would be no guarantee that the new body would not 'sit' on the assets in its control; a body invested with such powers might itself become difficult to oversee (Tömpe, see Sebök, 1989). Enterprise self-management was not to be abolished altogether, since it was felt that this would be a step backwards rather than forwards in the process of reform, and might lead to a revival of a form of state administration of the microeconomic sphere more akin to that which existed prior to the reforms of the mid-1980s (Auth, see Hajnóczy 1989b).

Nevertheless, the programme of the newly elected centre-right coalition government under József Antall, published on 22 May 1990, under the title 'Programme of National Revival', gave a clear indication of the new government's intentions to assert more firmly its role as owner. It proposed to abolish enterprise councils, initiate investigation into some of the transformations which had already taken place and, if necessary, reverse the situation (Government of Hungary 1990: 17). The programme promised to bring amendments to the existing legislation on enterprises, companies and transformation 'to modify the legal position of the state enterprises which have transformed into companies and to bring them under the control of the state administration' (Government of Hungary, p.26). The document also set out the main objectives and the direction of privatization, ruling out give-away methods and 'cross ownership' methods on the grounds that they would not create real owners, and asserting its intention to use the revenue from privatization to service foreign debt.

In July 1990, legislation on the SPA was modified; the SPA was removed from parliamentary control and placed under the direct authority of the government, the scope of its powers was extended and the possibility of appealing against its decisions through the courts was abolished.

The desire of the government to place privatization very securely under its own control was perhaps understandable in the light of public fears regarding spontaneous privatization and, possibly, the need to ensure that the SPA, as an organ set up by the previous, communist-led government, would in fact serve the aims of the new administration. At the same time, it was widely held that until real owners and real investors appeared on the scene, and until the supporting legislation and institutions of a market economy were in place and operational, some degree of supervision and planned, 'active' privatization on the part of the government, via the SPA, were needed. However, the highly-centralized privatization effort which resulted failed to bring about significant progress, hampered by bureaucracy, problems over asset valuation, and by the failure of the government to consolidate its strategy and pass legislation on privatization to update the 'Temporary Property Policy Guidelines'[15] (Wiesel 1990).

'ACTIVE' PRIVATIZATION PROGRAMMES

The SPA's First Privatization Programme, involving 20 large and reasonably profitable enterprises covering a wide range of economic activities, was begun in September 1990. The combined turnover of these enterprises totalled HUF 100 bn, and their book value was estimated at HUF 70 bn. The programme was spectacular in scope, and its aim was to attract as much interest as possible from foreign investors as well as public support within Hungary for privatization. Over 300 consultancy firms, including some of the world's top investment banks, tendered proposals for the valuation and transformation contracts for the enterprises in question, but despite this initial interest, the programme has been singularly unsuccessful. By October 1991, only four of the enterprises had been corporatized, and although by the end of 1992 this number had increased to 18 out of the original 20, only three of the firms (Ibusz, Pannonplast, Kunép) had been fully privatized.

Many experts now attribute the failure of the First Privatization Programme to the unrealistically high price expectations on the part of the SPA, which in turn may have been due to the political sensitivity of privatization in the aftermath of the controversy over 'spontaneous' privatization and to the fear of accusations of 'selling off the family silver'. At the same time, the foreign consultants took rather a long time to carry out transformation and draw up their recommendations for privatization and during this period the collapse of the CMEA markets and the deepening recession in Hungary drastically reduced the value of the firms. As a result, some of the original enterprises have been corporatized as smaller units, some of which have been sold separately (Danubius, Hungar-Hotels) to offset debts and thus present liability-free packages to potential investors. Additional complications and delays have been caused by the need to take into account the claims of municipalities, which are entitled to receive shares in the transformed enterprises equivalent to the value of the real estate on which the properties are

TABLE 9.1 First Privatization Programme of the SPA

Name of SOE	Value of assets (mn.HUF)	Description	Method
1. Centrum Áruházak	5218.9	Department stores	Public resale of a minimum 40% of shares and a strategic foreign partner
2. Danubius Szállodavállalat	6640.0	Hotels and catering	Public sale and strategic foreign partner
3. Erdögép	146.4	Forest machinery	Employee share ownership
4. Gamma Müvek	1753.7	Medical and tech./ computer instruments	Split the enterprise into units with the more successful sold to strategic foreign partners; the rest to private investors
5. Hollóházi Porcelángyár	484.1	Porcelain	Strategic foreign partner
6. Hungar-Hotels	10935.6	Hotels and catering	Public sale and strategic foreign partner
7. Hungexpo	1654.0	Exhibitions and foreign trade	Strategic foreign partner
8. IBUSZ	2144.3	Tourism, financial services, and foreign currency	Public sale of 37% of shares
9. IDEX	4400.0	Foreign trade in industrial products	Public sale and strategic foreign partner
10. INTERGLOB	1062.0	Transport and packing	Strategic foreign partner
11. KUER Nyomda	1566.1	Printing	Strategic foreign partner
12. Kunep	515.0	Housing and social construction	Strategic foreign partner
13. MEH Tröszt	3769.0	Scrap collection and conversion	N/A
14. Pannonia Szállodavállalat	6201.0	Hotels and catering	Public sale and strategic foreign partner
15. Pannonplast	4122.3	Industrial and household plastics	Strategic foreign partner
16. PIETRA	973.5	Building materials	Strategic foreign partner
17. Richter Gedeon	17481.4	Pharmaceuticals, cosmetics and other chemicals	Strategic foreign partner
18. Salgglas	1724.3	Glass	Strategic foreign partner
19. TRITEX	694.3	Clothing wholesaler	Strategic foreign partner
20. Volán-TEFU	2404.9	Transport	Strategic foreign partner
TOTAL	73890.8		

Source: SPA – Background information to the First Privatization Programme, September, 1990; and SPA Newsletter, January 1991.

TABLE 9.2 Second Privatization Programme

First Group

Name of SOE (holding)	Book value of assets (HUF mn)	Number of Assoc's (end-'89)	Number of Employees (end-'89)	Description
1. Casvaipari Vállalat	1121.96	12	2268	Screws producer
2. Csepel Müvek Ruhaipari Gép- és Krárgy.	1105.49	10	1977	Garments, industrial machinery, and bicycles
3. Elegant Május 1. Ruhagyar	699.34	4	2356	Garment producer
4. Élelmiszergépipari Vállalat	1094.27	7	2657	Food processing machinery
5. Épitögépgyárto Vállalat	333.05	12	2268	Construction machinery
6. GANZ Szerszámgyár	452.52	5	208	Machine tools
7. GRABOCENTER Sz. V.V.	2633.60	4	2837	Cotton weaving and synthetic leather
8. Információtechnikai V.	456.67	33	502	Information technology
9. MOM	2030.10	14	3738	Optical products
10. SZATMAR Butorgyár	331.14	6	887	Furniture
11. Szék- és Kárpitosipari Vállalat	404.83	11	1802	Chairs and upholstery
12. Szerszámgépipari Müvek	2947.05	17	3610	Machine tools
Total	13610.02	135	25110	

Second Group

Name of SOE (holding)	Book value of assets (HUF mn)	Description
1. Bajatex	562.26	Textiles
2. Budaflax	n.a.	Textiles
3. Budapest Harisnyagyár	815.59	Textiles
4. Budapest Butoripari Vállalat	868.50	Furniture
5. Budapest Finomkötöttérugyár	364.21	Textiles
6. DUNA Élelmiszer és Vegyiáru Kereskedelmi Vállalat	1052.83	Wholesaler in food and chemicals
7. Hodmezövásárhelyi Mezögép	384.93	Engineering
8. Magyar Aszfalt	848.00	Road construction
9. Nyiregyházi Mezögrzd. Gépgyár Vállalat	371.55	Engineering
10. REANAL Finomvegyszergyár	1013.42	Chemicals
11. Üvegipari Müvek	5000.29	Glass
Total	11281.88	

Source: SPA reports to the Hungarian Parliament

located, and to allow employees their statutory right (see below) to bid for up to 10 per cent of the shares in the companies at a reduced rate.

Table 9.1 gives details of the enterprises included in the First Privatization Programme, their respective book values and the proposed form of privatization. No consolidated data on the progress of privatization in these cases is available, since the programme which brought them together has been abandoned and they are now being handled on a case-by-case basis.

The Second Privatization Programme (Table 9.2) was launched in March 1991. Its aim was to tackle the problem of the 'empty shell' companies which had been created through spontaneous privatization, where a significant portion (over 50 per cent) of the former enterprise's assets had been transferred as a contribution in kind or leased to subsidiary companies or joint ventures and where, in the most extreme cases, the former enterprise had become no more than a holding company. Some 80 such enterprises were to be included in the programme; enterprises which had already drawn up transformation and privatization plans, and enterprises which for other reasons ('reasons of national interest') were not included in the government's privatization plans at least in the immediate future, were excluded. An initial, pilot group of 12 such enterprises was proposed (see table) with combined assets worth almost HUF 14 bn spread over 115 smaller companies, but again, the programme failed to produce results. One of the main reasons, in this case, was that closer examination of the shell companies revealed a morass of legal and financial problems. Again, a case-by-case approach has been adopted by the SPA; some of the sub-companies created with enterprise assets have been or will be privatized separately or absorbed into other programmes (self-privatization, etc.), and those of the erstwhile enterprise headquarters which cannot be privatized will be put into the hands of the receivers.

Other 'active' privatization programmes were proposed in spring and summer 1991 for specific industries, notably 35 enterprises in the construction industry and the 15 so-called 'historic' state vineyards, while another targeted a number of enterprises in sectors badly affected by the collapse of the CMEA and Soviet markets. Consultants and investment banks were called in to assess the privatization prospects for each case. However, although SPA reports in 1992 (SPA 1992c: 7,9) still mentioned these under separate rubrics as SPA 'programmes', in practice they have been abandoned and the firms dealt with individually or absorbed into other schemes.

In the hope of accelerating privatization, the SPA started a programme of investor-initiated privatization in February 1991. The initial interest in this programme was widespread, with almost 250 offers registered in the first few months, mainly from foreign investors, and covering a wide range of 'packages' ranging from a few shares to entire enterprises. Nevertheless, in these cases also progress remained slow. The SPA's attempts to introduce competition into the process by calling an open or closed tender frequently revealed that the foreign investors were reluctant to compete, and a further complication, reported in one of the SPA's own documents (SPA 1992c), was that the management of the enterprises in question tended to drag their heels, which meant that they had to be taken under the administrative control of the state. At the end of 1991, around 20 cases had been completed, and a further 70–80 were under consideration. Following the introduction of 'self-privatization', however, this programme likewise faded into oblivion.

4. Decentralized privatization

Reporting on its activities after the first six months, the SPA said that 'In the process of privatization ... the role of enterprise-initiated self privatization — or so-called spontaneous privatization — has been the most significant'. The same report described at length the disadvantages of 'administratively prescribed and enforced privatization', and gave pride of place to the task of 'making the process of spontaneous privatization smoother and better organized' (cited in Voszka 1991c). This has remained the case.

Partly as a result of this awareness, and in an effort to harness the momentum of enterprise-initiated privatization, but partly also as a response to the increasing criticism of its slow and bureaucratic approach which peaked in a wave of controversy in the summer of 1991, the SPA announced its intention to introduce 'self-privatization'. In June 1991 the SPA invited applications from independent consultancy firms with a minimum HUF 10 mn capital and experience in asset valuation to participate in the first round of decentralized privatization. Eighty-four consultants were selected and signed a 'framework contract' with the SPA to undertake the corporatization (transformation) and privatization of a selected number of enterprises virtually independently of the SPA, which in turn undertook to approve the transformations within 30 days and to intervene only in the event of gross anomalies. Enterprises eligible for inclusion in the first round were small to medium-sized, with up to 300 employees and an annual turnover of no more than 300 million HUF. The initial list involved just over 300 such enterprises, but this was gradually extended, so that by June 1992, nine months after the launch of the programme, their number totalled 437 and the combined book value of their assets was around HUF 20 bn (Zsubori 1992b).

By the end of March 1992, 66 of the 84 consultancy firms had entered into a contract with some 292 enterprises, but the number of transformations was only 43, while actual privatizations numbered no more than five, four of which were employee buy-outs. Given that the consultants' recompense was tied to completed privatization transactions, with additional bonuses for transactions completed before 31 March 1992, after which commission decreased on a monthly sliding scale, these results were somewhat disappointing. However, since in the vast majority of cases the process had at least got under way — a fact which was deemed a major success in itself — the overall results were considered sufficiently promising for a second round of decentralized privatization to be initiated in May 1992, this time involving larger enterprises with an annual turnover of up to HUF 1 bn and up to 1000 employees. It was hoped that around 600 enterprises would participate in this round, but by the end of December 1992 their number stood at 278, although the total book value of their assets was more substantial, at around HUF 70 bn (Zsubori 1992b).

Figures up to December 1992 (see Table 9.3), showed that out of the total of just over 700 firms concerned, only 50 had been privatized, 47 in the first batch and only 3 in the second. Foreign capital was involved in 42 cases, the rest coming from domestic investors, mainly from employees of the firms. Of the firms participating in the first round, some 200 had transformed into corporate entities, but only a dozen in the second round had got as far as preparing articles of association (Zsubori 1992c). The first round failed to meet its optimistic completion deadline of 31 March 1993, although there was a sharp upswing — from 80 to 167 — in the number of transactions concluded during February and March. Progress in the case of firms in the second round remains slow, with only eight sale contracts concluded as of the end of May 1993.

Some of the problems cited both by the SPA and by some of the consultancy firms in connection with 'self-privatization' include the time required in preparation of the transformation process[16], compounded by delays — of up to several months — over the registration of the new company, mainly as a consequence of the fact that the Court of Registration is heavily overburdened. Another problem has been the time taken to ensure that the process is 'competitive', including the invitation of bids from enterprise employees, for which 30 days is allowed, and the further delays caused by all too frequent conflicts with the local municipalities over shares/dividends due to them in respect of land and property belonging to the municipality but used by the enterprise. In addition, the consultants have been understandably fearful of being accused of selling at too low a price (not to mention the fact that their commission is related to the price achieved); 80 per cent of the nominal value of the enterprise is stipulated in the case of the second

TABLE 9.3 Self-privatization up to the end of 1992

	First round	Second round
Number of enterprises taking part	423	277
Of which (per cent):		
Contract concluded	85.3	63.2
Transformed	53.2	11.6
Sold	17.7	–
Undergoing bankruptcy procedures	8.7	7.9
Liquidated	12.1	4.3
Book value of the enterprises (HUF bn)	30.786	67.398
For transformed enterprises:		
Original book value of assets	16.846	11.118
Revalued assets	20.805	12.197
Sectoral distribution of enterprises (per cent)		
Industry	35.2	71.1
Trade and other services	59.8	22.0
Other	5.0	6.9
Income from selling the SPA shareholding (HUF bn)	3.057	–
Of which (HUF bn):		
To foreign owners	0.983	–
To domestic owners	2.074	–
Of which, to workers:	0.963	–

Source: Pénzügykutató Rt. (1993)

group, but there are indications that the SPA (Zsubori 1992c) is willing to accept as little as 60 per cent in the case of firms in the first group if, at the end of the competitive tendering process, this is the value accorded to the firm by the 'market'. There also seems to be a growing awareness that procrastination can only reduce the value of the assets, and the chances of finding investors for them, a fact which is becoming painfully clear as a growing number of the firms originally included in the programmes have been forced to declare themselves bankrupt in the course of 1992 as a result of the strict bankruptcy law which came into force at the beginning of the year, or are now in the hands of the receivers[17].

While it was perhaps naive on the part of those responsible for privatization in Hungary to expect a major breakthrough as a result of decentralization (especially since the combined assets involved so far amount to no more than 5 per cent of the total assets in state-ownership), it is generally felt that 'privatizated privatization' is the most practical and least bureaucratic approach. There are plans to extend the programme further and to introduce measures to enable more domestic investors to participate; interest rates on borrowing (notably the so-called 'existence-loans' or E-loans, specifically introduced to promote domestic capital investment in privatization) have already been reduced, and a guarantee fund was set up in December 1992, thus taking some of the pressure off commercial banks and enabling them to ease the collateral requirements on smaller investors. Other measures include the recent introduction of 'privatization by leasing' (discussed in more detail below), which the SPA plans to extend to include firms in the 'self-privatization' programmes.

5. Pre-privatization

Another important task assigned to the SPA was that of privatizing the retail, catering and consumer services sectors, legislation for which was drawn up by the previous government and enacted in September 1990. Privatization in these sectors was expected to proceed quickly and smoothly, but the process was soon submerged in administrative problems and political conflict, while the would-be small entrepreneurs failed to emerge in the numbers originally hoped for.

The first problem was establishing the number of units suitable for privatization according to the statutory provisions, which specified a limit of 10 employees in the case of retail outlets and 15 in the case of catering establishments. In addition, outlets belonging to a chain of stores, those 'for the management of which special qualifications are required', e.g. pharmacies, pawnbrokers, travel agencies, and hard currency shops, along with several other shops operating in factories, prisons, and army premises, were excluded. The number finally arrived at by this process of elimination was just over 10,000, relatively low by comparison with the 53,500 outlets registered statistically.

The next, and rather more problematic issue to emerge was the complex network of ownership relationships involved. In over 70 per cent of the cases, the businesses concerned were founded by the local councils, but managed by state-owned enterprises, which in turn paid a rent (although this was mainly nominal) to 'Real Estate Holding Companies' set up by the councils; the remaining 30 per cent were founded by the SOEs, but again often using premises belonging to the councils. Some 4,700 of the outlets in the programme had been leased by the enterprises to private entrepreneurs under the measures introduced in the 1980s. As a result, privatization in the majority of cases meant not the sale of the assets but the sale of the right to lease the business (since the SPA acquired the right to dispose only of whatever had 'belonged' to the enterprises, while the property itself remained in the hands of the municipalities).

The obstacles were manifold. On the one hand, the enterprises had little interest in cooperating since they would lose their function as 'middleman'; on the other, the municipalities, no longer relying on funding allocated by the state, as the old councils had, were expected instead to generate income for their activities from the property assigned to them under the new legislation[18]. Financial pressures to increase the rent on their premises (to 'realistic', though sometimes to exaggerated levels) collided, however, with the legislation providing that the rent on the free-hold stated at the time of the auction remain static for a period of 10 years. Protracted legal battles ensued[19].

The auction mechanism was duly set up at the beginning of 1991, but the promised credit scheme, 'existence-loans', devised to facilitate the purchase of businesses under the pre-privatization programme by Hungarian individuals and small groups (foreigners were not allowed to participate in the auctions), was not launched until March 1991. By the end of June, only around 500 auctions had taken place, less than 300 of which had resulted in the sale of the freehold lease (and only 70 of the property itself). Parliament passed a resolution requiring the SPA, together with the Ministry of Industry and Trade, to take steps to speed up the valuation process of the businesses and preparation of the auctions, and to examine possibilities of inviting those 4,700 traders currently operating businesses under contracts to buy those outlets at the asking price without having to participate in open bidding.

The latter proposal created another spate of legal wrangles, which were only resolved in spring 1992, with the enactment of legislation permitting sale without auction, by which time most of the contracts — some 3,000 — had already expired. It is expected that the majority of the remaining 1,700 will be privatized in this way, many through employee or management buyouts, since the process involves less risk than bidding at auction.

Other problems included the general lack of demand on the part of the Hungarian public, especially as the recession deepened and retail sales continued to fall; in addition, many would-be entrepreneurs preferred to start from scratch rather than buy former state-owned assets, particularly given the problems emerging regarding the behaviour of the municipalities and the uncertainty which that engendered. Many others (Félix 1991) held back in the hope that the asking price would be reduced if the first auctions failed, while still others were unable to obtain borrowing facilities, either due to the tough terms and high collateral required under the E-loans scheme, or simply because they were not deemed creditworthy.

Simplified procedures, introduced towards the end of 1991, including the introduction of the possibility to buy through a kind of hire-purchase arrangement

TABLE 9.4 Results of pre-privatization in 1991, 1992

	1991	1992	Total
Registered enterprises	373	44	417
Registered shops	10,240	520	10,760
Privatized shops (incl. leased)	3133	4504	7637
Gross sales proceeds (HUF bn)	5.1	6.1	11.2
Sales price as a percentage of the initial asking price	134.0	156.4	144.6

Source: Pénzügykutató Rt. (1993)

(also, somewhat confusingly, called 'leasing') which reduced the pressure on small investors to raise the cash or take on crippling loan repayments at the outset, did help accelerate pre-privatization and the year-end figures showed a marked improvement in the number of transactions concluded: 2,120 out of a total of over 3,200 auctions held.

Further delays were caused in the summer of 1992 by the announcement of forthcoming measures to ease interest rates on borrowing under the E-loan scheme and to institute a guarantee fund to enable the commercial banks to reduce collateral requirements on the loans administered. Interest rates on E-loans were finally reduced in March 1992 from 75 per cent to 60 per cent of the central bank's base rate, and the ceiling on the amount borrowed was removed. This was duly followed by an upswing in borrowing; while in 1991 the total amount of E-loans granted by the banks was around HUF 1 bn, the amount borrowed in the first nine months of 1992 totalled HUF 5.3 bn (*Heti Világgazdaság* 1992).

As of 1 October 1992, the SPA had almost fulfilled its obligation, in the strict sense of the Pre-privatization Act, to 'initiate' the process in all cases by 18 September. In 9,317 cases (out of the total of 10,193 registered up to then) the assets had been valued and auctions announced. However, only just over one half of these (5,214) had actually changed hands, leaving the fate of 49 per cent of the outlets still unsettled. The revised E-loan scheme has played a major part in the transactions completed; out of the 3,378 shops sold through auction, E-loans were used in 2,224 cases. (*Heti Világgazdaság* 1992). Table 9.4 summarizes the position up to the end of 1992. At the end of March 1993, by which time the SPA hoped to have completed the pre-privatization process, just over 75 per cent (7,637) of outlets had changed hands. In 70 per cent of cases, however, only the leasehold had been purchased.

6. Compensation and related matters

6.1 RESTITUTION

Following the election of the new coalition government in Hungary, one of the issues which dominated political debate was that of restitution of property expropriated under the former regime and the restoration of pre-war property rights. Not only was the government committed 'morally' to settling the issue, it was important also in the sense that until ownership of assets was reasonably settled, it would be difficult to begin the privatization process. This proved to be considerably more complicated than was at first assumed, and the protracted legal and procedural debate which ensued has affected the course of privatization in a multiplicity of ways.

The restitution debate centred at first primarily on the question of land reform, a very sensitive issue in agrarian Hungary, and in the smallholders' lobby within the governing coalition. But it soon became clear that restitution could not be made in respect of agricultural land without dealing with the former owners of other types of real estate (e.g. housing, business premises, etc.). As a result of a ruling to this effect by the Constitutional Court[20] at the beginning of October 1990, it was decided, somewhat reluctantly on the part of the coalition partners, that restitution in kind (of the actual properties formerly owned) should be ruled out. The only exception made has been the relatively clear-cut case of properties formerly belonging to churches and religious communities, where restitution of buildings and real estate (not productive assets — e.g. agricultural land) will be granted, provided that these are to be used for religious, educational, social, or health-care activities (Varga 1992). Out of the 6,000 claims received from 13 religious communities, 400 had been settled by the end of 1992.

In the other cases, former owners — or their direct heirs — receive interest-bearing compensation vouchers which can be used to purchase state-owned assets, including housing (from the local municipalities) and land (from the agricultural cooperatives), or preferential shares in selected enterprises on the Stock Exchange. Alternatively, vouchers may be used to obtain a fixed life-annuity or pension from the Social Security. They may also be sold freely, and a lively secondary market for the vouchers has developed. The ceiling on individual compensation claims is HUF 5 mn.

Due to the complexity of the issue, the first Compensation Act did not come into force until August 1991; the process of setting up the National Office for Compensation and the Settlement of Damages and the infrastructure for processing compensation claims, issuing vouchers and establishing the mechanisms for public auctions has meant further delays. Under the first Compensation Act, which covers cases of expropriation or confiscation of property from 1949 onwards, a total of 827,026 claims was received.

In the course of the debate on restitution it was recognized that, in the interests of equity, those who had suffered political injustice between 1939 and 1949 at the hands of the pre-communist regime should also be entitled to compensation; there was also a strong case for granting compensation in cases of persons 'deprived of their lives or their liberty for political reasons'. Further legislation was accordingly passed, in the course of 1992, to provide for these two groups. Under the Second Compensation Act, 71,248 claims have been registered, 57,710 of which are from Hungarians living abroad; under the Third, some 330,000 claims had been received at the end of 1992, and a further 20,000 are expected (*Heti Világgazdaság* 1993a). The Ministry of Finance estimates that the final value of compensation vouchers issued will total approximately HUF 60 bn.

AGRICULTURE

The sector possibly most affected by the legislation on compensation is agriculture. This is partly due to the volume of compensation claims which related to agricultural land, 35 per cent of which was farmed by cooperatives[21], but it was also affected in the less direct, but no less significant sense that the long delays in passing and implementing legislation on compensation meant corresponding delays in settling the issue of land reform in general and the reform of cooperatives in particular. When the first Compensation Act came into effect, Parliament declared a moratorium preventing agricultural cooperatives and state farms from changing their legal status (transforming to corporate entities, a process which many had begun, using the provisions of the Transformation Act) before 30 November 1991. This was then extended until the end of the year, but it was not until early in January 1992 that the Law on Cooperatives (which also applied to non-agricultural cooperatives in retail trade, industry, housing, etc.) and legislation governing the procedures of their transformation — the so-called Transition Act — were passed.

As a result of this legislation, the agricultural cooperatives were faced with a tight timetable in which to carry out a complex series of reform manoeuvres, beginning with the process of asset valuation, after which the ownership title to land and other assets had to be allocated to individual members — or their heirs — and a portion of their land assigned for auction under the compensation law. In recognition of the fact that membership of the cooperative had for many years been compulsory, the legislation allowed for members to withdraw which, as one observer has pointed out (Félix 1992a), is very close to being another form of compensation. Such persons are able to stake their claim in land or in vouchers entitling them to bid for physical assets of the cooperative in a two-stage auction process. This phase of the process was expected to be completed by the middle of 1992. By 31 January 1993, the cooperatives were to have completed their transformation process, the precise nature of which would depend on the decision of the members (Félix 1992a).

In the event, while 85-90 per cent of the former agricultural cooperatives had managed to complete their transformation by January 1993, it appears that a surprisingly large number have decided to continue operating as cooperatives and have re-formed according to the new legislation. This was to some extent expected, given the relatively small average size of the farms (4.5 hectares) obtained by individuals and the advanced age of the majority (around 70 per cent) of former cooperative members, making individual farming largely unfeasible. It seems, however, that this development has also been influenced by the bankruptcy law; almost a quarter of the cooperatives have either declared themselves bankrupt or are in the process of liquidation. The creditors have tended, in cases where agreement has been reached, to opt for keeping the cooperatives' assets intact, thus effectively restricting the choices open to individual members (Bonyhádi 1993).

The process of auctioning land subject to the compensation law began on 24 August 1992. By the deadline for registering compensation claims specifically related to agricultural land, 15 August, the Compensation Office had received

129,000 claims; this was only 15 per cent of those potentially eligible. In total, 47 million gold crowns' worth of land has been made available for auction in exchange for compensation vouchers[22]. At the end of December 1992, a total of 19,638 persons had acquired land through auction. The process accelerated at the beginning of 1993, and the total had jumped to 30,000 by 8 February, although this still represents only a small fraction of the total land to be auctioned. The process was supposed to have been completed by the end of the first quarter of 1993 (*Heti Világgazdaság* 1993a), but the end of 1993 turned out to be a more realistic target.

The privatization of state farms is only marginally less complicated than that of the cooperatives, and here too there have been considerable delays; it was hoped that the process would be completed by the end of September 1992, but in reality it has only just begun.

In Hungary, almost 20 per cent of agricultural land was owned by 130 state farms, whose combined assets are estimated to be worth around HUF 100 bn. In spring 1992, 106 farms were placed under the administration of the SPA, which appointed a 'commissioner' (in most cases the director of the farm itself) to draw up decentralization proposals for the purpose of dividing the farms up into smaller units potentially capable of operating as independent businesses[23]. Fifteen of the farms had already transformed (10 of them under the self-privatization programme); six are currently in the hands of the receivers, and three are being wound up completely. In the autumn of 1992, the government decided that 24 of the state farms — principally those with genetic research facilities, forests, and one fish farm — should remain at least partially in state-ownership in the longer term; these have now been transferred to the State Asset Management Company (see below) (*Heti Világgazdaság* 1993a; Kopint-Datorg, 24 Sept, 1992).

In theory at least, everything else is to be sold off. As of December 1992, it was estimated that former state farm assets worth between HUF 7 and 8 bn (out of a total of approximately 33 bn)[24] had been sold to new owners through the decentralization process, and the transformation of the rest is expected to be completed by the end of April 1993. However, there are certain complications. Employees of state farms are each to receive 20 gold crowns' worth of land in compensation, and it is not yet clear how many hectares this will involve. Moreover, while buildings, machinery, vineyards, orchards, etc. may be sold, the land itself is to be leased out, but in the absence of a functioning agricultural land market the prices and procedures for leasing have proved difficult to settle. At the same time, potential investors — particularly the handful of foreign investors who have registered interest (Félix 1993) — find it difficult to understand why they will be unable to buy the land, and this will remain unclear until Parliament passes the Land Act, debate on which has yet to take place[25].

Overall, despite the problems and the complexity of the legal, financial and organizational issues involved, the land ownership reform currently taking place is expected to prove even more radical than the reform which took place in the post-war period. However, although around 800,000 new landowners will emerge as a result of this process, placing around 90 per cent of all farmland in private ownership, it is expected that collective farming — whether as a cooperative or as a company — will continue to play an important part in Hungarian agriculture (see *Heti Világgazdaság* 1993b).

HOUSING

Another area affected by compensation is that of housing privatization. According to the statistical data for 1986, out of a total of 3,891,000 dwellings in Hungary, only just over 20 per cent (782,900) were owned by the state and administered by the local councils. The rather low proportion of public housing stock in Hungary compared to other former socialist countries was due to a variety of factors. First, much of the housing stock in Hungary had never been nationalized; second, as early as 1969, a government decree introduced the possibility for tenants to buy the flats they rented from the state; third, a sequence of measures introduced as a result of the liquidity crisis in Hungary in the early 1980s, by which time it had become clear that the government was increasingly unable to build sufficient dwellings to meet demands, led to a rapid increase in private housing construction to the extent that by 1988, out of a total of 50,566 new dwellings constructed in that year, 32,462 were built privately as opposed to 18,104 by the state and housing cooperatives (*Statisztikai Zsebkönyv* 1990, Central Statistical Office).

Privatization only began to gain momentum, however, towards the end of the 1980s, when successive modifications to the existing legislation extended the range of 'privatizable' housing and introduced financial terms favouring the tenants of such properties. As a consequence of this, the number of dwellings sold saw a rapid increase during 1990 and 1991. In addition, the Compensation Act of June 1991 made it possible to use compensation vouchers towards the purchase of housing. While this has undoubtedly contributed to the momentum of housing privatization, it is not yet clear to what extent compensation vouchers have been used for this purpose (see Szabó 1992).

For the municipalities, to which the ownership and management of former 'council' housing stock was transferred in September 1991, housing privatization has presented a number of problems. First, the income from the rent paid by tenants in council housing had for decades failed to cover the cost of repairs and maintenance; as a result, the housing stock inherited by the municipalities is in a very poor state of repair, and some sources estimate that as many as 150,000 council homes nationwide had had no renovation work carried out on them since 1950 (Szabó 1992). The conditions of sale set down by law reflected this situation: housing which had been renovated more than 15 years ago could be sold at 15 per cent of its market value; where renovation had taken place over five years previously, the selling price was 30 per cent of market value, and if renovation work had been carried out within the previous five years, it could be sold for 40 per cent of its value. As a consequence, although the municipalities had an interest in selling off housing stock as a means of reducing the burden of long overdue and costly renovations inherited, the income obtained from privatization has not been substantial. The use of compensation vouchers reduces the municipalities' income still further, since they are bound to accept these vouchers at face value plus accrued interest, while the market value of the vouchers is only 75-80 per cent of their face value. In addition, it is not yet clear what the municipalities will be able to use the vouchers for (see Szabady 1992).

Against the background of soaring property prices and business rents, especially in the commercial districts of Budapest, the former tenants seem undeterred by the burden of renovations which falls to them and the level of interest on the part of tenants to purchase their homes has continued undiminished[26]. However, fears that the best of the housing — and possibly as much as 50-70 per cent of former public housing stock in the capital — will be sold off, leaving the unsaleable remainder in the hands of the municipalities, have led to the suspension of sales in many localities, with the municipalities using their powers of discretion as owners to draw up lists of properties which may not be sold. This particularly affects properties in Budapest city centre, where there is some controversy over the possible intention of municipalities (i.e. the district councils within the city) to stall the process in the hope of being able to relocate incumbent tenants and provide much more remunerative accommodation for businesses through the sale or lease of the premises.

New and long-awaited legislation regulating the sale and rental of public sector housing and business premises was passed at the beginning of July. Although it makes uniform provision and thus eliminates the worst of the discrepancies between the actions of different local municipalities — e.g. the level of rent increases, arbitrary decision on which properties to sell and which to retain[27] — it is not yet clear how far it will go towards resolving the problems outlined above.

7. Institutional ownership and management of corporate assets

Several forms of institutional ownership of assets previously in state hands have developed in Hungary; these are worth mentioning here either because they have had (or are likely to have) a direct impact on the privatization process or because they represent a significant part (not least in terms of the considerable value of the assets involved) of the emerging jigsaw puzzle of ownership reform as a whole.

The first and most obvious case is that of the local municipalities, to which the transfer of assets worth an estimated HUF 3000 bn is now nearing completion. The process began with the Law on Municipalities passed at the end of September 1990, which transferred to the new local authorities real estate which had formerly been under the control of the councils or council institutions, with the exception of historical monuments and nature reserves. The second stage of the process took rather longer; it was another year before legislation on the transfer of assets to the municipalities was passed (September 1991), and even longer before it could be implemented. According to the provisions of this second law, public housing stock and non-residential premises were transferred to the new local authorities, along with local public services such as water and drainage, chimney sweeping, undertakers and burial services, real estate management, street cleaning and garbage removal. As illustrated in the foregoing sections of this chapter, the sequencing and implementation of other aspects of ownership reform and privatization often collided with the transfer of assets to the municipalities, resulting in inevitable delays, legal wrangles and political conflicts, not to mention considerable difficulties for the financial management of the local authorities. It is likely to be some time yet before the situation settles.

The Social Security service (*Társadalombiztosítás*) is also to receive a substantial portion of assets through two separate processes. First, in its Property Policy Guidelines, finally updated and passed in July 1992, the government pledged the transfer of assets worth HUF 300 bn to the Social Security over the next two years; this is most likely to be in the form of shares in companies in the portfolio of the State Property Agency and the State Asset Management Company (see below). Before any transfer of this type could take place, the organizational structures and regulations on investment and management of the assets had first to be established. This part of the process is virtually complete, and the bodies which will handle the Social Security's asset portfolio were expected to be functioning by early 1993, once the government had approved the regulatory framework. In late November 1992, the SPA offered the Social Security an initial package of shares worth HUF 8 bn in 28 firms, but objections were raised since the majority of the firms in question belonged to 'crisis sectors'. The Social Security administration has therefore accepted only a small fraction of the share package initially offered. It is expected that the Social Security will farm out the management of part of its portfolio to private asset management companies. Even when the transfer has been completed successfully, it is unlikely that the income from the shares will exceed HUF 25–30 bn annually, which, compared to the Social Security service's annual budget of HUF 600 bn, is scarcely significant, while the Social Security deficit currently stands at tens of billions of HUF (Zsubori 1993: 13).

The Social Security funds were also owed some HUF 94 bn (as of December 1992) by enterprises, and this figure is increasing. The moratorium permitted by the bankruptcy legislation with regard to payments by enterprises which declare themselves bankrupt, combined with the fact that the Social Security is well down the list of priority creditors to whom payment is due if a firm goes into liquidation, mean that the prospects of reclaiming these debts are slim. In an effort to alleviate the situation, the Social Security 'Exchange' was set up in August 1992, enabling debtor firms to offer real estate or other fixed assets or equity in lieu of payment. These may then either be sold to cover the debt or kept in 'pawn' until the debt, rescheduled by mutual agreement, has been paid in full.

The Treasury Property Management Organization was set up by the Finance Ministry in December 1990 to manage property formerly used by the Soviet Army, by communist political organizations and by the disbanded workers' militia[28]. Little information is available on the properties under the management of this body, on their value, or on how many of the 'usable' buildings have since been requisitioned or acquired by ministries and local authorities[29]. In May 1992 the government issued regulations governing the use and sale of properties 'vacated as a result of the withdrawal of the Soviet armed forces', but it appears that attempts to sell the properties met with little success (Szántó 1992). In addition, the legislation on long-term state property passed in August 1992 transferred to the Treasury shareholdings of between 25 and 50 per cent in state farms with gene-banks for seed development, and some state forests. Legislation regulating the use of Treasury assets is still awaited.

By far the most important institution in the context of privatization and ownership reform is the State Asset Management Company (SAMCo) set up in October 1992 to manage assets remaining in state-ownership in the long term.

The notion of setting up a separate body to manage state-owned corporate assets was first aired in the spring of 1991 by Finance Minister Mihály Kupa in a draft bill on privatization strategy supplementing his four-year economic programme (Kocsis 1991a). In the political climate at that time, it should be remembered, there was widespread dissatisfaction regarding the progress of privatization and increasing tension with respect to the powers of the SPA, which — in the absence of coherent government strategy on privatization to replace the twice-extended Temporary Property Policy Guidelines — had found itself in the position of being the *de facto* policy-making body on privatization issues. The idea of establishing a 'State Ownership Institute' which would divest the SPA of decision-making powers over certain state assets ('A Pénzügyministérium...') was thus perceived (and perhaps to some extent intended) as a direct attack on the SPA. The concept, predictably, gave rise to heated debate. The SPA published a report (Karsai 1991: 13) defending its activities, disputing the logic of the Finance Ministry and warning of the danger that setting up a new and all-powerful institution would mean not a devolution or redistribution of power, but an even greater centralization or 'statification' of the privatization process than the SPA had often been accused of. The Finance Minister also came under attack from many quarters, suspected of attempting to bring privatization under his direct control and thus build up a dangerous concentration of power (Kocsis 1991a).

After a period of uncomfortable silence on the issue of privatization in the autumn, the Finance Ministry finally published its draft 'Government Strategy on Ownership and Privatization' in September 1991. The preamble of this document stated that 'privatization cannot be based on centralized considerations...the power-base of the state supervisory system set up 18 months ago has already become too broad...' (Kocsis 1991a), and the bill outlined concrete proposals for a body which would separate institutionally 'the task of exercising state-ownership and that of executing privatization'. Rounds of ministerial bargaining then ensued to reach agreement on the nature and status of the proposed State Ownership Institute (SOI), and it was finally agreed that the new body should have responsibility for managing assets which were to remain in state-ownership in the longer term. A list of these was to be drawn up by the various ministries for government approval. Meanwhile the SPA, in somewhat modified form, would continue as a separate entity, alongside rather than responsible to the SOI, taking responsibility for privatization.

The next stage of the debate was concerned with two main issues. The first was whether the organizational framework of the proposed body should be a traditional budget-funded government institution, or whether, following the model of some Western countries, it should be a commercial holding company. Under a barrage of objections to the first alternative, mainly on the grounds that it would provide the government administration with too many opportunities to influence the SOI, and therefore also the sectors of the economy under its management, the government opted for the latter (Kocsis 1991b). Other reservations included the fact that the leadership of the new State Ownership Company was to be selected by the Prime Minister, and the fear that although it would be more difficult to dictate from above the economic operation of individual firms, there would be little safeguard against politically motivated redistribution of revenue from these companies (Kocsis 1991b).

The second bone of contention was the reasoning behind the proposals submitted by the ministries regarding which enterprises or 'strategic' sectors should be retained in state-ownership; the problem of the extent to which political and personal interests could influence the drafting of the list, rather than 'strategic' considerations which are in any case not always easy to identify; and the problem of the likely effect and possible dangers for the economy of long term state-ownership in general (Karsai 1992b).

However, despite the controversy surrounding the government's motivation in setting up such an organization, it must be acknowledged that so far only Hungary has recognized the need to establish some form of coherent asset management strategy for property which — whether simply due to the fact that privatization has not proceeded as quickly as was hoped or expected in 1991, or as a result of genuine strategic decisions to retain a state share in certain sectors or industries — will remain in state hands in the longer term.

Legislation on the new body, now entitled the State Asset Management Company (SAMCo) came into effect on 28 August 1992. The new 'super-holding company' will take the form of a private joint stock company in which the state is the exclusive shareholder, headed by an 11-member board of directors working in liaison with a 7-member supervisory committee. After some considerable delay and more than one 'false alarm', the list of companies to be transferred to SAMCo was finally published in the *Hungarian Gazette* along with the text of the legislation, and administrative arrangements began for the launch of the new body within the tight 60-day deadline stipulated by law (26 October 1992).

The companies to be transferred to the new holding company have been selected according to the following criteria:

1. companies of strategic importance or vital to the national economy;
2. companies which provide an important public service or which can only operate efficiently within a 'uniform research, production or distribution system';
3. companies whose privatization would be an exceptionally long and complicated process (Kopint-Datorg 1992: 2).

According to the legislation, the status of the companies under the control of SAMCo is to be reviewed on a two-yearly basis. The present list involves 157 companies, 36 of which are to remain in 100 per cent state-ownership; most of these are organizations engaged in activities related to defence and criminal justice, but the list also includes the state gambling company, Szerencsejáték Rt., the National Educational Textbook Publishing Company, the Hungarian

Railways (MAV), the Post Office and a newspaper publishing company. The list also includes major shareholdings in the energy sector, infrastructure and public utilities, basic materials and manufacturing, the engineering and chemicals industry, and pharmaceuticals. The state will also retain minority shares in 'traditional' Hungarian companies with internationally renowned brand names, such as the Herend and Zsolnay porcelain companies, Pick and Herz salami, the paprika-producing firms in Szeged and Kalocsa and the Tokaj wine-producing state farm. Others included are state farms with genetic research facilities or special breeding programmes, industrial, agricultural and water research institutes, sports facilities and cultural sector companies such as library supplies, film studios and film distribution, music publishers and two other publishing companies, the latter on the grounds that they provide a 'public service' (although this is seen by some as an indication of the government's desire to keep a considerable degree of control over Hungarian cultural life). For the time being the state is also to retain between 25 and 50 per cent shareholdings in financial institutions and insurance companies, but this is to be reduced to a maximum of 25 per cent by 1997.

Not all of these shareholdings are to be managed by SAMCo; a number of them are to be transferred to the Treasury (see above), while others will be the responsibility of the ministries, supervised by ministers without portfolio appointed for this purpose. The Ministry of the Environment, Water and Communications, for example, will be responsible for the railways, the Post Office and the national bus company, Volánbusz. The Ministry of Welfare will take charge of the Pomáz Institute of Occupational Therapy, while the Finance Ministry will manage Reorg (the successor to the old State Rehabilitation Organization), the Centre of Financial Institutions and the State Development Institute. The Ministry of International Economic Relations will have responsibility for two major companies involved in research and information services related to international trade, and the Ministry of Agriculture will look after companies handling animal waste processing, animal breeding, and quality control.

Table 9.5 gives a more detailed list of the companies, and the proportion of shares in each, which are to remain in state ownership in the long term.

The figures often quoted with respect to the value of the assets which will be transferred to SAMCo are somewhat confusing, since two distinct elements are involved. The first point to mention in this regard is that the assets of the companies will be transferred in their entirety to SAMCo, but only the portion which the state intends to retain in the long term is counted as the assets which make up the registered capital of the new body; this was estimated at between HUF 350 and 480 bn by Pál Teleki, the first director of SAMCo (Karsai 1992c), although others have placed the figure as high as 550 bn, and this was topped up by a contribution of HUF 2bn from the state budget. The other element is composed of the remainder, the 'privatizable' assets of the firms; these are estimated to be worth around HUF 1000 bn[30]. Around 110 of the 157 firms were still either just beginning or in the process of transformation (corporatization) at the beginning of 1993, and work has only recently begun at SAMCo to draw up full balance sheets of the firms (including the investments they hold in several hundred other companies), so it will be some time before a full and realistic financial

TABLE 9.5 Holdings by SAMCo and various ministries

SAMCo. (about 160 companies)		
Energy sector		
MOL plc	oil and gas	50% + 1 vote
MVM plc	electricity	50% + 1 vote
Mineralimpex plc		50% + 1 vote
Regional gas supply companies (5)		25% + 1 vote
Infrastructure, public utilities		
Regional water supply companies (5)		50% + 1 vote
Mahart Shipping Company		50% + 1 vote
Malév Hungarian Airlines		50% + 1 vote
Hungarocamion	road freight	50% + 1 vote
Matáv plc	telecommunications	50% + 1 vote
Hungarian Broadcasting Company		50% + 1 vote
Interlighter		25%
Basic materials and manufacturing		
Hungalu plc	aluminium	25% + 1 vote
Dunaferr	steel	25% + 1 vote
Chemicals		
Borsodchem Rt.		25% + 1 vote
Füzföi Nitrokémiai Ipartelepek		25% + 1 vote
Pharmaceutical companies		25% + 1 vote
Except: Richter Gedeon Rt.		50% + 1 vote
Protection of trade marks, security and other reasons (21 companies)		Between 5% and 100%
State Farms (with gene banks or other special features; incl. state forests; 45 companies altogether)		Between 25% + 1 vote and 100%; mostly 50% + 1 vote
Human infrastructure		
Publishing companies, film studios, etc. (20 companies)		Mostly 25% + 1 vote
Banks, financial institutions (10 companies)		Between 20% and 50% + 1 vote
Ministries (63 companies)		
Ministry of Transport, Communications and Water (32 companies)		Mostly 50% + 1 vote
Justice Ministry (12 companies)		100%
Defence Ministry (9 companies)		100%
Others (10 companies)		100% or 50% + 1 vote

Source: Magyar Közlöny, No. 88, August 28th 1992, reporting Government Decree 126/1992; and Hungarian Business Brief, September 1992

picture can be obtained. What is clear, however, is that the sheer volume of the assets in the hands of SAMCo is enormous, and that the impact the new organization will have on the economy as a whole will be significant.

Despite reassurances to the contrary from the Director of SAMCo, there are still widespread fears that the new holding company will, like its Italian counterpart, be open to political manipulation (Valentiny 1991,1992). Many leading economists (e.g. Tardos, the re-formed Blue Ribbon Commission — see Balassa 1992: 14.) argue that a more appropriate — and more 'market-oriented' — means of managing assets remaining in state-ownership in the long term would be to involve not one state-owned holding company, but several private asset-management firms. This may yet be an option open to SAMCo at a later date, perhaps in the course of the two-year review process, but such steps are unlikely to be taken until it is clear how much of the assets currently under its control can be privatized quickly, and what the prospects for the rest will be once restructuring requirements have been assessed. Although SAMCo has the right to privatize assets, it is unclear how it will relate to the SPA in these matters. At the same time, however, the government expects to receive revenue to the tune of HUF 34 bn from the organization in its first year of operation, which places the latter under considerable pressure to move quickly.

8. Recent developments — a turn-around in privatization policy?

The most recent developments in privatization policy and practice in Hungary seem to indicate a change in direction from the original, avowedly 'market-oriented' and revenue-centred privatization (sale of assets through a competitive bidding process) to more 'populist' methods and aims, with revenue to the government taking a less prominent role, at least in the shorter term. Before drawing general conclusions on the privatization process in Hungary, it is useful to examine briefly some of these new schemes and their objectives, and to assess their implications.

EMPLOYEE SHARE OWNERSHIP PROGRAMMES (ESOPs)

Provision was made for Employee Share Ownership in the Company Law and a basic regulatory framework set out in the original (1990) Temporary Property Policy Guidelines, which stated that Employee Share Ownership could be applied 'in an experimental way... in a few cases where the possibility presents itself', as a means of assisting the privatization of state assets. Up to 10 per cent (and in exceptional cases, 15 per cent) of enterprise assets are offered at preferential rates (50 per cent) for this purpose. Legislation on ESOPs was long delayed, and finally passed by Parliament in June 1992. However, the 'self-privatization' contract (autumn 1991) allowed specifically for priority to be given to bids from groups of employees wishing to set up such a scheme. The number of firms taking this option saw some increase as a consequence; at the end of 1991, however, only in 34 of the firms which had been privatized (6 per cent) was employee share ownership involved, while the average share owned by the employees was a mere 4.1 per cent, far below the 10 per cent allowed for by law (Vanicsek 1992). The progressive relaxation of borrowing terms, the introduction of further incentives and measures allowing the combination of ESOPs and other techniques (e.g. leasing, see below), along with the clarification of legal regulations (the law on state property passed in August 1992 placed even greater emphasis on employee ownership 'to extend the small property-owning section of society'), appear to have made ESOPs increasingly popular recently. Some degree of employee ownership has been involved in around half the cases of enterprises privatized under the self-privatization scheme alone, and the proportional share owned by employees has increased substantially. In more than a few instances, using a combination of ESOP and other techniques, employees have gained a majority shareholding in their companies. There are fears that extensive employee ownership will be detrimental to many firms, since the employee-owners are more interested in keeping their jobs secure and increasing wages, and this in many cases is delaying the painful but necessary restructuring of the firms. And it is principally on this that the success of the ESOP ventures will depend, since otherwise the value of the shares in their hands will rapidly decrease (Diczházi 1993).

PRIVATIZATION BY LEASING

The 'leasing' method has been under discussion at the SPA since spring 1992, and the legislation passed that year allowed it to go ahead. Its principal aim is to counteract the lack of domestic capital for privatization, and to provide something 'to fall back on' in instances where privatization by direct sale to investors has failed and is unlikely to be successful until the firm is restructured. It is hoped that this method will put an end to some of the uncertainties created by the lack of progress with privatization, the decline in output and in the value of the assets of these firms, and the failure of management to instigate change before new owners take over, all of which are having a disastrous effect on the economy as a whole.

The basic principles of the leasing method are as follows: a majority (up to 100 per cent) stake in the company is transferred by the SPA to the lessee, who is then entitled to exercise all business rights over the firm except the right to sell or transfer ownership of the assets[31]. The 'owner' remains the SPA, until the end of the leasing contract or until such time as the leasing fee has been paid in full. Only Hungarian 'natural' persons (i.e. not legal entities or companies) may compete for the leasing contract, and the contract will be granted to the person or group (managers and/or groups of employees are envisaged) who present the best restructuring proposals and offer the highest leasing payment. Lessees must agree, as a minimum, to maintain the value of the assets under their control and may not pay out dividends for the duration of the contract, which will be between five and eight years depending on the value of the assets, unless the lessee is able to raise capital from external sources to pay off the remaining amount in full before the end of the contract. While an initial down-payment is not required, the lessee must be able to furnish a guarantee equivalent in value to the first year's instalment payment, and the package includes generous interest rates and tax relief on repayments. The process of setting up the leasing mechanism is still in its early stages; the SPA published a list of eight firms late in 1992 for a trial run (shown in Table 9.6), although the leasing option will only be offered in cases where a first round of tender bidding fails to find cash buyers, so it is still too early to assess its impact.

PRIVATIZATION VOUCHERS

With vouchers both hailed and condemned as the most radical turn-around in privatization policy, the minister without portfolio responsible for privatization,

TABLE 9.6 Privatization by leasing

Company name and type of business	Registered capital (HUF mn)	SPA share (%)	Number of employees
Békéscsabai Kötöttárugyár Rt. (knitwear)	441.8	93.5	1574
Budapesti Köolajipari Gépgyárto Rt. (machinery for the oil industry)	844.0	69.0	750
Karamell Sütö- és Édesipari Rt. (bakery products and confectionary)	444.9	82.7	776
Lörinci Textil Kft. (textiles)	249.0	95.6	230
PROMONTORVIN Borgazdasági Rt. (wine)	580.5	36.7	300
SR Soproni Ruhagyár Rt. (clothing)	310.0	76.7	1411
START Autojavito és Kereskedelmi Kft. (car repairs and sales)	29.7	86.5	60
URÁNIA Ruházati Kereskedelmi Kft. (clothing trade)	90.0	92.4	84

Source: Figyelő 17 December 1992, p. 25

Tamás Szabó, insists that the issue is not a 'give-away' akin to the Czechoslovak coupon privatization programme. His controversial 'Strategy for a breakthrough in privatization', which called for an end to the 'revenue-centred' practice of the SPA and introduced the idea of a credit voucher scheme as a means of 'creating the widest possible range of domestic owners' and allowing for the possibility of participating in the privatization process without cash and 'without risk to the personal assets of the public', divided the cabinet when it was introduced in October 1992. The scheme allows any Hungarian citizen to purchase vouchers up to the value of HUF 100,000 in return for a down-payment of 1 per cent of the total value of the vouchers, and repayment terms will be more favourable than those for E-loans (a parallel scheme will allow for letters of credit to be used to supplement cash bids from bigger investors). Around one third of Hungary's population are expected to avail themselves of the opportunity. The many critics of the scheme argue that it represents a move away from recognition of the need to create 'real owners' capable of injecting capital into enterprise restructuring and of developing new markets (Kurcz 1993), as opposed to artificially created and weak owners who would take any profit out of the firm, and as such it is unlikely to achieve its desired aim of accelerating effective privatization. It is also argued that if there is no restriction on the trading of the vouchers, the scheme could lead to inflation, and there is concern that, from the point of view of the budget, voucher privatization would be disastrous.

The proposals have nevertheless been accepted in principle and a committee is currently working out the regulatory framework for voucher privatization. Free distribution of shares may not be on the cards, but the expectation on the part of many in Hungary that the government would eventually resort to adopting measures equivalent to free distribution helps to explain the lack of interest by the Hungarian public towards participation in privatization (Karsai 1993a).

There are evidently a number of motives behind the introduction or promotion of all these schemes, besides the practical necessity to find ways of increasing

.omestic participation in privatization, increasing the number of actors in the economy and creating some form of private ownership — even by artificial means — to get the ailing economy going again. The apparent change in direction may also be a tacit recognition of the fact that many of the assets will be impossible to privatize by any of the means originally conceived, or at least that they cannot be sold for more than people (the market) are willing to pay for them, which may be minimal. In addition, much of the available investment capital (both domestic and foreign) has already been used up, and neither investors nor the domestic population, with its limited resources, are willing to risk their money on 'lame duck' firms. In all these respects, it could be argued that the more 'populist' orientation of privatization policy may be the only realistic option left open to the government.

At the same time, however, the greater emphasis on 'populist' schemes has certain discernible political motives. On the one hand, the implementation of these schemes will undoubtedly produce a radical improvement in the privatization statistics, at least on paper, whereas otherwise the government would fall substantially short of its target of a 50 per cent reduction in state-owned assets by 1994, the year of the next general elections. The emphasis on favouring domestic ownership may also be an attempt to win the voters' favour through the popular appeal of introducing a greater element of 'equity' into participation in privatization, and there is certainly political mileage to be gained in this. It also offers concessions to the right and the left alike, on the one hand allaying the — largely unfounded — fears of the right (most notably from lobby groups within the coalition government itself) regarding extensive foreign ownership in the Hungarian economy, while on the other, introducing the possibility of a 'socialized' form of ownership distinctly Liska-esque in flavour[32]. Whatever the case may be, the new policy orientation certainly seems to indicate that the government is yielding to the somewhat hazy but very real ideological pressure (and Hungary is not unique in this) to compensate the populace on as wide a scale as possible for four decades of economic injustice. As one satirical cartoonist has put it: for 40 years they said that the means of production were owned by the people; now they'll have the papers to prove it.

9. Concluding comments

Hungary's experience of privatization so far has shown the difficulties involved in centralized planning of the privatization process, both in terms of speed and sequencing, and in terms of the methods and aims adopted. The government's initial stance and its expectations of privatization have progressively changed on almost all counts.

On the one hand, centrally managed, state-administered privatization has proved singularly unsuccessful. Although there is still a large state apparatus concerned with privatization, the number and the role of other, especially private, institutions in the privatization process has increased dramatically. As the legislative and regulatory framework was adapted and consolidated (notably concerning competition and anti-trust laws, financial auditing, etc) and fears of abuse by enterprise management abated, 'spontaneous privatization' was eventually institutionalized under the more reassuring guise of 'decentralized' or 'self-privatization' and allowed to take its course.

The development of cross-ownership, which began in the early days of so-called spontaneous privatization and to which the government was equally hostile at first, has continued[33]. Moreover, several parallel processes have enhanced its development. The most notable of these is the widespread exchange of debt for equity which is occurring with increased frequency as more and more firms are forced into bankruptcy or liquidation as a result of extremely strict bankruptcy legislation which came into force at the beginning of 1992. One effect of this will be changes in the ownership structure of financial institutions, in which enterprises and cooperatives owned a 35 per cent share at the end of 1991 (Mihályi 1992b), and this could have a positive impact on the banks' ability to put pressure on firms to restructure. The extent of privatization by liquidation is not yet clear, but it is expected to represent a substantial part of the eventual overall patchwork of ownership in Hungary.

The remainder of the patchwork will include a multitude of 'small' property owners created as a result of the compensation process, through employee share ownership schemes and, it can be assumed, through the other, 'populist' schemes described above. These, finally, will be supplemented by a number of institutional owners, which, at least for some time to come, are likely to remain a major force in the economy, although it is far from clear whether they will prove 'effective' owners.

It is difficult, however, to assess accurately the extent to which privatization has actually taken place. Rapidly changing circumstances and on-going reform of data-collection procedures have made it difficult for the Central Statistical Office (KSH) to keep track of changes in ownership, and of how these are affecting the economy as a whole. Taking privatization in its broadest sense of privatizing the economy, encouraging private ownership and increasing the number of independent actors in the economic sphere, the picture appears positive; indeed the changes made over the past three years since the government of József Antall came to power seem little short of miraculous.

A new, burgeoning private sector is already reckoned to account for a substantial portion of GDP (around 25 per cent in 1991 and around 32 per cent in 1992 according to some Hungarian observers), while the number of firms operating as legal entities totalled 69,386 at the end of December, 1992, compared with 15,235 at the end of 1989/90 (KSH, Kopint). However, these figures also include firms (the precise number of which is not known) which were set up during the wave of 'company-founding mania' at the end of 1991 in an effort to beat the deadline for eligibility for preferential tax rates[34], and which as yet only exist on paper or are only partially operational. The numbers also camouflage those state enterprises which have transformed into corporate entities, thus disguising the number of enterprises (or proportion of the state's shares in transformed enterprises) which have actually changed hands. The picture is further blurred by the 'invisible' privatization which has taken place alongside the 'official' privatization of state assets; by this we refer to the setting up of ostensibly new companies using the intellectual assets, markets, business contacts, and land, premises and equipment leased from the old enterprise[35]. Recent estimates suggest that this area where the 'new' private sector and the old state sector overlap accounts for a much greater proportion of 'privatization' than had previously been thought.

Estimates of privatization in its narrower sense of the transfer to private ownership of former state-owned assets vary somewhat, but it is clear that the figure is lower than had been hoped; the State Property Agency puts the figure at around 10 per cent of state-owned assets at the end of 1992, which is well below the government's stated target of 50 per cent by 1994.

Notes

1. It should be noted that the Czechoslovak reform package, unlike Hungary's NEM, also contained proposals for radical political reform.
2. According to official figures, US$ 5.5 bn in foreign direct investment flowed into Hungary between 1990 and June 1993, 1–1.3 bn of which was in connection with privatization, despite the increasing number and range of opportunities opening up for investors through privatization 'from Rostock to Vladivostok' (Mihályi 1992a) and despite the relatively high cost of labour in Hungary.
3. In contrast to other countries in the region, Hungary did not opt to have its debt rescheduled or to default on repayments, but to fulfil its debt service commitments in full in order to maintain the country's credit-worthiness. This was the policy of the pre-democratic government and it was simply continued by the government of József Antall. For details of the debate surrounding Hungary's external debt and a discussion of its macroeconomic implications, see Obláth, 1992.
4. For example by defaulting on the external debt accumulated by the former regime (see Obláth, 1992); or by the 're-nationalization' of enterprises which had gained a large degree of autonomy and certain 'quasi-ownership rights' as a result of successive reforms in order to clarify the state's position as owner (see Hajnóczy 1989a). Voszka (1991c) has argued that the present government has attempted both openly and covertly — but all in all rather unsuccessfully — to renationalize or 'restatify' the economy in ways which failed to recognize and take advantage of the momentum of privatization and which in fact have delayed the process.
5. Although the level of foreign direct investment in Hungary prior to 1989 (a little over US$ 500 mn) seems minimal compared to present levels (US$ 4bn at end 1992), it should be noted that the bulk of that investment came from a number of renowned and influential Western firms.
6. Lengyel (1988) edited a volume of distinctive studies on property ownership reform in Hungary by a number of Hungarian economists; Köhegyi (1991) analyses the different strands of the academic and political debate on ownership reform in Hungary. The discussion in 'concepts' in Section 2 of this chapter draws heavily on these two works.
7. Liska's work (the best-known of which is Ökonosztát, written in 1965) and its impact on reform thinking in Hungary are discussed in detail by Lengyel (1988).
8. Proponents of some form of enterprise self management (such as Károly Attila Soós (see Köhegyi 1991: 88; Tamás Bauer (see Lengyel 1988: 24) tended to argue that self-management should not be judged solely on the basis of the Yugoslavian experience. On the other hand, a common argument among economists was that since it was not possible to reverse the process which had put an end to private ownership and since traditional forms of state ownership had proved ineffective, then a middle way was called for. The introduction of self-management was not so much regarded as the best

way forward, but as the lesser of evils: a further devolution of administrative control to the enterprises, continuing the spirit of the 1968 reform — liberalization rather than ownership reform.

9. These figures are slightly misleading, in that they are based on the numbers of enterprises only; if one takes into account the number of employees and the scale of production capacity in the 'strategic' enterprises, then the proportion is closer to 50–50.

10. This tax break for new company foundations was discontinued from January 1, 1992.

11. Éva Voszka's well-documented analysis of the behaviour of enterprise management under the effects of the economic policies of the Németh government strongly indicates that, initially at least, many enterprise managers saw the founding of new companies as a 'last resort' (Voszka 1991c: 176).

12. Cited in Voszka 1991c: 178.

13. The term 'spontaneous' is something of a misnomer in that, besides the indirect pressure on enterprises to transform, the government administration did in fact have at its disposal various means by which it could influence enterprise transformations both in the case of self-governing enterprises and in that of enterprises under ministerial supervision. Its attitude, however, seems to have been one of benign neglect. For a full discussion of the role of the state administration in the enterprise transformation process, see Voszka 1991c: 180ff.

14. There remains very little available data on how much 'spontaneous privatization' was actually taking place. According to Voszka (cited in Frydman *et al.* 1993), unpublished figures of the Ministry of Industry and Trade indicate that between 1987 and 1990 40% of SOEs in industry, construction and trade had founded companies with an average of 10% of their assets. The actual number of 'new' companies founded in this way ran into hundreds.

15. These guidelines were twice extended and were no longer effectively in force after September 1991, though no new, comprehensive measures were enacted to replace them until August 1992. The SPA was thus in the awkward and conflict-ridden position of having to operate on the one hand in an *ex lex* state, while on the other being the *de facto* policy-maker on privatization.

16. Complications included the need to sift out those enterprise units (e.g. retail outlets, catering units, etc.) which fell under the pre-privatization programme.

17. As of December 1992, the number of 'self-privatizing' firms affected by bankruptcy and liquidation exceeded the number of successful transactions. In the first round, 52 companies with assets valued at HUF 4.5bn had declared themselves bankrupt, while a further 47, with assets worth HUF 2.5bn had gone into liquidation. Out of the second batch of companies, the numbers affected were 34 (HUF 10bn) and 8 (HUF 1.5bn) respectively (see Zsubori 1992c).

18. Additional problems and confusion were created by the fact that the legislation transferring assets to the municipalities did not come into effect until September 1991, one year after the new municipalities were elected.

19. In many cases the municipalities won, if only as a result of the pressure exerted on the new leaseholders through the threat that planning permission for renovation and reconstruction work on the premises would be withheld (Félix 1992b).

20. The restitution of land but not of other fixed assets was declared unconstitutional since it would involve unlawful discrimination between Hungarian citizens.

21. Around 50% of agricultural land was never nationalized, but stayed in private ownership; the remaining 15% was owned by state farms.

22. The value of a given piece of land is expressed in gold crowns (currently set at HUF 3,000) according to its quality, output, and location.

23. State farms functioned like large enterprises, often with a multiplicity of activities, and assets ranging from hotels to distilleries to plant maintenance workshops, with the different units often far apart geographically.

24. Note that the selling prices actually achieved have been on average 10-20% less than the original valuations; there has been some confusion over the availability of credits for the purchase of agricultural assets.

25. The issue of whether foreigners should be allowed to acquire ownership of farmland is a sensitive one in Hungary at present for several reasons, and it is doubtful that any legislation permitting more than land leasing by foreigners will be passed. First, there is strong political pressure (especially in the run-up to the general election in spring 1994) from within the coalition government itself — not to mention from the right-wing lobby — to protect domestic agriculture and the rural social structure, which has been already hard hit by three consecutive years of drought combined with radical structural transformation and decline in demand on agricultural markets. Second, until the compensation process and assignment of ownership title to the land has been completed and a land market emerges, the dangers posed by foreign speculation are enormous. At the same time, however, there is also a need to find sufficiently liberal legislative solutions so as not to deter much-needed foreign agricultural investment.

26. From 1989 to end May, 1993, the local municipalities had sold some 210,000 of former public housing stock apartments.

27. Besides freezing public housing rents till mid-1994, the new law allows tenants of local municipality housing five years (from January 1994 to end of 1998) to decide whether they wish to buy, and the purchase price until that time is stipulated as 50% of market value. The sale of remaining public housing stock by municipalities is to be prohibited for a further five years (until the end of 2004), after which these properties (except pensioners' flats) may be sold freely on the open market. Similar provisions are made with respect to business premises currently rented/leased from the municipalities. Lessees will be able to buy such premises at a maximum of 60% of market value until the end of 1997, after which the right to buy will be offered (until end of 1998) to the community of residents of any building in which the business premises are situated. There will be no restriction on municipalities selling such premises from 1 January, 1999.

28. The organization is also responsible for properties used by central government budget-funded bodies and by the ministries, e.g. universities and colleges, clinics, courts, police stations, etc. As such, it has some similarities with the UK's Property Services Agency.

29. The figures given in the 1992 report of the research group Financial Research Ltd. (Pénzügykutató Rt.) are unusually vague, putting the number of Treasury properties at between 1500 and 2000, and their total value at around HUF 100-110 bn. (Pénzügykutató Rt, 1993)

30. The combined assets of the oil and gas companies, the electricity corporation and Hungarian Telecommunications alone are worth an estimated HUF 800 bn.

31. Presumably this implies that the lessee could not use the leased assets as security for a business loan, since this would risk a transfer of ownership in the event of a default.

32. István Siklaky, one of the theorists behind the privatization voucher scheme, was an earlier devotee of Liska's social birthright ideas (see Karsai 1993a).

33. Mihályi 1992 and others have illustrated this process, predicted by Matolcsy, in detail (see Matolcsy 1988b; Lengyel 1988; Köhegyi 1991).

34. See note 10.

35. This is partly an extension of the VGMKs set up in the early 1980s, and has been facilitated by enterprise attempts to avoid bankruptcy.

References

Auth, H. and **Krokos, J.** (1989) Gyanus átalakulások, *Figyelő*, 9 February, p. 3.

Babus, E. (1993) Lakógyürés, *Heti Világgazdaság*, 1993/28, 10 July, p. 82.

Balassa, A. (1992) Kék szalag: Privatizált vagyonkezelést, *Figyelő*, 1992/44, 29 October, p. 14.

Bokros, L. (1989) Egy társadalom védelmében (in two parts), *Figyelő*, 1989/38, 21 September, p. 3, and 1989/39, 28 September, p. 3.

Bonyhádi, P. (1993) Atalakulási törvény: pro farm, *Figyelő*, 1993/3, 21 January, p. 19.

Central Statistical Office (KSH), *Statisztikai Zsebkönyv* (various issues), *Havi Statisztikai Közlemények* (various issues) *Magyar Statisztikai Évkönyv* (various issues).

Consultative Committee on Economic Management (1988) A szocialista piacgazdaság megteremtése, *Figyelő*, 1988/49, 8 December, p. 1, 17-20.

Csillag, I. (1988) A Reprivatizáció, in Pénzügykutató Rt., *Tulajdonreform*, p. 129f.

Diczházi, B. (1992) Tények és adatok, *Figyelő*, 1992/50, 10 December, p. 13.

Diczházi, B. (1993) Az MRP bajjal járhat, *Figyelő*, 1993/10, 11 March, p. 7.

Félix, P. (1991) Rémségek kicsiny boltjai, *Heti Világgazdaság*, 1991/46, 16 November, p. 79.

Félix, P. (1992a) Törvények a szövetkezetekről: pótkárpótlás, *Heti Világgazdaság*, 1992/3, 18 January, p. 86.

Félix, P. (1992b) Elöprivatizáció: Megy az üzlet, *Heti Világgazdaság*, 1992/23, 6 June, p. 107.

Félix, P. (1993) Bérlet a csödhöz, *Heti Világgazdaság*, 1993/8, 20 February, p. 83.

Ferber, K. (1991) Az AV közbelép (Interview with Zoltán Nagy, of the Finance Ministry Policy Office), *Figyelő*, 1991/28, 11 July, p. 15.

Frydman, R., Rapaczynski, A. and **Earle, J.** (1993) *The Privatization Process in Central Europe*, Central European University Press, Budapest.

Gatsios, K. (1992) Privatization in Hungary: past, present and future, *CEPR Discussion Paper*, No. 642, March 1992.

Gazdasági Reformbizottság (1989) A gazdasági átalakítás és stabilizáció 3 éves programjának tervezete, *Figyelő* 1989/18, pp. 9-12.

Government of the Republic of Hungary (1990) A Nemzeti Megújhodás Programja — A Kormányprogram irányelvei.

Hajnóczy, A. (1989a) Privatizálás patthelyzetben?, Interview with Henrik Auth, *Figyelő* 1989/38, 21 September, p. 7.

Hajnóczy, A. (1989b) Megkezdödött a gazdasági hatalom újrafelosztása, Interview with Henrik Auth, *Figyelő* 1989/47, 23 November, p. 7.

Hare, P. (1990) Reform of enterprise regulation in Hungary — from 'tutelage' to market, *European Economy*, No. 43, Brussels: Commission of European Communities.

Hare, P. and **Révész, T.** (1992) Hungary's transition to the market: the case against a 'big bang', *Economic Policy*, 14.

Heti Világgazdaság (1992) Boltcsinálta vállalkozók, 1992/43, 24 October, p. 86.

Heti Világgazdaság (1993a) Késik a vagyoni kárpótlás, 1993/8, 20 February, p. 15.

Heti Világgazdaság (1993b) Földaprózódás, 1993/10, 6 March, p. 8.

Kállay, L. (1992) A láthatatlan privatizáció, *Heti Világgazdaság*, 1992/16, 18 April, p. 10.

Karsai, G. (1991) Ahogy a Vigadó utcából látszik (excerpts from a report by the SPA for the government's economic cabinet), *Figyelő*, 1991/28, p. 13-14.

Karsai, G. (1992a) Privatizáció : mitöl kell félnünk?, Interview with Lajos Csepi, *Figyelő*, 1992/4, p. 1,19.

Karsai, G. (1992b) Törvényjavaslatok azállami vagyonról, *Figyelő*, 1992/11, 12 March, p. 1, 4.

Karsai, G. (1992c) Szervezet, töke, müködés: az AV Rt lesz a legerösebb gazdasági lobby?, Interview with the director of the State Asset Management Company, *Figyelő*, 1992/51, 17 December, p. 12.

Karsai, G. (1993a) Hiteljegy: A társadalmi örökség reinkarnációja?, (Inteview with István Siklaky), *Figyelő*, 1992/4, 28 January, p. 15.

Karsai, G. (1993b) Munkavállalói résztulajdonosi program — Diczházi: Az MRP bajjal járhat, (Interview with Bertalan Diczházi, Vice-chairman of the State Property Agency), *Figyelő*, 1993/10, 11 March, p. 7.

Kevevári, B. (1988) Az új tulajdonos: A vagyon pénztár (In three parts), *Figyelő*, 1988/45, 46, 47, Nov. 10, 17, 24, 1988, p. 7.

Kocsis, G. (1989a) (ed.) Ha megfogta, hadd vigye?, interview with Márton Tardos, *Heti Világgazdaság*, 1989/39, 30 September, p. 67.

Kocsis, G. (1991a) Privatizációs kormánystratégia — a legnagyobb közös megosztó, *Heti Világgazdaság*, 1991/39, 28 September, p. 78.

Kocsis, G. (1991b) Allami Tulajdonosi Intézet — Agyonkezelö központ, *Heti Világgazdaság*, 1991/48, 30 November, p. 78.

Kocsis, G. (1991c) Egyszerüsített privatizáció — vészkijárat, *Heti Vilaggazdaság*, 1991/50, 14 December, p. 84.

Kocsis, G. (1992a) Elveszejtö illuziók, *Heti Világgazdaság*, 1992/12, 21 March 21, p. 82.

Kocsis, G. (1992b) Allami Vagyonkezelö Rt. — Kézrátétel, *Heti Világgazdaság*, 1992/26, 27 June, p. 83.

Köhegyi, K. (1991) A tulajdonosi szerkezet átalakítás nak hazai koncepciói, Pénzügykutató Részvénytársaság, *Évkönyv* 1991, Budapest, pp. 81-101 (originally published in *Külgazdaság*, **4**, 1991).

Kopint-Datorg (1992) Law on State Property, *Hungarian Business Brief*, **19**, 24 September, 1992, p. 1.

Kurcz, A. (1993) Kelendö részvénytarsaságok privatizációja... avagy kárpótlási részvények pakettje?, *Figyelő*, 1993/17, 29 April, p. 17, 18.

Lengyel, L. (1988) A tulajdonviták története és a reform, in Lengyel, L. (ed.) *Tulajdonreform*, Pénzügykutató Részvénytársaság, Budapest, p. 21f.

Matolcsy, G. (1988a) A vagyonérdekeltség kulcsa, *Figyelő*, 1988/14, 7 April, p. 3.

Matolcsy, G. (1988b) Változatok a tulajdonreformra, in Lengyel, L. (ed.) *Tulajdonreform*, Pénzügykutató Részvénytársaság, Budapest, p. 107f.

Matolcsy, G. (1991) Lábadoz saink évei. A magyar privatizáció. Trendek, tények, privatizációs példák, Privatizációs Kutatóintézet, Budapest.

Mihályi, P. (1992a) Magyar privatizálás, *Budapesti Könyvszemle* (BUKSZ), **4**(1), pp. 48–53.

Mihályi, P. (1992b) Hungary: a unique approach to privatization — past, present and future, in Székely, I. P. and Newbery, D. M. G. (eds.), *Hungary: An Economy in Transition*, CEPR, Cambridge University Press, Cambridge.

Obláth, G. (1992) Hungary's foreign debt: controversies and macroeconomic problems, in Székely, I. P. and Newbery, D. M. G. (eds.), *Hungary: An Economy in Transition*, CEPR, Cambridge University Press, Cambridge.

Pénzügykutató Rt. (1993) Jelentések az alagútból (Reports from the tunnel), Budapest, May.

A Pénzügyminisztérium privatizációs javaslata, *Figyelő* 1991/28, 11 July, p. 15.

Réti, P. (1989) Allami vagyoneladás. Ebül szerzett jószág, *Heti Világgazdaság*, 1989/39, 30 September, p. 66.

Sárközy, T. (1989) Egy törvény védelmében (in two parts), *Figyelő* 1989/34, 24 August, p. 3, and 1989/35, 31 August, p. 3.

Sebök, E. (1989) Az állam nem manipulálhat tovább, Interview with István Tömpe, *Figyelő* 1989/36, 7 September, p. 5.

State Property Agency (1991) *Privatization and Foreign Investment in Hungary,* Budapest, March.

State Property Agency (1992a) Megkezdödött a decentralizált privatizáció második üteme, *Privinfo,* **2,** May 1992, p. 3-15.

State Property Agency (1992b) Uj vagyonpolitikai irányelvek, *Privinfo,* **2,** May, p. 25.

State Property Agency (1992c) Report on privatization trends and developments, State Property Agency, Budapest, (Internal report), Summer.

Szabady, A. (1992) Laksák rpótlási jegyért, *Figyelő,* 1992/34-35, 27 August, p. 27.

Szabó, G. (1992) A romlás világai, *Heti Világgazdaság,* 1992/23, 6 June, p. 109.

Szántó, A. (1992) Kincstári Vagyonkezelö Szervezet: Es mégis mozog, *Heti Világgazdaság,* 1992/27, 4 July, p. 71.

Székely, I. P. and **Newbery, D.M.G.** (eds) (1992) *Hungary: An Economy in Transition,* CEPR, Cambridge University Press, Cambridge.

Tardos, M. (1989) A Tulajdon, *Közgazdasági Szemle,* **12,** pp. 1405–23..

Tardos, M. (1990) A privatizáció privatizációja, *Heti Világgazdaság,* 1990/36, p. 66.

Tömpe, I. (1992) Hittük, amit hittünk, történt, amit tapasztaltunk, *Figyelő,* 1992/27, 2 July, p. 7.

Valentiny, P. (1991) Hungarian privatization in international perspective, in *Public Enterprise,* **11**(2-3), June-September, p. 141.

Valentiny, P. (1992) Gazdasági modernizáció és válságkezelés, *Külgazdaság,* 1992/11.

Vanicsek, M. (1992) Munkavállalói tulajdonlás: Távol a tüztöl, *Figyelő,* 1992/12, 19 March, p. 7.

Varga, A. (1992) Egyházfinanszírozás: Elszakadás három lépcsöben, *Figyelő,* 1992/52-53, 23 December, p. 41.

Varga G. (1988) Társaságok tára, interview with Miklós Pulai and Tamás Sárközi on the draft law on economic associations, *Figyelő,* 28 April, pp. 3, 4.

Voszka, E. (1991a) Vállalati önállósulások, *Heti Világgazdaság,* 1991/13, 30 March, p. 87.

Voszka, É. (1991b) Homályból homályba — A tulajdonosi szerkezet talakulása a nagyiparban, Pénzügykutató Részvénytársaság, *Evkönyv* 1991 (also published in *Társadalmi Szemle,* **5,** 1991).

Voszka, É. (1991c) A 'Spontaneit stól' a 'központosításig' — és tovább?', Pénzügykutató Részvénytársaság, *Evkönyv* 1991 (also published in *Külgazdaság,* 9, 1991).

Voszka, É. (1992) Mire jó a társasággá alakulás?, *Figyelő* 1992/50, 10 December, p. 12.

Wiesel, I. (1990) Privatizálni pedig kell, Interview with István Tömpe, Director of the SPA, *Figyelő,* 1990/28, p. 9.

Zsubori, E. (1992a) Önprivatizáció — Felsöbb osztályba léphet, *Figyelő,* 1992/12, 19 March, p. 7.

Zsubori, E. (1992b) Decentralizált privatizáció, második menet — a kiválasztottak szabadsága, *Figyelő,* 1992/23, 4 June, p. 19.

Zsubori, E. (1992c) Az önprivatizáció állása: hétszáz induló, félszáz befútó, *Figyelő,* 1992/49, 3 December, p. 22.

Zsubori, E. (1992d) Indul a TB-Börze: bedobják a törülközöt is?, *Figyelő,* 1992/33, 13 August, 1992, p. 17.

Zsubori, E. (1993) Késlekedö TB-vagyonátadás: mire lesz elég a juss?, *Figyelő,* 1993/4, 28 January, p. 13.

CHAPTER TEN

Privatization in Poland 1989–1993: policies, methods, and results

Stanisław Gomułka and Piotr Jasiński*

An ownership reform intended to transform an economy based on predominantly state ownership and central coordination to one based largely on private ownership and market coordination is an economic and social process of the most fundamental nature. Our principal concern in this chapter will be privatization in the narrow sense, defined as the transfer from state to private owners of full ownership rights. In Poland from 1989 to 1993, such a transfer has been a significant, but not yet the dominant cause, of the observed fast increase in the share of the private sector in total GDP, a principal measure of privatization in the broad sense. An endogenous growth of the private sector, commercialization of the co-operative sector, and mass leasing of small businesses have so far been the main causes of the share's increase. A discussion of these causes will be our second major concern.

The chapter starts with a brief overview of the changes in the ownership structure of the Polish economy. The next two sections describe briefly the ownership changes that preceded the Act on the Privatization of State-owned Enterprises of 13 July 1990. These sections also summarize the ideas underlying the competing privatization blueprints proposed in 1989 and 1990. Sections 4 and 5 are the core of the chapter. They report on the process of implementation of this Act, discussing various forms and methods of privatization. Section 6 discusses the privatization plans for 1994–5, involving above all mass privatization of large enterprises and privatization implications of the Pact on Enterprises. Implementation of these plans is expected to accelerate the privatization process so much as probably to ensure that Poland's ownership structure will be similar to that of the European Community before the end of the 1990s. Section 7 discusses constraints to privatization. Section 8 concludes with a tentative assessment of the results of efforts undertaken so far.

* The critical comments and positive suggestions by a number of readers of earlier drafts of this chapter have proved most useful in preparing the final version. The authors wish to thank in particular Leszek Balcerowicz of the Warsaw School of Economics, Saul Estrin of the London Business School, Wladyslaw W. Jermakowicz of the School of Business, University of Southern Indiana, and Mark Schaffer of the Centre for Economic Performance at the London School of Economics.

1. Growth of the private sector

Like the other countries of Central and Eastern Europe, Poland started the process of systemic transformation when its economy was dominated by state-owned enterprises (SOEs) and enterprises indirectly controlled by the state (mostly co-operatives). The political control over such enterprises was fairly tight, exercised ultimately by the Communist Party. However, the share of the GDP produced by the socialized sector peaked long before Tadeusz Mazowiecki formed his Solidarity-led government in September 1989. The share of the GDP produced by the private sector outside agriculture started to increase in the late 1970s and has grown more or less continuously since then[1]. The private sector consisted mainly of unincorporated businesses in crafts, services, and retail trading. In 1976 the so-called Polonia partnerships were allowed, i.e. firms owned by Poles or people of Polish origin not resident in Poland. In 1977 the first three firms were registered; by the end of 1980 their number had increased to only 46, employing 1560 people[2]. In 1985 a major legal reform took place: the Commercial Code of 1934 was returned into force. The real turning point for the private sector was, however, the 1988 Act on Economic Activities, introduced by the Rakowski government. Under the Mazowiecki government (September 1989 to December 1990), the growth of the private sector rapidly accelerated (Table 10.1). By the end of 1993 the private sector already employed about 60 per cent of those in work, compared with 44 per cent in 1989, and, in 1993, produced 50 per cent of GDP[3], compared with 28.6 per cent in 1989 (Table 10.2).

By far the most important element so far in privatizing the Polish economy has been what is known as *organic privatization* (Gomułka 1993a), which is one form

TABLE 10.1 Growth of the private sector in Poland, 1980–1993

	1980	1989	1990	1991	1992	1993
			% of the GDP			
Private sector		28.6	30.9	42.1	45.0	50.0
Private sector proper	17.5	19.2	23.0	n.a.	n.a.	n.a.
State sector	82.5*	71.4	69.1	57.9	55.0	50.0
			Number of registered firms in the private sector			
All private firms	460,333 (1981)	857,430	1,201,933	1,493,701	1,719,304	1,901,704
Cooperatives (excl. banks)	n.a.	16,691	16,650	17,374	18,284	n.a.
Domestic incorporated firms	–	15,681	33,239	47,690	58,218	66,457
Foreign incorporated firms	–	429	1645	4796	10,131	15,053
Polonia companies	46	841	862	787	716	n.a.
Unincorporated businesses	481,000	826,533	1,135,492	1,420,002	1,630,800	1,783,900

Source: Central Statistical Office, Ciechocińska (1992), and own calculations.
*Includes co-operatives

TABLE 10.2 Poland, employment by economic sector and ownership category, 1989–93

	1989	1990	1991	1992	1993
LEVEL (MILLIONS, END-YEAR)					
Non-agriculture	13.5	12.4	11.8	11.4	11.4
State	9.6	8.2	7.3	6.6	6.1
Private	3.9	4.2	4.5	4.8	5.3
Private sector proper	1.8	2.3	3.0	4.1	n.a.
Cooperatives, etc	2.1	1.9	1.5	1.2	n.a.
Agriculture	4.8	4.7	4.6	4.5	4.5
State	0.6	0.5	0.4	0.4	0.4
Private, incl. cooperatives	4.2	4.2	4.2	4.2	4.2
PRIVATE SECTOR (PRIVATE PROPER AND CO-OPERATIVES) SHARE OF EMPLOYMENT (%, END-YEAR)					
Total economy outside private agriculture	31.2	33.6	40.3	44.4	46.2
Total economy	44.3	49.1	53.0	56.6	60.0
Trade	72.7	82.2	88.3	90.7	92.5
Industry	29.1	31.2	35.8	40.5	46.9
Construction	37.4	42.1	59.5	71.9	80.9
Transport	14.3	15.2	26.0	25.4	28.5
Communal services	29.9	30.0	40.3	44.4	n.a.

Source: Central Statistical Office, in particular Informacja o Sytuacji Spoleczno-Gospodarczej Kraju, Rok 1993, Warsaw, 28 January 1994.

of *privatization from below* (Kawalec, 1989). Organic privatization involves setting up new private businesses, either incorporated or unincorporated, by both Polish and foreign investors, and the autonomous growth of existing private businesses. This privatization is in part fuelled by *asset privatization*, whereby some unused inventories and fixed assets of state enterprises are sold very cheaply to private owners. Second in importance was mass leasing of state and cooperative assets by small private businesses, also a form of privatization from below. Third in importance was what one could call *statutory privatization*. Following the dissolution of their central administration, cooperatives have been commercialized and are now considered to belong to the private sector (Section 4.2). Fourth, by the end of 1993, 977 non-agriculture SOEs were privatized (Section 5).

2. The privatization debate and developments before September 1989

In November 1988, a conference was held at the Central School of Planning and Statistics in Warsaw, entitled 'Proposed Transformations of the Polish Economy'. That conference marked the first serious academic discussion on privatization in a Polish context, during which some rather specific, and in those days revolutionary, proposals were put forward. Stefan Kawalec proposed turning state-owned firms into joint stock companies, and selling shares in these companies to the public. By contrast, Janusz Lewandowski and Jan Szomburg advocated a free distribution of shares of state-owned enterprises[4]. The dilemma as to whether the state-owned assets should be sold or distributed free of charge became subsequently a permanent feature of both theoretical and policy discussions.

These discussions, initially purely theoretical, were already accompanied by 'spontaneous privatization' (the polite Hungarian term) or *'nomenklatura'* privatization (*uwłaszczenie nomenklatury*, the apt Polish term). This privatization was a consequence both of a deepening economic crisis and of an ideological and a discipline crisis within the Communist Party.

Two kinds of actions were particularly popular. The first involved a low valuation of assets contributed by the state enterprise and a high valuation of the contributions in kind made by the private partner(s)[5]. The second route of *nomenklatura* privatization was based on contractual relationships between old state enterprises and the newly established *'nomenklatura* joint-stock companies'[6], in which state managers would have personal stakes. The manager might then lease the plant and machinery of the state enterprise at highly favourable terms to such a private company, allowing it to earn exceptionally high rates of return. The profits of the state enterprise could be also transferred to the private firm by way of giving it exclusive rights on selling the SOE's output. The best way to bias such a contract in favour of the private firm was to use highly favourable transfer prices (Winiecki 1992).

The *nomenklatura* privatization led to public outrage, following reports in the mass media. However, it would appear that the process consisted above all in exploiting legal gaps. Irregularities could and in some cases most likely did occur in evaluating the assets as well as in what can be labelled 'conflicts of interest', but their illegality was very difficult to prove and very few deals were in fact declared null and void. Even though *nomenklatura* privatization had some positive aspects (Ciechocińska 1992, Mizsei 1992), this route to capitalism proved politically unacceptable and was blocked by the Mazowiecki government in late 1989 and early 1990.

3. Policy controversies and the Privatization Act of 1990

Soon after Tadeusz Mazowiecki formed his Solidarity-led coalition government, an economic programme was announced. In clear break with the Round Table agreement of April 1989, the programme proclaimed a return to capitalism as its ultimate goal.

Though a key player in bringing the communist rule in Central and Eastern Europe to an end, Solidarity was above all a trade union and, as such, could not and did not have the return to full blooded capitalism as its principal objective. Things were additionally complicated by the earlier attempts to reform the Polish economy, which in the 1980s went almost unequivocally in the direction of self-management. At the same time, the demise of the Communist Party deprived members of the old *nomenklatura* of effective power and created at the enterprise level a vacuum which was filled by a triumvirate of the management, the workers' council, and the trade unions. In many cases the Solidarity union controlled the workers' council and the council controlled the management, making it difficult for the latter to propose and implement adjustment programmes which were costly in the short run. This legitimized the opinion that enterprises *de facto* belonged to their employees and therefore the formal property rights should also be transferred to them or, at least, that they should have a decisive say in designing and implementing the privatization policy. The Balcerowicz team, in charge of economic policy, became scared of the prospect of Poland choosing the 'third way' by default. Convinced that workers' ownership is inferior, the team confronted the self-management activists and their exaggerated ownership claims. However, the Act on state-owned enterprises of 25 September 1981 was still in force and it was not considered politically feasible for the Solidarity-led government to repeal it. Instead the legal powers of workers' councils had to be taken into account in designing privatization techniques.

THE EARLY PROPOSALS

The Mazowiecki government was already in 1989 presented with two privatization proposals, which this time had a real chance of being implemented. First Gomułka (1990, 1992) suggested that all the SOEs should be turned immediately into joint stock companies and that the government should create a network of intermediaries, which he called investment banks, but which would effectively be open-ended mutual investment funds. To avoid the valuation problem, the shares of the companies taking part in that scheme would be distributed equally among funds, with 10 to 20 per cent to be retained by workers. The shares could be swapped among funds, but they were to be gradually sold at a speed decided by the authorities. The funds themselves were eventually to be privatized. Soon afterwards Beksiak and three other Polish economists (Beksiak *et al.* 1990) presented an all-embracing programme of economic transformation, of which privatization was an integral part. At the start of the privatization process, employees would be given 20 per cent of shares. In this way a clearly identifiable group of shareholders would emerge from the start to reduce the costs of control over management. The State Treasury would own the remaining 80 per cent but without voting rights. Over time, as the remaining shares are sold or distributed free of charge, new controlling shareholder groups would emerge.

In the spring of 1990 it became clear, however, that the formation of many new intermediaries was beyond the capabilities of the government. The lack of suitable personnel and facilities was the stumbling block. In response to this formidable constraint, a programme was born based on two principles: (1) many paths, particularly for small and medium size firms and (2) use of some of the existing institutions and new domestic and foreign management groups for the purpose of mass privatization programme for large enterprises.

Already in October 1989, the Government Plenipotentiary for Ownership Transformation, Krzysztof Lis, was appointed at the Ministry of Finance to propose the necessary initial legislation. This would provide a general framework, and not be specific as to the methods of privatization. The work on selecting the enterprises for a UK-type privatization began almost at the same time.

In March 1990 the proposed text of the Act on the Privatization of State-owned Enterprises was approved by the Council of Ministers and sent to the *Sejm,* where a special committee was formed and met every day for three months to discuss the law. The main opponents, not so much of privatization as of the government proposals, were MPs involved in the self-management movement, who at the same time presented their own draft of the act[7].

The Act on the Privatization of State-owned Enterprises and the Office of the Minister of Privatization Act[8] were finally passed by the Sejm on 13 July 1990 and came into force on 1 August 1990[9]. Fig. 10.1 illustrates the overall structure of the

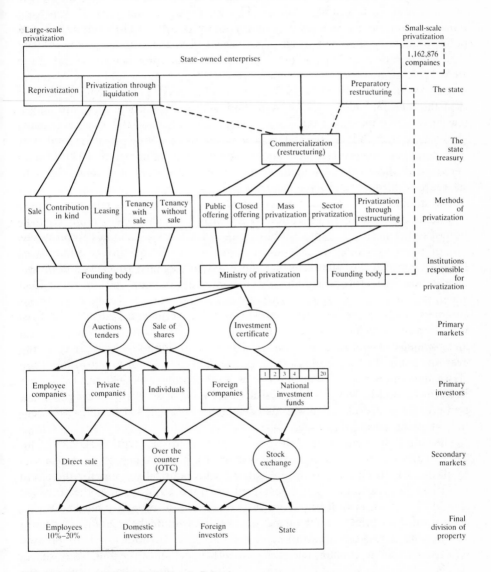

FIG. 10.1 The model of privatization in Poland
Source: Jermakowicz (1992)

privatization processes. Their description and an assessment of the results achieved will be given in section 5.

THE WAR OF PRIVATIZATION BLUEPRINTS, SUMMER 1990

The slow supply response of state enterprises in 1990 reinforced the point that the liberalization and stabilization policies of the Polish government rest on soft microeconomic foundations and may not be sustainable for long. Strong and self-interested advocates for profits and long-term net worth of state enterprises continued to be absent and, instead, incentives to increase the short-term income of the workforces became stronger. The Privatization Act of 1990 was very pluralistic and could be a legal basis for many policies. Reform designers and policy makers became convinced of an urgent need for a privatization strategy that could produce quickly, within five years or so, certainly before the end of the 1990s, private owners for most state property, ones who would have entrepreneurial talent and possibly also financial capital needed for restructuring. But then the questions were, first, how to find such owners where there are only a few successful domestic capitalists and, second, in what socially acceptable manner to hand over to them the state assets, where there is little private capital. The various policy blueprints which were proposed in the summer of 1990 differed above all in the way they sought to answer these two questions, especially with reference to medium and large enterprises.

The initial privatizers, led by Krzysztof Lis, were keen to rely on classical (Western) methods of privatization. They proposed mass-scale commercialization of state enterprises, rapid establishment of the stock exchange, careful valuation of enterprises and their sale through auctions and public offers. Similarly to Hungarian privatizers, the Lis group was essentially against vouchers and investment funds. The strategy had already encountered a difficulty in December 1989 when, in order not to antagonize trade unions and workers' councils, the mass commercialization proposal was rejected by the government. Instead, incentives were created to induce state enterprises to accept voluntary commercialization, and compulsory commercialization was left as an option to be used rarely. However, the main objection to Lis's strategy was that the pace of privatization using classical methods would be much too slow. In the summer of 1990, this led Leszek Balcerowicz and his key advisers to seek novel ways of accelerating the privatization process. An acceleration was also demanded by Lech Wałęsa in his presidential campaign during that time.

The hottest debate concerned the privatization of large enterprises (URM 1990). The use of vouchers was accepted as necessary for providing access to state assets to all (adult) citizens, and therefore gaining vital political support for the entire privatization programme. There remained the question of whether the vouchers should be named, in order to avoid their early sale in secondary markets and a collapse of share prices, or not named, in order to facilitate the creation of a capital market and a rapid concentration of shareholding. In both cases, to provide effective oversight for enterprise managements on behalf of the millions of shareholders, it became necessary to propose setting up intermediaries. But various blueprints differed as to the minimum number of these institutions, whether they should be state or market created, which if any of the existing institutions (banks, pension funds) could play such a role, what should be the rules for distributing the enterprise shares between intermediaries, and what role to offer to foreign management funds. Creating a small number of holding companies in the role of such intermediaries was administratively attractive, but could make them similar to old ministries or production associations, capable of engaging in monopolistic practices. Since the bankruptcy of such a holding company would be inconceivable, there was also the danger that the soft budget constraint that has long bedevilled the socialist economies might be recreated in a different guise.

The involvement of government in creating the intermediaries would help in terms of resources, supervision and trust, but care should be taken not to make them excessively bureaucratic. Western experts, particularly the British privatization advisers Warburg (1990), noted that mutual funds in Western countries act typically as passive investors. Poland needed active investors who would take control of the restructuring activities. This led to the idea of selecting one fund for each enterprise as a dominant shareholder.

Finally, there was the delicate matter of the extent and forms of involvement of foreign ownership and management. Already in early 1990 it was proposed and broadly accepted as a long-term aim that the economy-wide foreign ownership be substantial but possibly not more than 20 per cent (Gomulka 1990a). It was also hoped that there would be a considerable direct foreign investment ; a target of 50 billion US$ was thought feasible for the total inflow of foreign capital in the 1990s. Instead of selling state assets cheaply to foreigners, it was proposed to involve Western management companies in running the intermediaries (Frydman and Rapaczynski 1990, 1991). These companies, it was argued, have the standing necessary to attract foreign credits for restructuring and the know-how necessary to arrange production of attractive goods at competitive prices. Following such restructuring, the market value of Polish enterprises would increase sharply and, according to this argument, it would then be the right time for Polish shareholders to exercise the option of selling their stock to foreign buyers. These ideas influenced the scheme for 'mass privatization' of large enterprises (section 6).

The blueprints also differed with respect to a number of technical (rather than policy) issues. These included the specification of incentives for managements of the intermediaries; the appointment procedures for these managements; the rules for selecting enterprises; who and how would be selling enterprise shares to intermediaries and the shares of intermediaries to the public for privatization coupons; what other state property, apart from large enterprises in the mass privatization programme, could be bought for coupons; the precise rights of shareholders and the duties of intermediaries. One of the more controversial issues turned out to be the use of 'special' credit to augment the coupon capital. Some proposed to link the size of the credit in a fixed ratio to investor's own capital (Gomulka 1990a). Others proposed to offer such credit to all adults (Wałęsa's proposal of '10,000 US$ for everyone' was also made in the summer of 1990 during his presidential campaign), or to no-one (this was essentially the position of Balcerowicz). This particular issue was again hotly debated in 1993 and by the end of that year was still awaiting a clear resolution.

4. Mass privatization of small-scale businesses

Two important forms of privatization, especially in the early stages of the process, have been *municipal privatization* and the transformation of co-operatives. Both involved small-scale businesses and were therefore called *small privatization*. Analysis of these forms is, however, very difficult because reliable data are exceptionally scarce and dispersed. It also runs into similar conceptual problems as privatization in general on account of being sometimes mixed up with the organic growth of the private sector.

MUNICIPAL PRIVATIZATION

Most municipal privatizations concern retail trade. They were made possible by the Act on Economic Activities of December 1988 and the Act regulating the rental of trade premises, as amended in June 1990. Most of these premises belonged to municipal authorities and almost all of them changed their users but not their owners. The state and municipally owned retail and wholesale trade firms or nominal cooperatives, previously occupying the municipally owned trading premises, lost them, in a more or less competitive process, to private entrepreneurs, at the same time losing their workforces[10]. By the end of 1991, 33,786 premises owned by local councils moved from public to private users (Tamowicz *et al.* 1992), but only 1074 (3.2 per cent) of them were actually sold. It has led to a form of privatization from below of retail and wholesale trade, based on leasing arrangements[11]. The previously dominating firms, which are being privatized using techniques described in section 5, continue to trade on the premises which they actually owned.

In the first half of 1990, only 9 per cent of rent contracts, signed with the local councils and cooperatives, were based on open auctions and within the next 12 months this share fell to 4 per cent[12]. In all other cases some more or less transparent administrative procedures were applied and those who worked previously on the premises involved were offered preferential financial terms.

The legislation introduced in the spring of 1990 gave the local authorities the right to hold property. The ownership rights of some SOEs and state budgetary entities were transferred to local authorities on the territory of which they were located. Most of them were either public services or public utilities. Local authorities, in turn, were obliged to decide till the end of 1992 whether these enterprises were to be joint-stock companies, fully owned by the local council and with councillors acting as board directors, or budgetary units[13]. Both legal forms, however, could become transitory stages on the way towards privatization. Since privatization usually demands more expertise than most local authorities have at their disposal, once the necessary decision is taken, they are allowed to sign a contract with the MOP to have privatization services provided by the Ministry's officials and experts.

COOPERATIVES

Under the communist regime, cooperatives had in fact very little to do with group ownership; they were *de facto* — and not only from the point of view of the statistical classification used — a part of the public sector. At the same time they constituted a large[14] and very diversified class of economic agents, embracing housing cooperatives, labour cooperatives, dairy cooperatives, agricultural production cooperatives, cooperatives for the disabled, and cooperative banks. What is even more important, there existed cooperatives of legal persons as well as of natural persons. All of them were highly centralized and it was only in the 1980s that some genuine small cooperatives were set up.

This state of affairs provoked a quick reaction from the Mazowiecki government. The Cooperative Law was already amended in January 1990 in order to restructure and democratize the cooperative sector of the Polish economy. The amendments brought forward the election of new member representatives and liquidated all cooperative bureaucracy at the regional and national levels (Bandyk 1991). Other legislative changes intended to provide a legal basis for ownership changes in this sector, particularly for the transformation of cooperatives into companies registered under the Commercial Code, were still being debated in 1993, and new amendments to the Cooperative Law are expected in 1994[15].

5. Methods and results of privatization in the narrow sense

The methods and techniques of proper privatization which have been used in Poland include: capital privatization, privatization through liquidation using either the Privatization Act or the law on state-owned enterprises, the 'privatization express', sectoral (branch) privatization and privatization through restructuring. This section discusses all of these as well as privatization of banks and insurance companies and privatization in agriculture, which constitute special cases.

CAPITAL PRIVATIZATION

Capital privatization usually starts with the decision of the Ministry of Privatization (MOP, in Polish called the Ministry of Ownership Changes), to transform an SOE into a joint stock company with the state as single shareholder. In exceptional cases such a decision can be taken unilaterally by the Prime Minister[16], but normally the initiative belongs either to the SOE concerned, i.e. to its executive director and the employee council (after having obtained the opinion of the general assembly of the employees (delegates) as well as the opinion of its Founding Body), or to its Founding Body — typically a minister — with the consent of the SOE (Article 5 of the Privatization Act).

Initially a company emerging from such a transformation remains exclusively owned by the State Treasury. It assumes all the rights and duties of the transformed SOE and the Commercial Code applies (Articles 7 and 8). Yet privatization implies that shares are disposed to third parties and the MOP is given two years to do it, assuming that proper asset valuation has been completed and the legal status of a company's assets determined. It can choose one of the following three possibilities: an auction, a public offer, and negotiation after a public invitation (Article 23, para. 1)[17].

The subscription for the first public offer started on 30 November 1990. Part of the shares in five companies — 4.33 million out of the total of 6.5 million shares — were offered to the private sector (because state legal persons had to have special permission to purchase privatization shares)[18]. From then until the end

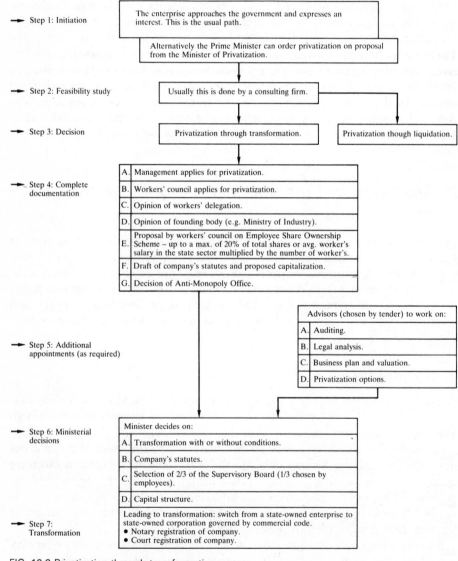

FIG. 10.2 Privatization through transformation
Source: Jermakowicz (1992)

of 1993 this method of finding buyers for all or some shares in privatized companies was used in 18 cases (but only in one case in 1992) and their shares are traded, together with those in four other companies, on the Warsaw Stock Exchange, which began trading on 16 April 1991[19].

Far more successful, especially more recently and from the point of view of state revenue, were trade sales, especially those in which foreign investors were the buyers, and leveraged buy-outs (LBOs)[20].

Altogether, by the end of 1993, 98 cases of 'individual capital privatizations' were completed (see Table 10.3). The sum total of payments received by the Treasury from 'individual capital privatizations' until then was equal to about $520 mln.

PRIVATIZATION THROUGH LIQUIDATION USING THE PRIVATIZATION ACT

The space devoted in the Act — 26 articles on 'capital privatization' against only 6 on 'liquidation privatization' — reflected the priorities and expectations of the official privatizers in the early 1990. These priorities were challenged within the government in the summer 1990. The developments which followed passing the Act have reflected the new approach, stressing techniques which were capable of accelerating the process (see section 3 above). In terms of the number of privatized medium-size SOEs, privatization through liquidation has proved to be the most effective technique, and leasing the most popular procedure of its implementation[21].

The very name 'liquidation privatization' is misleading insofar as the SOEs privatized in this way are in fact in a relatively good financial position. Under this procedure, a given enterprise is dissolved or wound up as a SOE[22], and its former employees set up a new company, with or without the participation of outside investors. This new company then takes control over all or some[23] of the assets of the liquidated enterprise. More precisely, to quote the Act;

> a Founding Body, after obtaining the consent of the Minister of Privatization, may rule that a SOE be wound up in order to:
> - sell its assets, or integrated parts of the enterprise's assets,
> - use the enterprise's assets or integrated parts of its assets as a contribution to a company,
> - allow the enterprise's assets or integrated parts of its assets to be let against payment for a specified time (Article 37, para. 1).

Until the end of 1993, this technique was applied in 917 SOEs, 73.5 per cent of which were to use leasing, and the process was completed in 707 of them.

The popularity of this type of privatization among employees stems from two reasons: they are treated preferentially in terms of access to assets[24], and only some money must be paid out of their own pockets. On the other hand, unlike cases in which the techniques described in the previous and the next sub-section were used, this kind of privatization is usually accompanied by a far reaching restructuring, both before and after ownership transformation. That is, this procedure is usually undertaken with a prepared business plan. From this point

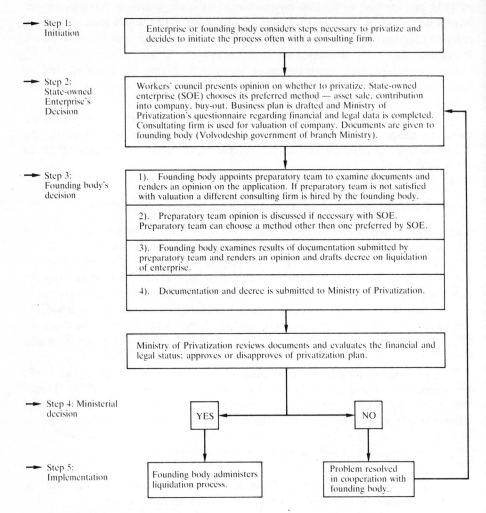

Step 1:
Initiation

Enterprise or founding body considers steps necessary to privatize and decides to initiate the process often with a consulting firm.

Step 2:
State-owned
Enterprise's
Decision

Workers' council presents opinion on whether to privatize. State-owned enterprise (SOE) chooses its preferred method — asset sale, contribution into company, buy-out. Business plan is drafted and Ministry of Privatization's questionnaire regarding financial and legal data is completed. Consultating firm is used for valuation of company. Documents are given to founding body (Volvodeship government of branch Ministry).

Step 3:
Founding body's
decision

1). Founding body appoints preparatory team to examine documents and renders an opinion on the application. If preparatory team is not satisfied with valuation a different consulting firm is hired by the founding body.

2). Preparatory team opinion is discussed if necessary with SOE. Preparatory team can choose a method other then one preferred by SOE.

3). Founding body examines results of documentation submitted by preparatory team and renders an opinion and drafts decree on liquidation of enterprise.

4). Documentation and decree is submitted to Ministry of Privatization.

Ministry of Privatization reviews documents and evaluates the financial and legal status; approves or disapproves of privatization plan.

Step 4: Ministerial
decision

YES   NO

Step 5:
Implementation

Founding body administers liquidation process.

Problem resolved in cooperation with founding body.

FIG. 10.3 Privatization through liquidation
Source: Jermakowicz (1992)

of view it is a pity that, because of limited access to credit, the size of liquidated SOEs is usually the most important factor limiting more frequent use of this technique. Further developments will, however, depend on the extent to which the present tendency to restrict trade in stocks and shares is overcome, thus allowing more dynamic growth of these companies.

PRIVATIZATION THROUGH LIQUIDATION USING THE LAW ON STATE-OWNED ENTERPRISES

A sharply increased level of international and domestic competition in 1991, the second year of transition, has led to a rapid deterioration in the financial position of many SOEs[25]. This situation had to be taken into account in designing privatization policy. The bankruptcy of an SOE, triggered for example by not paying the so-called dividenda tax, did not imply that some or even all of its assets could not be used profitably, especially if they were to be transferred to the private sector. Such a transfer is a form of privatization, but the legal instrument used is the Act on state-owned enterprises of 25 September 1981, with later amendments, not the Privatization Act.

In practice things are organized in the following way. The Act under consideration, Article 20, foresees the following situations in which an SOE can be liquidated:

1. The after-tax profits are not high enough to pay the 'dividend'[26];
2. The court or the administrative authorities banned all previous activities of the given SOE and no new activities had been started;
3. The government-appointed receiver proposes liquidation;
4. Stocks, shares and/or bonds plus assets leased or rented constitute more than a half of all assets of the given SOEs[27].

If any of these situations happens, the founding ministry may decide, either on its own or when solicited by the managers, to liquidate the enterprise[28]. Out of 1082 enterprises liquidated in this way until 31 December 1993, 87 were declared bankrupt and their assets and liabilities were taken care of by the courts. In other cases a liquidator is appointed to decide what to do with the assets, which may either be auctioned off or become a contribution in kind to a new company, set up, for example, by former employees. However, by the end of 1993 only 15.1 per cent of the liquidations in question, i.e. 172 out of 1082, ended up in striking the enterprise off the SOE register (see Table 10.3). This outcome indicates that it is easier to liquidate an enterprise than to find alternative uses for its assets. Recession and excess supply of second-hand capital goods are possible explanations for this state of affairs. At the same time cases of selling a (bankrupt) enterprise for a

TABLE 10.3 Number of privatized state-owned enterprises

	Total	Capital privatization	Mass privatization	Liquidation privatization	
				Art. 19	Art. 37
31.12.1990	6 (130)	6 (58)	0	0 (28)	0 (44)
30.06.1991	113 (505)	13 (162)	0	21 (173)	79 (170)
31.12.1991	188 (1258)	30 (244)	0 (64)	44 (534)	114 (416)
30.06.1992	385 (1724)	36 (286)	0 (178)	78 (708)	271 (542)
31.12.1992	570 (2052)	53 (301)	0 (183)	118 (853)	399 (715)
30.06.1993	781 (2265)	77 (316)	0 (185)	123 (967)	581 (797)
31.12.1193	977 (2521)	98 (336)	0 (186)	172 (1082)	707 (917)

Source: Central Statistical Office, Dynamika Prywatyzacji, various issues; own calculations
Note: Figures in brackets refer to the number of enterprises qualified to take part in the privatization programme

symbolic price are still sporadic. The authorities are aware that waiting too long for a buyer willing to pay a higher price may result in a rapid depreciation of assets, even to the point that nobody would be ready to accept them as a gift. But they often prefer to risk this rather than be accused of colluding with the buyer at the public expense.

'PRIVATIZATION EXPRESS'

The sections above described the standard privatization techniques adopted in Poland. However, within a limited legal framework provided by the Privatization Act and the Enterprise Act, more imaginative approaches are also possible, and the MOP has been trying to make use of at least some of them. The most relevant initiatives are presented below.

'Privatization express' is a form of 'liquidation privatization' aiming to speed up the sales of small and medium size SOEs (employing up to 500 people) to Polish investors[29].

It works as follows[30]. Founding bodies propose which firms they would like to be sold in this way, but each of their choices has to be approved by the MOP. When all necessary documents are ready, the sale of an enterprise is announced and after two weeks a commission staffed by people from the founding ministry negotiates the sale, taking into account prices offered[31], structure of payments, level and structure of employment, and investment potential of the buyer (Latuch and Głogowski 1992).

By the end of 1992 the 'express' sales of 103 firms were announced, 45 of them were completed, and negotiations are still going on in 23 cases. This may appear slightly disappointing, but an important conclusion to be drawn from this experience is that various forms of auctions, very attractive from the theoretical point of view[32], are likely to fail if too many conditions, the lowest acceptable price included, are imposed.

SECTORAL (BRANCH) PRIVATIZATION

In principle, a sectoral (branch) privatization may be either capital privatization or liquidation privatization. What makes it a distinct form of privatization is an attempt to exploit economies of scale, to the extent that problems faced by all enterprises in the given (sector of) industry are common or similar. For the MOP it is also easier, under the sectoral approach, to shape the future market and ownership structure of these industries, taking into account the requirements of competition policy and capital investment. In other words, sectoral (branch) privatizations combine ownership transformation with restructuring and with industrial policy.

Sectoral (branch) privatizations are to be based on detailed industrial studies of 34 sectors, ranging from petrochemicals and paper to sugar and beer. These are commissioned by the MOP from domestic and foreign consulting firms and investment banks. Authors of the studies are supposed to participate actively in subsequent privatizations, among others helping to find core investors.

So far now there has been one clear success story, the detergent products industry. Since privatization the industry includes several international producers.[33]. Another example of a successfully completed sectoral privatization is the car industry, with Fiat, General Motors, Peugeot and Volkswagen participating. Unfortunately, sectoral (branch) privatizations were considerably slowed down in the first half of 1992 under the Olszewski's Premiership, which resulted in many sectoral studies that were already prepared becoming out of date.

A special case concerns foreign trade companies. These are a remnant of the old system, when foreign trade was monopolized by the state. Some of them have nevertheless managed to adjust well to the new reality[34]. Out of 54 such companies, by the end of 1992 11 had already been privatized, 7 were being sold, and 5 were undergoing liquidation. Restructuring had started in four of them, and the rest were at various preparatory stages.

BANKS AND INSURANCE COMPANIES

Banks and insurance companies constitute a special case, firstly because their founding organ is the Finance Ministry and, secondly because their privatization is considered to be an opportunity to restructure these two crucial areas for creating the institutional framework of the nascent capital market in Poland.

Under the old system Poland, like all the other Soviet-type economies (STEs), had the so-called monobank and a few specialized banks. In 1988 the former was divided, along regional lines, into nine commercial banks[35]. Despite the fact that since 1988 scores of new banks have been created, their combined market share is still less than 5 per cent.

The decision of the Council of Ministers of 14 May 1991 made possible the transformation of the nine commercial banks into joint stock companies, with the Treasury the single shareholder[36]. Their subsequent privatization is expected to take place within the next three to five years. Public offers of the first two — Bank Śląski in Katowice and Wielkopolski Bank Kredytowy in Poznań — have taken place in 1993. To help the process along, the end result of which is to be an efficient banking system of West European quality, seven of the nine commercial banks were paired with various banks from the EC. The government intends to retain the majority of the bank shares in Polish ownership, while encouraging some of the foreign banks to buy shares of their supervisees[37]. To proceed with these privatizations, two fundamental problems have to be solved first: under-capitalization of banks and bad debts of enterprises. The new Act on Financial Restructuring of Banks and Enterprises, dated 19 December 1992, aims to deal with these two related problems. In particular, it allows for debt-for-equity swaps and an injection of capital from the budget, the World Bank and the G-24 Stabilization Fund.

Despite the fact that many new insurance companies have been created in the years 1990-1993, this market is still dominated by two firms: PZU SA and TUiR Warta SA, controlling respectively 70 and 16 per cent[38]. The main problem to be solved is the division of the PZU SA. The document presented by the government in December 1992[39] proposed that two nation-wide companies would be created, both having 50 per cent of shares in all regional branches[40]. The restructuring process is to be finished by the end of 1994. Privatization by a public offer should take place in 1995. In the case of the TUiR Warta SA, the aim of having the majority of its shares in private hands will be achieved by issuing new shares, offered to the public. Eventually the shares now held by the Treasury will also be sold.

As insurance companies are usually important institutional investors, privatization of the PZU and Warta is expected to help in speeding up the process of privatization of other companies and the development of capital markets, particularly the stock exchange.

PRIVATIZATION WITH RESTRUCTURING

This privatization technique was prompted by the increasing number of small and medium SOEs which were considered viable in the medium and long term, but for various reasons were currently in deep trouble. To meet the problem, in summer 1991 a restructuring team was created under the leadership of W. Jermakowicz and T. Stankiewicz. It developed a new technique which combines privatization with restructuring (Stankiewicz and Jermakowicz 1991). Management teams — individuals and/or institutions, domestic and/or foreign — would be invited to compete with each other in terms of restructuring plans and assessments of how much a given enterprise is worth. Restructuring would be carried out by the management team which wins the competition and the ultimate goal is to sell the restructured enterprise.

Although legally an enterprise under such restructuring remains, until the moment of its sale, owned by the State Treasury, this technique was designed to assure the best possible incentive structure for the winning management team. Apart from salaries, the managers would receive the share of after tax profits which corresponds to their own contribution to the capital of the company as well as, after the contract has been implemented, a share of the revenue from selling the enterprise. The share is 70 per cent of the increase in enterprise value resulting from the restructuring effort of the management team. Both shares are parts of the contract.

In the autumn of 1992 the first 15 SOEs were selected to participate in the programme, which is organized by Deloitte and Touche[41]. First contracts were awarded in 1993. Whether it works in practice remains to be seen, but financial restrictions imposed on the possible participants as well as fears of dysfunctional or collusive behaviour seem to be the most important obstacles to more extensive use of this method.

PRIVATIZATION IN AGRICULTURE

In 1989 71.7 per cent of agricultural land was in private hands, while 3.9 per cent was cultivated by cooperatives. The rest was owned by the state and organized in state-owned farms, known as PGRs. At that time 959 PGRs[42] owned 3.507

million hectares of land and employed 441,000 people. The systemic reforms of 1989–1990 led most of them to the verge of bankruptcy in 1991 and 1992. To solve the ownership problem in this sector of the economy, a special Agency of the State Treasury (*Agencja Własności Rolnej Skarbu Państwa* — AWRSP) was created. Its main task is to take over all PGRs, and find for them either outright buyers or leasees. By the end of 1993, 1557 PGRs became 'treasury farms'. Only 58,600 hectares were actually sold[43]. It seems that limited outside demand for land is emerging as an important barrier. Therefore it was proposed that each employee should be given a 0.4 hectare plot free of charge. This would help them to survive the most difficult period, and would in the process dispose of 100,000 hectares.

Despite the AWRSP's effectiveness in taking over the PGRs and despite high expectations, the process of ownership changes in agriculture will be long and complicated. The main barrier is financial; the PGRs are heavily indebted, their assets are often over-valued, and the price of credit is still very high. The unsolved reprivatization problems and gaps in legal documentation further slow down any progress. Finally, the whole process is causing serious social problems and the attitudes to privatization of those involved is often highly emotional (Olko-Bagieńska *et al.* 1992).

6. Privatization in 1993 and prospects for 1994–1995

Some of the plans of the Polish government in general and of the MOP in particular have already been mentioned in this chapter. All of them were listed and summarized in two documents: the *Memorandum of the Government of Poland on Economic Policy* (CM 1992b), prepared for the IMF in December 1992, and in the *Proposals for the privatization in 1993* (CM 1992a), sent for approval to Parliament in the same month[44]. Their implementation will be strongly affected by the Pact on Enterprises, a product of negotiations between the government, trade unions and employers. This Pact includes, *inter alia*, amendments to the Act of 13 July 1990.

All approaches to privatization, described above, continued in 1993. It is envisaged that in the years 1993–1994 1500–2000 SOEs, of about 7000 still remaining, will be commercialized and that privatization with restructuring will finally commence. Thirteen sectoral (branch) privatizations will also continue. 'Privatization express' should transfer to the private sector about 40 SOEs and debt-for-equity swaps will be encouraged, but initially limited to domestic banks and investors. Classical 'capital privatization' will result in only 8 to 10 public offers. Some 400 SOEs will take part in 'liquidation privatization' of the first type, i.e. they will be wound up in order to be privatized. The assets of almost 90 per cent of them will be leased using liberalized procedures compared to those in 1992. Bankruptcy liquidation will affect an additional 200 SOEs.

The most important issues in 1993 were, however, mass privatization of large SOEs, and reprivatization.

MASS PRIVATIZATION

Mass privatization is typically understood as (almost) free distribution of shares of a large number of state-owned enterprises, usually medium and large-scale, directly or through intermediaries in the form of mutual investment funds, banks, pension funds or holdings. In the West it was once advocated by Milton Friedman and Samuel Brittan, but never really tried in practice. In the context of the SOEs it was first proposed, as has been mentioned, by Lewandowski and Szomburg[45]. Despite many objections formulated by the critics of their proposal, it slowly gained political currency. Among other things, the Act of 13 July 1990 contains a clause, inserted at the very late stage of the parliamentary debate, which reads as follows:

The Parliament, on a motion of the Council of Ministers, shall pass a resolution regarding the issue and value of Privatization Coupons which can be used to pay for:

a. acquiring shares issued as a result of the transformation of an SOE;
b. acquiring title to participation in financial institutions (Mutual Investment Funds) which will have at their disposal shares created as a result of the transformation of SOEs;
c. acquiring enterprises or integrated parts of the assets of SOEs ... .

The Privatization Coupons issued ... will be distributed free of charge in equal volume among all citizens of the Republic of Poland resident in the country. (Article 25, para. 1 and 2).

The initially slow pace of ownership changes and the slow adaptation of SOEs to the new economic environment won support for mass privatization from three key figures: Lech Wałęsa, Tadeusz Mazowiecki and Leszek Balcerowicz. Once Janusz Lewandowski became Minister of Privatization in the Bielecki government (end of 1990 until end of 1991), an acceleration of privatization along this route seemed likely. In the event this apparently simple idea proved to be a logistic nightmare. What is more, all attempts to translate it into law which would make the general provisions of the Act specific and operational suffered from continuous political turbulence. The parliamentary election of 27 October 1991 made any serious discussion impossible, not to mention drafting the necessary legislation. Tomasz Gruszecki, responsible for ownership changes in the Olszewski government (December 1991–June 1992), restarted work on the draft but finished it only in June 1992, when the government fell. It was therefore Janusz Lewandowski again, returned to office in July 1992, whose task it was in 1993 to win the approval of the Polish Parliament for mass privatization of this kind. He achieved this objective in April and May 1993, when, respectively, the Sejm and the Senate approved the Law on National Investment Funds and their privatization.

The implementation of the mass privatization programme will be organized as follows. The key intermediary institutions are to be the National Investment

Funds (NIFs). There are to be about 30 of them (initially 20) and they are supposed to combine the activities of three different financial institutions known in the West: venture capital/turn around agencies, holding companies, and closed-end funds (Jermakowicz and Jermakowicz 1992). Each fund is to have a board of directors, a majority of them Polish citizens, appointed by a special selection committee[46]. These boards will supervise fund managers, who in turn will play the role of effective owners with respect to companies taking part in mass privatization. They are supposed to maximize the long-term worth of assets managed by their funds on behalf of the millions of small individual owners, and will be remunerated accordingly[47].

The NIFs will receive 60 per cent of shares in participating companies, but only 27 per cent of them will be distributed equally among all NIFs. The remaining 33 per cent will be bid for, and will go to one NIF, so that each NIF becomes a core investor (or dominant shareholder) in about 10 to 20 companies[48]. Employees of the participating enterprises will be given 15 per cent of shares in their enterprises (Art. 46.2).

The NIFs will themselves be joint stock companies owned by Polish citizens who will exchange their participation certificates for shares of the NIFs, once they become quoted by the Warsaw Stock Exchange. These certificates will be distributed at a nominal registration fee of 10 per cent of the average monthly wage to all eligible people who choose to participate in the programme[49]. The exchange of certificates for shares will however be possible only after one full year of working of the scheme, when first company reports will be ready for assessment. In the meantime, secondary trading in certificates among citizens (sales of certificates for cash) and in the shares of privatized companies among funds (swaps of shares for shares) will be allowed.

The government objectives of this programme are as follows: (1) accelerating restructuring of the enterprises involved, (2) further developing capital markets, (3) lessening the pressure on wages and subsidies, (4) attracting higher foreign investment, (5) increasing the long-term worth of the enterprises and job security for the employees (MOP 1992b). It remains to be seen whether all these objectives will be achieved. The energy of the MOP has so far concentrated, perhaps excessively, on perfecting the legal framework within which the NIFs are supposed to operate, creating in consequence a system which is quite complicated for a society with, until recently, almost no experience of capital markets. Another important question mark is raised by the possibility that the NIFs may constitute a powerful pressure group *vis-à-vis* the government. However, the really central question is whether the few funds will be capable of providing efficient oversight. This is related to the incentives for, and the control of, the managers of such funds. An incentive structure chosen is to supplement a management fee with stocks: 1 per cent for each year and 5 per cent at the end of the 10 year period (MOP 1993).

The first SOEs to be privatized in this way were selected as early as autumn 1991 and transformed into joint stock companies fully owned by the Treasury. The process has continued since then and, in early 1994, about 400 out of the envisaged 600 were selected for the programme and transformed into such companies. The sales of the 400 account for about 20 per cent of total public enterprise sector sales. According to the Law on National Investment Funds and their privatization these 400 enterprises will constitute the first tranche. The other 200 enterprises are to follow, depending on decisions of the enterprises themselves regarding whether or not they want to participate. The fact that the Pact on Enterprises is to force SOEs to decide about the method of their privatization within a fairly short period of time after the Pact comes into force, has already influenced many SOEs to join the mass privatization programme. The mere prospect of inevitable privatization is also accelerating the process of adjustment and restructuring.

THE PACT ON ENTERPRISES

The Pact on Enterprises, was proposed by Jacek Kuroń, Minister for Labour and Social Security in the Suchocka government, in July 1992. Negotiations between the government, almost all trade unions and the representatives of employers took place from October to December of that year. The tripartite Pact was signed on 22 February 1993 and is the first agreement of that kind in the post-communist countries. The Pact has been codified in 13 pieces of proposed parliamentary legislation, to be considered in 1994.

The Pact has three parts regarding labour issues, financial matters and privatization. In order to speed up privatization, workers are to be given a period of time, yet to be specified, to choose a form of it. If they fail to do so, the MOP will be free, and indeed obliged, to take the decision. Financial terms for leasing agreements under liquidation privatization will be eased. What is more, ownership rights will be transferred before all payments are made, giving enterprises better access to bank credit. Instead of being entitled to purchase 20 per cent of shares at a 50 per cent discount, workers will be given 15 per cent of shares free of charge. The right of employees to elect some members of the supervisory board will be a permanent one. Finally, the excess-wage and 'dividenda' taxes[50] will be phased out and a new tripartite commission will be set up to negotiate nationwide pay agreements.

7. Constraints to privatization

Bolton and Roland (1992) divide all major constraints to privatization into five categories: stock-flow, fiscal, informational, administrative and political. This is a useful categorization and in this section we shall briefly comment on these constraints and discuss their impact in Poland.

The *stock-flow constraint* has already been mentioned. It denotes the fact that the stock of assets to be sold is large compared to the flow of new savings of households or the flow of future profits of enterprises. Since excessive lengthening of the period of privatization was not acceptable to Polish reformers, there remained two other options: selling to foreigners at full prices and to domestic investors at give-away prices.

The *fiscal constraint* is typically a serious problem during transition. As the economy shrinks, social expenditures increase, and enterprises profits fall, a large budget deficit tends to emerge. One way of reducing the deficit could be to sell much of state assets at 'reasonable' prices. This would require slowing down the pace of privatization. Keeping the deficit low is needed to achieve macroeconomic stability, while privatization is needed to speed up microeconomic restructuring. Therefore the fiscal constraint considerations may imply that there exists a trade-off between macroeconomic stability and privatization. An additional support for the presence of such a trade-off is derived from the evidence of a relatively large incidence of tax avoidance in the private sector.

These arguments are, however, easy to overstate. The tax avoidance is serious only in the sector of very small private enterprises, those employing less than five workers. Such enterprises are typically new ventures rather than the products of state-driven privatization. A major cause of the fiscal problem is also 'tax strikes' by powerful state enterprises. Privatization of these may in fact help to meet the problem. Some larger private firms, especially with foreign participation, are offered tax incentives. But the incentives operate for a short period of time, and their purpose is to induce greater investment and therefore to increase future tax revenue. Selling state enterprises to poor domestic investors at full prices, for cash or against future profits (no-cash bids, advocated by Bolton and Roland, 1992), has the disadvantage of reducing private resources needed for restructuring of the privatized enterprises. The strategy would amount to making use of scarce private savings for the purpose of financing public consumption.

The fiscal implications were considered by the Polish reformers in the summer of 1990, when privatization policies were formulated, and again in 1991–93, when budget deficits became a problem. The policy chosen was that efficient and speedy privatization rather than large revenue from privatization from domestic investors should be the dominant concern of the MOP. At the same time it was decided to reduce the scale of tax privileges to joint ventures and to strengthen tax discipline in the private sector. The introduction of VAT in July 1993 was also intended to achieve the latter end. At the same time the government was ready to meet some categories of budgetary obligations with the shares of state enterprises. Already in 1990 the London Club of creditors was informed that stock-debt swaps could be one of the debt reduction instruments. In 1992 the parliament offered the government to settle with shares outstanding pay obligations to the employees of budgetary units and some categories of pensioners. The first tranche of nearly 400 large state enterprises under the mass privatization programme of 1993, worth about $4 billion, is to be used in part for this purpose. The state shares will also be used to compensate former owners for nationalization of their property. A wider use of shares as a way of payment to pensioners was considered in 1991, but rejected on the grounds that it would be opposed by pensioners themselves.

The *informational constraint* relates to limited ability to value enterprises in the new (market) environment. This is less of a problem if assets are given away or auctioned off. In those situations it was accepted that the book value can be a rough guide.

Ascribing excessive importance to the concept of book value or, alternatively, stressing the need to provide independent assessments of the value of assets has nevertheless proved time consuming. Repeated controls by the NIK, a state audit office, caused central privatizers to become over-cautious. This was particularly damaging because privatization in Poland has from the very beginning been highly centralized[51], partly because of bad experiences with *nomenklatura* privatization.

Administrative constraints have caused a serious bottleneck. The constraints favoured the choice of simple privatization techniques and forced the use of outside consultants, some of them foreigners. In order to make better use of local resources many privatization offices were set up throughout the country.

The category of *political constraint* brings us to the problem of the attitudes of Polish society towards privatization. Paradoxically, public support for privatization had been at its strongest before the process of systemic transformation started. A CBOS survey of spring 1989 showed that 97.9 per cent of workers and 99.2 per cent of managers favoured privatization in the handicraft sector, retail trading and small-scale industrial enterprises, while privatization of large industrial enterprises, the least favourably viewed, was supported by, respectively, 58.9 and 56.6 per cent of the members of the two groups. In February 1990 those accepting the view that privatization was necessary in Poland still outnumbered its opponents by a ratio of 5:1 (56.3 per cent against 11 per cent of respondents), but only 14.7 per cent were prepared to invest their savings in shares of privatized companies.

Two and a half years after the Privatization Act was passed, privatization is still perceived as something unavoidable, but, again according to CBOS, between January 1991 and December 1992 the proportion of people thinking that privatization is good for the Polish economy diminished from 47 per cent to 32 per cent and the share of people rejecting this view increased from 5 per cent to 19 per cent[52]. On the other hand, only 4 per cent of those surveyed wanted to work in a privatized firm and only 14 per cent were prepared to view the privatization of their own firm with hope rather than with fears[53]. The following are the primary concerns:

1. The distribution of state assets, in the form of shares or the revenue from their sales, may not be 'just';
2. High unemployment may be a by-product of privatization; and
3. Too large a share of the economy may become foreign-owned or otherwise come under the control of foreigners.

Concern (3) was particularly strong at the start of the reform. However, it became subsequently evident that foreign capital is not eager to invade Poland. Advantages of attracting foreign capital and foreign management services to improve competitiveness and save employment have also been noted. Consequently this particular concern ceased to be a major factor, though it influenced somewhat the content of the mass privatization bill (see section 6).

Privatization in Poland, looked at as an exercise in the redistribution of wealth, does not present a clear picture. It is still too early to identify those who gain most. Slogans on the need to create a middle class are used often. But in practice the first move belongs typically to the workers and not to prospective investors. The desire to cushion the possible negative effects of privatization, the fears of which so far proved unfounded, often takes precedence over the efforts to create opportunities for entrepreneurship.

The distrust, and even fear, which found their expression in the CBOS surveys quoted above, are quite understandable, but they were reinforced by political in-fighting, especially during the presidential election campaign of November and December 1990 and prior to the parliamentary elections of 27 October 1991 and 19 September 1993. The three elections resulted in many changes of government. As a consequence, apart from Krzysztof Lis who set up the privatization bureaucracy in 1989 and 1990 but never became cabinet minister, ministers in charge of privatization were Waldemar Kuczyński (autumn 1990), Janusz Lewandowski (twice: 1991 and from July 1992 to September 1993), Tomasz Gruszecki (the first half of 1992) and Wiesław Kaczmarek (from October 1993). This lack of continuity at the top was accompanied by many changes at lower levels of the ministerial hierarchy. Also important have been legislative delays, illustrated best by the fate of the laws on mass privatization and reprivatization.

8. A tentative assessment: concluding remarks

The measures typically used to assess the progress of privatization are the shares of the private sector in employment, capital ownership, output and investment. If we take the share of the GDP produced by the private sector, 50 per cent in 1993, or the share of the private sector employment, 60 per cent in 1993, it is evident that a very considerable success has been achieved. But if we compare the result with expectations as reflected in successive government programmes, some disappointment would be justified.

The question of whether privatization improves economic efficiency is now easy to answer for whole economies in the long run, but can be difficult with respect to particular enterprises in the shortrun, and be so even in relatively stable economies like the UK one (Yarrow 1989). The very process of fast systemic transformation as well as the sheer scale and complexity of the East European undertaking makes the comparison task virtually impossible. Higher consumer satisfaction from the wider range and higher quality of products and the much improved performance of the trade sector is in good measure due to privatization. But this improvement is probably not captured fully by the official statistics.

Three studies deserve attention. For 1991 Dąbrowski et al. (1992b) investigated 20 enterprises and for the period ending on 30 June 1992 the sample was increased to 55 enterprises (Dąbrowski et al. 1992c), all of them at different stages of the ownership transformation process. The researchers were interested in almost all aspects of privatization, beginning with the question of who initiated the procedure and ending with the present distribution of shares. Although the profitability of privatized companies declined over the investigated period of time, this decline was smaller than for the economy as a whole. This is particularly true for those enterprises that underwent capital privatization. The two reports confirm that the main problem of privatization in Poland is politics and the state administration. But what makes their overall assessment relatively optimistic are efforts undertaken by many privatized companies to reorganize themselves, to introduce production modifications and to extend the scope of their activities.

The third study is by Macieja (1993). It reports the results of a survey in which 55 companies privatized by liquidation took part. The founding body for all of them was the Ministry of Industry and Trade. Unlike Dąbrowski *et al.* (1992b and 1992c), Macieja's study is much more critical about liquidation privatization. He even comes to the view that management and worker buy-outs do not improve economic efficiency of privatized companies. It seems, however, that this disturbing conclusion does not really follow from the data presented by the author. He fails to compare the results from the sample with those for the economy as a whole and for the relevant sectors, in consequence ignoring the fact that the business environment was quite different in 1991 and 1992. Moreover, the very fact of privatization liberates the privatized enterprises from *popiwek* and therefore the management may initially accommodate demands for a wage increase.

These remarks are not supposed to imply that the picture is in fact a very rosy one. There are, in particular, problems with sufficient cash flow to finance large investment programmes necessary to compete with high quality imports. Initially it was common to be excessively optimistic about future profits stream. The fact that the leased assets could not be used as a collateral for bank credit made these problems more troublesome, but changes envisaged in the Pact on Enterprises should help to solve them (section 6).

The pace of Polish privatization, through the application of a wide variety of routes described in this chapter, is nevertheless extraordinary by Western experience, as it is revolutionary by historical experience of the country and the region.

This fast privatization has on the supply side been the primary factor accounting for the recovery in Polish GDP, 1.5 per cent growth in 1992 and 4 per cent growth in 1993. Much of this growth has taken place in the industrial private sector, as Table 10.4 portrays.

During 1992–93, privatization proper — in the form of direct transfer of ownership — is, in Poland, at best able to explain the fall of output of the state industry. The key source of industrial recovery, the largest in Central and Eastern Europe so far, has clearly been the very fast organic growth of the private sector. The explanation of its success lies not in the high volume of investment, but in the good choice of investment projects which have been typically extremely capital-saving. Labour productivity, wages and profit margins are about the same in both

TABLE 10.4 Poland: Industrial sales 1991–93, constant prices

	1991	1992	1993
LEVEL (total 1991 = 100)			
State	74.4	71.9	67.2
Private	25.6	32.0	43.1
Total	100.0	103.9	110.3
GROWTH RATE (in %)			
State		−3.3	−6.5
Private		23.4	34.7
Total		3.9	6.2

Source: Central Statistical Office, *Informacja, Rok 1993*, p.81, Warszawa, 27 January 1994.

sectors, but the capital/output ratios — both average and marginal — appear to be many times lower in the private sector. Consequently, the profitability of investment is also many times higher in the private sector.

Although privatization aims to limit politicians' interference with day-to-day running of the economy at the microeconomic level, the process itself can be implemented only by state institutions through political means. The very concept of private property is sometimes ambiguous and embodied in various legal arrangements. This indeterminacy is made worse by transition-related shocks, which increase uncertainty and social anxiety. Consequently many advise against a new shock which rapid privatization may cause.

The early dilemma as to whether to privatize or to liberalize and stabilize the economy first was, in 1989, decided in favour of liberalization and stabilization. The recession which followed became an important background which had an impact on privatization policies and their implementation. The effects can be observed at both the micro and macro levels.

At a microeconomic level, the phenomenon of so-called soft budget constraint survived the 'controlled shock therapy' of January 1990. However, it is much less pervasive than it was, being limited largely to tax arrears, and is heavily concentrated (Gomulka 1993b; and Jasiński 1993). The debts and liabilities make the purchase of a state firm less attractive. But any financial restructuring, usually a necessary precondition for the transaction, is usually complex and time consuming. Also, to the extent that the persistence of the soft budget constraint translates into a poor macroeconomic environment, investors' response to offers put forward by the MOP may be affected.

The as yet unsatisfactory structure of the privatization law is best illustrated by the issue of reprivatization. As many as five drafts of the Reprivatization Act have already been proposed, both by the government and the MPs. The real cause of delays seems to be the lack of political will to solve the problem[54]. The main controversy revolves around the problem of the form and extent of compensation[55]. This is, however, a political problem *par excellence*, which brings us back to the tangled issue of the relationship between politics and privatization in Poland.

Notes

1. Efforts to collectivize Polish agriculture never really succeeded; what was collectivized in the period of Stalinism was reversed after 1956. This meant that some 80 per cent of arable land was in the private sector. Activities of farmers were still controlled by means of compulsory deliveries of products, fixed prices, centralized distribution of material supplies and rationing of mechanized equipment.
2. By 1989 their number had increased to 841 and they were employing 100,240 people, less than 1 per cent of the workforce.
3. These figures do not include the parallel or under-reported sector of the private economy. It is widely presumed that this sector has been growing since 1989.
4. Kawalec (1989) and Lewandowski and Szomburg (1989), later modified in Lewandowski and Szomburg (1990, 1991). For a critical assessment of the two models of

privatisation see Jasiński (1990). It is worth noting that other speakers at the same conference either preferred reorganization of SOEs (Święcicki 1988) or still advocated self-management (Dąbrowski 1988).

5. When the partner was a foreign investor, this kind of 'sweetheart deal' would often involve giving the foreign partner a stake in the enterprise and, in return, the manager would be appointed to an attractive position in the new venture (Gruszecki 1990).

6. Socialized institutions (state enterprise, cooperative, association, administrative agency acting on behalf of the Treasury) which establish connections with the manager of such an entity, the manager having the status of a partner in the company. These persons — managers, presidents, directors — are members of the *nomenklatura*. There were also 'weaker' forms of *nomenklatura* companies, in which the president, manager or director do not become formally partners, but are members of the supervisory board or are additionally employed in the company's management, deriving various benefits from such an arrangement (Gruszecki 1990).

7. The main differences between the two projects were: 'the scope of legislation, the institutional framework of the privatization process, including political control over its progress; the choice of procedures for privatization, and the role and importance of employee shareholding and other legal and financial measures intended to ensure private ownership' (Błaszczyk and Gruszecki 1991: 24). The Sejm decided to use the government proposal as their basis for discussion but the final version contained solutions from both documents.

8. For full texts of both documents see Economic Commission for Europe (1992), p. 115–130, and for the detailed structure of the MOP see Frydman *et al.* (1993).

9. They were made operational by seven instructions of enactment, issued by the Council of Ministers and the Minister of Privatization (initially Ownership Changes) in October and November 1990 (Błaszczyk and Gruszecki 1991: 51–56).

10. A similar process went on in crafts and services, and there is no doubt that in manufacturing 'small privatization' was substantially helped by the provisions and implementation of the act on the privatization of SOEs (Bednarski 1991).

11. 'Under the existing rules, the sale of such premises is not possible, because the rules do not permit the sale of shop space which constitutes a part of a larger building. And it is in large buildings where most shops are found' (Bednarski 1991: 11). On the other hand, however, there are ways of dealing with the uncertainty allegedly faced by shopkeepers because of such an arrangement.

12. A similar picture emerges from the survey reported in Tamowicz *et al.* (1992). The authors analyzed decisions taken by 24 urban local councils (*gminy miejskie*) and only one of them decided to go for a market solution based on open auctions.

13. On the one hand, local councils are liable for any debts incurred or damages caused by budgetary units. On the other hand, budgetary units were not subject to the *popiwek* regulations, i.e. to the tax on above norm increases of wages, still in force at the beginning of 1994.

14. In 1989 they employed 2.203 m people.

15. The most important problems which have to be solved follow from the indivisibility of most of a cooperative's assets and from the typically huge discrepancy between the original share fund and the actual share capital.

16. Until the end of 1993 such decisions were taken only in respect to SOEs which are to take part in the mass privatization programme.

17. Article 23, para. 2 reads as follows: 'In specific cases, the Council of Ministers, on a motion of the Minister of Privatization, can permit State Treasury shares to be sold in a different manner from those specified in para. 1'.

18. According to the Privatization Act employees are entitled to buy up to 20 per cent of shares at a 50 per cent discount, subject to the total value of the discount not exceeding one year's wages.

19. It may be of interest to notice that, in real terms, expressed as a ratio of the price of 15 December 1992, to the subscription price of December 1990, adjusted for inflation (128 per cent), share prices of the first five companies privatized by public offer were as follows: Exbud 1.11; Próchnik 0.38; Kable — 0.23; Krosno 0.21; Tonsil — 0.15. These results were hardly encouraging for the purchase of shares of privatized companies. An extraordinary boom on the Warsaw Stock Exchange, in these and all other shares, however, took place in the course of 1993.

20. In fact, the very first privatization, the meat processing company Zakłady Mięsne in Inowrocław, was a leveraged buy-out. Makowski (1990) gives a very detailed account of this pioneering enterprise.

21. In the case of leasing ownership rights can, but do not have to, be transferred to the lessees at the end of the contract. Nevertheless, since control rights are fully transferred from the very beginning, it seems appropriate to treat this as real privatization. What is more, the planned amendments to the Pact on privatization envisage changing leasing into deferred payments once 30 or 40 per cent of payments have been made.

22. Strictly speaking, from the legal point of view privatization of SOEs as SOEs was impossible: an SOE could neither sell itself nor be sold as a whole, and any revenue from selling its assets had to stay in the given SOE, preserving in this way its value. That is why, to be privatised, a SOE had to be either transformed into a company (commercialized) or liquidated (Gruszecki 1990).

23. They have to constitute at least 20 per cent of the book value of the liquidated enterprise.

24. Preferential treatment enjoyed by employees consists in that Art. 37, par. 1.3 can be used only if most employees become stakeholders in the new company to which *the enterprise's assets or integrated parts of its assets [are] to be let against payment for a specified time.*

25. On the behaviour of Polish SOEs since 1989 see, *inter alia*, Schaffer (1992,1993), Dąbrowski *et al.* (1990, 1991a and b, 1992a), Maj (1991), Mayhew and Seabright (1992), Wawrzyniak (1992), Pinto *et al.* (1992, 1993).

26. Under the Pact on Enterprise, to be implemented in the second half of 1994 (see section 8), the dividend tax is to be discontinued.

27. *Inter alia*, this is to avoid creating empty shell-type SOEs after they set up a joint venture.

28. An approval from the MOP is also necessary, this was only a formality and not a single case has been rejected up until now.

29. Foreign investors purchase only those enterprises which are located in regions particularly affected by unemployment. More generally, in those regions the rules of 'express privatization' are much more liberal (Latuch and Głogowski 1992).

30. The legal basis for this procedure is provided by the Act on the Privatization of State-owned Enterprises (Article 37, para. 1) and by the Act on State-owned Enterprises (Article 18a, para. 2 and 3).

31. It is usually equal to three year profits, but not less than 75 per cent of the book value, adjusted for the value of the land.

32. See, e.g., Maskin (1992), Bolton and Roland (1992).

33. The most important producers are Unilever, Henkle and Benckiser. Another important company in this industry, Procter and Gamble, preferred initially to import its products, but in the late 1992 it began constructing a new plant.

34. Most of them were already joint-stock companies and their privatization was much easier because it was enough to diminish the proportion of shares owned by the Treasury by simply issuing new shares and selling them exclusively to private firms and/or the public. If fact, precisely this method was used in the case of Universal, which had most of its shares in private hands already under the Rakowski government.

35. The establishment of an investment bank in 1993, to conduct the remaining NBP commercial activities, would complete the process of separating commercial from regulatory functions of the central bank.

36. The cases of other state owned banks, BGŻ, PKO, BP, PKO SA and Bank Handlowy etc. are too complicated for any realistic scenario to be proposed at the present time.

37. An agreement on the debt repayment with the London Club — commercial banks whom Poland owes about 13 billion US$ — would help the process along. The negotiations restarted in February 1993 and an outline agreement was reached in March 1994.

38. PZU is still fully owned by the Treasury, while a new issue of shares in TUiR Warta reduced the proportion of shares held by the Treasury to 48.5 per cent. The main private contestants Westa and Westa-Life, which won almost 10 per cent of the insurance market in Poland, had their licences withdrawn in the autumn of 1992 and went into receivership, which further complicates the prospects for increasing competition, as foreign firms' entry will be severely restricted until 1999.

39. CM (1992a). See also *Rzeczpospolita*, 306 (3344), 31.12.1992–1.01.1993.

40. An alternative and most likely cheaper proposal, put forward by PZU's management, advocates setting up one nation-wide company, taking over 50 per cent of the present structure, and five smaller companies based on regional branches.

41. For the list of selected enterprises, see *Prywatyzacja*, 12/92, p. 3–4.

42. By the end of 1991 the number of PGRs increased to 1409.

43. Central Statistical Office, *Iformacje* 1993; p. 70, Warsaw, 27 January 1994.

44. The Act on the Privatization of SOEs (art. 2, para. 2) requires that the government's plans for and reports on the progress of privatization are presented to the Sejm for approval.

45. Gomułka (1989) can be also interpreted in this way. The papers by Balcerowicz (1990a and b), Olex (1990) Kawalec (1990a), Bieć and Gomułka (1990), Sachs and Berg (1990), Lipton and Sachs (1990) represent somewhat different variations of the same central proposal. Suggestions by Hinds (1991), Frydman and Rapaczyński (1991), Tirole (1991, 1992), and Blanchard *et al.* (1991) belong to the same family. All these schemes, different as they were, expected financial intermediaries, either holdings, banks or mutual investment funds, to play a key role in solving the agency problem. Technical papers by EBRD (1990 and 1991) and Warburg (1990), among others, have been useful early inputs in the formulation of the policy.

46. Members of the selection committee were be appointed by the Parliament (4 by Sejm and 1 by Senate), 2 by nationwide trade unions (one by each of them) and by the Council of Ministers (12).

47. Out of about 200 firms which were offered the possibility of providing the executive teams, 35 expressed their readiness to participate in the selection process by submitting detailed offers. The authors of best offers will be awarded contracts to run NIFs. Obviously, no contract can be signed before the final legal framework is ready and binding.

48. Of the remaining 40 per cent of shares, 15 per cent will be given free of charge to the employees, who at present are entitled to buy 20 per cent of shares at a 50 per cent discount, and 30 per cent will be kept by the Treasury (18 per cent of these shares will be used to pay pensions and salaries of state employees).

49. It is estimated that if 10 million people pay for their certificates, the cost of organizing mass privatization in Poland will not exceed $20 million, while the registration fees paid in would amount to $200 million. The estimated book value of assets per certificate would be about $500.
50. The former is a highly progressive tax on excess wages, the latter is a tax levied on a certain category of capital assets.
51. The MOP has 13 regional offices, but their role in the process is almost exclusively subsidiary. The central privatisers numbered less than 30 for most of 1990. The staff of the MOC increased during 1991–1992 to reach about 200, still a very small number by the East German standards.
52. In August 1991, the respective ratios were equal to 25 and 27 per cent.
53. This mixture of general support and of the desire not to be affected by this kind of change seems to be consistent with what the Polish public opinion thinks about market economy in general (Kolarska-Bobińska 1990).
54. In principle, when the act of taking away the property violated the then existing law, no new regulation is necessary and the matter can be settled by administrative decisions of respective ministers. From 1 January 1992 till the end of August 1992, 552 decisions were declared null and void. Nevertheless, even though this procedure proved in some cases relatively straightforward and successful, many other claims have to go through numerous appeals, which takes a lot of time and is very costly. That is why even in these cases there is a need for an overall legal regulation.
55. *Rzeczpospolita*, 91 (3435), 19.04.1993, p.I. It is worth noting that the whole problem has also an international aspect: 73.6 per cent of claims refer to property on the territory of the former Soviet Union, for which, according to the agreement signed between the government of Poland and the USRR, the claimants were to be compensated by the Polish government. On the other hand, 149 claims were put forward by people currently living abroad, mostly in Germany (MOP 1992a).

References

Balcerowicz, L. (1990a) Principles of accelerated privatization, mimeo, 1 June.

Balcerowicz, L. (1990b) Privatization of large-scale enterprises, mimeo, 24 August.

Bandyk, C. (1991) *Privatization in Poland. Program, Achievements and Foreign Investment Policy*, Ministry of Privatization, Warsaw.

Bednarski, M. (1991) Small Privatization in Poland, *PPRG Discussion Paper No. 7*, Department of Economics, Warsaw University.

Beksiak, J. and **Winiecki, J.** (1990) Comparative analysis of our programme and the Polish Government Programme, in Beksiak, J. *et al.* (eds) *The Polish Transformation: Programme and Progress*, Centre for Research into Communist Economies, London, pp. 19-59.

Berg, A. (1992) The logistics of privatization in Poland, paper for the conference on Transition in Eastern Europe, NBER, Cambridge, Mass., 26–29 February.

Bieć, A. and **Gomułka, S.** (1990) State-driven privatization: how to combine speed with economic efficiency and political concerns, memo to L. Balcerowicz, September.

Blanchard O.J. *et al.* (1991) *Reform in Eastern Europe*, MIT Press, Cambridge, Mass.

Błaszczyk, B. and **Gruszecki, T.** (1991) *Privatization in Poland. Laws and Institutions (April 1990–January 1991)*, Stefan Batory Foundation, Warsaw.

Bolton, P. and **Roland, G.** (1992) Privatization policies in Central and Eastern Europe, *Economic Policy*, **15**, pp. 275–310.

Ciechocińska, M. (1992) Development of the private sector in Poland in 1989–90, *Communist Economies and Economic Transformation*, **2** (4), pp. 215–36.

Corbo, V., Coricelli, F. and **Bossak, J.** (eds.) (1991) *Reforming Central and East European Economies. Initial Results and Challenges*, The World Bank, Washington D.C.

Council of Ministers (CM) (1992a) *Main Directions of Privatization in 1993*, Warsaw.

Council of Ministers (CM) (1992b) *Memorandum of Government of Poland on Economic Policy*, Warsaw.

Dąbrowski, J. M. *et al.* (1990) *State Enterprise Adjustment. Poland, January–June 1990*, The Research Center for Marketing and Property Reform, Gdansk–Warsaw, pp. 48–52.

Dąbrowski, J.M. *et al.* (1991a) *State-owned enterprises in 1990–Research Findings*, Instytut Badań nad Gospodarką Rynkową i Prawami Własności, Gdansk.

Dąbrowski, J. M. *et al.* (1991b) *Collapse of the public sector–The Stage of Truth.* (First half of 1991), Instytut Badań nad Gospodarką Rynkową, Gdansk.

Dąbrowski, J. M. *et al.* (1992a) *State-owned Enterprises in Their Second Year of Economic Transformation. Research Findings*, The Gdansk Institute for Market Economics, Gdansk.

Dąbrowski, J. M. *et al.* (1992b) *Privatization Process in the Polish Economy in 1991*, The Gdańsk Institute for Market Economics, Gdansk.

Dąbrowski, J. M. *et al.* (1992c) *Privatization of the Polish State-owned Enterprises. The Second Report*, The Gdansk Institute for Market Economics, Gdansk.

Dąbrowski, M. (1988) Group ownership as a way of transforming state ownership, paper for the seminar on Transformation Proposals for Polish Economy, SGPiS, Warsaw, 17–18 November.

EBRD (1990) Polish mutual funds feasibility analysis and implementation: proposed terms of reference, mimeo, 17 December.

EBRD (1991) Technical assistance project for mass privatization in Poland, response to Polish Government's request for assistance, mimeo, 4 January.

Economic Commission for Europe (1992) *Legal Aspect of Privatization in Industry*, United Nations, New York.

Frydman, R., Rapaczyński, A. Earle, J. S. *et al.* (1993) *The Privatization Process in Central Europe*, CEU Press, Budapest, London, New York.

Frydman, R., and **Rapaczynski, A.** (1990) Memorandum to S. Gomułka on finance ministry privatization proposals, 27 August.

Frydman, R. and **Rapaczynski, A.** (1991) Markets and institutions in large-scale privatization: an approach to economic and social transformation in Eastern Europe, in Corbo, V. *et al.* (eds.) (1991), pp. 253–74.

Gomułka, S. (1989, 1992) How to create a capital market in a socialist country for the purpose of privatization, in Prindl, A. R. (ed.), (1992). (Polish version written in July 1989 and published in *Studia Ekonomiczne*, **25** (1990), pp. 80–93.)

Gomułka, S. (1990a) Directions of Poland's economic policies 1990–1993, mimeo, April, written for and discussed by Economic Committee of the Council of Ministers.

Gomułka, S. (1990b) Comments on L. Balcerowicz, Privatization of large-scale enterprises, 24 August, memo to Balcerowicz.

Gomułka, S. (1992) Polish economic reform, 1990–91: principles, policies and outcomes, *Cambridge Journal of Economics*, **16**, pp. 355–372

Gomułka, S. (1993a) Poland: glass half full, in Portes, R. (ed.) (1993)

Gomułka, S. (1993b) The financial situation of Polish enterprises in 1992–93 and its impact on monetary and fiscal policies, mimeo, LSE, London and Poland's Ministry of Finance, Studies and Analysis no. 6, CASE, Warsaw.

Gomułka, S. and **Polonsky, A.** (eds.) (1990) *Polish Paradoxes*, Routledge, London.

Grosfeld, I. (1992) The paradox of transformation: an evolutionary case for a breakthrough in privatization, mimeo, DELTA, Paris, November.

Gruszecki, T. (1990) *Privatization. Initial Conditions and Analysis of the Government Programme (August 1989–mid–April 1990)*, Stefan Batory Foundation, Warsaw.

Gruszecki, T. (1991) Privatization in Poland in 1990, *Communist Economies and Economic Transformation*, **2** (3), pp. 141–54.

Gultekin, G. and **Wilson, G.** (1990) Comments on a plan for free distribution of shares to citizens through mutual funds, mimeo, 10 August.

Hinds, M. (1991) A note on the privatization of socialized enterprises in Poland, in Corbo, V. *et al.* (eds.) (1991), pp. 275–88.

Jasiński, P. (1990) Two models of Privatization in Poland. A critical assessment, *Communist Economies*, **3** (2), pp. 373–401.

Jasiński, P. (1992a) The transfer and redefinition of property rights: theoretical analysis of transferring property rights and transformational privatization in the post-STEs, *Communist Economies and Economic Transformation*, **2** (4), pp. 163–90.

Jasiński, P. (1992b) Impact of the transfer of property rights on economic efficiency of the enterprise, *Ekonomista*, **5/6**, pp. 709–29.

Jasiński, P. (1993) *Regulating Finances of State-owned Enterprises in Central and Eastern Europe. The Soft Budget Constraint under Central Planning, Market Socialism and in the Process of Systemic Transformation*, Regulatory Policy Institute, Oxford.

Jasiński, P. and **Welfens, P. J. J.** (1994) *Privatization and Foreign Direct Investment in Transforming Economies. Theoretical and Policy Issues of Systemic Transformation in an International Perspective*, forthcoming Dartmouth Press, Aldershot.

Jermakowicz, E. K. and **Jermakowicz, W. W.** (1992) *Mass Privatization Programs in the Czech and Slovak Federal Republic (CSFR), Poland, and the Federation of Russia*, Proceedings of the 29th Annual meeting of the Academy of International Business Society of the Midwest Business Administration Association, Chicago.

Jermakowicz, W. (1992) *Privatization in Poland: Aims and Methods*, Centrum Prywatyzacji, Warsaw.

Kawalec, S. (1989) Privatization of the Polish Economy, *Communist Economies*, **1**(3), pp. 241–56.

Kawalec, S. (1990a) Holding companies as a means of accelerating privatization in Poland, mimeo, 7 March.

Kawalec, S. (1990b) Employee ownership, state treasury ownership: dubious solutions, *Communist Economies*, **2**(1), pp. 83–93.

Kolarska-Bobińska, L. (1990) The myth of the market and the reality of reform, in Gomułka, S. and Polonsky, A. (eds) (1990), pp. 160–79.

Kołodko, G. W. (ed.) (1991) *Fiscal Policy, Stabilization, Transformation*, Instytut Finansów, Warsaw.

Latuch, B. and **Głogowski, K.** (1992) Privatization express, *Prywatyzacja*, **7** (22), pp. 6–7.

Lewandowski, J. and **Szomburg, J.** (1989) Property rights as a basis for social and economic reforms, *Communist Economies*, **3** (1), pp. 257–68.

Lewandowski, J., and **Szomburg, J.** (1990) *Privatization strategy*, Instytut Badań nad Gospodarką Rynkową, Gdansk.

Lewandowski, J. and **Szomburg, J.** (1991) The strategy for privatization, in: *The Social and Political Consequence of Decentralization and Privatization*, (1991), pp. 25–38.

Levitas, A. (1992) The trials and tribulations of property reform in Poland: from *state-led to firm-led privatization*, 1989–1991, paper for the conference on The Political Economy of Privatization in Eastern Europe, Asia and Latin America, Brown University, 23–24 April.

Lipton, D. and **Sachs, J.** (1990) Privatization in Eastern Europe: the case of Poland, *Brookings Papers on Economic Activity*, **2**, pp. 293–341.

Lipton, D. and **Sachs, J.** (1991) Privatization in Eastern Europe: the case of Poland, in Corbo, V. *et al.* (eds.) (1991), pp. 231–252.

Lis, K. (1989) *Programme of Ownership Changes in the Polish Economy*, December, Warsaw, mimeo.

Lis, K. (1990) Privatization programme of the Polish economy, mimeo, discussed by the Government Privatization Group on 28 August.

Macieja, J. (1993) Privatization without efficiency, *Rzeczpospolita–Ekonomia i rynek*, **4** (3348), 4 January 1993, p. III.

Maj, H. (1991) Process of microeconomic adjustment. Behaviour of enterprises under stabilization policy, in: Kołodko, G. W. (ed.) (1991), pp. 67–90.

Makowski, H. (1990) *How to privatize an enterprise. Practical advice*, Ino-press, Inowrocław.

Maskin, E. S. (1992) Auctions and privatization, in Siebert, H. (ed.) (1992), pp. 115–36.

Mayhew, K. and **Seabright, P.** (1992) Incentive and the management of enterprises in economic transition: capital markets are not enough, *Oxford Review of Economic Policy*, **8**, pp. 105–29.

Mizsei, K. (1992) Privatization in Eastern Europe: a comparative study of Poland and Hungary, *Soviet Studies*, 44, pp. 283–96.

MOP (1990) *Privatization Programme of the Government of Poland*, 26 October, second version dated November, Warsaw.

MOP (Drygalski) (1991) *Privatization of Small and Medium size Enterprises: Risks and Proposed Changes of Strategy*, 25 April, discussed at a policy meeting chaired by Deputy Prime Minister L. Balcerowicz, Warsaw.

MOP (1992a) *Report on Privatization in Poland*, Warsaw.

MOP (1992b) *The Government Programme of Privatization*, 11 February, Warsaw.

MOP (1993) *Mass Privatization Programme*. Consultation document, June, Warsaw.

Olex, M. J. (1990) Mutual funds and second-stage privatization, memo to L. Balcerowicz and S. Kawalec, copies from L. Balcerowicz to J. Rostowski, A. Berg and S. Gomułka, 20 June.

Olko-Bagieńska, T. *et al.* (1992) *Ownership changes in state-owned farms in Poland*, Fundacja im. Freidricha Eberta, Warsaw.

Ordover, J. and **Wellisz, S.** (1990) Privatization plans for Poland, a memo to L. Balcerowicz, S. Kawalec and K. Lis, 20 August.

Pawłowicz, L. (ed.) (1990) *Principles of Privatization of Co-operatives*, The Research Center for Marketization and Property Reform, Gdansk–Warsaw.

Pawłowicz, L. (ed.) (1991) *Transformation and Changes of the Ownership Structure of Co-operatives*, Instytut Badań nad Gospodarką Rynkową, Gdansk.

Pejovich, S. (1990) *The Economics of Property Rights: Towards a Theory of Comparative Systems*, Kluwer Academic Publishers, Dordrecht.

Pinto, B. *et al.* (1992) *Microeconomic Response to the Economic Transformation Program: Evidence from the Largest Polish SOEs*, World Bank Resident Mission, Warsaw.

Pinto, B. *et al.* (1993), *Microeconomic Response to the Economic Transformation Program: Evidence from the Largest Polish SOEs. The Second Report*, World Bank Resident Mission, Warsaw.

Portes, R. (ed.) (1993) *Economic Transformation in Central Europe: A Progress Report*, Office for Official Publications of the European Community, Brussels, and CEPR, London.

Prindl, A. R. (ed.) (1992) *Banking and Finance in Eastern Europe*, Woodhead-Faulkner, London.

Sachs, J. and **Berg, A.** (1990) A program for privatization of state-owned enterprises, a memo to L. Balcerowicz and S. Kawalec, 14 August.

Schaffer, M. (1992) The Polish State-owned enterprise sector and the recession in 1990, *Comparative Economics Studies*, Spring.

Schaffer, M. (1993) The enterprise sector and the emergence of the Polish fiscal crises 1990–91, CEP Working Paper, No 280, LSE, *Economica,* forthcoming.

Schmieding, H. (1992) Alternative approaches to privatization: some notes on the debate, in Siebert, H. (ed.) (1992) pp. 97-108.

Siebert, H. (ed.) (1992) *Privatization*, J.C.B. Mohr (Paul Siebeck), Tübingen.

Social and Political Consequence of Decentralization and Privatization (1991) Meeting Report, Gdansk.

Staniszkis, J. (1990) Poland's economic dilemma: 'de-articulation' or 'ownership reform', in: Gomułka, S. and Polonsky, A. (eds) (1990) pp. 180–97.

Stankiewicz, T. and **Jermakowicz, W.** (1991) *The Management Contract (the so-called Business Contract) as used in the Restructuring Program for Treasury-owned Joint Stock Companies*, Centrum Prywatyzacji, Warsaw.

Świątkowski-Cannon, L. (1992) Privatization strategy in Poland and its political context, paper for the conference on 'Transition to Democracy in Poland', Stanford University, Palo Alto, 23–24 November.

Święcicki, M. (1988) Ownership reform, paper for the seminar on Transformation Proposals for Polish Economy, SGPiS, Warsaw, mimeo, 17–18 November.

Święcicki, M. (1990) Comments on L. Balcerowicz, Privatization of large-scale enterprises, 29 August.

Tamowicz, P. *et al.* (1992) *Small privatization–Polish experiences 1990–1991*, Instytut Badań nad Gospodarką Rynkową, Gdansk.

Tirole, J. (1991) Privatization in Eastern Europe: incentives and the economics of transition, *NBER Macroeconomics Annual*, pp: 221–59 .

Tirole, J. (1992) *Ownership and Incentives in a Transition Economy*, Document de Travail 10, Institut D'Economie Industrielle, Université des Sciences Sociales de Toulouse.

URM (Office of the Council of Ministers) (1990) Minutes of a strategy meeting on August 28, Warsaw, concerning the privatization policy, present: L. Balcerowicz, A. Bieć, K. Lis, J. Koźmiński, S. Kawalec, W. Kuczyński, S. Gomułka, W. Góralczyk, G. Jędrzejczak, J. Kwaśniewski, M. Olex, J. Rostowski and J. Małkowski (the order of names as in the official document).

URM (Office of the Council of Ministers) (1991) Review of the privatization problems, 19 April, Warsaw.

URM (Office of the Council of Ministers) privatization experts (1991) Proposed actions to accelerate and increase effectiveness of ownership changes, mimeo, 5 May.

Warburg S. G. (1990) Western institutional investment: strength but a tragic weakness, Report to L. Balcerowicz, copies from L. Balcerowicz to K. Lis, S. Gomułka, J. Rostowski, J. Kozmiński and A. Bieć, mimeo, 24 August.

Wawrzyniak, B. (ed.) (1992) *Difficult Change: Behaviour of Enterprises in the Transformation Process*, Fundacja im. Friedrich Eberta, Warsaw.

Winiecki, J. (1992) *Privatization in Poland. A Comparative Perspective*, Kieler Studies 248, J.C.B. Mohr (Paul Siebeck), Tübingen.

Yarrow, G. (1989) Privatization and economic performance in Britain, *Carnegie–Rochester Conference Series on Public Policy,* **31**, pp. 303–44.

CHAPTER ELEVEN

Privatization in the former Soviet Union and the new Russia

Alexander Bim, Derek Jones and Thomas Weisskopf*

In this chapter we present a survey of the policies, processes and results of privatization in the waning years of the Soviet Union and the first years of the independent Russian Federation. Section 1 begins by providing a simple analytical framework in the form of a classification of alternative privatization policy choices. Section 2 presents a brief history of the early moves toward privatization in the former Soviet Union in the context of Mikhail Gorbachev's economic reform policies. Section 3 discusses the more rapid development of privatization policy and its results in independent Russia under Boris Yeltsin. We conclude in section 4 with an overall evaluation of the process of Russian privatization to date.[1]

1. An analytical framework

In describing and analyzing the process of privatization in societies in transition from a centrally planned to a market economy, it is useful to begin with an understanding of alternative methods by which privatization may be accomplished. Toward this end we highlight a series of two-way choices between alternative privatization policy options and discuss briefly some of the considerations weighing in favour of one or the other option. Our formulation of alternative methods of privatization is designed to capture the key choices facing policy-makers in the context of the former Soviet Union. We begin therefore by defining privatization very broadly to include any process which reduces the role of state-owned and centrally controlled enterprises in favour of the development of firms which are in various respects independent of the state.[2] This permits us to consider the full range of alternatives to the traditional state enterprise that dominated the Soviet economy, including mixed as well as full-fledged private forms of enterprise organization.

*This paper is based in part upon materials collected and compiled for an initial report (Bim *et al.*, 1992). Jones acknowledges partial support from IRIS and Weisskopf acknowledges partial support from a grant by the University Council on International Academic Affairs of the University of Michigan.

First, the development of non-state enterprises can be accomplished either through the *emergence of new non-state enterprises* or through the *transformation of existing state enterprises* (or parts thereof) into non-state enterprises. The complexity of transforming existing enterprises whose economic performance has been unsatisfactory would appear to favour a policy of encouraging the formation of entirely new enterprises, whose competition with existing enterprises could eventually drive the latter to improve their performance or go out of business. In the rather chaotic economic conditions characterizing the transition from a centrally planned to a market economy, however, it is very difficult to form major new enterprises, and it is even more difficult to assure that the logic of market competition will encourage the survival of the fittest. The transformation of existing enterprises is therefore bound to be an indispensable element in economic reform, however successful entrepreneurs prove to be in establishing new businesses in response to new market opportunities.

Second, whether a non-state enterprise is an entirely new undertaking or the result of the transformation of a state enterprise, the bulk of the assets of the non-state enterprise may be *owned* by parties independent of the state or they may be *leased* from state agencies by independent operators. Economic theory suggests that in most circumstances economic efficiency is best served when enterprise decision-makers have ownership rights over the assets whose use they control. A case can be made for leasing state assets, however, when and where it is difficult to administer a fair and equitable transfer of state property into non-state hands and/or when the outright purchase of state assets imposes a huge financial burden on independent operators of an enterprise.

In cases of non-state enterprises whose assets are primarily owned rather than leased, it is useful to identify a third set of choices that illuminate different forms of property and entrepreneurship. Here we address first the choice between open and closed firms; then we consider a further distinction in each of these two cases. An *open joint-stock company* issues publicly traded ownership shares, the company's assets are owned by individuals in proportion to their share holdings, and the company is controlled by those who own a controlling packet of shares (who may be insiders — i.e., enterprise managers or workers — or outsiders). A *closely held firm* is owned and operated by a person or group of people closely attached to the firm as owner(s) and/or manager(s); there may or may not be separable ownership shares, but if there are they are not publicly traded and/or they carry no control rights.

The case for open joint-stock companies — and an active capital market in company shares — rests mainly on the putative advantages of such a system in raising private capital funds, in allocating these funds flexibly among competing enterprises, and in disciplining enterprise managers. Critics question whether stock markets actually perform such functions effectively, especially in the context of formerly centrally planned economies with very undeveloped capital market institutions. Advocates of closely held firms argue that such firms are more likely to be characterized by a focused, tightly-knit, 'flesh-and-blood' ownership group with a strong stake in enterprise performance, as compared with the alternative of external shareholder ownership of joint-stock companies.

In the case of open joint-stock companies it is important to distinguish between two alternative possibilities with respect to the exercise of effective control over enterprise operation: control by *insiders* or by *outsiders*. Insiders include all the people working in the enterprise. An insider-controlled firm may be effectively controlled by its managers, by its workers, or by some combination of the two; in the case of workers control may be exercised either directly or indirectly through the election of representatives to a workers' council. Outsiders include those whose attachment to the enterprise is based on an ownership stake rather than on work within the enterprise. They may be individual owners or shareholders, or they may be institutional shareholders (i.e. financial intermediaries such as banks, mutual funds, holding companies and investment trusts). Individually owned firms can be controlled either by insiders or by outsiders, but of course collectively owned firms are necessarily controlled by insiders.

Outsider control means that enterprise decisions will be guided primarily by the objective of maximizing the return on investors' capital. The case for outsider control is based on its putative advantages with respect to economic performance. Outsiders can be expected to push more rapidly and more ruthlessly than insiders for the restructuring of an enterprise, forcing the liquidation of unprofitable assets and the dismissal of redundant workers. Outsiders may well also have better access to private capital markets to mobilize new resources to invest in their enterprises.

Insider control, on the other hand, implies that the security and stability of the enterprise and its work force will weigh more heavily in decision-making. The fact that insider control is more conducive to enterprise stability and long-term employment relationships may contribute to better economic performance in a number of ways. Greater enterprise stability may encourage more salvaging of still useful capital stock, and it may help to avoid a cascade of business failures due to the shutdown of one key enterprise in a productive structure still characterized by an inflexible network of input sources and output outlets.[3] More stable employment patterns may result in greater utilization of the accumulated experience and firm-specific knowledge of enterprise managers and workers, and they seem likely to enhance worker motivation to contribute to the long-term improvement of the firm. The case for insider control rests also on the proposition that there are significant social and economic gains at the society-wide level in reducing the burden of economic dislocation and unemployment through greater employment security and stability at the enterprise level.

In the case of closely held firms it is useful to distinguish between two alternative forms of ownership: *individual* and *collective* ownership. The assets of individually owned firms are divisible and separable; there may be one or many asset owners, these owners may be insiders or outsiders, and individuals may buy, hold or sell different kinds and amounts of ownership stakes. The assets of a collectively owned firm are indivisible and inseparable; all the people working in the firm (with the possible exception of certain categories of employees, e.g. temporary workers) *ipso facto* share in the ownership and control of the firm. Collectively owned closely held firms are thus the enterprise form in which workers are most likely to be able to exercise a significant degree of control over enterprise decision-making.

Economic theorists are generally very sceptical about the economic performance characteristics of firms that are collectively owned and controlled by their workers, arguing that the perceived interests of enterprise workers are likely to conflict in a number of important respects with the long-term interests of their enterprise and the economy as a whole. It is held that workers will have a bias against capital investment, that they will tend to push for wage increases at the expense of enterprise profits, and that they will resist layoffs when these are needed to increase micro-level productivity or macro-level rationality. Worker ownership and control, however, need not take the form of such a collective enterprise; the kinds of concerns just raised can be alleviated — if not eliminated — by vesting significant ownership and control rights in workers through individual rather than collective forms of ownership. Indeed, a growing body of theoretical analysis and empirical evidence suggests that worker ownership and participation in management can enhance economic performance through the stimulating of higher labour productivity — by promoting worker cooperation with managers, by encouraging mutual monitoring among workers, and by fostering a more positive attitude toward work in general.

A final key choice in privatization policy arises where an independently owned firm is formed by the transformation of a state enterprise; it concerns the mechanism by which the state divests itself of the enterprise assets. On the one hand, these state-owned assets may be turned over to the new owners via *market sale*. This choice includes various kinds of sales procedures; e.g. competitive auctions of enterprise assets or shares, commercial tender competitions, insider asset buyouts. What is important is that the new owners provide a *quid pro quo* in the form of significant resources of their own in order to acquire assets previously owned by the state (though their purchase of these assets may be facilitated by various kinds of credit arrangements).

On the other hand, the assets of a state enterprise may be turned over to its new owners by way of *concessional transfer*. This choice includes outright gifts or transfers at a nominal charge well below any reasonable assessment of the value of the assets transferred. In the case of closely held firms the most likely beneficiaries would be insiders, because there is unlikely to be any justification for turning over state enterprises on highly concessional terms to outsiders. In the case of open joint-stock companies, shares are initially held by a state agency; concessional transfer involves the subsequent transfer of these shares to prospective shareholders free or at a concessional charge. The most likely recipients of such shares would be either enterprise insiders or citizens at large, in the latter case through mass distribution of 'vouchers', providing citizens with a means to purchase shares (either directly as individual investors or indirectly through financial intermediaries).

The sale of state assets at a market or near-market price may well involve time-consuming asset evaluation, credit extension and/or bidding mechanisms; indeed, there may be no prospective purchasers of the less attractive state properties. Market sale has the advantages, however, of raising state revenues from the privatization process, and of disposing of state property in a relatively fair manner. Concessional transfer, on the other hand, involves less of an administrative and organizational burden; share transfers to enterprise insiders can be achieved

TABLE 11.1 Key choices in privatization policy

---

1. Emergence of new non-state enterprises vs. Transformation of existing state enterprises
2. Assets owned by parties independent of the state vs. Assets leased from the state by independent operators
3. Property and entrepreneurship in owned non-state enterprises:
   Open joint-stock companies vs. Closely-held firms
   (a) Joint-stock companies: controlled by outsiders or insiders
   (b) Closely held firms: owned individually or collectively
4. Divestment of state assets via market sale vs. Divestment of state assets via concessional transfer

---

quite readily, and even share transfers to all citizens can be accomplished more quickly on a large-scale than the sale of shares to new investors. But concessional transfer does not enable the state to receive significant receipts from the process of privatization. And concessional transfer is highly inequitable unless all members of society — through some kind of *per capita* voucher distribution scheme — receive equal shares of state property.

Table 11.1 summarizes our framework of key choices in privatization policy. In subsequent sections of the chapter we will make use of this classification scheme to characterize and distinguish various methods of privatization that have been proposed and/or implemented in the Soviet Union and in the Russian Federation.

2. Privatization in the Soviet Union

Mikhail Gorbachev was appointed General Secretary of the Communist Party of the Soviet Union in March 1985, but it was not until 1987 that the economic reforms associated with his programme of *perestroika* began to be implemented. In terms of economic reform in general, and privatization policy in particular, it is useful to distinguish between an early *perestroika* period running from 1987 to 1990 and a later period running from 1990 up to the demise of the Soviet Union in late 1991 (in the wake of the failed coup of August 1991). A third, clearly distinct period in the history of economic reform begins with the collapse of the Soviet Union in late 1991 and the establishment of an independent Russian Federation. We discuss the *perestroika* periods in the Soviet Union in this section and turn to the Russian period in the following section.

THE EARLY PERESTROIKA PERIOD

The most important pieces of reform legislation bearing on issues of privatization in the early period were: the Law on State Enterprises, introduced in mid-1987 to cover the activity of all state units; a series of laws regulating cooperatives culminating in the final Law on Cooperatives, passed in mid-1988; and the Decree on Leasing and Lease Relations, enacted in mid-1989.[4] The Law on State Enterprises paved the way for a considerable degree of decentralization in the operation of the centrally planned Soviet economy, giving greater autonomy to state enterprise managers and greater influence over enterprise affairs to employees (organized in each enterprise into a 'worker collective', which includes all employees working within a given enterprise except for top administrative officers). The laws on cooperatives in effect served to legalize much of the 'second economy' of semi-legal private and cooperative enterprises, which had already been operating on a substantial scale primarily in the service sector. The final such law legalized the operation of cooperative enterprises in virtually all fields and gave a significant boost to the non-state sector, although it still required that non-state enterprise assets be leased from the state or owned collectively by all the workers engaged in production. The Decree on Leasing (along with related acts and decrees) spurred the development of enterprises in which enterprise managers and workers could independently operate assets leased from the state.

What Gorbachev was clearly trying to accomplish with his early *perestroika* reforms was to revitalize the Soviet socialist economy by altering the pattern of operational control and thereby the incentives facing managers and workers, but without any changeover to capitalist forms of property ownership in productive assets. In effect he was trying to convert the system from a centrally planned to a more marketized form of socialism, while encouraging the development of new 'hybrid' forms of enterprise organization whose structure lies somewhere between the traditional Soviet state enterprise and a conventional capitalist firm.[5]

Between 1987 and 1990 the most important hybrid enterprise forms to develop in the Soviet Union were the new *producing cooperatives* (the adjective serves to distinguish them from the collective farms and consumer cooperatives which had long operated in the Soviet Union under close state supervision) and the new *leased enterprises*.[6] In terms of the classification introduced in the previous section, the new cooperatives represent entirely new non-state enterprises, whose assets were sometimes primarily owned by the independent cooperators and at other times primarily leased from the state, constituted as closely held firms and characterized by collective ownership and effective control by insiders. For the most part they were relatively small enterprises, averaging about 25 workers, operating principally in construction and service industries. Leased enterprises represent a case of transformed state enterprises (or parts thereof), whose initial assets were entirely leased from a 'parent' state enterprise (although newly formed assets could be collectively owned), under the control of insider managers (usually) and/or workers (occasionally). These leased enterprises were typically much bigger than cooperatives, averaging close to 700 workers each, and their spheres of activity ranged widely across all sectors of the economy.

Table 11.2 presents official data on the changes in enterprise organizational form which took place in the Soviet Union between 1985 and 1990. During this time the share of traditional forms of state enterprise dropped by roughly 8 percentage points. Most of this change was accounted for by the emergence of new producing cooperatives and leased enterprises (3.8 per cent and 2.7 per cent of total employment in 1990, respectively); while the proportion of people primarily engaged in family farm plots also registered an increase (from 3.2 per cent to 4.6 per cent).[7]

TABLE 11.2 Distribution of employment by enterprise organizational form in the Soviet Union: 1985–1990

	1985		1990	
Total	100%		100%	
Traditional Forms	96.8		88.6	
State enterprises		81.4		74.0
Collective farms		12.2		11.2
Consumer cooperatives		3.2		3.2
Hybrid Forms	0.0		6.5	
Producing cooperatives		0.0		3.8
Leased enterprises		0.0		2.7
Joint ventures		0.0		0.1
Private Enterprise	3.3		4.9	
Family farm plots		3.2		4.6
New private farms		0.0		0.1
Individual working activity		0.1		0.2

Source: State Statistics Committee of the USSR, Narodnoe Khoziaistvo USSR v 1990 g. (Moscow, 1991), p. 51; and Ekonomika i Zhizn', No. 43 (October 1991), p. 7 (for leased enterprises and joint ventures).

THE LATE PERESTROIKA PERIOD

The new forms of property and entrepreneurship which began to develop in the Soviet Union up to 1990 — notably cooperatives and leased enterprises — did not emerge from any clearly articulated conception or government programme of privatization. During this early *perestroika* period the goals of economic reform were not envisaged in such a radical manner. The first call for privatization as an urgent economic reform task was sounded in the well-known '500-Day Plan' of Stanislav Shatalin and Grigor Yavlinsky in the autumn of 1990. Yet even this plan did not contain any detailed programme of privatization, and in any event it ultimately failed to receive political support.

The economic programmes of the last two administrations serving in the Soviet Union under (then) President Gorbachev — those of Nikolai Ryzhkov (autumn 1990) and Valentin Pavlov (spring 1991) — contained calls for privatization at the rhetorical level. But in both cases what was primarily intended was the autonomization of government enterprises by means of their transformation into leased enterprises or into various forms of government joint-stock companies under the continuing strong regulatory influence or control of branch ministries. The Law on Ownership in the Soviet Union passed in 1990 envisaged a type of collective enterprise resembling the Yugoslavian model of quasi-worker-ownership, as opposed to Western models of employee ownership in which workers actually own separate shares of their own enterprises. This law did go further than earlier reform measures under Gorbachev, however, in providing the operators of leased enterprises with the opportunity to buy out the assets they leased from the state and thereby create independent collectively owned enterprises.

The first government of independent Russia — the administration of Premier Ivan Silayev, under President Boris Yeltsin — proposed in mid-1991 a whole series of concrete measures for privatization within the framework of a programme to overcome the ongoing economic crisis. These measures have generally been associated with the name of Yevgeny Saburov, who drew up an ambitious privatization plan that included a scheme of individual privatization accounts to enable citizens to acquire company shares.

In July 1991 the Supreme Soviet of the Russian Federation (the Russian Parliament) enacted a major Law on the Privatization of State and Municipal Enterprises in the Russian Federation, setting out general principles of privatization and authorizing the establishment of implementing agencies. This marked the first practical step in a systematic process of privatization in Russia, to be based on the Saburov plan. The next steps were never taken, however, because the failed coup attempt against Soviet President Gorbachev in August 1991 set in motion events that led to the collapse of the Soviet Union as well as to the resignation of Russian Premier Silayev and his administration. In its stead Russian President Yeltsin appointed a new administration with an economic team led by First Deputy Prime Minister Yegor Gaidar, who spearheaded new and more radical approaches to economic reform.

In spite of the absence of a systematic program for widespread privatization of state enterprises, the overall process of privatization did move forward in the Soviet Union in the last year before its collapse. As far as small-scale establishments are concerned, the growth of non-state enterprise came primarily as a result of the formation of new businesses. The number of producing cooperatives peaked in 1990, but during the following year a significant minority of these cooperatives were able to drop the facade of cooperation and convert themselves into private firms under new legislation on the formation of 'small enterprises'. In addition, some new private small enterprises — including private farms — were also formed directly by individual entrepreneurs. The transformation of small-scale state establishments was begun in 1991, largely under the auspices of municipal and local authorities. Such small-scale establishments as shops, restaurants, and service outlets (many of which were previously operated by larger state enterprises or agencies) began to be 'commercialized' — i.e. given independent juridical and economic status — and a few of these were even sold to their worker collectives or to individual entrepreneurs.

The transformation of medium to large-scale state enterprises proceeded slowly, but there were a number of significant developments before the end of 1991. First, under the provisions of the 1990 Soviet Law on Ownership the managers and workers of a small number of leased enterprises were able to buy out their leased assets on rather favourable terms and form independent collectively owned enterprises. Second, the phenomenon of *nomenklatura* privatization, which had already emerged in 1990, increased significantly in 1991. This phenomenon takes different forms. The most common is the conversion of state enterprises into joint-stock companies, in which the major shareholders are insider managers and/or closely affiliated public officials and agencies. Another is the formation, out of former branch ministries, of new corporate complexes of related state enterprises — now labelled 'concerns', 'consortiums', 'associations', etc. This

TABLE 11.3 Distribution of employment by enterprise organizational form in the Soviet Union: 1990–1991

	1990*		1991*	
Total	100%		100%	
Traditional Forms	90.7		84.8	
State enterprises		78.7		72.9
Collective farms		10.7		10.6
Consumer cooperatives		1.3		1.3
Hybrid Forms	5.7		10.4	
Producing cooperatives		2.9		2.4
Leased enterprises		2.7		6.6
Joint ventures		0.1		0.2
Joint-stock companies and corporate complexes		0.0		0.5
Private Enterprise	3.6		4.8	

Source: Ekonomika i Zhizn', No. 43 (October 1991), p. 7.
*The figures are for January–September of each year.

is done in such a way that the old ministry bureaucrats and enterprise managers end up acquiring significant property rights in state assets on very favourable terms.

Table 11.3 presents data on changes in enterprise organizational form in the Soviet Union between 1990 and 1991. According to these data, the share of traditional forms of state enterprise dropped by about 6 percentage points within this one year. This change was accounted for largely by a jump in the proportion of employment in leased enterprises from 2.7 per cent to 6.6 per cent; but the emergence of joint-stock companies and corporate complexes (reflecting the rise of nomenklatura privatization) also contributed over a percentage point to the increase in employment in hybrid enterprises. Finally, the proportion of employment in full-fledged private enterprises also rose by more than a percentage point between 1990 and 1991.[8]

Nomenklatura privatization accelerated sharply in the last quarter of 1991 (beyond the period represented in Table 11.3), because of the collapse of central authority in the Soviet Union and the generally chaotic political and economic conditions surrounding the transition of the former republics to independence. As effective authority moved not only from the centre of the old Soviet Union to the former republics, but also from the centre of the newly independent republics themselves to their own regions and localities, regional and local authorities increasingly asserted ownership rights over state assets. This enabled regional and local bureaucrats to participate in the process of nomenklatura privatization of medium- and large-scale enterprises; it also enabled many localities — e.g. the major Russian cities of Moscow and St Petersburg — to step up the process of privatization of small-scale establishments as well as residential housing.

3. Privatization in independent Russia

The second administration of President Yeltsin, under the economic leadership of Acting Prime Minister Gaidar, rejected the earlier Saburov plan for privatization. Some elements of the 1991 Russian Law on Privatization, however, were maintained, for example, the entrusting of the State Committee for the Administration of State Property (*Goskomimushchestvo*, or GKI), to the leadership of Chairman Anatoly Chubais, with primary responsibility for organizing the whole process of privatization. Prior to developing a comprehensive programme for privatization of state enterprises, the new administration in late 1991 tried to speed up the existing processes of privatization of small establishments and to reclaim government ownership rights in the large enterprises that had undergone *nomenklatura* privatization, so as to prepare these latter firms for an orderly process of privatization. Further, it undertook the work of assigning government property to federal, regional/local, or municipal authorities, and it sought to develop regulations governing the reform of property relations in land and in housing. In these efforts the administration was only partially successful; further progress would have to await major new legislative initiatives.

A first important step toward implementation of systematic mass privatization was the issuing in December 1991 by President Yeltsin of a decree on Basic Provisions of the Privatization Programme for the Russian Federation in 1992. This document determined the composition of enterprises to be subject to privatization, dividing state enterprises and organizations at all levels of government into those subject to compulsory privatization, those subject to voluntary privatization, those whose privatization had first to be approved by a particular governmental authority, and those whose privatization was prohibited. In the first three cases some practical procedures for carrying out the privatization were also spelled out; primary emphasis was given to the acceleration of privatization of small-scale enterprises by a variety of methods, while mechanisms for the widespread privatization of larger enterprises remained to be worked out in detail.

In June 1992, after protracted debate and numerous modifications and compromises, the Russian Parliament passed the final Government Programme of Privatization for the Russian Federation in 1992. This is the single most important policy document governing the privatization process in Russia; it spells out in great detail the procedures and options available for the privatization of the great bulk of small-scale state enterprises and a substantial proportion of the larger ones. Later decrees and provisions issued by the second (Gaidar) and third (Chernomyrdin)[9] administrations under President Yeltsin have clarified and elaborated many provisions of the 1992 government programme, but all of these subsequent documents have remained close to the spirit and the letter of the June 1992 programme. The key provisions of this programme are examined below.

In early 1993 the (third) Yeltsin administration presented to parliament a government programme of Privatization for 1993 to succeed the 1992 government programme. This document proposed to widen the scope and accelerate the pace of privatization of state enterprises. After a somewhat unfavourable reception in the Russian Parliament, the government undertook to introduce further modifications and prepared to submit a revised version of the 1993 programme to the parliament in the summer of 1993. The ultimate fate of the 1993 programme will hinge on the outcome of the continuing struggle with opposition forces in parliament over the nature and speed of the privatization process. In the meantime, the 1992 government programme continued to govern the privatization process in 1993.

THE STRUGGLE OVER PRIVATIZATION POLICY IN RUSSIA

From the launching of Gorbachev's *perestroika* policies in the Soviet Union to the current efforts of Yeltsin's economic reformers to bring about a fundamental transformation of the Russian economy, there have been sharp clashes and conflicts over the direction of economic reform in general and over the question of ownership in particular. While almost everyone now accepts the inevitability, if not always the desirability, of the transition from a centrally planned to a market economy, and the transition from public to private forms of ownership, the precise nature, speed and outcome of the latter transition remains highly contested.

The 1992 government programme represented the outcome of a protracted struggle over privatization policy between major forces in the Russian political arena. The complexity of contemporary Russian politics defies any easy categorization of such forces, but as far as economic policy is concerned it is useful to distinguish three camps. The 'radical reformers' are led by new-generation economists such as Gaidar and Chubais and enjoy strong backing from international agencies such as the World Bank and the International Monetary Fund; they favour the most rapid possible transition to a capitalist market economy. The 'gradual reformers' are strongly supported by the so-called 'industrial lobby' (led by the Union of Industrialists and Entrepreneurs under Arkadii Volsky) and also have considerable support among trade union and worker collective leaders; they favour a gradual transition to a market economy, retaining a mix of different forms of enterprise organization. The 'conservatives' are supported by many old Communist Party apparatchiks and some elements of the new nationalist right wing; they favour a strong role for the state both in political and in economic affairs.

As President Yeltsin took the reins of power in newly independent Russia in late 1991, he entrusted the formation of economic policy to a group of radical reformers; they spearheaded the policy of 'shock therapy' (comprehensive price liberalization and stringent macroeconomic policy) in early 1992, and dominated the preparation of the administration's mass privatization policy. The latter policy, however, could not simply be implemented by administrative decree; it called for the passage of enabling legislation in the Russian Parliament, where the radical reformers constitute only a minority. The majority in parliament are supporters either of gradual reform toward a market economy or of a return to an economic system dominated by the state. Because the conservatives are relatively weak, both in parliament and in terms of public support, they have tended to align themselves on issues of economic policy with the gradualists among the reformers. Thus the struggle over privatization policy shaped up as a battle between the radical and the gradual reformers over the nature and the pace of the transfer of state enterprises into non-state hands.

With respect to the privatization of small-scale enterprises there was general agreement on the desirability of proceeding rapidly with the process of commercialization and privatization. Differences of opinion centred mainly around two questions: (1) whether small establishments should be sold via auctions and tender competitions to the highest bidder, or be transferred on concessional terms to worker collectives; and (2) whether new private farms should be formed on the basis of full-fledged private property in land or long-term leasing of land from governmental authorities. By and large the radical reformers prevailed with respect to the first issue, ruling out highly concessional transfer of enterprises to their workers. They failed, however, to prevail on the second issue: agrarian reform legislation passed by the Russian Parliament in November 1992 finally legalized the purchase and sale of land, but only under rather restrictive conditions with respect to the size, price, and use of the land parcels.[10]

With respect to the privatization of larger-scale enterprises there have been continuing sharp conflicts between radical and gradualist reformers. The radicals wish to turn these state enterprises into open joint-stock companies under conditions of share purchase which favour the acquisition of control by new external domestic or foreign investors. The gradual reformers, on the other hand, prefer to turn state enterprises into non-state companies owned and operated by their former managers, with a strong voice for workers.

The outsider-control model preferred by radical reformers has several possible variants, depending on the ultimate locus of effective control and the terms on which shares are made available to buyers. The simplest variant is for the government to sell shares of corporatized state enterprises in an open market, with the hope that a 'strategic investor' (domestic or foreign) will turn up and take over control, or in the expectation that an active stock market would discipline management even in a context where share ownership is widely dispersed among many small investors. A more complex variant involves the establishment of strong financial intermediary institutions (holding companies, mutual funds, etc.), which would be expected to buy controlling packets of shares in companies and proceed to restructure and monitor them. Either of these variants could be combined with a mass voucher programme, in which citizens are enabled to participate in the purchase of enterprise or investment fund shares through free privatization vouchers distributed by the government.

The insider-control model preferred by gradual reformers also comes in several variants, depending on the enterprise ownership structure and the terms on which shares are made available to buyers. Enterprises could be structured as open joint-stock companies in which managers and/or workers have acquired sufficient shares to exercise effective control, or they could be closely held firms. In the latter case, managers and/or workers could individually own separable shares (without making voting shares available to outsiders to any significant extent) or they could collectively own and control the firm. Most proponents of insider control have also argued for transfer of state assets on terms quite concessional to enterprise insiders, on the grounds that it is these insiders who have contributed most to the formation of the assets of any given enterprise.

The 1992 government programme, as finally enacted in June 1992, represented something of a compromise between the radical and gradual reformers. The programme adopted a multi-track approach to privatization, distinguishing between small-scale, medium- to large-scale, and 'strategic' enterprises. The most relevant provisions are outlined in the following paragraphs.[11]

Small-scale enterprises — i.e. those with up to 200 employees and a book value of capital of less than 10 million rubles (at January 1992 prices) — were to be privatized primarily through competitive auctions (in which worker collectives as well as individual investors may bid for unconditional purchase), or through commercial tender competitions (where bids must include commitments to meet certain employment or investment conditions); there were also provisions for the buy-out of leased assets by leased enterprises. Thus market sale was clearly indicated rather than concessional transfer.

Virtually all small-scale enterprises in Russia (a total of more than 200,000) were targeted for privatization; it was hoped that more than half of them would be privatized by the end of 1992 and that the rest would follow in 1993. Most of these enterprises are involved in service, construction, and transportation activities; roughly half of them are engaged in retail trade (shops), public catering (restaurants) and other consumer services. Because most small-scale enterprises are owned by local and municipal authorities, their privatization was to be carried out by local property committees and funds (operating under the overall supervision of the GKI). In most arrangements for 'small privatization' certain benefits or discounts were made available to enterprise workers as opposed to citizens at large.

Medium- to large-scale enterprises — with from 1,000 to 10,000 employees or a book value of capital from 50 to 150 million rubles (at January 1992 prices) — were to be privatized through conversion into open joint-stock companies and subsequent sale of most of the shares initially held by government agencies. Enterprises falling between the small-scale and medium- to large-scale definitional limits could be privatized in the manner prescribed for either category. The 1992 government programme mandated the corporatization approach for roughly 6000 enterprises, representing more than two-thirds of Russia's productive capacity and including the bulk of the industrial sector.[12] Before the end of 1992 each of these enterprises was required to submit its own plan for privatization to one of 80 regional property committees set up by the GKI, and it was hoped that most of them would be privatized by the end of 1993. Enterprise employees, voting as members of their worker collective,[13] could choose from among the following three privatization options, all of which involve individual shareholder ownership of open joint-stock companies:

Option 1: a minority ownership share for insiders (workers and managers). Insiders receive 25 per cent of all shares free of charge, but these are non-voting (unless and until sold). Workers have the opportunity to buy another 10 per cent of (voting) shares, and administrative officers have the opportunity to buy another 5 per cent of (voting) shares, at highly concessional rates. The remaining shares — at least 60 per cent of the total and 80 per cent of voting shares — are to be sold through public auctions in which foreigners as well as domestic citizens can participate.

Option 2: a controlling ownership share for insiders. Insiders can buy voting shares up to 51 per cent of the total authorized capital, at a charge of 1.7 times the book value of the assets (a rate that is generally quite concessional); however, they are precluded from obtaining credit toward such share purchases from any state financial institution. The remaining shares are to be sold through public auctions.

Option 3: a contract with a subgroup of insiders. A group of administrative officers and/or workers enter into a one-year agreement to restructure the enterprise with a view to avoiding bankruptcy. If they are successful they gain, in exchange, the right to buy 20 per cent of the enterprise shares at the (highly concessional) book value of the assets. If this option is selected, all administrative officers and workers gain the right to purchase up to 20 per cent of enterprise shares at a highly concessional rate.

The second or third of the above options could be selected by enterprise employees only if supported by at least two thirds of the voting members of the worker collective, failing which the first option (clearly preferred by the authors of the privatization programme) was to go into effect.

Strategic enterprises — including those with more than 10,000 employees and a book value of capital of more than 150 million rubles (at January 1992 prices), as well as those in 'strategic industries' — were to be privatized, if at all, only with the approval of the GKI and/or other governmental authorities. Excluded from privatization (at least in the initial phase covered by the 1992 programme) were most natural resource-based enterprises, electricity generation stations as well as space and nuclear facilities. Some of these enterprises could be corporatized, but the state was to retain a controlling packet of shares — at least for the time being — in most enterprises in the energy, communications and military sectors, and foreign investors were excluded from some enterprises in these sectors.

A major feature of the whole 1992 government programme for privatization was the introduction of a mass voucher programme whereby 'privatization tokens' would be distributed to all citizens to enable them to participate in the acquisition of claims to state assets. Every one of Russia's 148 million citizens was to receive a free privatization voucher with a nominal value of 10,000 rubles. The total value of the vouchers represented roughly 35 per cent of the book value of the 6,000 medium- and large-scale enterprises due to be corporatized by the end of 1992 and privatized by the end of 1993. The intention was thus to transfer a significant share of state assets to the general public at a fully concessional rate. The privatization vouchers can be used to buy shares in joint-stock companies on the privatization list or to bid on enterprises at auctions; they can be deposited in investment funds; or they can be sold for cash to any buyer.

In structuring their preferred Option 1 for the privatization of medium- to large-scale enterprises, the radical reformers preparing privatization policy for the Yeltsin administration decided to encourage an outsider-control variant relying on strategic non-institutional investors rather than strong financial intermediary institutions. To meet worker claims on state assets they included the provision granting workers 25 per cent of the shares free of charge, but these shares were made non-voting in order to prevent workers from obtaining a controlling packet. To meet citizen claims on the nation's capital stock they undertook the mass voucher privatization scheme under which citizens on an equal basis could gain access to a substantial fraction of the assets of enterprises subject to privatization. Investment funds were permitted to be established, but limits were set on their ability to acquire citizen vouchers and they were not allowed to purchase more than 10 per cent of the shares of any single corporatized enterprise. The rejection of a major role in enterprise governance for strong financial intermediaries reflected the radical reformers' suspicions that such institutions could not be established or operated without coming under the excessively politicized influence of the state.

Some of the most outspoken opponents of radical reform pushed initially for an insider-control variant involving closely held collectively owned firms, with state enterprises to be transferred on concessional terms to their own managers and workers. This was the idea behind the kind of buy-out of initially leased enterprises that began to occur in 1990, and it also appeared to be the direction in which the Soviet Union was moving under Gorbachev;[14] even now it is still favoured by many leaders of worker collectives and their political allies. As the debate evolved both within and outside the Russian Parliament, however, most of the gradual reformers were increasingly ready to settle for the transformation of state enterprises into closely held individually owned firms under the control of managers and workers, with asset ownership to be transferred on terms favourable to the latter. In the face of the evident inequity of denying a claim to state property by the large numbers of people not working in the enterprise sector (and of benefiting employees in the enterprise sector very unequally, depending on the value of the assets in their own enterprise), many proponents of insider control agreed that insiders must ultimately pay for their acquisition of valuable assets at something approaching market prices, and that some of the revenues from the sale of state assets should be used for the benefit of citizens not in a position to acquire any such assets.

The end result of the struggle between radical and gradual reformers in parliament was a further compromise in the form of Option 2, which enables insiders to acquire a controlling packet of shares in the newly created joint-stock companies, but on terms that were only partly concessional to insiders, with no access to government credit, and only by at least a two-thirds majority vote of members of enterprise worker collectives.

Although the choice among options for privatization of medium- to large-scale entreprises was in several ways skewed in favour of the Option 1 preferred by the radical reformers, the results of voting by worker collectives in late 1992 and early 1993 were actually more often in favour of Option 2. Emboldened both by this display of worker commitment to insider control, and by the weakened political position of the radical reformers after the December 1992 session of the Congress of People's Deputies (which led to the resignation of Acting Prime Minister Gaidar), a task force organized by prominent members of the Russian Parliament drafted a proposal for a fourth privatization option. As compared with Option 2, Option 4 would greatly facilitate and accelerate the transformation of state enterprises into insider-controlled companies; 90 per cent of the shares of an enterprise would be made available in a closed subscription for purchase by worker collectives at book value (thus on highly favourable terms), while only the remaining 10 per cent of enterprise shares would be made available for purchase by outsiders on the open capital market. Proponents claimed that the proceeds from this kind of privatization would still be great enough to provide substantial benefits for the fraction of the population not employed in the enterprise sector. This option represents an intermediate form of insider-oriented privatization, located between the establishment of enterprises owned collectively by insiders and the establishment of joint-stock companies in which insiders have limited advantages over outsiders in acquiring shares.

Needless to say, the new proposal has led to further sharp debate between radical and gradual reformers since its presentation to the Russian Parliament in January 1993 as an alternative to the 1993 government programme for privatization prepared by radical reformers under the direction of GKI Chairman Chubais. Although there are strong differences of opinion on these and other economic policy issues within both the legislative and the executive branches, the approach to privatization reflected in the government programmes of 1992 and 1993 retains strong support among economic policy-makers in the Yeltsin administration, while the alternative Option 4 has a strong base of support in the Russian Parliament. The fate of Option 4 remains uncertain at the time of writing, but President Yeltsin's victory in the 25 April referendum has clearly strengthened the position of the radical reformers, and they appear likely to prevail on matters of privatization policy into the foreseeable future.

THE PROGRESS OF PRIVATIZATION TO DATE

To provide an overview of the evolution of patterns of ownership in Russia, we begin by presenting evidence on changes in enterprise form in the Russian Federation between 1990 and 1992 in Table 11.3, in the same format as in Table 11.2 for the Soviet Union. According to the figures in the table, the share of traditional forms of state enterprise dropped by about 7 percentage points from 1990 to 1991 and by another 8 per cent from 1991 to 1992. The change between 1990 and 1991 (the last year of the Soviet Russian Republic) was accounted for largely by an increase of almost 5 per cent in the proportion of employment in hybrid forms of enterprise; but these latter made a net contribution of only 3 per cent to the decline in traditional enterprise employment between 1991 and 1992 (the first year of the independent Russian nation). It is noteworthy, however, that the proportion of employment represented by joint-stock companies and corporate complexes actually increased by 4 percentage points between 1991 and 1992; we continue to list these as hybrid rather than (fully) private enterprises because up to

TABLE 11.4 Distribution of employment by enterprise organizational form in the Russian Federation: 1990–1992

	1990		1991		1992*	
Total	100%		100%		100%	
Traditional Forms	90.6		83.7		75.6	
State enterprises		83.2		76.2		68.8
Collective farms and consumer cooperatives		7.4		7.5		6.8
Hybrid Forms	7.7		12.6		15.3	
Producing cooperatives		3.5		3.4		2.9
Leased enterprises		3.8		7.6		6.6
Joint ventures		0.1		0.1		0.3
Joint-stock companies and corporate complexes		0.3		1.5		5.5
Private Enterprise	1.7		3.7		9.1	
Small businesses		0.1		1.1		4.3
Private farms, plots, etc.		1.6		2.6		4.8

Sources: IMF, Economic Review: Russian Federation (Washington, D.C., April 1992); unpublished data from the State Statistics Committee of the Russian Federation; and authors' calculations.
*The figures are for January–September 1992.

the end of 1992 their shares remained almost exclusively in the hands of government agencies and/or enterprise insiders.

According to Table 11.4 the growth in (full-fledged) private enterprise lifted the private employment proportion by 2 percentage points from 1990 to 1991 and by more than 5 percentage points from 1991 to 1992. This increase in private sector activity was accounted for both by new small businesses and by new private farms.[15]

As noted earlier, the privatization of small-scale enterprises had begun well before the 1992 government programme was finalized in June 1992. As of the end of April of that year, roughly 13 per cent of the state enterprises scheduled for privatization had submitted privatization applications, but only about 1.5 per cent had actually completed the privatization process. The total revenues received by government authorities from privatization sales by the end of April amounted only to about 3 billion rubles, as compared with the goal of 92 billion rubles set for 1992 in the December 1991 Yeltsin decree on Basic Provisions for privatization.[16]

Table 11.4 displays information on the pace of privatization of retail trade, public catering, and other consumer service establishments, which together account for roughly half of all of the small-scale enterprises in Russia. Figures are given separately for two different steps in the process of removing establishments from direct state control. First there is commercialization, the process whereby an establishment, which previously had no juridical or financial independence from the state enterprise or agency under whose auspices it was operated, gains the rights of an independent legal entity with its own economic accounts; typically such a commercialized enterprise is operated collectively by

TABLE 11.5 Commercialization and privatization of retail trade and service establishments in the Russian Federation

	1 Oct 1991	22 Jan 1992	1 May 1992	1 Oct 1992
Retail trade (shops)				
• commercialized	12,100	15,700	38,700	39,900
• privatized	66	n.a.	1180	10,814
Public catering (restaurants)				
• commercialized	3500	5200	9100	10,100
• privatized	28	n.a.	316	3174
Other consumer services (workplaces)				
• commercialized	2500	4900	17,500	21,900
• privatized	33	n.a.	906	6800

Sources: Data from the Russian State Statistics Committee.

its workers and continues to rent its premises and other assets from the local or municipal government, though it may eventually buy out some or all of these assets. Then there is full-fledged privatization, in which all ownership rights are transferred from the state to a non-state entity. The data for 1 October 1991, indicate that very few — only 127 — state service establishments had been fully privatized by the end of the *perestroika* period; most of these establishments are owned privately by individuals, but some are owned collectively by all their workers.

The data in Table 11.5 suggest that the commercialization of retail trade and service establishments did not begin to lead to much privatization of such establishments until the second half of 1992. By 1 October 1992, over 20,000 such

TABLE 11.6 Privatization of state enterprises in the Russian Federation as of 1 January 1993

	Enterprises subject to Privatization	Enterprises Privatized	Percentage of Enterprises Privatized	Proceeds* from Privatization
All sectors	217,694	46,815	21.5	157,152
Industry	78,714	10,208	13.0	42,436
Light industry	2284	752	32.9	7146
Food processing	4991	1507	30.2	6464
Construction	14,555	2178	15.0	6955
Agriculture	13,817	1457	10.5	2565
Others	43,067	4314	10.0	19,295
Services	138,980	36,607	26.3	114,716
Retail trade	53,500	18,387	34.4	72,721
Public catering	20,537	4373	21.3	10,220
Consumer service	27,676	10,660	38.5	16,493
Others	37,267	3187	8.6	15,282

Sources: Data from the Russian State Property Committee, and authors' calculations.
*In millions of rubles at current prices.

establishments had been fully privatized in independent Russia, and the figure surpassed 33,000 by the end of the year, representing roughly one third of all such establishments scheduled for privatization (see Table 11.6). There has been very substantial geographic variation in the extent of commercialization and privatization of retail trade and service establishments, with the most rapid rate of change generally being registered in the large cities of Western Russia (Bim *et al.* 1993b, Tables 7 and 8). The most common method of privatization of small retail trade and service establishments in Russia has been through commercial tender competitions; but the buy-out of leased assets and competitive auctions has also been relatively common (Bim *et al.* 1993b, Table 9). In the majority of cases the newly privatized enterprises are owned by their own workers.[17]

In Table 11.6 presents the latest comprehensive GKI data available to us on the privatization of state enterprises in Russia, broken down by sector of the economy. Out of 218,000 state enterprises to be privatized, some 47,000 — a little over 20 per cent — had been privatized by 1 January 1993.[18] Unofficial estimates reported in the financial press suggest that this number surpassed 60,000 by the end of the first quarter of 1993; and at the rate of privatization established in early 1993 about half of all Russia's small-scale enterprises would be privatized by midsummer of 1993.[19] The pace of privatization has clearly been more rapid in service than in industrial activities, which is not surprising given the typically smaller size and value of service establishments. According to Table 11.5 a total of 157 billion rubles was realized by government authorities for the sale of privatized enterprise assets during the year 1992; this represents very roughly 15 billion rubles at January 1992 prices, or little more than 15 per cent of the 92 billion ruble target for privatization proceeds in 1992.[20]

Aside from small-scale enterprises, the second main arena of privatization in Russia up to the end of 1992 was the agricultural sector. Although state and collective farms have remained dominant in Russian agriculture, there has been significant growth in the number of new private commercial farms — typically based on lifetime or long-term leasing of land from collective farms and/or municipal and local authorities. The growth of private farms in 1991 and 1992 is tracked in Table 11.7. At the beginning of the year 1991 only 4400 private farms

TABLE 11.7 Growth of private farms in the Russian Federation

Date	Number of Farms	Total Area (thousand hectares)	Average Area (hectares)
1 Jan 1991	4432	199	45
1 Mar 1991	8931	395	44
1 July 1991	25,159	1094	44
1 Oct 1991	na	na	na
1 Jan 1992	49,006	2058	42
1 Apr 1992	94,132	3859	41
1 July 1992	127,233	5344	42
1 Oct 1992	148,681	6245	42
1 Jan 1993	183,663	7840	43

Sources: Data from the Russian State Statistics Committee, and authors' calculations.

had been registered across Russia; but the number of private farms rose by 45,000 during the year 1991 and by more than 130,000 during the year 1992. By 1 December 1992, a total of 184,000 private farms occupied a total area of 7.8 million hectares, at an average area of 43 hectares per farm. Yet these new farms accounted overall for only about 2 per cent of the cultivated land in Russia; by comparison, the traditional farm sector of small family plots accounts for about 3 per cent of all agricultural land (World Bank 1992: 200). Moreover, the new farms accounted for no more than 1–2 per cent of total agricultural production in Russia in 1992.[21]

Turning to the privatization of medium- to large-scale enterprises, it has already been mentioned that the 1992 government programme mandated the corporatization of roughly 6,000 enterprises by the end of 1992, based on the particular privatization option to be selected (from among three alternatives) by each enterprise worker collective. It was hoped that most of the designated enterprises would be privatized by the end of 1993. By the end of 1992 each adult Russian citizen was to receive a privatization voucher with a nominal value of 10,000 rubles, which could be used *inter alia* to bid for shares in the corporatized enterprises.

Given the ambitious nature of these mass privatization plans, it is hardly surprising that the original timetable has not been met.[22] The designated enterprises began to hold votes by their worker collectives and to submit privatization plans in late 1992, but only about 600 were transformed into joint-stock companies by the end of 1992; it was estimated that almost 2000 of these enterprises had completed their corporatization by the end of June 1993 and that another 3000 would be completed by the end of 1993. Thus far the worker collectives of enterprises being corporatized have most often chosen the second privatization option, which enables workers and managers to buy up to 51 per cent of the shares and maintain insider control of the enterprise.[23]

The distribution of privatization vouchers was begun in October 1992 and virtually completed by January 1993; during this time they were fetching between 4,000 and 6,000 rubles in the secondary market (roughly half their face value), though apparently most people were not selling them immediately for cash. The first auction of shares under the voucher programme took place on 9 December 1992, at the Bolshevik Biscuit Company in Moscow. Bolshevik workers and managers had already purchased 51 per cent of the company's equity in a closed subscription at 1.7 times its early 1992 book value (following privatization Option 2), and on 9 December a two-week period of public voucher bidding on another 44 per cent of the equity was initiated.[24] Most of the publicly auctioned Bolshevik shares were purchased by enterprise workers, managers, pensioners and their families, thus reinforcing insider control of the enterprise.

Such public auctions of shares for privatization tokens under the voucher programme continued apace in the following months, involving enterprises of all sizes. Auctions were held for just 18 enterprises in December 1992, but the monthly rate increased rapidly and by June 1993 shares in 2,418 enterprises had been sold in voucher-based auctions, of which roughly 700 were in the medium- to large-scale category (Boycko *et al.* 1993, Tables 2 and 3). These latter included a few of the very biggest of Russia's industrial enterprises; for example, the giant

ZIL Company — with 15 plants and over 100,000 employees across the country — began in March a nationwide sale of 35 per cent of its assets for vouchers.

Several hundred investment funds had been registered in Russia by mid-1993, and this number was expected to continue to grow. These funds can accumulate citizen vouchers in exchange for shares of their own equity, and use the vouchers to bid for enterprise shares; but current legislation prohibits any such fund from holding more than 10 per cent of the shares — or investing more than 5 per cent of its own assets — in any one enterprise. It was estimated in April 1993 that some 15 per cent to 20 per cent of all privatization vouchers had been invested either in enterprises or in investment funds.

The overall results of the privatization process in Russia through May 1993 have been mixed. Clearly the privatization of small-scale enterprises is well on its way to completion, if not by the end of 1993 then surely within the following year. The privatization of medium- to large-scale enterprises, however, has been somewhat slower and remains quite incomplete. By mid-1993 about a third of the 6000 enterprises scheduled for corporatization and privatization in the 1992 government programme had been transformed into joint-stock companies; less than half of the latter had offered shares in public voucher-based auctions. Many important state enterprises — especially in the military-industrial complex — were not even mandated for privatization under the 1992 programme, and their future remained uncertain in mid-1993.

4. Conclusion

From the launching of Mikhail Gorbachev's economic reform policies of *perestroika* in 1987 until the demise of the Soviet Union in late 1991, privatization in the Soviet Union developed in two stages. In the first stage, until 1990, the main thrust of privatization policy was to decentralize control of state enterprises within the continuing context of a centrally administered socialist economy; some new forms of non-state enterprise were encouraged (e.g. cooperatives), but these were limited in scope and scale. In the second stage economic policy-makers began to articulate plans for the divestment of state assets and the development of independent private enterprise on a substantial scale. By the end of 1991, however, privatization had not proceeded very far, and it mainly took the form of leased enterprises (whose assets were still owned by state authorities) or *nomenklatura* privatization (the conversion of state enterprises into joint-stock companies whose controlling shareholders are present or former government officials). It was only with the demise of the Soviet Union and the rise of independent Russia, under President Boris Yeltsin, that the era of widespread privatization really began.

The approach to privatization favoured by the radical reformers who gained the upper hand in the Yeltsin administration once Russia became independent calls for outsider control of individually owned open joint-stock companies; this is reflected in their preferred privatization Option 1 for medium- to large-scale enterprises under the 1992 government programme for privatization. Many gradual reformers favoured instead a very different approach to the transformation of such state enterprises, aiming at insider control of closely held collectively owned firms. This approach has been resisted by economic decision-makers in the Yeltsin Administration, but an alternative and more moderate version — involving insider control of individually owned joint-stock companies — was incorporated as Option 2 into the 1992 government programme.

The approach of the radical reformers clearly stresses the goals of economic efficiency and dynamism over the goals of economic stability and security. The idea is to promote restructuring and rationalization at the enterprise level, even though this is likely to generate — at least in the short run — a great deal of dislocation and unemployment. The approach of the gradual reformers, by contrast, puts considerably more weight on stability and security. In spite of the efforts by the radical reformers to elicit the choice of Option 1 in voting by worker collectives in medium- to large-scale enterprises, votes up to mid-1993 have gone heavily in favour of Option 2. This outcome clearly reflects a very strong commitment by workers to maintaining a degree of stability and security through insider control.

The economic merits of outsider *versus* insider control depend on the relative importance of the potential efficiency gains and losses associated with each form of control, for example the gains from radical firm restructuring *versus* the gains from preserving enterprise stability and long-term employment relations (see section 1). These relative gains will surely differ from one enterprise to another, depending on the particular circumstances; so one cannot make a universally applicable case for one form of control over another. It has become clear, however, that insider control — whatever its merits or demerits — is likely to be a fact of life in most medium to large-scale enterprises in Russia for a long time to come. The radical reformers' effort to attract strategic external investors appears unlikely to succeed, not only because of the preferences of voting workers for insider control, but also because there are few potential outside investors ready and able to take on responsibility for management of transformed state enterprises. The bulk of the domestic population lost all of its savings in the inflationary spiral of the past few years, and even with vouchers does not have enough resources to purchase any more than a few shares in large joint-stock companies. Those Russians who possess large amounts of investible funds (mostly traders and speculators who have benefited from the opening up of markets in a highly volatile and inflationary economic environment) generally find it much more profitable to continue their lucrative short-horizon trading activities than to invest their money in long-term restructuring of failing enterprises. Potential foreign investors are scared away by the enormous political and economic uncertainty that continues to characterize contemporary Russia; such foreign investments as there are tend to flow into the primary product extraction and service sectors (where there are prospects for quicker profits and where success is less dependent on the whole economic environment) rather than into manufacturing industry.

The situation, however, has slightly changed in the summer of 1993. Some private companies, including newly created commercial banks, have expressed interest in the privatization of former state enterprises. There are already cases where large packages of shares have been bought through auctions and tenders by purely private outside investors who have managed to accumulate their capital through trading and speculation. This is important in that it opens up new possibilities for outside control over privatized enterprises in Russia as a significant form of property structure and enterprise governance. Thus 'free' potential capital now already exists and is showing interest in the process of privatization. Of course the prospects of channelling financial capital into the productive sphere will depend on many different factors, of which two are especially important. First — whether privatization procedures will be developed so as to stimulate outsider access to a controlling block of enterprise shares; otherwise it is very unlikely that outsiders will be interested in investing their money. Second — whether the current managers of the enterprises will be interested enough in new capital investment so as to accept a redistribution of shares to outsiders; this requires that the government cease providing preferential credits to enterprises.

External control of state enterprises on a large scale would appear to be impossible without a major government-led effort to create and support outside investors on an institutional basis. In order to take control out of the hands of insiders, the Russian government would have to encourage private holding companies and/or mutual funds to take over control of large numbers of transformed state enterprises. Far from encouraging the development of large external institutional investors, however, the policy actually followed by the Yeltsin administrations has very much restricted the role of institutional investors like voucher investment funds. This has made it all the more likely that government agencies will continue to hold a substantial fraction of the shares of corporatized state enterprises in which insider managers are exercising control. Such a pattern of ownership and control makes it especially difficult to overcome the well-known problems associated with soft budget constraints.

Contributing to the problems besetting the government programme of privatization has been an overall erosion of the authority of the federal government. This has made it all the more difficult to ensure reasonably fair access to shares on the part of outsiders; the rank and file of the *nomenklatura* are often able to arrange privatization deals in ways that benefit themselves at the expense of the public interest in higher privatization proceeds, if not outsider control. The under-developed state of of capital markets has also seriously hampered the operation of the government programme of mass privatization. To succeed as intended this approach requires good information-gathering, accounting and regulatory institutions which are only very slowly developing in the Russian economic environment.

The predominance of insider control of privatized enterprises in Russia at the present time reflects not only problems in the tactics of the radical reformers. It reflects also an underlying reality confronting their basic strategy, namely the strong desire of a large proportion of the Russian people for stability and security. Even where and when it makes good economic sense to promote efficiency and dynamism through outsider control, the goals of stability and security cannot be ignored or given only secondary consideration. Popular demands for these latter goals will surely surface in one way or another, as they have in the struggle over privatization options in Russia. It follows that any effort to dislodge insiders from control of transformed state enterprises would have to be accompanied by an effective society-wide programme for dealing with the dislocation and unemployment that results from external control. Although the radical reformers in the Yeltsin administration do pay at least lip service to the importance of dealing with problems of unemployment, their overall economic strategy (including sharp cuts in government spending) raises real doubts about their desire and/or ability to compensate dismissed employees for their loss of employment and enterprise-based social services. Thus it does little or nothing to relieve enterprise managers of the implicit obligation to keep on providing employment and social services to their workers.

Turning from the question of control to the terms of transfer of state property, we confront issues of social justice: who deserves to inherit the property accumulated by the state on the (nominal) behalf of the people? Proponents of mass voucher programmes argue persuasively that such a concessional transfer is more than just either concessional transfer to insiders or market sale of state assets, for a voucher system allows all segments of the population equal access to the nation's capital stock, whether or not they have an inside status and whether or not they have somehow accumulated investible funds. The authors of the 1992 government programme for privatization in Russia did indeed undertake a mass voucher privatization scheme, in order both to enlist citizen interest in the privatization process and to assure the public of its fairness. While the Russian voucher programme is consistent in principle with these objectives, the degree of distributive justice it brings about in practice is limited in two important respects. First, the privatization vouchers enable citizens to participate in acquiring only a fraction of the nation's assets; the rest go on somewhat preferential terms to enterprise insiders, are subject to market sale, or remain in state hands. Second, the underdeveloped condition of capital markets, as well as the scarcity of reliable information about investment opportunities, serve to erode the real value of the vouchers for the average citizen investor.

Given the strong pressures for continued insider control of transformed Russian state enterprises, what will be critical is the economic environment in which insider managers control their enterprises, for example how much competition they will face in product markets, what kind of access they will have to investible funds, and how well they and their workforce will be motivated to improve enterprise performance. The single most critical issue may well be where to find the funds to undertake new capital formation, for without such investment no programme for restructuring can succeed. The Yeltsin administration reformers had hoped that external investors would supply the needed capital in the process of acquiring control over enterprises. Major changes in the structure of ownership rights in these enterprises were expected, through resultant changes in incentives to save and invest, to lead to significant increases in real saving and real investment.[25] But the paucity of external investors casts great doubt on the success of such an approach. Moreover, the very low level of proceeds realized by governmental agencies from the privatization process has weakened the capacity of the state to play a major role in making ingestible funds to the non-state sector (or to undertake public infra-structural investment).[26]

In the last analysis, the success of the privatization process in Russia will not be measured — as it so often is now — in terms of the percentage of former state enterprises that have been transferred into non-state hands. Instead, it will be measured in terms of the success of such enterprises in restructuring and improving their economic performance, in producing needed goods and services, and in providing the basis for economic and social stability. In order to achieve these goals, privatization policies and procedures will need to be developed in such a way as to attract outside capital inflows, to stimulate effective competition, to improve the motivation of enterprise workers and managers, and to facilitate the utilization of existing productive assets as well as the formation of new labour skills and physical capital.

Notes

1. The process of privatization in contemporary Russia is of course ongoing and continuously evolving; our survey in this chapter necessarily takes account of developments only up to the time of the paper's completion in the summer of 1993.
2. We recognize that the term 'privatization' is often defined more narrowly to connote the transfer of enterprise ownership from the public to the private sector, but our broader definition allows us to encompass the whole evolution of Soviet and Russian policy in this area.
3. See Leijonhufvud (1993) for an insightful analysis of these issues.
4. See Desai (1992) for a review of the evolution of *perestroika* economic reform policies and Bim *et al.* (1992) for further details on legislation relevant to privatization.
5. See Bim *et al.* (1993a) for an analysis of 'hybrid' forms of enterprise organization in the Soviet and Russian context.
6. We draw in this paragraph on the detailed survey of new cooperatives and leased enterprise provided by Bim *et al.* (1993a).
7. It should be stressed that the figures in Table 11.2 do not provide a precise measure of the overall significance of non-state economic activity, because they ignore the widespread semi-legal 'second economy' which engaged at least the part-time efforts of a large fraction of the Soviet population. One can, however, give credence to the trends displayed in the table.
8. As in the case of Table 11.2, the figures in Table 11.3 ignore the 'second economy'. There are also some inconsistencies between Tables 11.2 and 11.3, which reflect the different sources of data. Thus the figures in Table 11.3 do not provide an accurate measure of the existing employment structure, but they should provide a reasonably good indication of trends in employment over time.
9. Viktor Chernomyrdin succeeded Yegor Gaidar as Prime Minister of Russia in December 1992.
10. See Wegren (1993) for an account of the evolution of Russian agrarian reform legislation.
11. For a more detailed summary and discussion of this and other documents relating to the Russian privatization programme, see World Bank (1992: 85–92), Bush (1992, 1993); and *Transition*, Vol. 3, No. 10 (November 1992), pp. 6-7.
12. An additional 18,000 enterprises were estimated by the GKI to fall into the intermediate range (book value of fixed capital from 1 to 50 million roubles, or of less than 1 million roubles but with more than 200 employees) where corporatization is possible but not mandatory. See Bim *et al.* (1992, Table 3.3–1).
13. The legislation actually defines somewhat more broadly the members of a worker collective eligible to vote (and to receive employee benefits and discounts): employees

holding their principal job at the enterprise; persons who are entitled to be re-employed at the enterprise, according to the laws of the Russian Federation; pensioners who have retired from the enterprise, or former workers of the enterprise who have worked there not less than 10 years in the case of men and 7.5 years in the case of women, and who retired voluntarily or as a result of staff cuts; and persons discharged from the enterprise as a result of staff cuts after 1 January 1992.

14. Transformation of leased state enterprises into non-state collectively owned firms through the buy-out of assets on favourable terms was first allowed under the 1990 Soviet Law on Ownership, and it remained one of several permissible privatization mechanisms in the 1991 Russian Law on Privatization.

15. As in the case of Tables 11.2 and 11.3, the figures in Table 11.4 do not reflect activity in the 'second economy'. In the transition from the Russian Republic to independent Russia, much of the restrictive legislation that drove private business into the semi-legal and illegal realms of the second economy lost its force. Although a good deal of such activity remains unrecorded, if not illegal, some of it has been channelled into legitimate private business. Thus the figures in Table 11.4 probably overstate the rate of growth of private business activity in Russia between 1991 and 1992, while continuing to understate the level in all years.

16. The figures cited in this paragraph are GKI data presented in Bim *et al.* (1992, Table 2.1–5).

17. According to *Russian Economic Trends*, (1993) **2**(1), 'at the end of 1992 worker collectives owned 60 per cent of the shares in privatized small-scale enterprises, other firms owned 27 per cent and individuals owned 13 per cent' (p. 51).

18. These GKI data refer to state enterprises of all sizes, but the vast majority — and virtually all of those already privatized by January 1993 — are small-scale enterprises.

19. A report in *Ekonomika i Zhizn'* #17 (April 1993), p. 4, indicated that 11,000 small-scale enterprises were privatized in January and February 1993. GKI Chairman Chubais is quoted in *Transition*, Vol. 4, No. 2 (March 1993) as declaring in Washington on 19 March that almost 50 per cent of Russian small businesses were already privately owned at that time; but elsewhere the number of private small enterprises has been estimated at about 60,000 in March, a figure quite consistent with earlier data but amounting to less than 30 per cent of the small establishments scheduled for privatization.

20. Since most of the enterprises were privatized in the second half of the year, and since price inflation for small enterprise assets is estimated by GKI at roughly 1000 per cent through the first three quarters of the year, it is reasonable to divide the value of assets sold throughout the year by about 10 to arrive at an estimate of the real value of assets sold in January 1992 prices.

21. Wegren (1993), p. 53, footnote 53, cites estimates that in 1992 new private farms produced about 2 per cent of all the grain purchased by the state and less than 1 per cent of the potatoes, vegetables, meat, poultry and milk produced in the country.

22. The information on the progress of privatization in medium- to large-scale enterprises, provided in this and the following paragraphs, is drawn primarily from reports in *Transition*, Vol. 4, No. 2 (March 1993), pp. 1–4, and from Bush (1993); more recent information was obtained from Boycko *et al.* (1993) and from periodic reports from the financial press in Russia and abroad.

23. According to *Russian Economic Trends*, (1993) **2**(1), by the end of 1992 64 per cent of workers' collectives in medium- to large-scale firms had chosen Option 2, 34 per cent had chosen Option 1 and 2 per cent Option 3 (p. 51). Boycko *et al.* (1993) report that as of July 1993 the corresponding figures were 68 per cent for Option 2, 31 per cent for Option 1 and 1 per cent for Option 3 (Table 2).

24. The proportion of enterprise equity that could be sold for privatization checks was increased from 35 per cent to 80 per cent in October 1992 in order to increase interest in (and the value of) vouchers.
25. This approach clearly reflects the supply-side notion that the best way to revitalize an economy is to let the market take care of things under clearly defined property rights, rather than to enlist government in an effort to mobilize real resources and channel them into desired activities.
26. The low level of government proceeds from privatization is due both to the large amount of state property turned over simply in exchange for vouchers and to the concessional prices at which much of the remaining state property is sold. As noted in section 3, privatization proceeds for 1992 amounts to only about 15 per cent of the original target.

References

Bim, A. S., Jones, D. C. and **Weisskopf, T. E.** (1992) New forms of property and entrepreneurship in the former Soviet Union: experience, tendencies, and problems, report prepared at the Institute of Market Economy, Russian Academy of Sciences, Moscow.

Bim, A. S., Jones, D. C. and **Weisskopf, T. E.** (1993a) Hybrid forms of enterprise organization in the former USSR and the Russian Federation, *Comparative Economic Studies*, **35** (1), pp. 1–37.

Bim, A. S., Jones, D. C. and **Weisskopf, T. E.** (1993b) The growth of private enterprise and institutional change in the former USSR and the New Russia, working paper, University of Michigan.

Boycko, M., Shleifer, A. and **Vishny, R. W.** (1993) Privatizing Russia, paper prepared for the Brookings Panel on Economic Activity, September 9–10.

Bush, K. (1992) Russian privatization programme accelerated, *RFE/RL Research Report*, **1** (30), pp. 43–45.

Bush, K. (1993) Industrial privatization in Russia: A progress report, *RFE/RL Research Report*, **2** (7), pp. 32–34.

Desai, P. (1992) *Perestroika in Perspective* 2nd edn. Princeton University Press, Princeton, N.J.

Leijonhufvud, A. (1993) The nature of the depression in the former Soviet Union, *New Left Review*, **199**, pp. 120–126.

Wegren, S. K. (1993) Trends in Russian agrarian reform, *RFE/RL Research Report*, **2** (13), pp. 46–56.

World Bank (1992) *Russian Economic Reform: Crossing the Threshold of Structural Change*, The World Bank, Washington, D.C.

CHAPTER TWELVE

Economic system reforms and privatization in Romania

Avner Ben-Ner and John Michael Montias*

1. Introduction

As the Romanian government gradually withdraws from its pervasive control of economic life, built up during more than a hundred years of state 'interventionism', the habits and mentalities left over from the past are restricting the opportunities for smooth and rapid system change. Some of these habits and mentalities are the legacies of centuries of foreign (principally Turkish Ottoman) domination, the delayed emancipation from serfdom of its peasant population, the social and technological backwardness inherent in the country's peripheral situation *vis-a-vis* developed Western nations, and the protracted predominance of its rural economy. The values and attitudes of the Romanian population were also shaped by the extreme nationalism of its governing elites, which gave birth to the policies for which Romania was already notorious at the beginning of the 20th century. These policies initially took the form of discrimination against foreigners (in the sale of land and in employment), in high tariffs, and in subsidies to industry. From the 1930s on, they were carried out through strict quotas, bilateral balancing agreements, and restrictions on the importation of foreign capital (Spulber 1966: pp 21, 69–75). The dominant position of the state in economic life went hand in hand with citizens' attempts to avoid state controls, if necessary by corrupting government officials. The state's weak legitimacy, and the concomitant lack of respect for the laws of the land, as well as the corruptibility of its officials (particularly at lower levels of the bureaucracy), are problems that it must still cope with today.

In this chapter we examine the changes in the economic system and policies that took place in the three and a half years since the December 1989 revolution.

*Information presented in this chapter is based on published sources (cited in the footnotes and in the bibliography) and on unpublished Romanian documents and interviews conducted by the authors in the second half of July 1993 (Ben- Ner) and in the first week of August 1993 (Montias). In addition both authors visited Poland and conducted interviews in Warsaw during the second half of June (1993). Ben-Ner acknowledges support for travel from the International Program Development at the Carlson School of Management at the University of Minnesota. Montias's research was supported by a travel grant from the International Research and Exchanges Board, with funds provided by the US Department of State (title VIII) and the National Endowment for the Humanities. None of the organizations cited above is responsible for the views expressed by the authors. Helpful comments were made by Saul Estrin, Egon Neuberger and participants at a seminar at Yale University. The chapter was written while Ben-Ner was a visiting professor at the Department of Economics and the Institution for Social and Policy Studies at Yale University.

Special attention is paid to developments in the organization and ownership of firms, since it is the microeconomic aspects of the system where the changes are most difficult to achieve and the potential gains are greatest. Since the communist regime raised the guiding role of the state in the economy to unprecedented heights, we need to describe briefly the system and the policies they instituted (in Section 2) before we can deal with the post-1989 macroeconomic reforms that altered both system and policies, as the new government proceeded to dismantle the controls that had tightly swaddled the economy (Section 3). In Section 4 we describe in detail and evaluate the organizational reforms and privatization that have taken place since the beginning of 1990. The last section presents a general evaluation of the macro and microeconomic strategies of systemic transition in Romania.

2. The Romanian economy under communism

The communist regime imposed on the population in 1945 inherited a backward rural economy, along with a number of high-cost industries that had been built up behind the walls of protectionism. Its nascent petrochemical and machine-building industries, including armaments, had been boosted by wartime demands, at a time when Romania was allied with the axis powers. But nearly three-quarters of its population was still engaged in agriculture, eking out a living from small, inefficient farms. The new communist leaders aspired to create a modern industrial base in the country, in imitation of the Soviet universalist model, with a dominant priority assigned to heavy industry. In the first post-war period, however, the goal of industrialization on a wide spectrum had to give way to the exigencies of Soviet domination. Stalin's government, having decided to treat Romania as a defeated axis power, even though it had switched to the allied side late in the war, demanded and received reparations and joint control of the country's petroleum and lumber resources through Soviet–Romanian joint companies. These joint companies were dissolved a year after Stalin's death, at considerable cost to the Romanians. After the Soviets withdrew their troops from Romania in 1958, the Romanian leaders finally acquired the autonomy to conduct their own economic policies. Their refusal to specialize in agriculture and in the food-processing and light industries, and to de-emphasize the metallurgical and heavy engineering industries (for which they had inadequate resources), created considerable friction within the Soviet-dominated Council for Mutual Economic Assistance (CMEA) (Montias 1967: 193–225). In spite of the pressures exerted by the Soviet Union and by the more developed members of CMEA, Gheorghe Gheorghiu-Dej and his successor Nicolae Ceausescu pursued policies aimed at a 'complex, multilateral development', by which was meant the deployment of light and heavy industries along a broad front, irrespective of international comparative advantage. Priority was given to the metallurgical, heavy-engineering, and petrochemical industries. Investments, which, together with inventory accumulation, were boosted to 30–35 per cent of net material product, were directed mainly to industry and transportation. Agriculture was neglected, especially cattle-breeding and horticulture. As a result of these highly concentrated efforts, industrial output rose rapidly — typically at 8 to 10 per cent per year, on the basis of somewhat inflated official claims — while agriculture and services grew slowly or not at all.[1]

The country became even more autarkic in its external economic relations than it had been in the pre-war period. Preferential trade with fellow members of CMEA, to the extent that Romania cooperated with the organization, further distorted the patterns of its exchanges with the world. During the 1970s, Romania received credits from Western banks and from international organizations like the IMF. The country's external debt reached a high of $9 billion in 1981. Imports of extremely energy-intensive equipment, combined with Romania's inability to produce high-quality products that would be competitive on Western markets, and the inroads made in Romania's markets by the newly industrialized countries of Asia, lowered the returns on debt-financed investments to extremely low (in some cases, negative) levels. The high interest rates of the early 1980s further undermined Romania's ability to repay its foreign debts. Unlike Poland, however, which eventually had to declare a moratorium on its debts, Romania, at Ceausescu's bidding, had to go through the excruciating process of repaying all its debts within eight years, much sooner than it was compelled to by its creditors. Imports were cut to the bone, and exports, particularly of consumer goods and of Romania's best machinery, were expanded without regard to cost. The combination of lower machinery imports and higher machinery exports reduced the replacement of worn out and obsolete capital to unprecedented levels.

The communist regime's policies were implemented via rigidly enforced central commands. The efficiency of allocation suffered from 'voluntaristic' decision-making at the highest levels of the Party, poor coordination among firms producing and consuming inputs, and inadequate or misdirected incentives given to workers and management. Unlike other East European countries, Romania did not decentralize decision-making to the level of government-owned firms (henceforth GOFs), had no significant private sector, and did not rely on markets to any meaningful extent. Politically the most repressive regime in communist Eastern Europe (with the exception of Albania) since the early 1970s, Romania, as of 1989, did not have the semblance of an autonomous political class. The only muffled expressions of dissent came from individuals within the party and intellectual elites. Despite the worsening economic conditions of the late 1980s, popular protests were rare and confined primarily to miners.

Living standards, especially after 1980, fell to low levels both as a result of the high-investment, high-export, low-import policies approved by Ceausescu and of the inefficiencies that pervaded the system. In early 1989 the government announced triumphantly that all foreign debts had been repaid. At the same time it made clear that there would be no relief for consumers, who were suffering from extreme deprivation.[2] On 22 December a popular uprising, abetted by disgruntled party members (some of whom had been shifted to minor posts in the wake of disputes with the leadership) forced Ceausescu and his wife to flee Bucharest and abandon power.[3]

3. The economy since 1990

Since the December 1989 revolution, the freely elected parliament and the various centre-left governments that it has named have been committed to a policy of removing the restrictions that had virtually eliminated private enterprise in industry and trade and severely limited it in agriculture (almost all of the country's farming area was cultivated by state farms or cooperatives with compulsory membership). In this spirit it has attempted to sell to private interests, including foreigners, some of the assets that it owned; it has pursued a policy of freeing prices from administrative controls and of eliminating subsidies for consumer goods and services; and it has begun to develop an institutional framework and initiated policies necessary for the operation of a market economy. The formal mechanisms associated with comprehensive central economic planning were abolished as early as 1990, but some informal rationing of inputs to GOFs persisted until at least 1992.

The first actions of the revolutionary government (the Council of the National Salvation Front) were directed at improving the lot of the population in the domains of consumption, work, and personal freedom. This was accomplished, for example, by halting the export of foodstuffs, importing coffee and other necessities, curbing the output of energy-guzzling industries and eliminating quantity restrictions on the use of energy by consumers and municipalities and reducing its price, removing price controls on private sales by peasants, reducing the length of the work week from 46 to 40 hours, curtailing the activities of the secret police, and permitting freedom of the press and other forms of expression. A few months after the revolution, a quarter of the agricultural cooperatives' land was already transferred to private cultivation, the permissible area for private cultivation was doubled, and forced deliveries were abolished. Various decrees and laws were hastily adopted in February and March of 1990, making provisions for (1) the privatization of farm land, (2) the founding of private non-farm enterprises by Romanian nationals (which were limited in size and in their access to inputs), (3) the creation of joint enterprises with foreign participants, and (4) the conversion of most GOFs to private or state-private firms. These measures, which were widely popular, produced enough support, particularly in the rural areas, to ensure an overwhelming (80 per cent of the vote) victory for the party of the National Salvation Front in the parliamentary elections of May 1990.

OUTPUT AND EMPLOYMENT

Economic developments since the revolution can be summarized as follows. Industrial output in 1990, compared to 1989, was down 18 per cent; by December 1991, it had fallen by 44 per cent; in December 1992, it had shrunk to a little less than half of its 1989 level. The decline seems to have been arrested at the end of 1992. By March 1993 the index stood at 52 per cent of the average for 1989. All branches of industry have contracted since 1989. Even the output of the foodprocessing and textile industries barely exceeded 50 per cent of their base level in March 1993. Hardest hit were the metallurgical and petroleum-processing industries which were down 58 per cent and 65 per cent, respectively, from 1989 levels

(National Bank of Romania 1993: 5). These were the industries that had been most over-extended during the communist period.

In 1990 and 1991, employment in industry hardly decreased. At the beginning of 1992, unemployment, expressed as a percentage of the economically active population was 2.7 per cent (3.4 per cent including unemployed persons who were not entitled to government aid) (Guvernul Romaniei, 1992: 39). In the course of 1992, industry began to shed labour on a larger scale. By July 1993 unemployment rose to 9.5 per cent. Labour productivity in industry, which had been going down steadily in 1990 and 1991, rapidly recovered in the second half of 1992, as employment fell and output began to stabilize (NBR, 1993: 3). By June 1993, hourly productivity was down only 13 per cent from the October 1990 level and 7 per cent on a per-employee basis (interview information). Farm output has also fallen, though less spectacularly than in industry. It rose by 10.4 per cent in 1990 as compared to the previous year, then fell 4.7 per cent in 1991 and 8.7 per cent in 1992 (in part due to a bad weather spell). Altogether GDP declined by 7.4 per cent in 1990, 13.7 per cent in 1991, and 15.4 per cent in 1992 (Government of Romania 1993, Annex).

Generally, the fall in output can be traced to the following causes: (1) the collapse of trade with CMEA members (the decline in exports affecting the output of exporting branches directly, and the decline of imports, particularly of cheap fuels, depressing the output of import-dependent industries); (2) the closing of factories or their component parts due to high inefficiency, pollution or shortages of domestic inputs; (3) the lack of internal demand (due to competition of imports and to the growth of small private domestic manufacturers whose output is not fully recorded in the official statistics); (4) labour problems, including the reduction in the working week and a decline in discipline in GOFs which depressed productivity; (5) the difficulties due to the elimination of central planning as a coordinating mechanism in the absence of efficiently functioning markets, due to the slow emergence of supporting institutions; and (6) difficulties encountered by GOFs in adjusting to market processes. These points are discussed later in the chapter.

FOREIGN TRADE

Total exports, expressed in current US dollars, dropped sharply in 1990 and 1991 (by 20 per cent and 26 per cent, respectively). Imports rose by over 50 per cent in 1990, as the government went into foreign debt to relieve the shortage of domestic goods; they then fell by 40 per cent in 1991 in the wake of an extreme foreign exchange crisis. After this see-saw, both exports and imports stabilized approximately at the previous year's level in 1992. The current account deficit in the balance of payments rose to $3.5 billion in 1990 (which may be contrasted with the surpluses accumulated in the last years of the Ceausescu regime). It then declined to about $1.1 billion in 1991 and 1992, to rise again to the rate of $2 billion a year in the first semester of 1993, a sign that the problems that afflicted the economy two years earlier might be recurring (NBR 1993: 29). Since late 1991 all trade has been carried out in convertible currencies, in contrast to 1990 when exports in 'convertible rubles' (in trade with CMEA countries) still amounted to

35 per cent of total exports and imports from CMEA to 45 per cent (NBR 1993: 29). We will return to the current account deficit and the exchange rate policy after a brief discussion of the inflation.

PRICES AND WAGES

Since November 1990 when liberalization of retail prices began in earnest, monthly price increases have varied between 6 and 26.5 per cent (with a typical monthly change of 10 per cent). Altogether, in March 1993, the retail price index stood at 1,752 (October 1990 = 100). Food prices were about 20 times higher than they were in that base month and non-food prices 16 times (NBR 1993: 7). The high variance in month-to-month increases in both wholesale and retail prices may be explained by the administrative nature of the liberalizing process. Producers and retailers are not so much free to set prices at the level that would maximize profits as they are periodically allowed to increase their prices to cover costs. In an apparent move to restrict the effects of local monopolies in trade, retailers, until mid-1993, could only include in their price accounting a 'commercial margin' (*adauga comerciala*) that was set at a maximum of 30 per cent. In marked opposition to Poland, where the prices of goods were set free at one fell swoop in January 1990, it has taken the Romanian government nearly three years to get to the same point. The uncertainty about the episodic run-ups of prices in Romania has undoubtedly fed inflationary expectations.

Average wages also rose rapidly, but they did not keep up with the price increases. They were about 11 times higher in March 1993 than in October 1990 (12 times in industry) (NBR 1993: 6). A comparison of the changes in wages and in retail prices suggests that real wages fell by over 30 per cent. But this calculation is partially misleading. In October 1990, long queues for most foodstuffs and empty shelves for industrial products made retail prices virtually void of meaning. In contrast, most goods are now readily available. Black-market prices were much higher than official levels, and the black market has virtually disappeared. The statistics of per-household consumption indicate that there was a 10 to 15 per cent decline in the quantities of basic foodstuffs purchased by households in the Statistical Commission's sample from the first half of 1991 to the first half of 1992, which was the worst year of the transition to liberalized prices. The decline has been largely arrested according to the results of the sample for the first three months of 1993, with small declines in some categories and increases in other categories (Comisia nationala pentru statistica June 1993). In our view, the only people who suffered anything like the full drop in statistical real wages are those who, in the initial period, had the time to stand in queues (including pensioners, non-working individuals and those with relatively more time to spare) or those who could obtain goods by virtue of their special connections.[4]

What are the causes of the inflation? Linked to each other are the following three factors.

1. The budget deficit has fluctuated around 5-10 per cent of GDP. It is in large part generated by the decline in GOF output and productivity which

was not accompanied by a commensurate reduction in wages. This reduction in GOFs' profits along with widespread evasion of taxes on private firms and trade and of excises on imports, caused a decline in government revenues from taxes and levies.[5]

2. The National Bank, under pressure from the government, has financed the non-performing loans extended to GOFs in industry (chiefly in petroleum-processing, metallurgy, and machine building) with massive injections of credits; these credits were rapidly monetized and added to the purchasing power of the population.

3. Since mid-1991, wages have been nominally indexed at 80 per cent of price increases (when real wages fall below 80 per cent for a few months, nominal wages are raised to meet this target); this is the cost-push side of the inflation which also raises inflationary expectations.

Inflationary pressures would have been even more severe had an export surplus been generated (as was the case in Poland in 1990). But the deficit on the current account could only be sustained by lowering reserves and borrowing, mainly on short term from abroad, with negative consequences for the future. One important reason for the deficit on the current account has been the over-valuation of the exchange rate. The depreciation of the officially quoted leu (the Romanian currency) has systematically lagged behind the inflation. Since the middle of 1992, the rate is supposed to be set on a free auction market ('the interbank market'), but the government, by excluding bidders with low-priority requirements for foreign exchange, has kept the rate at least 20 per cent below the rate that would result if all citizens, as well as private and government firms, were allowed to bid freely on the exchange market, so that internal convertibility would be achieved. The unwillingness to let the market take over has, on balance, been bad for the economy. While it has moderated administrative price increases, in the sense that the increases in the price of imported goods that would have resulted from a more realistic devaluation of the currency were averted, it has contributed to the cumulative inflationary movement by undermining faith in the national currency. Romanian citizens have shifted their savings from lei to dollars and Deutsche Marks; more and more transactions have been carried out in these currencies. The unwillingness to hold lei has contributed to a rise in the velocity of money (M1 or M2) from 2.0 in 1990 to 5.5 in terms of GDP in 1992 (World Bank 1993). In Poland, the shock therapy applied in 1990 rapidly achieved internal convertibility; the exchange rate set early in that year, which initially undervalued the zloty, was maintained for 10 months (after that it was first devalued to a rate that was maintained for a few months and then later converted to a crawling peg, whereby the zloty was devalued every two months in line with the expected rate of inflation). By maintaining the 'anchor' for some months, inflationary expectations, at least in the initial period of 1990–91, were broken, and a significant trend away from the 'dollarization' of the economy occurred. A much lower rate of inflation than in Romania (2–3 per cent per month), despite a continued budget deficit, was an apparent consequence of this resolute policy.

FINANCIAL INSTITUTIONS

The transition to a market economy has been supported not only through the adoption of the economic policies described, but also through the introduction of various new institutions. The National Bank of Romania was transformed into a central bank with nominal independence from the government. The state-owned 'commercial banks', which were hived off the central bank, started to adopt prudential principles in lending compatible with the needs of a market economy. By the middle of 1993, three private and two mixed state-private banks had been established, along with five foreign-owned banks. A stock exchange is scheduled to open in 1994. But the most important changes in the economic system took place in the realm of the organization of production, discussed in the following section.

EVALUATION OF MACROECONOMIC REFORMS

Romania's system changes and economic policies have generally moved in the right direction toward the introduction of market-oriented institutions, the freeing of prices and the liberalization of markets, and the adoption of measures to control inflationary pressures, but they have been irresolute and protracted in their implementation. Political obstacles arising from opposition to liberalization in parliament and in the government administration itself, have been part of the problem. The liberalization of consumer goods' prices has periodically been halted, for fear that increases in the prices of essential goods would be socially intolerable. The elimination of direct and indirect subsidies to heavy industry has met with similar opposition, especially in the regions where the closing of plants would have taken place.

These apprehensions are easily understandable. But adjustments of prices to market levels have at times also been delayed owing to confusion between the one-time effects of price increases on the statistical rate of inflation and the factors leading to cumulative inflation. The inability to set interest rates on bank loans above the rate of inflation is a case in point. Higher interest rates tend to raise production costs and may contribute to one-time increases in prices, but, to the extent that they discourage loans for frivolous projects, they will dampen one of the principal forces that promote the inflation. Similarly, the government's reluctance to institute full-fledged convertibility is based, at least in part, on the mistaken belief that an overvalued exchange rate generating low import prices for 'essential' raw materials and foodstuffs is effective in combating the inflation. But again devaluation, coupled with a tight monetary policy aimed at dampening inflationary expectations, should have only a one-time impact on raising prices. The greater efficiency associated with the alignment of domestic on foreign prices should even reduce this one-time impact. Poland's shock therapy, in retrospect, appears to have been more effective in reducing the inflation than Romania's dithering. It is not evident that the social or economic adjustment costs resulting from Poland's trenchant policies have been higher than those associated with Romania's more timid initiatives.

While Romania's policies have been less decisive than Poland's, with the consequences that we have seen, they have still been more consistent and resolute in combating the inflation than, say, Russia's or Ukraine's, let alone of Albania where the government has almost totally lost the ability to initiate and carry out collective action.

4. Changes in the management of government-owned firms, privatization and entry of new firms

Three main types of changes in the organization of production have taken place. First, most GOFs were 'corporatized,' i.e. turned into profit-oriented, self-financing commercial companies with a nominally independent board of directors. The remaining firms were turned into autonomous state enterprises (*régies*). Second, a framework for privatization was put in place and the first steps towards privatization were taken: 30 per cent of the shares of corporatized GOFs were allocated to one of five private ownership funds, and the remaining shares were transferred to the state-ownership fund, which was charged with divesting itself of its shares (privatizing) within seven years. Third, provisions were made for the entry of new firms (domestic and foreign), and a large number of (mostly small) new firms were created. These changes were introduced through a series of laws and government decrees, the first of which date back to less than two months after the revolution.

THE LEGAL FRAMEWORK FOR ORGANIZATIONAL REFORMS, PRIVATE FIRMS, AND PRIVATIZATION

There are four landmark laws on firms, all of which were later amended and supplemented.[6] The first was introduced in August 1990 (Law 15).[7] It stipulates the conversion of GOFs in most industries from units subordinated to various ministries and subject to state planning into commercial joint-stock or limited-liability companies owned, for the time being, by the state. GOFs in the 'strategic branches of the economy' — armaments, electric power, mines, natural gas, the post office, railway, and a few others — have become autonomous state enterprises (*régies autonomes*, similar to some French government-owned firms, henceforth referred to as *régies*). The law, which was to be implemented within six months, also established the basic principles of privatization of commercial GOFs that were elaborated later, in the laws summarized below.

The second law was introduced in November 1990 (Law 31). This law emulates closely the French commercial code, effectively eliminating most legal impediments to private enterprise. The rules concerning the internal governance of various firms as well as provisions for their dissolution and merger are also similar to those in the French code.

The third law, passed in August 1991 (Law 5), specifies the methods by which commercial GOFs are to be privatized. The law stipulates the free distribution of five ownership certificates to each adult in Romania. Each certificate entitles its owner to a share in one of the five private ownership funds (POFs). Thirty per cent of the shares of each commercial GOF were scheduled for allocation to a POF, with the remaining 70 per cent to be assigned to a newly created state-ownership fund (SOF). The SOF was directed to sell to the public its holdings within seven years, and the POFs were required to become mutual funds. The state and private ownership funds were made responsible for managing the GOFs as shareholders until the process of privatization was completed.

The fourth law was introduced in April 1991 concerning foreign investment. It established the Romanian Development Agency as the primary institution for dealing with applications by foreign investors for a licence to operate in Romania. The law set various incentives for foreign investors, including exemptions of taxes on profits for five years in most industries. The law permits the repatriation of profits in foreign currency (all profits earned in foreign currency plus 8-15 per cent of the profits earned in lei) and the proceeds, in lei, due to the liquidation of their investments in Romania.[8] Foreign investors may be sole owners of firms in Romania or participate in joint ventures; they enjoy all the rights and obligations of Romanian firms.

CORPORATIZATION AND RESTRUCTURING OF GOVERNMENT-OWNED FIRMS

All GOFs were freed from comprehensive government control with the dismantling of the central planning mechanism in early 1990; the ministries to which they belonged lost their rights to dictate the actions of firms that were still their subordinates.[9] Although, as noted earlier, some price controls survived for many industrial products and their inputs until May of 1993, firms were free to decide on their production and financial affairs without interference from the newly created Ministry of Industry and Resources. Moreover, managers were allowed to participate in the efforts to restructure their firms, which frequently led to the formation of new firms from the constituent parts of the old ones.

At the end of the first half of 1993, there were approximately 6,400 commercial GOFs and 912 régies. These numbers are larger than in previous years due to the break-up of firms. As noted earlier, several large industrial firms were shut down, shedding perhaps as many as three quarters of a million employees.[10] In total, approximately 70 commercial GOFs and 14 régies were shut down.

The régies were intended to operate primarily as commercial entities sustained from their own sales. It appears, however, that their budgets regularly include subsidies designed to supplement their revenues from commercial sources. Whereas, by design, régies continue to be supervised by the ministries in charge of them, the corporatization and restructuring of commercial GOFs has turned them into largely autonomous firms. In this subsection we describe, on the basis of available information, some of the changes in the management and organization of GOFs that have occurred thus far. In the next subsection we examine the planned changes in the management of GOFs as they progress towards privatization.

In many GOFs, the loss of central control and guidance, which jeopardized the regular supply of inputs as well as outlets for output, resulted in disorientation. Managers with experience in production found it difficult to make decisions on product design, marketing, and financing in a new and volatile market environment that was evolving rapidly. Moreover, many managers were replaced, mainly by their employees, shortly after the revolution; the new managers were apparently less competent, and many old managers had to be reinstated.[11]

A common response in face of these adverse changes has been for managers to seek assistance from ministries to which they were formerly subordinate (or from the ministries that succeeded them after 1989). The assistance requested is of various kinds: to apply pressure on former suppliers to maintain their sales, to obtain critical inputs for themselves, to set advantageous prices, to facilitate the extension of credit to finance production, and to grant subsidies. Such assistance was often forthcoming, albeit in subversion of stated government policy. Subsidies to GOFs were grudgingly approved by the government. (Provision for subsidies had, in fact, been made in Law 15, although with a view toward their gradual elimination within five years from its enactment.) Subsidized credits at interest rates way below the inflation rate continue to be extended to GOFs in industry, transport, and communication.

For the most part, however, managers were left to their own devices. In addition to laying off some workers and placing others (sometimes entire factories) on extended vacations, managers looked for various ways to survive on the market. They used their old networks to seek continuation of their pre-1990 patterns of purchases and sales even if they did not have the funds to support them. One way to do so was for firms to extend credit to their customers. These inter-enterprise credits, which rose to very high levels in 1991 and 1992, have been periodically supported by the National Bank's injections of supplementary credit to keep alive the chain of payments. The government's attempts to wipe out arrears have not prevented the renewed extension of inter-enterprise credits, which amounted to nearly 2,000 billion lei in April 1993 (about the same level as that of bank credit outstanding). A bankruptcy law was enacted in 1992 (Law 76) according to which creditors can declare a firm bankrupt and seize its assets; but this has apparently not yet happened. One reason for this might be the difficulty in selling the seized assets, when several creditors compete for payment. In addition, the court system is limited in its ability to settle disputes.[12]

The condition of commercial GOFs is not entirely bleak, at least financially. According to government documents consulted by the authors, the GOF sector has been moderately profitable, though at lower levels than in the past and only at about one-quarter of the profitability of the private sector. In many firms management has succeeded in adapting to the new circumstances through learning-by-doing, reliance on consultants, and retraining personnel to teach them the way to do business in a market environment.[13]

PRIVATIZATION[14]

Large scale privatization

Certificates of ownership
The initial planning and execution of various aspects of the privatization process was entrusted to the National Agency for Privatization (NAP). The distribution

of certificates of ownership (COs) was completed by the end of 1992. Each adult received five COs, one in each POF. However, the COs can be traded and therefore accumulated in numbers in excess of the initial allocation. COs can be used to purchase shares in large commercial GOFs in which the issuing POF owns shares (when such firms will be presented for sale by the SOF), although COs can be used for the purchase of only up to 30 per cent of a firm's shares. Employees can use all their five initial COs to purchase shares in the firms in which they work.[15]

Trade in COs has hardly begun through the Romanian Foreign Trade Bank and private channels. At present, in the informal market for COs, their value has been very low (around $6 per CO), but it may well rise when the stock exchange opens in 1994.[16] To expedite the privatization of small firms, the administrative councils of the five POFs agreed in April 1993 to establish values for their COs, ranging between 23,000 and 29,000 lei per CO (about $30 to $37). These nominal values, as we have seen, are greatly in excess of current market values. Holders of COs may hold on to them but cannot receive dividends for the first three years (presumably 1993-5). If they keep them for the full five years, the COs will become shares in their respective POFs, which in turn will be transformed into share-issuing mutual funds.

The pilot privatization

In the interest of gaining experience with privatization as well as to generate understanding of and support for the process, the NAP was charged with a pilot privatization project targeted at up to 0.5 per cent of the small- and medium-sized commercial GOFs. This percentage amounted to 32 firms which were selected to represent economically viable firms. The selection of the firms was done with the guidance of foreign consultants. By the middle of 1993, 22 firms had been privatized by the NAP. The terms of each sale include a price, the period during which it will be paid, and a commitment by the buyers to make certain investments and maintain a certain level of employment. In seven cases the price was close to the estimated book value of the firm, whereas in many other cases it was higher. The duration of payment is between two and four years. Investment commitments, to be carried out typically within three years, vary from a small fraction of the equity to much more sizable sums.

Of the 22 privatized firms, 14 were purchased by employees and management through what is universally known in Romania by its English acronym MEBO — management and employee buy-out.[17] A MEBO is carried out by a voluntarily constituted association of employees which negotiates with the seller. In order to participate in negotiations over a MEBO, the association must represent at least three-quarters of management, or two-thirds of management and 15 per cent of the employees, or 51 per cent of the employees. The typical MEBO firm employs a few hundred employees, although one has 2,337 employees and another 1,538. There is no information about the distribution of shares between management and employees, but apparently employees hold a majority of shares in most cases. In another five cases employees have ownership stakes.[18] The three remaining cases include a joint venture between a foreign investor and the Romanian state (81 per cent and 19 per cent, respectively), a purchase by a Romanian–Canadian company, and a firm with 51 per cent owned by individual investors and 49 per cent by a foreign investor.

The private ownership funds

The five POFs and the SOF began operation in early 1993. The POFs received 30 per cent of the shares of all 6,400 commercial GOFs, and the SOF received the remaining shares. The POFs are based in five different regions of the country. The principles underlying the allocation of shares to POFs are the following: (1) geographical concentration, to facilitate control over firms that serve a parti- cular region; (2) industrial concentration, to allow for some specialization among POFs' staffs; and (3) industrial diffusion in the financial and insurance industries, in order to create competition, and in the 'distressed industries' (chemicals and petrochemicals, metallurgical, and machine building), to spread the risk of failure of firms there. Thus whereas the SOF owns 70 per cent of the shares of all commercial GOFs, each POF has the remaining 30 per cent of the shares in all commercial GOFs in agriculture, building and construction and local service industries in its region; the remaining 30 per cent in all commercial GOFs in designated industries; and 6 per cent (one-fifth of 30 per cent) of the shares of each GOF in the 'critical' financial and insurance industries as well as in distressed industries. Thus each POF has sizable holdings in numerous firms.[19]

Each POF is governed by a seven-member administrative council (appointed by the government and approved by the parliament) that meets monthly. The size of the staff, both current and targeted, is very small; the Bucharest based POF number 4 has 60 employees, with a target of 170 employees. POFs' key functions are to maximize the financial value of their owners' shares, to participate with the SOF and the NAP in planning further privatization of the shares owned by the SOF, and to update quarterly the valuation of the certificates of ownership. There are two primary means to pursue the objective of maximization of the value of their holdings. First, POFs may engage in control over GOFs by appointing representatives to Shareholders' General Assemblies (which will be constituted in late 1993). The POF representatives will work under a contract which stipulates fees for being present at, and reporting about, the two annual regular and any extraordinary meetings (100,000 lei, or currently a little over $100), and a pre- mium of 5 per cent on profits in excess of projected profits (the method of projection is undefined). The premium will not be paid if no dividends are distributed (i.e., if all profits are reinvested or distributed to management and employees).[20] Second, POFs can invest dividends in privatized firms (as two have done in a case mentioned above), in real estate, in foreign companies, etc.

The state ownership fund

The SOF is governed by an administrative council consisting of the president of the NAP, and an additional 16 members appointed by the President, the Council of Ministers, and the two houses of the Parliament. It has four principal functions with respect to GOFs: (1) to govern all the commercial GOFs for which, with 70 per cent of the shares, it is the major shareholder; (2) to carry out the privatization of its holdings within seven years by selling annually 10 per cent of its shares; (3) to restructure weak GOFs (by appointing new management, redesigning the organizational structure, changing product lines, breaking firms up, etc.) in preparation for their privatization, and (4) to close down non-viable GOFs. In addition, the SOF has to manage the financial assets that accrue from the sale of GOFs and to control the payments of buyers, most of whom purchase the firms on credit from the SOF.

With primary responsibility for all commercial GOFs (numbering about 6,400), the SOF's immediate task is to appoint approximately 11,000 representatives to Shareholders' General Assemblies. The SOF's contract with its representatives differs from that of the POFs' contracts mainly in that it holds out incentives that depend on the dividends paid by the firms. The management of firms will work under a management contract of the type used in some Scandinavian countries; the exact nature of this contract is currently being debated in parliament.[21] In July 1993 the SOF had about 80 employees, with a target employment of 900. The organization of the SOF has not been finalized yet, but it will probably have divisions for strategy (preparing annually the list of firms for privatization), shareholding (governance of firms), financing (providing credit for Romanian buyers), and restructuring. The shareholding division will probably be organized on a geographic basis and the restructuring division on an industrial basis.

In the short time since it began its operation, the SOF has focused on the privatization of small firms employing a few dozen to a few hundred employees. It had privatized 66 firms employing a total of 15,536 employees by early July 1993, at a rate of nearly two firms a day. Almost all of these firms were privatized through MEBOs, with terms of payment of 15 per cent down and the rest to be paid within approximately seven years, with variable requirements for future investments. Privatization of some 1,100 firms with more than 1,000 employees (jointly employing 65 per cent of all the employees in commercial GOFs) is yet to begin.[22]

Small scale privatization

Perhaps the most important accomplishment thus far of the privatization programme was the privatization of assets owned by GOFs, such as equipment, small production facilities, buildings, hotels, restaurants, stores, and warehouses. Assets for sale or lease are published frequently in daily newspapers and auctions are taking place daily throughout the country. The auctions are at first open only to Romanian citizens; in the case of unsold assets a second auction is held where foreigners are allowed to participate. Employees (active or retired) receive preferential treatment in these auctions. As noted in the next subsection, this type of privatization has an important role in the entry of new private firms.

There have been many accusations of corruption in the sale of assets. One frequently alleged form of corruption occurs when managers collude with purchasers. A recent case involves the transportation minister who has been accused of selling most of the merchant navy to a foreign buyer for a low price in return for favours.

Privatization in agriculture

Property relations in agriculture began to change in the next few months after the revolution. One third of the land cultivated by cooperative farms had been turned over to their members by mid-1990 (Vatasescu 1990: 6). In the next two years, most of the remaining cooperatives were liquidated at the initiative of their members and managers. This organizational change seems to have resulted in some decline in output, which was aggravated by adverse atmospheric conditions. Whereas in 1990 the usage of fertilizers (both chemical and natural) was essentially the same as in the previous year, it fell drastically in 1991 (no data are yet available for 1992). The farms that have been created, like those that resulted from the inter-war land reform, are very small.

Because of the difficulty in adjudicating among conflicting claims — some of them more than a half century old — the government has not given the peasants who now cultivate the land full title to its ownership. This not only discourages investments in the land — owing to the uncertainty about the ultimate disposal of the parcels distributed — but it makes it virtually impossible for farmers to obtain bank credit since they cannot use their land as collateral.[23] The assignment and use of the heavy machinery possessed by the government-owned machine-tractor stations has also presented problems. Most of this equipment is too expensive to be owned by small farms. For the time being the government has been encouraging the formation of user cooperatives (somewhat akin to the defunct 'Agricultural Circles' in Poland) to make joint use of the equipment. The government, which has retained ownership over some 20 per cent of the land in extant state farms, has been reluctant to allow the creation of large private farms, presumably for political reasons. Until a market for land is created, where owners of plots who are too old or too far removed from the land to cultivate it efficiently will be able to cede them to those who can do so, the farm sector will operate below its full potential.

ENTRY AND EXIT OF NEW DOMESTIC PRIVATE FIRMS[24]

The rapid growth of the private sector can be partly inferred from the very rapid growth in the number of registered private firms. By the end of June 1993 there were 266,061 private commercial companies and 3,961 cooperatives, and another 25,078 individuals registered as traders (not including farmers who sell on farmers' markets and artisans, who do not have to register).[25] Most new firms are small. A rough calculation indicates that in June 1993 the average capitalization of a new private firm was around one million lei, amounting to approximately $1,250, or about 17 times the average monthly wage.[26]

The majority of new firms appear to rely on existing assets — structures, machinery and equipment — which they buy, lease or rent from state agencies or GOFs. In trade, where most new firms are concentrated, many GOFs lease assets and use the proceeds to pay wages or to finance investments.[27]

The government estimates that more than 3.6 million employees worked in the private sector at the end of 1992 (out of a workforce of about 10 million people). The private sector's share in the 1992 GDP is said to be about 25 per cent

(Government of Romania 1933: 33).[28] Private firms accounted for 26.1 per cent of exports and 32.3 per cent of imports; they carried out 44.9 per cent of domestic retail sales and 26 per cent of services. By May 1993, their share of domestic retail sales had surpassed 50 per cent.[29]

For all the massive entry of new firms, there has been extremely little exit. Between the end of 1990 and the end of 1992 approximately 800 private firms were 'deregistered.' The rate of deregistrations has increased over this period and has intensified further in 1993, with about 150 deregistrations during the month of June alone. (In developed market economies approximately one-half of firms go out of business within five years of registration, with a peak of deregistrations occurring within two to three years of entry.) By mid 1993, the great majority of Romanian private firms had been registered for less than two years, so the peak of vulnerability, if it resembles that in other countries, has not yet been reached. With so many private firms being young and inexperienced, there is a distinct possibility that a rash of failures may afflict Romania (as well as other transition economies) in the near future, causing additional economic and social turmoil. The severity of the problem may be alleviated by the fact that there is so much unsatisfied demand for goods and services that fewer firms will go under than would under more stable conditions. Many new firms will also be established to take advantage of the pent-up demand.

ENTRY OF NEW FOREIGN FIRMS AND JOINT VENTURES

Foreigners played an active role in the formation of new firms in Romania. At the end of 1989 there were only six joint ventures, all by law with minority foreign ownership. Since the revolution, some 23,873 commercial companies with foreign participation have been registered in Romania, with a total of $479 million in subscribed capital in foreign exchange (as of the end of June 1993).[30] In June 1993 of 10,028 newly formed commercial companies, 1,023 were with foreign partici-pation. Foreign investments tend to go to the large cities: 22.3 per cent of the firms founded in Bucharest in June 1993 were foreign, compared to 10 per cent of the newly formed commercial companies for the country as a whole.

The per-firm level of most foreign investments in Romania is very small, although still larger than in firms founded by Romanian citizens. The 1,023 foreign firms and joint ventures formed in June 1993 had a combined capitaliza-tion of $6.5 million in foreign exchange, with the larger ventures going to the bigger cities (e.g. $10,000 per firm in Bucharest). Several large investments in the telecommunications and petroleum industries hold out the promise of transfer of technology in areas that are critical to Romania's development.[31] Italy, Germany and France are the largest investors, followed by the USA.

Foreign investors seem to come to Romania for several reasons. In Eastern Europe, Romania's population of 23 million is second in size only to Poland. In addition to its own market potential, Romania is also a potential bridge link for Western companies wishing to trade with the former Soviet Union. The popula-tion is well educated and technically trained and the wage rate is among the lowest in Europe. Romania has mineral deposits which may be commercially exploited in the future.

The most common complaints by foreign investors concern the low level of development of communications and transport and the slow operation of the Romanian bureaucracy, which is staffed by people who are unfamiliar with market processes (and expect occasional bribes to facilitate transactions). In addition, foreign investors complain that the repatriation of foreign currency requires prior application to a commercial bank authorized to bid for dollars or marks at the daily auction organized by the National Bank, which may not honour all its purchase orders. Some foreign companies resort to exporting Romanian goods in order to obtain the requisite foreign currency for repatriation. This problem seems to affect mainly smaller companies as the large ones tend to reinvest their profits in Romania.[32]

EVALUATION OF ORGANIZATIONAL REFORMS AND PRIVATIZATION

As we have seen, the organization of production in Romania has changed considerably since the end of 1989. Agricultural cooperatives have been dismantled and the bulk of farm output now originates with private producers. The state-owned sector has shrunk by about 750,000 employees, although it still produces nearly all manufacturing output and a little more than half of all services in its 6,400 corporatized, largely independent, firms, and about 900 régies. The private sector has grown to employ more than one-third of employees, and is occupying increasingly important roles in commerce and in services. The growth of the private sector occurred almost entirely through entry of new small firms rather than through privatization of GOFs, although most of the tools, equipment, and structures used in the private sector come from the privatization of assets of GOFs, and the workforce of the private sector consists chiefly of employees who moved from the state sector. Privatization of GOFs has only just started. By early July 1993 less that one hundred small- and medium-sized firms had been privatized, involving some 35,000 employees, employees and management playing crucial ownership roles through the MEBO method of privatization. Domestic and foreign investors participated in the privatization of less than two dozen firms, in many instances in partnership with employees. The privatization process that will encompass another nearly 6,400 firms is planned to last for seven years. For reasons adduced in the next subsection, we consider the Romanian strategy of organizational reforms and privatization to be reasonable in Romania's present circumstances, although some of the problems that plague it may, if they are not overcome, be a serious source of inefficiencies.

An interpretation of the main features of the Romanian privatization process

The slow privatization process in industry allows the development of institutions, skills and financial capital that are crucial for the effective operation of a large private sector (Murrell and Wang 1993). The emergence of a private sector consisting of small firms is conducive to such a development; from among the entrepreneurs who will have acquired the skills and capital and the willingness and ability to take risks on a larger scale will come the investors who will purchase shares in GOFs. Meanwhile, financial intermediaries will acquire knowledge and experience in evaluating the risks faced by firms and become better lenders, and additional institutions that can support the accurate evaluation of firms and the dissemination of relevant information will come into being. These developments will permit a better match between prospective buyers and the GOFs they seek to purchase, in terms of the requisite entrepreneurial and managerial expertise, attitudes toward risk and the provision of financial capital, on the one hand, and the relevant characteristics of GOFs, on the other. Whereas the most egregious cases of firms generating waste and pollution were obvious and have been dealt with (by closing them or reducing their output), many other firms cannot be immediately evaluated, given the current skills available in Romania and the conditions that prevail there. In general, the current profitability of firms depends on the capital they presently employ, their organizational structure, the management they have, the marketing strategies they employ, and so on; these factors are not only difficult to evaluate, but they may change significantly as new economic conditions arise.

The considerations outlined above have apparently militated for the policy that firms should be privatized in a sequential fashion. The absence of institutions and mechanisms for the enforcement of direct or indirect control by private shareholders simultaneously in a large number of firms inspired the policy that, among the purchasers of GOFs, there should be a core investor with the interest and ability to expend resources in the exercise of control. These two policies generated a third one: the establishment of the SOF and POFs as core investors and privatizers.

With the elimination of central planning and the delay of large-scale privatization, decentralization of decision-making and the inculcation of a more cost-conscious outlook among the management and workforce of GOFs were necessary. The corporatization of GOFs probably helped in both respects. Managers of GOFs are undoubtedly now far less subject to control of government bureaucrats than they once were. Autonomy is a mixed blessing, because it allows managers to pursue their personal objectives at the expense of economic efficiency as well as of other stakeholders in GOFs. The main constraint on management autonomy is imposed by employees, although their influence is limited, especially compared to Poland. Under conditions of uncertainty about firms' future ownership, employees may press for higher wages even if this harms the long-term profitability of their firm; on the other hand, such pressure may have a positive impact on efficiency if it forces managers to pay closer attention to profits, possibly at the expense of their personal interests.

Unanticipated capital constraints and the emergence of MEBOs

Some constraints affecting the privatization process were anticipated incorrectly by policy makers. It turned out that much private domestic capital went into the immediately profitable new private sector where, as noted earlier, the profit rate has been estimated to be four times as high as in the GOF sector and that little was left for the purchase of GOFs.[33] In 1993, the government recognized a 'great discrepancy between the Romanian private capital resources that might be available to buy shares (estimated to amount to an annual average of 200 billion lei up to 1995) and the nominal value of shares scheduled to be offered for sale by the State Property Fund [the SOF] (which presently amounts to 530 billion lei)' (Government of Romania 1993: 23). Foreign capital, for a variety of reasons, is not available in sufficient quantities to make up for the lack of domestic capital (and if it were, foreign control of many domestic firms would probably be unacceptable to most Romanians). As the same government document stated it (p. 23), 'the difference between supply and demand on this capital market can be, in principle, covered by attracting foreign capital — either as direct and portfolio investments or as credits. Studies indicate that the situation on the international capital market is not favourable at this particular point in time. That is why, the Government considers that at least in the next two to three years it cannot count on foreign investments large enough (at least 300 billion lei annually) to cover the difference between the domestic demand and supply of shares'. Indeed, with total foreign investment now running about $700 million, it is unlikely that about $400 million dollars (the approximate equivalent of 300 billion lei) would now be available each year for the purchase of shares in GOFs.[34]

Thus the expectation of the availability of domestic capital and of foreign investments was apparently over-optimistic. In order to improve incentives for foreign investors, the government amended the existing law in June 1993 to allow for the repatriation of profits earned in lei. In order to move ahead with privatization despite the capital shortage, the government has been making provisions to increase the availability of capital through the participation of financial intermediaries on the future stock exchange market. But this is only a possibility for the future; for the time being, as we have seen, privatization is taking place mainly through MEBOs. This type of privatization creates instantaneous core investors — the employees and the management — with a strong interest in the firm and better familiarity with the affairs of the firm than any other party.[35] Insider investors are likely to be better debtors (less likely to walk away from their debts and declare default), and they are more easily identifiable than other potential 'good' investors. On the other hand, other investors, both domestic and foreign, may be deterred from investing in insider-controlled firms for the fear that insiders will take advantage of their special knowledge and control over the management at the expense of other investors. To promote MEBOs the government has offered (through the NAP and more recently through the SOF) the possibility of payment for the firm in instalments as well as at reduced prices.[36]

The scarcity of organizational skills and its consequences

The scarcity of organizational skills that the Romanian economy faces, frequently acknowledged by policy makers (e.g. in Government of Romania 1993, ch. 3), complicates the task of privatization. In order to use these skills most effectively the crucial restructuring and privatization process was concentrated in the NAP, SOF and POFs. However, in our view, the small staff of these organizations is inadequate for the execution of the tasks with which they were charged. They will not be able to exercise effective control over their firms, which, as a consequence, will be run by their managers as they see fit under the constraints imposed by employees. Since managers are not owners, their decisions are likely to have a negative impact on the investment and modernization plans of their firms. The effects of poor decisions will not be restricted to one or a few firms but will affect entire industries placed in the custody of the NAP, the SOF, and the POFs.

Further, it is necessary to strengthen the staff and skills of the POFs and the SOF as well as of the individual GOFs. Since it will take several years for the requisite skills to develop among Romanian nationals, it will be necessary to rely for some time on the skills of experienced foreign consultants.[37] The current reliance on foreign consultants is restricted to POFs and the management of the SOF; but it is the management in thousands of GOFs that could benefit immediately from improved organizational practices suited to a market environment. It would be greatly beneficial if temporary support services tailored to specific needs could be provided by foreign consultants to individual GOFs, possibly paid for by the SOF and POFs.

The problem of coordination among institutions in the privatization process

There are many areas in which the actions of the POFs and SOF (the NAP's role in future privatization is unclear) must be coordinated and their respective responsibilities more clearly demarcated. This concerns primarily the selection of the 10 per cent of firms due for privatization (that is, for sale of their SOF shares) each year, the restructuring of GOFs to be privatized, and the drawing up of management plans for GOFs. Currently coordination is attempted through the requirement that POFs and the SOF enter 'shareholders' agreements' that specify the conduct of their common affairs. However, this is widely regarded as a patch-up attempt due to the conflicting incentives faced by POF and SOF representatives in shareholders' assemblies of the kind that we have seen earlier. This may slow down the privatization process or cause a less careful evaluation and a less thorough restructuring of GOFs than needed. Some redefinition of the responsibilities of the POFs and the SOF is required in order to avoid unwanted consequences.[38]

Coordination may be achieved but with undesirable effects. The requirement that the POFs and SOF maximize the value of their shares, given the SOF's position as major shareholder and the concentration of POFs' holdings in certain industries, encourages these organizations to engage in collusion among the firms they control.[39] Given the absence of anti-trust legislation, this is not illegal currently in Romania. This suggests the more general problem of synchronization of legal and organizational reforms.

The problem of law and policy support for organizational reforms

A market system built on private ownership requires the support of a legal system that recognizes the key rights of ownership: the right to control owned assets, the right to dispose of their returns or benefits, and the right to dispose of the previous two rights (to sell or lease the assets). The system also requires mechanisms that support and enforce the exercise of these rights. In the case of the privatization process in agriculture the rights to control and returns were granted to peasants, but without the accompanying right to transfer (due to the lack of enabling legislation and other problems). Consequently, despite the fact that land holdings are small and fragmented, markets for the sale and the rental of land have not evolved (Brooks and Meurs 1993).

Firms where employees are major shareholders have different objectives than firms owned by outside investors and therefore experience different agency-managerial and technical-administrative problems. Their organizational structure, the way decision-making rights are allocated, the extent to which employees should be monitored, and the way in which incentives should be structured, ought to be adapted to these different objectives (Ben-Ner *et al.* 1993). There has been no apparent recognition of this issue, either by policy-makers or by those closest to the privatized firms — the NAP and SOF personnel and firm managers. There is no legislation dealing with the specific organizational needs of firms with substantial insider ownership in the same ways the law presently deals with the specific needs of single proprietorships, partnerships, and publicly traded companies. Romania is not unique in this sense (see Daviter *et al.* 1987), but because the government prescribes MEBOs as the method of privatization of thousands of GOFs (see Government of Romania 1993, ch. 3), the absence of appropriate legislation may adversely affect a substantial segment of the economy.

Laws upholding the right of transfer of ownership shares by employee owners are among the most urgently needed. Tradability ensures that employees' current decisions affect their future wealth, thus providing an incentive for making correct investment decisions. It also allows outside shareholders to participate in the ownership of employee-owned firms, since they can buy and sell at the same prices at which insiders do. But not all special needs of employee-owned firms can be addressed through the law. More importantly perhaps, the management and employees of these firms must become aware of their firms' needs and act upon them as knowledgeable and responsible owners who are ultimately in charge of running their firms. This is a new role for managers and employees and it will take time and effort to learn to adjust to it. External assistance will be important in this respect, too.[40]

5. Conclusions

The December 1989 revolution in Romania was driven by two fundamental aspirations: to improve standards of living and to alleviate political oppression. Most Romanian political agents, including the new leaders, thought that these aspirations could be realized through a market economy embedded in a democratic political system. Political oppression was largely eliminated by the beginning of 1990. Levels of living, which briefly improved in the year after the revolution, suffered a setback in 1991 and 1992. During the three and a half years since the revolution important steps were taken aimed at the introduction of a market economy and the transfer of control of firms from the state to private interests. There is a widespread perception that the transition in Romania has been too gradual and moderate, as compared to other East European countries. However, at the end of 1989 Romania had a hypercentralized planned economic system with virtually complete state-ownership of the means of production and a totalitarian political system, whereas Poland and Hungary had gone a long way in introducing markets and allowing private activities not only in agriculture (where the private sector was dominant in Poland), but also in commerce, services and even in production, and had political systems that were less intolerant of opposition than Romania's. With nearly 40 per cent of the Romanian labour force now in the private sector (as compared with about 50 per cent in Poland), with an operational market system (though less so in some respects than in some other East European countries), the depth of change in Romania during the past three and one-half years compares favourably with most other countries of East Europe and of the former Soviet Union.

An economic system consists of a web of institutions that set the rules for the determination of prices, the allocation of credit, the coordination of trade among enterprises and individuals, etc. These institutions are largely interdependent, and the degree to which they form a cohesive and coherent system affects the system's efficiency. Successful systemic transition calls for the elimination or transformation of existing institutions and the establishment of new ones to form together a coherent system. Given Romania's legacies and environment, its transition strategy has been generally sound. Nonetheless, the process has been fraught with difficulties. These are due, in part, to poor policy choices in both the macroeconomic and microeconomic arenas, as well as to the lack of resolution in the pursuit of their goals by policy makers.

Despite the sharp discussions in parliament and the split in the dominant party, there has been a considerable continuity in the broad strategy for system transition pursued by the government and in parliament's support for it. This political strength is probably the key factor that allowed the pursuit of a relatively slow and cautious transition strategy. The continuity in the Romanian transition strategy is most clearly illustrated in the government's pursuit of organizational reforms and privatization. The principles of these reforms were laid out in Law 15, less than eight months after the revolution. A specific framework for privatization was codified in law one year later. Although the details of the laws and of their implementation have been the subject of considerable debate, which have resulted in their subsequent amendment, the main laws and policies have remained remarkably unchanged, especially when compared to other Eastern European countries. There is only one exception: the evolution of MEBOs as the primary route of privatization. Apart from a brief mention of discounts to employees and managers buying up to 10 per cent of the shares in the firms in which they work, employee ownership was not mentioned in the original privatization law.

The process of organizational reform and privatization can therefore be viewed as the result of the government's pursuit, under considerable uncertainty, of a set of objectives subject to various constraints. Within the scope of the broad goal of transition to a market economy, the more immediate objectives regarding the organization of production and distribution for the transition period include: (1) the abandonment by the state of centralized control of the assets it owns and the transfer of most of them to private agents, domestic or foreign; (2) the continued operation of GOFs in areas the government considers to be of strategic importance or where the private sector may not serve as well the public interest; (3) the establishment of efficient governance mechanisms during the period of transition; (4) the assurance of approximately equal access of all citizens to state property; and (5) the imposition of approximately equal costs of transition on all citizens. The key constraints include: (1) the near absence of individuals with experience in running firms in a market system; (2) the expectation of comparatively limited foreign investment; (3) the very limited availability of domestic capital; (4) the absence of established institutions that are essential to the efficient running of firms in a market economy, such as investment banks, stock exchanges, auditing firms, commercial judges and lawyers, as well as information-gathering and processing represented by credit ratings, external audits of firms, etc.[41]

These objectives and constraints, which, in one form or another, have been articulated by Romanian policy makers (see, e.g. Government of Romania 1993), have apparently led to the adoption of a process of organizational reform and privatization that has the following key features: (1) slow and centralized execution of the privatization process in industry, (2) fast privatization in agriculture, (3) retention of government ownership of firms in certain industries, (4) insistence on the existence of core investors in privatized firms, (5) reliance on management and employees in the privatization of small- and medium-sized GOFs, (6) support for the entry of small private firms, and (7) encouragement of foreign investment. Capital constraints, both domestic and foreign, were a major factor in the preference given for privatization through MEBOs. Because these constraints were not correctly anticipated, the early planning for privatization did not include the MEBO option.

In addition to the intentional element, the systemic transition in Romania was shaped by various obstacles and political considerations. Generally, profound systemic change is potentially inhibited by three major problems: (1) the politicians' uncertainty as to the exact nature of the desired system, (2) their imperfect knowledge about the necessary institutions that might best support the system they want, and (3) difficulties in eliminating or transforming existing institutions and introducing new ones. The first two problems stem from the political agents' imperfect understanding of the market system, as well as from disagreements among them as to the precise features they want in such a system. The third problem arises from the different types and amounts of resources, including time, that it takes to reform or implement institutions (to abolish central planning, to privatize GOFs, to establish a new banking system, to pass laws), due to technical reasons (e.g. skill requirements) and to the varying extent of political support available for different components of the new system.

Several examples of these problems and the difficulties they have caused for the transition process in Romania were brought out in this paper, including the following: (1) The comparatively slow pace of macroeconomic system change in areas such as the price system and foreign exchange markets has temporarily and partially protected the purchasing power of pensioners and workers while perpetuating economic distortions, (2) The persistence of the central bank's influence on commercial banks, has resulted in heavily negative interest rates both on the savings of the general public and on loans to GOFs; this policy has enabled firms to remain solvent which should have been closed or downscaled and deprived more deserving firms, including private ones, of needed loans, (3) The policy restricting the wages of employees in GOFs attempted to limit the extent to which management and employees could 'strip' their firms; this has probably resulted in reduced incentives for better performance, as well as the departure of better employees for the private sector, thus weakening also GOFs that should not be weakened, (4) The rushed privatization in agriculture preceded the promulgation of laws that could support the efficient use of private farm land, (5) The privatization of GOFs through MEBOs was not accompanied by appropriate corporate laws. These examples are suggestive of the process through which a patchwork of reforms has been generated, reforms that are not all well-timed and that together combine to form a system that partly lacks coherence and is less efficient than it could be.[42]

There are important interdependencies between macroeconomic reforms on the one hand and organizational reforms and privatization on the other hand. The macroeconomic policies that resulted in rapid and variable inflation and in exchange rate uncertainty slow down privatization and foreign investment and adversely affect the reorganization of GOFs. Privatization is hampered by uncertainty which makes it difficult to reach agreement between the government and buyers on the value of firms. Foreign investors are less inclined to invest in Romania if the repatriated value of future profits made in Romania is very uncertain. Romanian policy makers do not appear to recognize sufficiently the inter-dependence between the macro and micro aspects of the economy.

External events also have a significant impact on the chances for successful transition in Romania. Exports to the West may have a double positive effect: they may act as a demand-side macroeconomic stimulus and as a setter of standards for technology and product quality to be followed by Romanian producers. The United States, by denying Romania, until very recently (November 1993), most favoured nation (MFN) status (which it enjoyed during most of the Ceausescu era) has made the country's transition for market more difficult, as have the other import restrictions it and the EEC have imposed.[43] Easier access to Western markets and credits may forestall the tendency to return to the practices suggested by the old slogan *prin noi insine* (through our own efforts alone), which induced Romania to engage in misguided autarkic adventures for more than a century.

Notes

1. The harvest statistics released after the Revolution of December 1989 revealed that official claims in this area had been especially exaggerated.
2. One of the authors who was in Bucharest in December 1989 can testify to unheated public buildings and extensive cuts in the electricity supply. The long queues for meat (despite the fact that it was rationed) and for most other foodstuffs added to the population's misery.
3. For more details about Romania's economic development during the communist period, see Montias (1967 and 1991) and Ben-Ner and Montias (1991). The operation of GOFs in this period is described in Earle and Sapatoru (1992).
4. According to the polls taken by the Romanian Institute of Public Opinion in January 1993, 43 per cent of respondents were convinced or strongly convinced that the

evolution of Romania was going in a bad direction, which was exactly the same as the percentage who were convinced that it was going in a good direction. As to what the government could do about the 'economic shock', 35 per cent of the respondents suggested that it could stop the increase in prices. 58 per cent of the respondents thought that Romania would not succeed in overcoming the economic crisis (16 per cent thought it would) (data provided to the authors by the Institute). None of these questions quite gets to the essential point: whether respondents thought they were better or worse off than they were three years ago.

5. A value-added tax, to be paid on all goods, was introduced in July 1993. It is expected that this tax will be easier to collect than the taxes on profits that it replaced.

6. A complete selection of laws, decrees and government decisions concerning the economic reform can be found in Curier Legislativ, *Organizarea si Aplicarea Reformei Economice*, no. 13 Editura Forum, Bucharest, 1993. A useful compilation in English of laws enacted by September, 1991 can be found in Romanian Development Agency, *Law Digest for Foreign Investors*, Bucharest, 1992.

7. Agricultural firms are covered by Law 36, not discussed here.

8. In June 1993 the law was amended and all restrictions on repatriation of profits were removed.

9. The shareholders' assembly and the board of directors of state-owned commercial companies were still appointed by the relevant ministry after Law 15 took effect; they will be replaced by the representatives of the private ownership funds and the state ownership fund (see next subsection).

10. A government document shows the following partial or complete closures in the chemical and petrochemical industries: Biosin (in Calafat) for 'economic inefficiency'; Famos (Suceava) for high pollution; Archim (Arad) for lack of natural gas; Romproteine (Curtea de Arges) for 'economic inefficiency'; four installations in Brazi, Telejean Media, and Pitesti for 'lack of resources to import petroleum'; 37 installations for the production of organic chemicals, for lack of raw materials and low economic efficiency; 9 installations for macromolecular products, for unstated reasons (probably the same as the preceding); and 3 installations for the production of caustic soda (about 40 per cent of total national capacity) for excessive energy consumption. In the metallurgical industry the same document lists 9 furnaces in Galati, Hunedoara, Resita, and Calan that were shut down owing to 'the reduction of internal demand and poor export prospects'; one coke battery was eliminated because of 'sub-average efficiency'; 16 Siemens-Martin hearths in Hunedoara, Resita, Otelul Rosu and 7 electric hearths in Tirgoviste and Cimpia Turzii were shut down because of 'the reduction in steel production, worn out and technologically obsolete equipment, and low efficiency', etc.

11. Problems of management competence were overshadowed in several industries by the sudden disappearance of traditional customers owing to the collapse of the Soviet bloc's CMEA, which had accounted for 40 per cent of Romania's exports. Domestic demand has also fallen for many products.

12. This is in sharp contrast to the situation in Hungary where a severe bankruptcy law has been promulgated and many state firms have been forced into bankruptcy. In Poland the bankruptcy law is less strict than in Hungary but still more effective than in Romania.

13. In an interview with one of the authors in May of 1991, the manager of a GOF producing porcelain goods complained both about the disruption in trade links and about the lack of market-oriented skills in his management team. More than two years later, he reported that the firm had recovered by making various price and quantity adjustments and other changes. The firm now produces as much as it did before the revolution, and with the same number of employees. In response to the

new value-added tax, the firm reduced its prices to remain competitive. In response to higher prices of gas, the usage of energy was reduced to a fifth of the previous level by purchasing a more efficient oven in the West. The decline in work discipline (which prompted the dismissal of 60 employees) and the deterioration in labour relations (including a strike against the management) that took place shortly after the revolution, were reversed. A monthly meeting between the firm management and union leaders was established (with a parallel structure in individual departments) to discuss the condition of the firm along with measures to improve productivity, and financial information is now shared. The union agreed to Saturday work and a profit-sharing plan is being implemented. The firm has no arrears problems, is profitable, and pays an average monthly wage that is 25 per cent in excess of the national official 'control wage'. The firm pays a penalty tax of 500 per cent on this excess wage bill.

14. Most of the details presented in this subsection are based on written materials from and interviews with officials of the National Agency for Privatization, the State Ownership Fund, and Private Ownership Fund number 4 (Muntenia).

15. Romanian citizens can use up to ten COs to purchase shares in large firms at a 10 per cent discount from the final established price; employees receive a 20 per cent discount for up to 10 per cent of their firm's outstanding shares.

16. In Russia, since 1992, citizens have been trading their vouchers for shares of corporatized firms. Shares valued at about 3 per cent of the value of the capital stock of industry calculated at early 1992 prices have been traded for vouchers. See Boycko *et al.* (1993); these authors also examine reasons for the low value of vouchers which apply to a considerable extent to the Romanian situation as well.

17. Ordinary Romanians interviewed by the authors, whether they knew English or not, could not say what MEBO stands for in English, but understood quite well what it means.

18. In one firm with 2,498 employees 45 per cent of equity is owned by employees, with the rest held by individual investors, two private banks, two POFs, and foreign investors. Another firm (with 1,700 employees) is 93 per cent owned by management and the rest by employees. Seventy per cent of a small firm (26 employees) was purchased through a MEBO, with the rest going to a private Romanian investor. In the case of two clothing manufacturing firms (employing 4,126 and 937 employees, respectively) foreign investors teamed up with the employees, their respective shares being 71 and 29 per cent in one company, and 85 and 15 per cent in the other.

19. POF number 4, for example, has shares in some 1,300 GOFs: in industries producing pharmaceuticals, cosmetics, materials for construction, and glass and ceramics, in addition to the financial and the distressed industries, and the local industries in its region.

20. Currently the law prescribes, within broad ranges, the allocation of profits to various uses. This law is likely to be repealed.

21. The management contract is being designed by parliament because, in this and other issues concerning GOFs, parliament regards itself as the representative of the Romanian people who own these firms via the SOF and POFs.

22. As noted earlier, a few firms with more than 1,000 employees were already privatized by NAP. The rate of privatization of GOFs was maintained through the end of 1993. However, the total of about 250 privatizations for 1993 represents only half of the projected number.

23. Some credits are channelled to small farmers through Romcereal, the trading organization which holds virtual monopsony of purchases of cereals and technical crops from the farm sector. Romcereal no longer has a legal monopsony on procurements – indeed

some competition has begun to develop – but it has a fleet of trucks, as well as warehouses and silos located all over the country, which enables it to dominate the market.

24. Unless otherwise noted, the data presented in this and the following subsections are derived from publications of the National Trade Register Office of the Chamber of Commerce and Industry of Romania.

25. The number of active firms cannot be made out from the available statistics. Since the fees and capitalization requirements for certain types of firms are very small and there is no penalty for being registered but inactive, these numbers are probably exaggerated. Hence the number of deregistered firms, reported in the next subsection, is understated.

26. This calculation is rough because the data on firm capitalization are classified according to the form of incorporation but not the type of ownership, whereas the data on the number of firms is broken down according to both criteria.

27. For example, many state-owned department stores lease some of their space to private firms which set up shop in their immediate vicinity. Such arrangements appear to reduce incentives for the state-owned store's employees to improve their own shop. First, rental income may bring them sufficient income (especially in view of the penalty for paying high wages). Second, investment in the shop may not accrue to them personally if it is eventually sold to somebody else (if it is sold to employees, the price may be raised to reflect the value of the investment).

28. If the two figures are consistent, this suggests that the value added per worker in private firms is lower than in GOFs, presumably reflecting the greater capital intensity in the latter.

29. These are government estimates. Employment in the private sector is not known with precision, primarily because many employees work in the 'informal sector'.

30. This sum does not include later investments, which bring the total foreign investment in Romania to approximately $700 million.

31. In August 1993 the joint venture between AT&T and Romtelecom has introduced international telephone calls via satellite. These calls can be accessed by any telephone in the country. This facility will obviate the extreme paucity of international trunk lines.

32. This paragraph is based on interviews with officials of the Romanian Development Agency and the National Bank of Romania.

33. At the end of 1989, 80 per cent of wage earners made less than $40 a month, and the total savings deposits and currency held by the public averaged about $35 per household. It is likely that more than the average amount of capital was available in the hands of those who had engaged in illicit activities under the former regime, most of whom seem to have channelled their capital into the new private sector.

34. Of course, the economic value of shares may diverge from the figure cited by the government, but as pointed out in the discussion of the pilot provatization, many firms were sold at above the nominal price based on the book value of GOFs.

35. This method 'has also the advantage of creating a favourable attitude toward privatization' (Government of Romania 1993: 24).

36. See Boycko et al. (1993) for a parallel analysis of Russian privatization through employee and management buyouts.

37. A domestic market for business consulting is developing, though the number of consultants is now small and apparently many are insufficiently qualified. Many potential customers of consulting services lack at the moment the resources to identify appropriate consultants or to pay for their services.

38. Some of our informants thought that these problems might induce the creation of coordinating bodies above the POFs and SOF, which, if they took the form of

holding companies, would pave the way toward economic recentralization. After the completion of this chapter the Romanian government announced the establishment of a new ministry in charge of coordination of economic reform and strategy, including privatization, following the advice of an international consulting firm.

39. When this possibility was suggested to an official of a POF, he responded that this would be against the interests of society at large.

40. For a discussion of additional legal and organizational issues concerning employee-owned firms in transition economies, see Ben-Ner (1993).

41. Of course, these are not the only objectives governments pursue. For a discussion of such objectives and the constraints under which they are pursued, see Montias et al. (1993), and Ben-Ner (1993) for a discussion in the specific context of organizational reforms. We do not seek here to explore the sources of these objectives and constraints and how they are expressed in the political arena. These objectives and constraints can be interpreted more narrowly or expansively. It is probably fair to say that the Romanian government's interpretation is more expansive than that of some other Eastern European governments and that it is more 'statist' or 'paternalistic' than other governments in the region, in keeping with its historical tradition.

42. The first example probably reflects a mixture of misunderstanding of the nature of inflation, as well as the pressure of potentially affected groups. The second example probably illustrates both an imperfect understanding of the role of interest rates on savings and investment decisions, as well as the pressure exercised by GOFs' management and employees. The third example appears to represent a concession to the need to continue to control GOFs which, before restructuring, are likely to behave in undesirable ways, and a lack of understanding of the incentive effects of this move. (Interviews with policy-makers indicated unawareness of this possibility.) The fourth and fifth examples seem to combine political expediency with lack of recognition of the existence of a need for special legislation.

43. In 1993 the World Bank suspended the last tranche, amounting to $150 million, of a $400 million loan. It has done so because of Romania's economic instability and high inflation rate, its over-valued exchange rate, its large government budget deficit, the growing deficit in foreign trade, and its slow privatization process. It was also perhaps motivated by the aim of strengthening the position of supporters of more liberal economic positions and of speeding up the pace of reforms. However, this suspension may not take into full consideration the sources of these problems, and may have the effect of increasing the resentment of Romanians to foreign intervention. It may thus contribute to an exacerbation of the political problems of the present government, the fall of which would in turn contribute to economic instability. Economic instability, in turn, would certainly slow down the transition.

APPENDIX 1   SANEX – A GOVERNMENT-OWNED FIRM IN CLUJ-NAPOCA (TRANSYLVANIA)

Sanex, a government-owned firm producing procelain goods, encountered numerous difficulties when the old system was discontinued. In an interview in May 1991, the general director (one of the few top managers in Cluj-Napoca not to be replaced after the revolution) complained both about the disruption in trade links caused by the radical change in the environment and about the lack of market-orientated skills in his management team. More than two years later he reported that his firm had managed to adjust to the numerous changes that affected its operations. During the intervening time, he and his team have done a lot of 'learning-by-doing' about finance and marketing, in addition to using the consulting services of their bankers (especially the Romanian Export Bank) and university professors (not everyone could cope with the new circumstances: the chief accountant left voluntarily for this reason).

The firm made both price and quantity adjustments. For example, in response to the new value-added tax imposed in July 1993, the firm reduced its prices to remain competitive. In an effort to adjust to new prices of gas the firm's usage of energy has been reduced to a fifth by purchasing a more efficient oven in the West. The firm also purchased (with credit from the Western seller) machinery that will improve efficiency and ease the work of employees. Unlike in previous years, the purchases were negotiated directly rather than through a government foreign trade company, although a ministry representative was present during negotiations as a consultant. The firm is now free of any external interference and makes all of its own decisions.

The firm now produces as much as it did before the revolution, and with the essentially same number of employees. Following the revolution there was a decline in discipline (such as an increase in theft and drunkenness), resulting in the dismissal of about 60 employees. Labour relations also deteriorated, culminating with a strike against management in 1991. After the strike a monthly meeting between the firm management and union leaders was established (with a parallel structure in individual departments) and financial information is now shared. Discussions at these meetings focus on the condition of the firm along with measures to improve productivity. One measure to which the union agreed is to work on Saturday, despite the government's repeal of compulsory Saturday work in early 1990. In addition, the union and management agreed to implement a gain sharing plan and are also expecting to put in place a plan for assessing penalties for low quality production. The management and the union are discussing a management and employee buyout, which both groups prefer to a privatization by other methods. The general director of the firm praises the cooperation with the union.

The firm has no arrears problems at all, is profitable, and pays an average monthly wage of 94,000 lei. This wage is 24,000 above the national official 'control wage'; government rules require that GOFs that pay in excess of this wage must pay a penalty, which in Sanex's case amounts to 500 per cent on 24,000 lei for each employee.

The main complaint of the general director was the high taxes the firm has to pay, which leave little for investment. He also lamented on the loss of business due to the boycott on Yugoslavia.

Source: Interview with one of the authors, July 1993 (follow-up of an interview in June 1991).

APPENDIX 2   COMPEXIT – A NEW PRIVATE FIRM IN CLUJ-NAPOCA
(TRANSYLVANIA)

One of those who later became a partner in Compexit took a management course
in 1990. One of the course assignments was to write a business plan for a new
firm. This plan became the basis for a new firm when in 1991 this person and four
acquaintances left their jobs in factories and government agencies. The five, along
with an Austrian partner, formed a firm that now employs 60 people and engages
in imports of consumer goods, mainly electronics and Czech Skoda cars, operates
a chain of foreign exchange offices (with another 50 employees), and is in the
process of opening a bank. They operate in facilities purchased and leased both
from government-owned firms and individuals.

The management described several problems that their firm faces. They claimed
that the tax holiday enjoyed by foreign investors discriminates against domestic
firms who have little surplus after left for investment. An obstacle to expansion is
their lack of know-how concerning assembly of imported parts and servicing the
goods they sell. (Given the structure of import tariffs, it is advantageous to import
parts, with 8 per cent import duties, and assemble them in Romania rather than
import finished goods with import duties of 80 per cent). They believe that the
short-run solution to the investment and know-how problems is to add foreign
partners to their firm. The management also complained about preferential treatment given to government-owned firms. For example, they felt it discriminatory
to require that they pay for import duties with a cashier's cheque at the border
after the goods arrive at the border and are assessed by the authorities, whereas
government-owned firms can pay with their own cheques, thus saving themselves
the trouble of traveling back and forth to their home towns to obtain cashier's
cheques. They also raised the issue of the long time it takes for cheques to clear
(more than a week for local cheques and twice as long for out-of-town cheques).
Another problem was the uncertainty induced by the frequent changes in laws.
Finally, the loss of traditional markets (Iraq, Libya and Yugoslavia) due to
international boycotts was mentioned. Interestingly, the problem of tele-commu-
nications was not seen as significant, and the number of telephones with direct
international access is increasing. Roads are in reasonable shape and are safe.

The management also mentioned a number of relatively problem free areas. One
of these was the availability of credit; they can get loans in foreign exchange from
state banks at 8 per cent with collateral in cars and real estate valued at 120 per
cent of the loan, and from the private banks at 20 per cent interest rate but with
easier requirements for collateral. The firm also has access to an ample supply of
well-qualified employees, though not of managers.

Source: Interview with one of the authors, July 1993.

APPENDIX 3   TOP TEN FOREIGN INVESTMENTS IN ROMANIA DURING THE FIRST HALF OF 1993

Partners (F: Foreign, D: Domestic)	Foreign Equity ($ million)	Area of Activity
F: Stima Engineering (Italy) D: Infratirea SA	21	Machine building
F: Companie Immobilier Phenix (France) D: Athenee Palace SA	13	Tourism
F: Agneta Zimmermann (Germany) D: Karmen Zimmermann	10	Mining, transport, commerce
F: Ozeksim Dis Tikaret D: Municipality of Galati	6.5	Food, commerce
F: Transpac (France) D: Romtelecom (RA)	5.5	Telecommunications
F: Conad (Bulgaria) D: Ric Impex SA	5.3	Light industry commerce
F: Teohari Leonida (Canada) D: Oarga Ilarie, Dorhoi Cantemir	4.3	Transport, food, commerce
F: Mantelli &C SPA (Italy) D: Silvafruct SA	2.4	Consumer goods
F: Abri Janos, Abri Mag (Hungary) D: Ro Max Tim	2.3	Electronics, transport, commerce
F: Darianne International Trading (Canada) D: Silvafruct SA	1.9	Transport, food, agriculture

Sources: Romanian Development Agency and Romania Economic Newsletter.
Notes: The majority of the shares of most of these ventures are owned by the foreign partners. Domestic companies with designation SA are mostly government-owned firms that will be privatized in the future, and the firm with designation RA is a government-owned firm intended to remain such. Of the remaining three Romanian partners one is a municipality and the other two private entrepreneurs. These are not the largest foreign investments in Romania. For example, in 1992 there were several relatively large foreign investments, several of them in petroleum exploration, including $44 million by Shell (Holland), $20 by Amoco (US) and $17 by Enterprise Oil (UK).

References

Ben-Ner, A. (1993) Organizational reforms in Central and Eastern Europe: a comparative perspective, Annals of Public and Cooperative Economics 64 (3), pp. 329–65.

Ben-Ner, A. and Montias, J. M. (1991) The introduction of markets in a hypercentralized economy: the case of Romania, Journal of Economic Perspectives, 5 (4) (Fall), pp. 163–70.

Ben-Ner, A., Montias, J. M. and Neuberger, E. (1993) Basic issues in organizations: a comparative perspective, Journal of Comparative Economics 17 (June) pp. 207–42.

Boycko, M., Shleifer, A. and Vishny, R. W. (1993) Privatizing Russia, Paper prepared for the Brookings Panel on Economic Activity, September 9–10.

Brooks, K. and **Meurs, M.** (1993) Romanian land reform in the earliest period of restitution, February-August, 1991: new patterns of land holding and use, Working Paper, The World Bank and American University.

Daviter, J., Gessner, V. and **Holand, A.** (1987) *Selbstverwaltungswirtschaft: gegen wirtschaft und recht? Techniche und okonomische problembetrachtungen*, Bielfeld: AJZ Druck und Verlag GmbH.

Earle, J. S. and **Sapatoru, D.** (1992) Privatization in a hypercentralized economy: the case of Romania, CERGE Working Paper no. 15 (October), Prague.

Montias, J. M. (1967) *Economic Development in Communist Romania*, Cambridge, Mass.: MIT Press.

Montias, J. M. (1991) The Romanian economy: a survey of current economic problems. *European Economy* (June), Commission of the European Communities.

Montias, J. M., Ben-Ner, A. and **Neuberger, E.** (1994) *Comparative Economics*, Harwood Academic Publishers (Encyclopedia of Economics Series, edited by J. Lesourne and H. Sonneschein), Chur, Switzerland.

Murrell, P. and **Wang, Y.** (1993) When privatization should be delayed: the effect of communist legacies on organizational and institutional reforms, *Journal of Comparative Economics*, **17** (2), pp. 385–406.

Olson, M. (1992) Why is economic performance even worse when communism is abolished?, IRIS Working Paper no. 28, College Park, Maryland.

Spulber, N. (1966) *The State and Economic Development in Eastern Europe*, Random House, New York.

Vatasescu, A. (1990) Informare asupra masurilor ce se impun pentru asigurarea populaties cu alimente, caldura si energie electrica in iarna 1990–1991, mimeograph, Bucharest (October 1).

CHAPTER THIRTEEN

Privatization in Bulgaria

Derek Jones and Charles Rock*

1. Introduction

In this chapter, the policies, processes and some of the economic effects of privatization in Bulgaria are examined. Our definition of privatization is very broad. As well as fully fledged forms of private ownership, we include *hybrid*[1] forms of economic organization in which, compared to state-owned and controlled firms, there is a large measure of operational control by non-state parties. In addition, enterprises which have emerged through the transformation of existing state-owned firms and firms which have been newly created are examined.[2]

The chapter is organized around the main phases of Bulgarian privatization. It focuses on the fourth (and continuing) period of privatization that began with the passage of the Transformation and Privatization law in the spring of 1992. Since privatization is inherently a political process intimately bound up with other economic policies, these episodes are discussed *inter alia* with the broad political and economic situation. Finally we offer a critical evaluation of the policies designed to foster privatization in Bulgaria.

2. The economic context and privatization initiatives before spring 1992

THE ECONOMIC CONTEXT

Before discussing the earlier phases of privatization, we briefly note two important features of the Bulgarian economy since the late 1980s, i.e. since discussion of the need for 'restructuring' (and in some cases, for 'privatization') first began. Unlike Poland, and even the former GDR and Hungary, there was no private sector in Bulgaria during the communist era. The starting point on the road to

*We have benefited from conversations and correspondence with Mario Nuti, Svilen Parvulov, Ognian Pishev, Mieke Meurs, Tom Weisskopf, Roumen Avramov and Zeljko Bogetic. Jones acknowledges help from IRIS, Rock benefited from a grant from IREX during 1991–92, and both authors are grateful for support from NSF SES–9223571.

privatization was one where almost all of the economy was state-owned. Also the cooperative sector (which was part of the socialized sector) was quite small compared to countries such as Poland; this was especially the case in the industrial sector. In turn this predominant type of industrial organization led to extraordinary economic concentration; giantism without small firms was the order of the day (Jones and Meurs 1991; Jones and Parvulov 1992).

Second, the beginnings of the transitional process in general (and privatization in particular) were marked by an economic context that was extraordinarily unfavourable, even when compared to many other Eastern and Central European economies. This is the case on matters such as: the level of external debt; the enormous dependence on CMEA markets; and severity of the disruption to trade and loss of markets because of the recent conflicts in the Balkan and Middle East region.

PRIVATIZATION UNDER ZHIVKOV

The key political change in recent Bulgarian history was the replacement of the dictator, Zhivkov, after a bloodless coup in November 1989. Until then, industrial policy under the old regime included a series of fairly modest innovations concerning what we are calling privatization. In this pre-history of privatization under the communists, several initiatives (mainly Decree 12 and 33) were introduced and supportive institutions were established (notably the Bulgarian Industrial Association) to foster the development of new firms within the state-owned sector. While these reforms led to the establishment of up to 700 new production units (Jones and Meurs 1991: 320–323), in practice only a minority of these firms were autonomous. However, the entry of some new non-state firms did represent a turning point in the postwar history of economic organization in Bulgaria, although in the aggregate these changes accounted for less than 1 per cent of total employment and thus barely affected the existing size distribution of firms.

Potentially a more important change was the introduction of Decree 56 in January 1989. This new commercial code re-established the right of new private firms to exist, to hire up to 10 permanent employees and to sell enterprise assets. Consequently by the end of February 1990 more than 14,000 (of a total of 15,500) *registered* firms were private firms. However, many new firms existed only on paper and those that did actually operate were typically quite tiny.

Also during this period a special agreement (signed by the Komsomol, Central Cooperative Union) of 1987–1988 re-established the right to operate what were essentially autonomous cooperatives. While most such firms acted to service collective farms, unfortunately the available data are extremely limited.

NOVEMBER 1989-END 1990: THE ERA OF WILD PRIVATIZATION

The political events of November 1989 were followed by the rapid emergence of political pluralism, much of which coalesced into the Union of Democratic Forces (UDF). However, it was the Bulgarian Socialist Party (the BSP, formerly the communists) that received a mandate in the free elections in June 1990. After unsuccessful attempts to form a coalition government, in September, the BSP was forced to establish a one-party government. During this time their popular support significantly eroded and in December 1990 the Socialist government fell. During this period (as in others) the privatization process in Bulgaria was in no way a thoughtfully planned and rationally unfolding process. Rather it reflected the shifting political sands during a period of persistent political struggle.

In fact the privatization process for much of this period was one of uncoordinated, *ad hoc* privatizations. This 'wild', 'quiet' or 'spontaneous privatization' involved the sale of portions of state-owned assets at their listed book value.[3] Due to accounting practices under the previous system, in many cases these values had little relationship to any probable market valuation. This period of privatization has been condemned by some as one of self-serving and scandalous grand theft on the part of managers and Communist Party members. However the scale of these privatizations is not clear since no data appear to exist. Moreover, even in well known cases, with Decree 56 and other enabling decrees making the legal regime murky, proving wilful fraud seems unlikely.[4]

END 1990 – OCT. 1991: SMALL PRIVATIZATION, RESTITUTION, AND THE NEW COOPERATIVE LAW

After the fall of the Socialist government, a coalition caretaker government headed by the UDF under Dimiter Popov emerged. As a result this period was also characterized by political deadlock and not much legislative activity took place.[5] In particular, a comprehensive privatization law was not enacted. At the same time, both the importance attached to privatization, as well as the ostensible objectives of the process, clearly changed during this period. The Popov government announced its commitment to rapid privatization with a specific timetable for early 1991. In addition, under the Popov administration (but even more so under the subsequent UDF government) privatization was conceived as having dual aims: that of securing economic efficiency but at the same time ensuring that the previous elite has fewer chances of re-emerging.

In terms of actual privatization, the hallmark of this period was the so-called *small privatization* of mostly service and retail units. This began at the very end of 1990 after the new more liberal ministers took office in December. Several small auctions (both open bid and solicited tenders) occurred on an irregular schedule. However, after the passage of a new commercial code (both replacing and accompanying portions of Decree 56), and in anticipation of the reasonably rapid passage of a comprehensive privatization law, these auctions were suspended in the last half of 1991. In any event many of the necessary steps preceding actual auctions had got bogged down and/or politicized in fights between municipalities and the federal government over ultimate ownership of assets that were to be sold. The small privatization program in fact led to very little transfer of ownership and little raising of revenue, with property sales including a few petrol stations.[6]

Also begun during this period was the process of restitution of land to former owners under the terms of the Law on Ownership and Use of Farmlands.[7] As such, restitution is one of the forms of privatization that has assumed great importance in Bulgaria. Unfortunately progress under the provisions of the restitution laws has proceeded slowly in this and in subsequent times. In turn, this has slowed down other forms of privatization. For example, as the claims of former owners are sorted out this naturally puts a brake on the selling of assets; it makes the situation as to what can and cannot be sold vague and unclear.

Another development was the passage of a New Cooperatives Law (July 1991). By repealing the 1983 law this measure abolished the control function that had been exercised by the old cooperative unions and, by providing for new governance structures, led to the reorganization of many 'old' cooperatives under the new statutes. Hence there was a modest growth of independent cooperatives during this period (Meurs and Rock 1993).

CHANGES IN OWNERSHIP FORMS: 1990–1991

The absence of any reliable system of gathering information on the consequences of these particular changes means that it is impossible to obtain accurate data on even basic indicators of the economic importance of these non-state forms of economic organization. Some things are known, however. Further growth of the small firm sector has continued during this period. The data show continuing large increases in the number of new firm registrations: by the end of 1990 there were 69,00 firms and this had grown (according to differing estimates) to between 130,000 and 180,000 by the end of 1991. It is also clear that most of these new ventures were in services and trade. But the absence of information on even the average number of permanent employees and average sales means that the overall economic significance of this economic activity is impossible to determine.[8]

It is also difficult to get reliable data on the pace of change in legal forms of ownership for firms that originated in the state-owned sector. However, survey data (see Jones 1993a) for a panel of manufacturing firms that began as SOEs, and which was representative of employment in such enterprises in the principal urban areas from 1988-1992, show that in 1988, 92.1 per cent of manufacturing firms were state-owned. By 1990 this had fallen slightly to 89.7 per cent with further declines in 1991 to 80 per cent and in 1992 to 76 per cent. These data also show that during the same period the percentage of joint stock companies in which the state had a significant (often a 100 per cent) ownership position increased steadily from 0.7 per cent in 1988 to 12.7 per cent in 1992. Finally, the survey shows that those cooperatives that regarded themselves as independent accounted for 5.7 per cent of the sample in 1988 and increased to 8.5 per cent of the sample by 1992. But fully fledged private firms were always a rarity in those manufacturing firms that were once state-owned; even by 1992 they represented only 1.8 per cent of the sample.

Within manufacturing, property forms have evolved at different rates and in different directions across industrial sectors. Thus in 1988 in engineering 98.5 per cent of all sample firms were state-owned; only one (of 132) firms was state-joint stock and one firm was an independent cooperative. By 1991 only 81.8 per cent were still fully fledged state firms, while 10.3 per cent were state-joint stock, 1.5 per cent were independent cooperative and 0.4 per cent were private. A year later the corresponding figures were 79.5, 16.7, 2.3 and 1.5. But in the food industry, in 1992 88 per cent of all enterprises remained fully state-owned and controlled. This contrasts with chemicals where by 1992 almost half of the sampled firms had moved away from a pure SOE form.

In principle, another way to gauge the extent of the impact of privatization is to examine data on joint ventures. Again, in practice, in the absence of centrally coordinated reporting requirements, the available data are very incomplete. However, the clear impression is that such activity is not very extensive.[9] Data derived from the same sample of manufacturing firms confirm the conclusion. During the period 1988–1992 that only 11 firms (about 2 per cent) had ever been involved in a joint venture. Interestingly, of these 11 only one joint venture was with a private firm. For the remainder all joint ventures were with firms that continued to be state-owned (and not transformed into a joint stock form) throughout the period.

3. Privatization since November 1991: the focus moves to large-scale privatization

Following new elections, in November 1991 for the first time a non-socialist party (the UDF) alone formed the government. At the same time, reflecting a continuing polarization of politics, the socialists gained almost as many seats as the UDF. Except for the ethnic-Turkish party (the Movement for Rights and Freedoms) not one of the more than 40 smaller parties secured any parliamentary representation. Furthermore, in presidential elections in January 1992, the UDF candidate Zhelu Zhelev was victorious, though the opposing candidate, supported by the BSP, received 46 per cent of votes cast. Thus for most of 1992 the situation was one in which the UDF, led by Prime Minister Phillip Dimitrov, was in the driving seat. However, since the balance of power was held by the Movement for Rights and Freedoms, the position was often tenuous, and it proved difficult to introduce new legislation and even more difficult to implement new laws effectively. Unsurprisingly the situation proved to be unstable and in November 1992 the UDF government fell. This political stalemate was resolved with the emergence of a new coalition government (in January 1993) under the leadership of Lyuben Berov, who was nominated by the party that represents the ethnic Turks, the Movement for Rights and Freedoms.

Against this backdrop the UDF government first reiterated its dedication to a comprehensive programme of rapid privatization. The key privatization measure to date was adopted on May 8 1992: the Transformation and Privatization Law. While this law was written and passed under significant pressure from international financial organizations in order to secure continued credits for the transition period, the law also reflected a continuing controversy over the appropriate type of privatization programme. Other enabling rulings were required to make the law workable and these only came into being in late 1992.[10]

The political process of creating the privatization law led to a compromise which now involves several groups and agencies in the actual process of privatization. The State Privatization Agency (SPA) was established to create annual plans and to carry out privatization of the larger (more than 10 million leva in long term assets) SOEs. This body has the role of overall monitor, reporting directly to the

Council of Ministers. However, many other actors are involved in the administration and management of the process. For example, consideration of an SOE
for privatization may be initiated by different interested parties: the Council of
Ministers and a special sub-committee of the National Assembly, certain ministries (most importantly Agriculture and Industry), specialized government agencies (e.g. the Committee on Telecommunications), municipal governments, special
privatization bodies created by municipalities, managers and workers, potential
buyers, and creditors. Also, the municipal councils handle privatization of municipal assets themselves.

The main method of privatization under the law is the sale of shares, with share
prices to be determined by competitive bidding. Apparently it was believed that
the sale of assets (rather than, for example, giving them away) would be likely to
lead to a better matching of assets and new systems of corporate control. At the
same time the law has always appeared to be quite flexible. For example, it
provides that the prices at which SOEs must be sold are subject to negotiation,
thereby acknowledging that in practice simple auctions may themselves have
problems.[11] In that process, the ultimate decision-maker (the SPA, the parliament and cabinet, or municipal governments depending on which SOE is being
transferred) may weigh heavily factors such as job creation or training, future
investments, and the impact on exports. Indeed such considerations may outweigh
the bid price and in some cases the SPA anticipates divesting of some enterprises
for only a nominal (one lev) payment. Leasing, renting, and management contracts with options to purchase may all be used instead of immediate sale.

The autumn 1992 Letter of Intent of the SPA stated that the main goals of
privatization are: (1) attracting foreign investors; (2) raising money for social
security and for reducing the government budget deficit; and (3) assisting in the
creation of efficient capital markets and financial institutions. The SPA hoped to
complete the task of privatizing 25 per cent of the large enterprises under its direct
jurisdiction by the end of 1995 (even though the law permits a five year period for
transfer). But the start of the process was delayed by the lack of enabling decrees
and by continuing instability of the government at the end of 1992 and in early
1993.

The 1992 Privatization Law grants two basic types of privilege or price reduction on assets purchased by employees. Each type depends on the type of SOE. In
all cases the maximum total price reduction per employee is constant and in no
case is the preference greater than one year's salary. One type permits employees
in *corporatized SOEs* [12] to buy a portion of their own firm at a 50 per cent
reduction on the assessed valuation price. The preference sale to employees
may only be for a maximum of 20 per cent of the enterprise's total shares (in
joint stock SOEs) or total capital (limited liability SOE). The total preference
reduction for any single employee is also restricted. It can be worth no more
than the employee's cumulative salary for between eight months to one year,
depending on tenure. A significant additional restriction on the value of these
preference purchases is that the acquired shares or portion of capital have no
voting power in determining the controlling supervisory board of the enterprise
(for a period of three years after purchase).

Different rules apply to SOEs which have remained as *directly owned SOEs* (i.e. neither joint stock nor limited liability corporations.)[13] In these cases, if at least 30 per cent of the employees wish to submit a bid to buy the company outright, they may do so. If their bid price for the SOE wins, their actual payment is reduced by 30 per cent. The same restriction on total preference reduction holds as with corporatized SOEs: a maximum value for the reduction of one year's salary. Hence, this type of worker buyout requires more cooperation among employees — at least 30 per cent must agree to submit a bid — and it also apparently allows employees to gain full control over the enterprise.

The privatization law and associated regulations also provide that 20 per cent of the shares (or stakes in a limited liability company) will be allocated to a Mutual Fund. An equivalent amount of cash may be given to the fund in lieu of shares. The law provides for this fund helping 'Bulgarians freely taking a part in privatization ... as well as contributing to the Social Insurance program and for compensating former owners whose specific property cannot be restituted' (Article 8).

Finally some brief words on the structure and functioning of the administrative side of the operation. Fundamentally, the law provides that the SPA is to be governed by a board of 11 members, each of whom has a four-year term. Six of the members are appointed by the National Assembly; the balance is appointed by the Council of Ministers. Beyond this, at the time of writing, the operational realities of the SPA are still in flux.[14] This was the case, for example, concerning both the establishment of particular divisions within the SPA, the size of the total staff and the number, location and functions of regional offices.

4. Overall evaluation

In evaluating the Bulgarian experience to date, the first thing that the previous account should demonstrate is that, as in most emerging market economies (and unlike the introduction of privatization in Western economies), privatization has not been introduced in Bulgaria as part of a carefully planned scheme. While since 1989 nearly all administrations have at least paid lip-service to the goal of privatization, a series of political struggles and economic crises has meant that other matters have typically claimed prior attention. Often the facilitating legislation that in fact was introduced was a response to a particular set of circumstances, sometimes reflecting what was practically possible and policy makers' assessment of the population's tolerance of transition costs. The Bulgarian experience also shows that the results of privatization laws are not easily predictable.

In attempting to gauge how the process of privatization is in fact faring in Bulgaria, the first difficulty is the absence of a single coordinating agency that collects information on all types of privatization. While this is particularly troublesome for small-scale privatization, the multiplicity of partners involved in large-scale privatization also sometimes leads to comparable difficulties in assembling reliable data. In addition despite its having been outlawed, there is much anecdotal evidence that 'wild' privatization continues (though the sophistication of the parties in camouflaging such schemes has conceivably improved.)

Moreover, as former SOEs drift towards privatization, a complex system of institutional cross-ownership seems to be emerging. Often through several layers of holding companies it appears that banks hold large stakes in firms and that companies have also secured stakes in each other. Penetrating these mazes of ownership patterns makes accurate assessments of changes in ownership regimes difficult. In turn, in the absence of general measures to facilitate conversion of these ownership claims into debt, the pace of the emergence of fully fledged large private firms may be slowed.

For functioning economic enterprises, overall it seems that relatively little has been achieved thus far in Bulgaria. In the sense of transferring ownership claims, privatization, certainly for large and probably for small firms, has been proceeding much more slowly than most had expected. Indeed, while there is disappointment with the pace and consequences of privatization elsewhere in the region, in Bulgaria this is perhaps especially acute. At the same time an important part of the privatization process, and a feature that is unusually prominent in Bulgaria (compared to many other countries), is the restitution legislation. While in terms of the transformation of SOEs into fully fledged private enterprises as yet little has happened in Bulgaria, there are many indications that firms of a more *hybrid* nature have begun to assume much greater significance in Bulgaria. Moreover there is preliminary evidence that the behaviour of state joint-stock companies differs in important respects from pure SOEs. (See Standing *et al.* 1993 for evidence on labour market outcomes.)

Turning to specific areas of activity and considering first large scale privatization, when the results are evaluated against the three objectives set by the SPA itself — attracting foreign investors, gaining revenues, and developing capital markets — it is fair to conclude that, to date, this form of privatization has not been a success. Fundamentally this is because there have been so few sales. At the time of writing (July 1993) no companies on the various select lists had actually been privatized. While a food processing plant was sold to a Belgian company (reported in the *Bulgarian Economic Review* May 21-June 3 1993), the legal process had still not been completed. Consequently, to date the law has produced very little in the way of attracting foreign investors or in garnering new revenue for the state. As of March 1993 it seems that the total revenue of the SPA was 600,000 lev (about $24,000) for the sale of a single warehouse, much less than the administrative costs of the exercise to date!

For various reasons there have been few sales. These include diverse political-cum- administrative problems in establishing the lists of firms to be privatized and the slowness in setting up the implementation bodies. Thus while earlier lists identified 292 firms as targeted for privatization by the end of 1993, at the time of writing the revised privatization programme identified a total between 318 and 322. (Given that 3356 SOEs remained at the end of 1991 this probably represents less than 10 per cent of the stock of SOEs today.) Of this total, 83 (large) SOEs are scheduled for privatization by the SPA with the balance of firms (of all sizes) to be handled by the branch ministries. (These lists represent a scaling back on earlier lists of firms that were to be privatized and the timetable for the targeted firms is not so pressing as under earlier schemes.)[15] However, the record to date would suggest that even these totals are much too ambitious. As of March 1992 it seems that only about 10 large firms were in the process of being privatized and that not a single firm had actually been privatized.[16] Based on this track record, without major new initiatives, it is unlikely that the different bodies will succeed in privatizing even half of the listed firms by the end of 1993.

There have also been problems caused by the absence of a single authority. The fact that several parties may initiate a change in practice seems often to have led to no-one taking any decisive action. The law leaves many issues unresolved and provides great latitude for interpretation, and consequent inevitable delays. Indeed, often it seems as if the law is more of an enabling piece of legislation than anything else. Reflecting the continuing uncertainties of the larger political context, the process continues to be politicized. Finally, capital markets are still quite embryonic in Bulgaria. For example, the volume of trading on the stock exchanges is still quite modest, certainly compared to volumes in Poland and Czechoslovakia.

Also there has been only a fraction of the amount of foreign investment that was anticipated by some.[17] This lack of foreign interest (and even domestic buying) reflects several factors. These include the general climate of political uncertainty, which has been greatly compounded by the problems arising from the handling of restitution claims and clearly identifying exactly what it is that the state has title to, so that it is able to sell. Even when these matters are resolved there is still the problem of the inability of foreigners to secure title to land. These difficulties are especially acute for particular enterprises, e.g. the uncertainties concerning the legal status of companies believed to have been privatized 'wild'. In addition, prospective buyers complain about the perceived inexperience of domestic partners in preparing business plans for consideration by foreign partners, problems of valuing assets and irritation suffered because of the slowness of the whole administrative process. Another important hindrance to the speed of privatization is that, as of June 1993, there was still no clear set of bankruptcy regulations in place.

Turning to other forms of privatization, in terms of fostering the entry of new private firms and, more generally, in terms of the fostering of economic pluralism the scorecard is probably not that great. On the one hand it is difficult to estimate how large is the activity of the private sector. Growth of registrations of new small private firms continued though the pace seems to have slowed markedly. By February 1992 there were about 200,000 new firms registered, and by mid 1992 about another 10,000 had been added. However, the absence of any reliable system of gathering information means that it is impossible to obtain accurate data on even basic indicators such as mean sales. But it seems clear that, at least in terms of employment, most new private firms remained small. Thus in the middle of 1992 there were only 130 private sector manufacturing firms with 10 or more permanent employees (Jones 1993b). In terms of industrial distribution, data obtained from the Union of Private Economic Enterprises (reported in Bartlett 1993) indicate that a surprising 25 per cent are in manufacturing, 24 per cent in services, 17 per cent in construction and 15 per cent in trade. Hence estimates of the size of the overall private sector range widely. While the official estimates vary from 5-7 per cent of GDP, unofficial claims have been made that the private sector accounts for up to 37 per cent of overall economic activity, with more than 50 per cent in some sectors such as retailing. Whatever the true figure, it is also clear that, in part because energies recently have been focused on the problem of trying to privatize large SOEs rapidly, the conditions conducive to the entry of new small firms have remained less than ideal. While much has been done to foster a private sector — e.g. the spate of new legislation — there does not seem to be sufficient appreciation of the extremely complex set of rules that must be created before a private sector will flourish. As many argue (e.g. Clague and Ransser 1992) it is clear that much more work is needed to determine precisely what are the impediments to the expansion of the private sector.

While the legal basis for restitution is now firmly in place, the process of implementation has proceeded slowly. Thus by the end of 1992 the National Statistical Institute estimated that only 46 per cent of more than 51,000 applications for restitution had resulted in property being returned to original owners. The total value of restituted property was almost 4 billion leva, averaging about 165,000 leva and representing about 3.5 per cent of 1991 GDP. In terms of land restitution, based on a survey by the National Public Opinion Centre, it appears that, as of May 1993, at most only about one third of those who have already taken possession of their land have received title to it.

Clearly the enormous uncertainty generated by this confused and chaotic situation has severely hampered restructuring, especially in agriculture. More generally, it is arguable that the new (former) owners of restituted property are often not necessarily the best equipped to manage the assets. While restitution may be 'fair', it is not obvious that it is efficient and a focus on restitution clearly hampered the ability of government to address other privatization issues. In addition property returned to former owners means that the state forgoes potential revenues and incurs various extra administrative costs. Hence Bulgaria may already have paid (and may continue to pay) a large price for a policy of insisting on physical restitution.

Finally we briefly consider some possible changes in the Bulgarian approach to privatization. While to date actual ownership changes in SOEs have been quite rare, without a dramatic change in policy, in the future this slow pace in the transfer of title is likely to continue. The need to speed up the process and to introduce some new initiatives has been recognized and, at the time of writing, two proposals for mass privatization were being seriously discussed, proposals associated with the Prime Minister Berov and his deputy Karabashev.

While details of the schemes are sometimes unclear,the Berov scheme seems closer to a Czech style plan and the Karabashev proposal more nearly resembles the Polish model. Under the Berov scheme, after payment of a 1250 leva downpayment, all Bulgarian citizens would be eligible to obtain deferred-payment, privatization bonds worth 25,000 leva, a 'balloon-mortgage' type of scheme. This contrasts with the Karabashev scheme which is restricted to citizens and permanent residents over 18, and uses a system of privatization points and convertible bonds. Under the Berov plan, foreign capital could participate freely in auctions of privatizable enterprises, whereas the other scheme prohibits this. Also the Berov scheme is grander, aiming to auction 600 large companies (rather than 200), worth about 185 million leva (rather than 65 million) and to do so in seven (rather than nine) months.

At the time of writing, a scheme which draws on both plans is being prepared by a team of experts for consideration by the Council of Ministers. Whatever the precise shape of the final plan, it remains to be seen whether, in the face of the erosion of parliamentary support, the government will be able to adopt new legislation. Even if this is done, questions must remain concerning machinery for implementation of new legislation.

In considering the nature of the next initiative on privatization, it appears that outsider control is unlikely to appear on a significant scale in the near future. At the same time, the law aims to provide for a measure of employee ownership. And there is some evidence (Rock 1993) that employees are to some degree at least interested in buying their firms, i.e. in taking steps towards achieving a measure of insider control. However the design of the current legislation and the implementation plans means that without large changes they are unlikely in fact to buy much stock. Under the present arrangements for corporatized SOEs, employees have no control rights during the three years when the discounted shares are non-voting. Clearly this places the burden of large risks on would-be employee-investors' shoulders. Moreover, even if they wish to, employees are seldom in a position to finance the acquisition of shares that they are eligible to buy. (Since 1989 average real earnings have fallen by more than a third. Also the rate of unemployment is approaching 20 per cent so that in a country with traditionally high male and female participation rates average family income has fallen markedly.) Yet there are no special credit programmes to enable employees to buy shares.

Given this, what is needed are mechanisms that, initially at least, provide for easier insider control. Hence a broader range of specific privatization techniques including ESOPs, mass privatization through citizen shares and management buyouts, needs to be considered.[18] For all of these, issues of providing credit for liquidity-constrained insiders assume great significance.

There is an issue of fairness since only workers in 'privatizable' SOEs are granted shares on preferential terms. Government actions to promote employee ownership more vigorously might be more politically feasible if these were accompanied by some form of preferences for 'citizen ownership' as well. That is, moving in the direction of facilitating more insider control together with citizen privatization will more likely lead to the process of mass privatization gaining broader support.

Some changes in the restitution law might also be considered. The restitution law, which promises to restore specific property, does have a deadline for filing claims. In practice, however, it is taking too long to establish legitimate title, especially when competing claims exist and documentation is often so poor. In turn this acts as a drag on progress elsewhere. Consequently it might be better to amend the law so that, after a set period beyond the expiration of the time for filing claims, there will be a rapid and clear-cut settlement via a system of equivalent compensation to former owners. Then the unresolved property issues would not have interfered with potential buyers' calculations of risk/value.

Yet even if the pace of (large scale) privatization is increased in Bulgaria, it will still take several years to complete the process of privatizing the bulk of the SOEs. Consequently a need clearly remains to improve the functioning of those enterprises which will effectively remain state-owned for some time. In any event, arguably even those enterprises that do change ownership form will not necessarily become suddenly more efficient. We disagree with those who implicitly seem to believe that a change in ownership alone will lead to a hardening of the budget constraint facing firms and to improvements in performance. In other words, the idea of privatization as a magic bullet that would solve all the hard economic problems needs to be reappraised and careful consideration to those other necessary corollary measures needs to be given.

Amongst these other measures arguably too little attention has been given to the internal restructuring of firms. For example the new Labour Code of January 1993 effectively removes provisions for employee involvement, provisions that did exist under previous edicts, including the old labour code. This is at variance with those participatory features of enterprise structures that a growing body of theoretical and empirical evidence indicates often lead to better incentives for the main actors within the new forms of economic organization (e.g. Blinder 1990). Moreover, this seems to be at odds with the preferences of Bulgarian employees for a measure of employee involvement in corporate governance (Jones 1993a; Rock 1993).

Notes

1. Unlike firms fully controlled and owned by the state, *hybrids* include leased firms, joint ventures, and joint stock companies. For fuller discussions see Bim *et al.* (1993).
2. We do not examine other 'marketization' policies including attempts to restructure management (and stabilization). On these see Rock (1992), World Bank (1991) and Wyzan (1993). Also space restrictions preclude examination of the role and evolution of important new institutional forms such as private housing and stock and commodity exchanges.
3. In fact there were some instances of wild privatization in the last year of the Zhivkov era. These occurred beginning in January 1989, soon after Decree 56 was introduced, and were helped by other minor laws facilitating asset transfer during 1989.
4. According to the April 1992 Privatization Law, transactions after 1 January 1990 which failed to have remuneration for the state-owned firm selling the asset are subject to annulment by courts (Clause 8).
5. However a major stabilization programme was introduced. Policies included: price liberalization, the decision to let the lev float, wage controls, and a tightening of macro fiscal and monetary policy. For more discussion and evaluation of the success of these policies see Wyzan (1992).
6. It seems that only about four (of an initial offering of more than 300) petrol stations, and about 60 smaller properties in retailing and distribution were sold. The auctions raised a little over $1 million, all from domestic buyers.
7. Beginning in late 1991, several laws were passed that outlined procedures for restitution of other assets. For land restitution, comparable measures had begun to be introduced during the first half of 1991.
8. Yet the vast majority clearly were tiny. Thus in 1991 Anachkova *et al.* (1992) estimate the average size of a new firm was three employees.
9. Estimates of the total number of joint ventures include 240 in mid-1991 (Frydman *et al.* 1992: 23) and 189 at the end of 1991, with another 20 developed by mid 1992 (Injova 1992: 4).

10. The main additional decrees were the Regulations of the Council of Ministers Concerning the Auctioning of State and Municipal Assets (SG 23/March 1991) and the Regulations of the Council of Ministers for the Establishment of the Privatization Agency (SG 12/January 1992). These and other measures were mainly concerned with the process of making bids, the special preference for shares for workers, and the valuation process.

11. This flexibility probably reflects the limitations imposed on this process because of the under-developed nature of Bulgarian capital markets as well as obvious market failures in the market for corporate control. Thus the more able managers or committed bodies of workers may have small initial endowments of wealth and are unable to borrow against future income. Similarly those who win auctions may simply be those who are richer (perhaps through illegal activities), and not necessarily likely to manage the privatized assets more intelligently in the future.

12. This happens mainly through the law on Incorporating Single-Owner Firms with State Property (July 1991).

13. This type of preference also applies to corporatized SOEs which have long-term assets worth less than $10 million leva (less than $US 0.5 million at current exchange rates). It can also apply to bankrupt SOEs.

14. The position was further complicated following the replacement in May 1993 of the five people previously appointed by the UDF with five nominees of the Berov government and the resignation of the Director of the SPA in August 1993.

15. While the national SPA is the main player, at the same time there are regional bodies and other actors who are also drawing up their plans. Thus the Greater Sofia Municipality approved a programme of the Sofia Privatization Agency for 1993 only in May 1993. This calls for 95 units to go private, 79 of which are distributive trade companies. The main technique will be auctions and tenders. The revenues raised will be distributed as follows: 50 per cent municipal investment fund, 30 per cent social security fund, 20 per cent into a loan fund.

16. At that time there had been only one case of privatization under the new law, that of a warehouse by the Ministry of Trade.

17. Data from the national account show that in 1990 foreign investment summed to $4 million and for 1991 $56 million. See *Planecon*, 1992.

18. The current law on employee discounted shares reflects a political struggle primarily over different conceptions of the relative importance of social justice and economic efficiency. Many have argued for a much bigger role for employee ownership (the current law is not overly generous), on the grounds of social justice. In our view the arguments on economic efficiency have often been misrepresented and misunderstood in the debate. Evidence exists (e.g. Blinder, 1990) that for superior economic performance via well-motivated insiders, participation in economic returns and in control need to be combined.

References

Agency for Economic Coordination and Development (1993) *Annual Report*, Sofia.

Anachkova, B., Jones, D. C. and **Parchev, I.** (1992) Who are the new entrepreneurs? mimeo., Department of Economics, Hamilton College, Clinton, N.Y.

Bartlett, W. (1933) A comparison of development of small firms in Bulgaria and Hungary, *MOCT-MOST*, 2, pp. 73–95.

Bim, A., Jones, D. C. and **Weisskopf, T.** (1933) Hybrid forms of enterprise in the former USSR and the Russian Republic, *Comparative Economic Studies*, **35** (1), pp. 1–37.

Blinder, A. (ed.) (1990) *Paying for Productivity*, Brookings, Washington, D.C.

Bogetic, Z. and **Fox, L.** (1993) Income policies during stabilization: a review and lessons from Bulgaria and Romania, *Comparative Economic Studies*, **35**(1), pp. 39–58.

Bogetic, Z. and **Wilton, J.** (1992) Bulgarian market reform: beating the odds, *Transition*, **3** (6), pp. 5–6

Bulgarian Economic Review, Sofia, various issues.

Clague, C. and **Rausser, G. C.** (eds.) (1992) *The Emergence of Market Economics in Eastern Europe*, Blackwell, Oxford.

Frydman, R. *et al.* (1992) *The Privatization Process in Central Europe*, Central Europe University Press, London.

Injova, R. (1992) Privatization in Bulgaria, Working paper, Agency for Economic Coordination and Development, Sofia.

Jones, D. C. (1992) The Bulgarian labour market in transition, *International Labor Review*, **130** (2), pp. 211–226.

Jones, D. C. (1993a) Trade union membership and employee participation in Bulgaria, 1989–1992, Working Paper No. 93/3, Department of Economics, Hamilton College, Clinton, N.Y.

Jones, D. C. (1993b) The nature and performance of small firms in Bulgaria, Working Paper, No. 93/10, Department of Economics, Hamilton College, Clinton, N.Y., and forthcoming in H. Brezinski and M. Fritsch (eds.) *Bottom Up Transformation in Eastern Europe*, Elgar.

Jones, D. C. and **Meurs, M.** (1991) On entry in socialist economies: evidence from Bulgaria, *Soviet Studies*, **43** (2), pp. 311–28.

Jones, D. C. and **Parvulov, S.** (1992) Industrial organization in a restructuring socialist economy: evidence from Bulgaria, forthcoming in *Empirica*.

Meurs, M. and **Rock, C.** (1993) Recent evolution and issues of Bulgaria cooperatives, in *Yearbook of Cooperative Enterprise*, Plunkett, London.

Planecon (1992) *Bulgarian Monthly Economic Monitor*, **8** (45–46), pp. 1–16.

Republic of Bulgaria (1992), Transformation and privatization of state-owned and municipal-owned enterprises Act, April 23, 1992 (SG No. 38/1992).

Rock, C. P. (1992) Employment, labour and privatization in Bulgaria's reforms: 1989 to mid-1992, unpublished manuscript, July.

Rock, C. P. (1994) Privatization in Bulgaria and employee ownership, mimeo, Department of Economics, Rollins College.

Standing, G., Sziraczki, G. and **Windell, J.** (1993) The Bulgarian labour flexibility survey: introduction, paper presented at Conference on Restructuring Labour Practices in Bulgarian Industry, Sofia, May 18–20.

World Bank (1991) *Bulgaria: Crisis and Transition to a Market Economy*, 2 vols., The World Bank, Washington D.C.

Wyzan, M. (1992) Bulgaria: shock therapy followed by a steep recession, *RFE/RL*, Nov. 13, pp. 46–52.

Wyzan, M. (1993) Stabilization policy in post-communist Bulgaria in Somogyi, L. (ed) *The Political Economy of the Transition Process in Eastern Europe*, Elgar, Aldershot.

Index

agriculture,
  Hungary, 198–200, 213–14
  Poland, 234–5, 242, 292
  Romania, 280, 281, 282, 292–3, 294, 298,
    300, 301, 302, 304
  Russia, 263, 270–1, 277
allocative efficiency, 94, 95
Antall, József, 186, 187
assets, sale of
  Bulgaria, 316–19, 323
  Hungary, 21 (*Fig. 1.2*), 37, 177–8,
    179–86
  Poland, 220, 239
  Romania, 292, 298
  Russia, 255
Auth, Henrik, 185, 186, 187
autonomous state enterprises (régies), 287,
  288

Balcerowicz, Leszek, 222, 224, 225, 236
banking, 6, 16, 54, 55, 58, 62–4
  Czech Republic, 169, 170, 172
  Poland, 233, 245
  Romania, 286, 301
bankruptcy laws
  Czech Republic, 156, 166–70
  Hungary, 303
  Poland, 303
  Romania, 289, 303
Bauer, Tamás, 182
Beksiak, J., 222
Bielecki, Krzysztof, 236
borrowing, 62–4
Brittan, Samuel, 236
Bulgaria, **311–24**
  communist resurgence, 18, 311–12
  cooperatives, 312, 314
  corporization, 316, 321, 323

current account, 10 (*Table 1.2*)
Decree, 56, 312, 313
economic progress 1990–3, 10 (*Table 1.2*),
  11 (*Fig. 1.1*)
employee ownership, 316–17, 321, 322, 323
foreign investment, 318, 319 323
free distribution, 21 (*Fig. 1.2*)
gross domestic product, 10 (*Table 1.2*), 11
  (*Fig. 1.1*)
hybrid forms, 311, 318
inflation, 10 (*Table 1.2*), 12
joint-stock companies, 314, 316, 317, 318
joint ventures, 315, 322
large-scale privatization, 317, 318
mass privatization, 320–21
Movement for Rights and Freedoms, 315
output drop, 11 (*Fig. 1.1*)
ownership changes, 314–17, 318, 320,
  321–22
political pluralism, 312–13, 315
pre-conditions and outcomes, 7–13 (*Tables
  1.1, 1.2, 1.3*), 312–13
private sector growth, 12 (*Table 1.3*),
  319–20
restitution, 21 (*Fig. 1.2*), 313–14, 318, 319,
  320, 321, 322
restructuring, 311, 322
sale of assets, 316–19, 323
small-scale privatization, 313, 314, 317
State Privatization Agency (SPA),
  315–16, 317, 323
state-owned enterprises (SOEs), 314–15,
  316–18, 320–21
unemployment, 10 (*Table 1.2*), 11, 321
Union of Democratic Forces (UDF), 312,
  313, 315, 323
'wild' privatization, 312–13, 317, 322

capital markets, 5, 6, 16, 17, 20, 22, 23, 36, 58, 74
capital privatization, 227–9, 235
Ceausescu, Nicolae, 18, 280, 281
centralization, 57, 60
certificates of ownership (COs), 289–90, 304
Chernomyrdin, Viktor, 261
Chubais, Anatoly, 261, 262, 267, 277
COMECON, 130, 131, 140, 141
commercialization, 34, 224, 269–70
communism, 83–5, 87, 221
    Bulgaria, 18, 311–12
    resurgence, 18
    Romania, 18, 280–1
    Russia, 18
competition, 14, 33, 36, 75, 76, 81
concessional transfer, 255
constitutional reform, 88–9
contract employment, 94
cooperatives,
    Bulgaria, 312, 314
    Hungary, 198
    Poland, 220, 226, 227, 244, 292
    Romania, 282, 292, 293
    Soviet Union, 257
corporization, 26, 27, 54–68, 74
    Bulgaria, 316, 321, 323
    Czech Republic, 157, 164–6
    Romania, 287, 288–9
Council for Mutual Economic Cooperation (CMEA), 5, 8–9, 16, 22, 188, 191, 280, 283
creditors, 62–4
cross-ownership, 162, 180–1, 211
Czech Republic,
    banking reform, 169, 170, 172
    bankruptcy law, 156, 166–70
    Consolidation Bank, 158 (Table 8.1), 169, 172
    corporization, 157, 164–6
    cross-ownership, 162
    current account, 10 (Table 1.2)
    foreign investment, 171–2
    founder ministries, 157, 158 (Table 8.1)
    gross domestic product, 10 (Table 1.2), 11 (Fig. 1.1)
    inflation, 10 (Table 1.2), 12
    investment funds, 164–6, 172, 173
    large-scale privatization, 156–63
    National Property Funds (NPFs), 157, 158 and Table 8.1, 159, 169, 172
    projects, 163–4
    share distribution, 160–3
    small-scale privatization, 156, 159

unemployment, 10 (Table 1.2), 11
voucher scheme, 160–6, 172
Czechoslovakia, 5, 6, 176, **154–75**
    communist collapse, 18
    constitutional blockage, 88
    control transfer, 59–61
    creditors, 62
    economic progress 1990–3, 10 (Table 1.2), 11 (Fig. 1.1)
    foreign investment, 35
    free distribution, 20, 21 (Fig. 1.2), 28
    legislation, 156–9
    output drop, 11 (Fig. 1.1), 156
    ownership rights, 27, 155–6, 157, 159
    pre-conditions and outcomes, 7–13 (Tables 1.1, 1.2, 1.3)
    price liberalization, 8
    private sector growth, 12 (Table 1.3), 13, 44
    restitution, 21 (Fig. 1.2), 89
    share transfer, 58, 59–61, 154, 157
    valuation problems, 155–6, 157
    voucher scheme, 20, 21 (Fig. 1.2), 23, 27, 36, 37, 46, 61, 90, 154, 155–6, 162 (Table 8.4), 173, 209
    See also Czech Republic; Slovakia

decentralization, 54, 56, 57, 192–4
deindustrialization, 127, 136–7, 148–50

East Germany, 6, 8, 127–53
    ATLAS project, 147–8
    communist collapse, 18
    decentralization, 138–9
    deindustrialization, 127, 136–7, 148–50
    employment subsidies, 128, 132, 141–2
    enterprise breaking-up, 140, 142
    enterprise evaluation, 139–40
    financial restructuring, 139–40, 142
    free distribution, 21 (Fig. 1.2)
    investment grants, 128, 131–2, 141
    management KGs, 145–7, 148, 150, 151–2
    management buy-ins (MBIs), 135 (Table 7.5), 144–5, 150
    management buy-outs (MBOs), 128, 135 (Table 7.5), 144, 150
    new owners, 135–6
    output drop, 129–30
    restitution, 21 (Fig. 1.2), 38, 132
    and reunification, 127, 129–32, 137–8
    sale of enterprises, 132–4
    sale to insiders, 144
    sale to outsiders, 128, 144–5

sale of state-owned firms, 20, 21 (*Fig. 1.2*), 37
subsidies, 131–2, 141–2, 150
supervisory boards, 138–9, 140
Treuhandanstalt, 32, 33, 57, 127–50
unemployment, 127–8, 136–7, 142
efficiency, 93, 96–8
effort, 92, 93–8, 106, 107–8, 113–18, 119–20
employee share ownership, 90, 222, 228, 244, 246, 316–17, 321, 322, 323
employment subsidies, 131–2, 141–2
entrepreneurs, 19, 86–7, 94–5, 99, 100–1, 106, 120
equity financing, 63
'existence-loans' (E-loans), 194, 195, 196

'fair wage hypothesis', 95
foreign investment, 35, 42, 47
    Bulgaria, 318, 319, 323
    Czech Republic, 171–2
    Czechoslovakia, 35
    Hungary, 35, 177, 184, 212
    Poland, 225, 245
    Romania, 280, 294, 296–7, 308
    Russia, 273, 275
free distribution, 23–4, 26, 28, 35, 54, 56
    Bulgaria, 21 (*Fig. 1.2*)
    Czechoslovakia, 20, 21 (*Fig. 1.2*), 28
    East Germany, 21 (*Fig. 1.2*)
    Poland, 21 (*Fig. 1.2*), 27, 28, 236
    Romania, 28
    Russia, 20, 21 (*Fig. 1.2*), 28
Friedman, Milton, 236

Gaidor, Yegor, 259, 261, 262, 267
Gheorghiu-Dej, Gheorghe, 280
Gomułka, Wladyslaw, 222, 225
Gorbachev, Mikhail, 252, 256, 257, 258, 259, 266, 272
government-owned firms (GOFs), 281, 282, 283, 284–5, 287, 288–9, 291, 295–6, 297, 304, 305
gross domestic product (GDP), 9, 10 (*Table 1.2*), 11 (*Fig. 1.1*), 71, 177
Gruszecki, Tomasz, 236, 241

Havel, Vaclav, 89
housing, 200–201, 214
Hungary, 4, 5, 6, **176–217**
    agriculture, 198–200, 213–14
    bankruptcy law, 307

Company Act (1988), 182, 183, 184
control transfer, 57
cooperatives, 198
cross-ownership, 180–1, 211
current account, 10 (*Table 1.2*)
decentralization, 192–4
economic progress 1990–3, 10 (*Table 1.2*), 11 (*Fig. 1.1*)
Economic Reform Committee, 185–6
Employment Share Ownership Programmes (ESOPs), 207–8
Enterprise Act (1984), 182, 184
'existence-loans' (E-loans), 194, 195, 196
external debt, 62, 177, 212
foreign investment, 35, 177, 184, 212
gross domestic product, 10 (*Table 1.2*), 11 (*Fig. 1.1*), 71, 177
housing, 200–201, 214
individual entrepreneurship, 180–1
inflation, 10 (*Table 1.2*), 12
institutional ownership, 180, 201–7
joint-stock companies, 180, 185
leasing, 208, 209 (*Table 9.6*), 214
legislation, 79–80, 182–8
Municipalities, Law on (1990), 201, 213
New Economic Mechanism (NEM), 176, 180, 183
output drop, 11 (*Fig. 1.1*), 71, 177
ownership rights, 177, 179–86, 194–5, 202–3
pre-conditions, 7 (*Table 1.1*)
pre-privatization, 194–6
private sector growth, 12 (*Table 1.3*), 13, 44
programmes, 188–92
public utilities, 77–80
reform process, 8, 9, 88, 177, 179–86
restitution, 38, 196–201, 213–14
sale of state-owned assets, 20, 21 (*Fig. 1.2*), 37, 179–86, 277–8
self-management, 180, 182–6, 212
self-privatization, 192–4, 213
Social Security, 202
'spontaneous' privatization, 183, 187, 213, 221
State Asset Management Company (SAMCo), 36, 199, 202, 203–7
State Holding Company (SHC), 78, 80
State Property Agency (SPA), 33, 57, 78, 184, 186–96, 202, 208, 212
state supervision, 25, 182–8, 201–7
Transformation Act (1989), 184
Treasury Property Management Organization, 202

Hungary (*continued*)
  unemployment, 10 (*Table 1.2*), 177
  voucher scheme, 208–10, 214

income distribution, 92, 95, 96–8, 99, 103, 119
industrialization, 86
inequality, 94, 97, 98, 104, 107, 108, 110
inflation, 9, 10 (*Table 1.2*), 12, 284–5, 286
insider-control privatization, 24–5, 37, 56,
  263, 264–5, 267, 273–5
insurance companies, 233–4
inter-enterprise credits, 289
International Monetary Fund (IMF), 79, 262,
  281
investment funds
  Czech Republic, 164–6, 172, 173
  Czechoslovakia, 59, 60
  Poland, 59–60
  Russia, 172, 272
investment grants, 128, 131–2, 141

Jermakowicz, W., 234
joint-stock companies,
  Bulgaria, 314, 316, 317, 318
  Hungary, 180, 185
  Poland, 222, 226, 233, 237
  Russia, 253–4, 260, 263, 264, 266, 267, 271,
    272, 273
  Soviet Union, 256

Kawalec, Stefan, 220, 243
Klaus, Vaclav, 90
Kombinats, 140, 144
Kuczyński, Waldemar, 241
Kuroń, Jacek, 238

labour, 97, 99–100
labourers, 95, 97, 98, 99–100, 107, 110. *See
  also* workers
land ownership, 292–3, 298
large-scale privatization,
  Bulgaria, 317, 318
  Czech Republic, 156–63
  Russia, 263, 271, 273
leasing,
  Hungary, 208, 209 (*Table 9.6*), 214
  Russia, 264, 277
  Soviet Union, 257, 258, 259, 264, 266
Lewandowski, Janusz, 220, 236, 241, 243
liquidization privatization, 229–32, 235, 242,
  244
Lis, Krzysztof, 222, 224, 241
Liska, Tibor, 181, 212

Little, Arthur D., 145
living standards, 281, 282, 284, 306

management buy-ins (MBIs), 135 (*Table 7.5*),
  144–5, 150
management buy-outs (MBOs), 128, 135 and
  Table 7.5, 136, 144, 150
management KGs, 145–7, 148, 150, 151–2
manager-employee buy-outs (MEBOs), 19,
  20, 24–5, 37, 290, 292, 295, 297, 298, 304
managers, 6, 14–16, 25, 99–100, 102, 104, 106,
  107, 120, 121, 185–6
market system, 17, 19, 32, 33, 59, 71, 95,
  96–7, 98–102, 121, 122
mass privatization, **54–68**
  Bulgaria, 320–21
  Poland, 222, 224, 225, 226–7, 236–8, 246
  Russia, 261
Matolcsy, G., 180, 181, 183
Mazowiecki, Tadeusz, 219, 221, 222, 227, 236
municipal privatization, 226, 244

nationalism, 84–5, 90
Németh, Miklós, 183, 184
nomenklatura, 23, 33, 83, 89, 221, 243, 259,
  260, 261, 272, 274

Olszewski, Jan, 233, 236
organic privatization, 219–20
output, 103, 105, 107, 108
output drop, 100, 101, 109
  Bulgaria, 11 (*Fig. 1.1*)
  Czechoslovakia, 11 (*Fig. 1.1*), 156
  East Germany, 129–30
  Hungary, 11 (*Fig. 1.1*) 71, 177
  Poland, 11 (*Fig. 1.1*)
  Romania, 11 (*Fig. 1.1*), 282–3
  Russia, 11 (*Fig. 1.1*), 12
outsider-control privatization, 24, 26, 37, 263,
  266, 273–5
ownership rights, 14, 20, 24, 26–8
  Czechoslovakia, 27, 155–6, 157, 159
  Hungary, 177, 179–86, 194–5, 202–3
  Poland, 27, 218, 226, 238, 244

Pavlov, Valentin, 258
perestroika, 256–60, 262, 272
Poland, 4, 5, 6, **218–51**
  administrative constraint, 240
  agriculture, 234–5, 243, 292
  asset privatization, 220, 239
  banking, 233, 245
  bankruptcy law, 307

capital privatization, 227–9, 235
communist collapse, 18, 221
constitutional conflict, 87–8
constraints, 238–41, 242
control transfer, 59–61
cooperatives, 220, 226, 227, 244, 292
creditors, 62
current account, 10 (*Table 1.2*)
economic progress 1990-3, 9, 10 (*Table 1.2*), 11 (*Fig. 1.1*)
employee share ownership, 90, 222, 228, 244, 246
employment, 62
fiscal constraint, 239
foreign ownership, 225, 245
founding ministries, 229, 231, 232
free distribution, 21 (*Fig. 1.2*), 27, 28, 236
gross domestic product, 10 (*Table 1.2*), 11 (*Fig. 1.1*)
inflation, 9, 10 (*Table 1.2*), 12, 286
informational constraint, 239
insurance companies, 233–4
intermediaries, 224–5
joint-stock companies, 222, 226, 233, 237
liquidation privatization, 229–32, 235, 242, 244
mass privatization, 222, 224, 225, 226–7, 236–8, 246
model of privatization, 223–5
municipal privatization, 226, 244
National Investment Funds (NIFs), 237
nomenklatura, 221, 243
organic privatization, 219–20
output drop, 11 (*Fig. 1.1*)
ownership rights, 27, 218, 226, 238, 244
ownership transformation, 227–9, 232, 236–8
Pact on Enterprises (1992), 218, 235, 238, 242, 245
political constraint, 240–1
pre-conditions and outcomes, 7–13 (*Tables 1.1, 1.2, 1.3*)
price liberalization, 8, 9, 242
private sector growth, 12 (*Table 1.3*), 44, 219–20, 243
'privatization express', 232, 235, 245
prospects, 235–8
public support, 240–1
reprivatization, 242, 246
restitution, 243, 246
restructuring, 232, 233, 234, 245
retail trade, 226
sectoral (branch) privatization, 232–3, 235

share transfer, 58, 59–61, 220–1, 222, 227–9, 236–8
small-scale privatization, 226–7, 243
soft budget constraint, 242
Solidarity, 219, 221, 222
stabilization, 9, 242
state-owned enterprises (SOEs), 219, 220–4, 226, 227, 229–32, 234, 235–7, 244
state-owned farms (PGRs), 234–5
statutory privatization, 220
stock-flow constraint, 238
tax rates, 17, 238, 246
trade union, 221–2
unemployment, 10 (*Table 1.2*), 11
voucher scheme, 21 (*Fig. 1.2*), 23, 27, 37, 224–5, 236
workers' councils, 221–2
political legitimation, 84–5
price control, 77
price liberalization, 8, 9, 16, 22, 111–13
private ownership funds (POFs), 288, 289, 290–1, 297, 298
private sector growth,
Bulgaria, 12 (*Table 1.3*), 319–20
Czechoslovakia, 12 (*Table 1.3*), 13, 44
Hungary, 12 (*Table 1.3*), 13, 44
Poland, 12 (*Table 1.3*), 44, 219–20, 243
Romania, 12 (*Table 1.3*), 293, 308
Russia, 12 (*Table 1.3*), 268
'privatization express', 232, 235, 245
public security markets, 64–6
public utilities, 69–82

régies (autonomous state enterprises), 287, 288
reprivatization, 242, 246
restitution, 26, 37–8, 89
Bulgaria, 21 (*Fig. 1.2*), 313–14, 318, 319, 320, 321, 322
Czechoslovakia, 21 (*Fig. 1.2*), 89
East Germany, 21 (*Fig. 1.2*), 38, 132
Hungary, 38, 196–201, 213–14
Poland, 243, 246
restructuring, 5, 6, 14, 15, 16, 35–6, 56, 57, 60, 139–40, 142, 234
retail trade, 226, 268–70
Romania, **279–310**
agriculture, 280, 281, 282, 292–3, 294, 298, 305, 306, 308
autonomous state enterprises (régies), 287, 288
banking, 286, 305
bankruptcy law, 289, 307

Romania (*continued*)
certificates of ownership (COs), 289–90, 304
communism, 280–1, 303
constraints, 301, 305
control transfer, 57
cooperatives, 282, 292, 293
corporization, 287, 288–9
current account, 10 (*Table 1.2*)
economic progress 1990–3, 10 (*Table 1.2*), 11 (*Fig. 1.1*), 282–7
exchange rates, 285, 286
foreign debts, 8, 281
foreign investments, 288, 294, 296–7, 304
foreign trade, 283
free distribution, 28
government-owned firms (GOFs), 281, 282, 283, 284–5, 287, 288–9, 291, 295–6, 297, 300, 301, 302
gross domestic product, 10 (*Table 1.2*), 11 (*Fig. 1.1*)
industrialization, 280–1, 282, 302–3
inflation, 10 (*Table 1.2*), 12, 284–5, 286
inter-enterprise credits, 289
land ownership, 292–3, 298
laws on firms, 287–8, 303
living standards, 281, 282, 284, 303
management, 288–9, 292, 303, 304
management and employee buy-outs (MEBOs), 290, 292, 295, 297, 298, 300
National Salvation Front, 282
organizational reforms, 287–99, 299–302
output drop, 11 (*Figs. 1.1*), 282–3
pre-conditions and outcomes, 7–13 (*Tables 1.1, 1.2, 1.3*)
prices, 284–5
private ownership funds (POFs), 288, 289, 290–1, 297, 298
private sector growth, 12 (*Table 1.3*), 293, 304
problems, 301–2, 305, 306
restructuring, 288–9
revolutionary economy, 282–7
sale of assets, 292, 298
sale to foreigners, 90
share transfer, 287, 290–1, 298, 303–4
state control, 279–80
state-ownership funds (SOFs), 288–92, 296, 297, 298
taxes, 285, 303, 304
unemployment, 10 (*Table 1.2*), 11, 283
wages, 284–5

Russia, **261–78**
agrarian reform, 263, 270–1, 277
concessional transfer, 255
constitutional conflict, 88–9
current account, 10 (*Table 1.2*), 12
economic progress 1990–3, 10 (*Table 1.2*), 11 (*Fig. 1.1*)
enterprise organization, 267–8
'500-Day Plan', 258
foreign investment, 273, 275
free distribution, 21 (*Fig. 1.2*), 28
gross domestic product, 9, 10 (*Table 1.2*), 11 (*Fig. 1.1*)
inflation, 10 (*Table 1.2*), 12
insider-control model, 263, 264–6, 267, 273–4
investment funds, 172, 272
joint-stock companies, 253–4, 260, 263, 264, 266, 267, 271, 272, 273
large-scale enterprises, 263, 271, 272
leased enterprises, 264, 277
management-worker buy-outs, 37, 46, 266
market sale, 255, 264
output drop, 11 (*Fig. 1.1*), 12
outsider-control model, 263, 266, 273–5
pre-conditions and outcomes, 7–13 (*Tables 1.1, 1.2, 1.3*)
price liberalization, 8
private sector growth, 12 (*Table 1.3*), 268
reform conflict, 262–7
retail trade and service, 268–70
sale of state assets, 255
share transfer, 255–6, 264–7, 271–2
small-scale enterprises, 263, 264, 270, 272, 277
state property transfer, 275, 278
unemployment, 10 (*Table 1.2*)
voucher scheme, 37, 263, 265, 266, 271–2, 275
worker collectives, 263, 264–5, 266–7, 271, 276–7.
See also Soviet Union
Ryzhkov, Nikolai, 258

Saburov, Yevgeny, 259, 261
Sachsenmilch AG, 136
Sárközy, Tamás, 183
sectoral privatization, 232–3, 235
self-management, 14, 180, 182–6, 212
self-privatization, 192–4, 213
share transfer, 90
    Czechoslovakia, 58, 59–61, 154, 157

Poland, 58, 59–61, 220–1, 222, 227–9, 236–8
Romania, 287, 290–1, 298, 303–4, 305
Russia, 255–6, 264–7, 271–2
Shatalin, Stanislav, 258
Silayev, Ivan, 259
Slovakia, 86, 157, 159, 160
small-scale privatization
    Bulgaria, 313, 314, 317
    Czech Republic, 156, 159
    Poland, 226–7, 243
    Russia, 263, 264, 270, 272, 277
Solidarity, 219, 221–2
Soós, Károly Attila, 180
Soviet Union, **252–60**, 272
    cooperatives, 257
    enterprise organization, 257, 258 (*Table 11.2*), 260 (*Table 11.3*)
    joint-stock companies, 256
    leased enterprises, 257, 258, 259, 264, 266
    nomenklatura privatization, 259, 260, 272
    perestroika, 256–60, 262, 272
    voucher scheme, 37
    workers' collectives, 257
    See also Russia
'spontaneous' privatization, 25, 183, 187, 213, 221
Stankiewicz, T., 234
state-owned enterprises (SOEs)
    Bulgaria, 314–15, 316–18, 320–21
    Poland, 219, 220–4, 226, 227, 229–32, 234, 235–7, 244
state-owned farms (PGRs), 234–5
state-owned firms, sale of, 20, 21 (*Fig. 1.2*), 37
state-ownership funds (SOFs), 288–92, 296, 297, 298
statutory privatization, 220
subsidies, 57–8, 131–2, 141–2, 150
Szabó, Tamás, 209
Szomburg, J., 220, 236, 243

Tardos, Márton, 180, 181
taxation, 17, 42, 43 and *Table 2.3*, 46, 47, 184, 238, 246, 285, 303
technical efficiency, 93, 94
Teleki, Pál, 205

Tömpe, István, 186
trade unions, 129, 221–2
Treuhandanstalt (THA), 127–8, 130, 132–5, 137 (*Table 7.6*), 138–52

unemployment
    Bulgaria, 10 (*Table 1.2*), 11, 321
    Czech Republic, 10 (*Table 1.2*), 11
    East Germany, 127–8, 136–7, 142
    Hungary, 10 (*Table 1.2*), 177
    Poland, 10 (*Table 1.2*), 11
    Romania, 10 (*Table 1.2*), 11, 283
    Russia, 10 (*Table 1.2*)
utility maximization, 113–18
utility regulation, 71–81

Volshky, Arkady, 87, 262
voucher scheme, 5, 25, 26–7, 33, 46
    Czech Republic, 160–6, 172
    Czechoslovakia, 20, 21 (*Fig. 1.2*), 23, 27, 36, 37, 46, 61, 90, 154, 155–6, 162 (*Table 8.4*), 173, 209
    Hungary, 208–10, 214
    Poland, 21 (*Fig. 1.2*), 23, 27, 37, 224–5, 236
    Russia, 37, 263, 265, 266, 271–2, 275
    Soviet Union, 37

wages, 16–17, 18, 102–3, 104, 107, 109–10, 129–30, 150
Wałeşa, Lec, 224, 225, 236
West Germany, 135, 136, 148, 152
    and reunification, 129–31, 137
    and THA, 137–9, 141, 149, 151
Western Employee Stock Ownership Plan (ESOP), 90
'wild' privatization, 312–13, 317, 322
workers (*see also* labourers)
    control by, 56
workers' collectives
    Russia, 263, 264–5, 266–7, 271, 276–7
    Soviet Union, 257
workers' councils, 221–2
World Bank, 79, 107, 262, 285, 310

Yavlinsky, Grigor, 258
Yeltsin, Boris, 13, 88, 89, 252, 259, 261, 262, 267, 268, 272